Holy Spirit Library
Cabrini College

Given in Memory of
RON BECHT
1944-2002

by the
Cabrini College Community

May 2002

Romantic Victorians

# Romantic Victorians

## English Literature, 1824–1840

Richard Cronin

First published 2002 by
PALGRAVE
Houndmills, Basingstoke, Hampshire RG21 6XS and
175 Fifth Avenue, New York, N. Y. 10010
Companies and representatives throughout the world

PALGRAVE is the new global academic imprint of
St. Martin's Press LLC Scholarly and Reference Division and
Palgrave Publishers Ltd (formerly Macmillan Press Ltd).

ISBN 0–333–96616–3

This book is printed on paper suitable for recycling and made from fully managed and sustained forest sources.

A catalogue record for this book is available from the British Library.

Library of Congress Cataloging-in-Publication Data
Cronin, Richard.
   Romantic Victorians/Richard Cronin.
      p. cm.
   ISBN 0–333–96616–3
      1. English literature—19th century—History and criticism.
   2. Romanticism—Great Britain. I. Title.
PR468.R65 C76 2001
820.9'145—dc21
                                                        2001036491

10   9   8   7   6   5   4   3   2   1
11   10   09   08   07   06   05   04   03   02

Printed and bound in Great Britain by
Antony Rowe Ltd, Chippenham, Wiltshire

*In memory of my father,*
*George Henry Cronin*

# Contents

# Acknowledgements

My primary debt is to the Arts and Humanities Research Board and to the University of Glasgow who between them funded a period of research leave in the academic year 1999–2000 without which this book would not have been written. My colleagues, Dorothy McMillan, Robert Cummings, Seamus Perry, Stephen Prickett, and Nicola Trott, kindly read my manuscript and made valuable suggestions for its improvement. I have also benefited from discussions with two other colleagues, Clifford Siskin and Janet Todd. These are all more than colleagues – they are friends – and if they feel that I have placed rather a high tax on friendship, they have paid it uncomplainingly. Dorothy McMillan has cheerfully accepted even greater impositions: she is not just my colleague and my friend but my wife. I am grateful, too, to the anonymous readers of the manuscript for their generosity, and even more grateful for their strictures. It still may not be the book that they would have liked me to write, but it is a better book for their comments.

This book has been very long in gestation. Early versions of some chapters have been given as conference papers, and some have appeared as articles. I am grateful to the conference organizers who allowed me to try out my work; amongst them, Lilla Crisafulli (three times; at Rome, Bologna, and Lerici), Nora Crook, John Goodridge, Simon Kovesi, Warwick Gould, Nicholas Roe (twice), Rebecca Stott, and John Sutherland. I am also grateful to the editors of *John Clare: New Voices*, the *Keats–Shelley Journal*, the *Keats-Shelley Review*, the *Philological Quarterly*, and *Victorian Poetry* for permission to re-use material that appeared in an earlier form in these publications. I am grateful too to all those who responded to those articles and conference papers, especially Stuart Curran, who has saved me from repeating a particularly egregious mistake.

# Introduction

This is a book about English literature in the years from 1824 to 1840. I have felt free to look before and after, whenever the need arises, but these are the years on which the book is focused. It is a shadowy stretch of time sandwiched between two far more colourful periods. In my old-fashioned primary school we were made to memorize the sequence of the English monarchs, beginning with Henry VII. It seems somehow appropriate that the hardest to remember, the historical equivalent of seven times eight in the multiplication tables, was William IV. In truth, there is little to remember about this younger brother of the Prince Regent, except that he had ten illegitimate children by the actress Mrs Jordan. He reigned from 1830 until 1837, and at his death the obituarists found it hard to find any strong feelings to express. *The Spectator* summed him up economically, 'His late Majesty, though at times a jovial and, for a king, an honest man, was a weak, ignorant, commonplace sort of person.' For many years the writers of his reign fared little better. Bulwer Lytton, then simply Edward Bulwer, was the most successful novelist, but he survives, it seems, only because his name has been affixed to a prize for bad writing. There are faint signs of a reawakening of interest. A few of his novels are now back in print, and there was a conference on his work in London in September 2000. But he is not the name he once was. The most famous poet was Felicia Hemans. She has benefited from the resurgence of interest in women poets. Two of her volumes are now back in print, Susan Wolfson has edited a generous selection of her poems, and her work figures in most accounts of nineteenth-century poetry.[1] But the new readiness to accept that her poetry ought to be discussed has been matched by a widespread puzzlement as to what kinds of thing might be said about it. A web discussion thread quite recently addressed itself to precisely this problem. The contributions were fascinating, but inconclusive.² The period's most celebrated prose writer is Thomas Carlyle, who remains greatly celebrated, but remains also little read.

These are among the writers that I shall discuss, along with others who seem to have fared still worse. As I write, remarkably, only *Sybil* of all Disraeli's novels remains in print. The poems of Beddoes and George Darley are available only in second-hand editions, as are novelists such as Thomas Lister and Robert Plumer Ward. But again there are signs of a change. A selection of Beddoes's poems has recently been published. A generous selection of Letitia Landon's poems was published in 1997, and Catherine Gore, wittiest of all the 1830s novelists, is once again in print. Mary Shelley may now be better known than she was while she was alive. All her novels are in print, several of them in editions that private readers can afford. Elizabeth Barrett Browning is, for the first time since her death, attracting more attention than her husband. The time seems right, then, for a reconsideration of the period, and I hope that this book will do something towards that.

But perhaps it would be truer to say that the years on which I focus are not really a neglected period of English literature. It is rather that they do not constitute a literary period at all, but something more in the way of a lacuna, a dash, or some other kind of punctuation mark. Literary periods are constituted in various ways, sometimes by the writers themselves, more often by literary historians. But once a period has been successfully constituted a number of forces are rapidly deployed to defend its borders: systems of library classification, the sectioning of publishers' catalogues, the production of anthologies and of monograph series, and the construction of university courses. Universities advertise for an eighteenth-century specialist, a Romanticist, or a Victorianist, because, once they are established, these courses need to be taught. So it is that the kind of knowledge that the study of literary texts produces is constrained, like all kinds of knowledge, by the institutional structures within which that study takes place. In the past twenty years there have been many more radical challenges to this system of constraints than any offered by this book. Most obviously, there has been a vigorous attempt to challenge the category literature itself, and to transform the traditional English department into a department of cultural studies. And yet, oddly but perhaps predictably, the new breed of cultural historians has tended to accept the period boundaries first posited by the traditional literary historians of the nineteenth and twentieth centuries. One consequence is that the period I have chosen to study has been neglected by Victorianists and Romanticists alike, 'both sides', as one of the few students of the poetry of these years suggests, being apt to 'take more interest in marking their natural boundaries than in mapping the roads between them', with the result that the period has been abandoned, 'a no-man's land that no one is fighting for'.[3]

My title conceals a confession. 'Romantic Victorians' does not fill a space: it does not even give it a name. That is because I do not wish to separate the writing of these years from what came before or from what came later, and that for two reasons. First, I wish to dispute various boundaries that have in the past twenty years been drawn not only between the study of one period and the study of another, but within the study of particular periods. For example, few would dispute that some of the most interesting work in the Romantic period has concerned itself with the discovery, or re-discovery of a female Romanticism, and yet the result has been, very often, simply to offer a choice between one version of Romanticism and another, each served by its own text-books and its own anthologies. One attraction of the period that I have chosen is that it covers a number of years in which it is possible neither to ignore the work of women writers nor to isolate their work from that of their male contemporaries. There is a similar if less fraught division, even more marked in Victorianists than Romanticists, between the study of poems and of prose fiction. There are divisions between those who confine their attention to the traditional literary genres and those who wish to bring into notice other kinds of writing, and there remain even clearer differences between those who wish to preserve the term 'literature' as a description properly applicable only to writings which have achieved a particular cultural status, and those who believe that the proper object of attention is all or any of the writing that was produced in the period. In the years between 1824 and 1840 none of these divisions is at all easy to sustain, and that in itself is a powerful reason to give the writing of those years closer attention.

So my purpose is to examine, in the words of my most important predecessor, Virgil Nemoianu, 'the peculiarly neglected English literature of the 1820s and 1830s'. But my ambitions are not just more modest than his, but very different. Nemoianu's study comprehends the literature of all Europe in these years, and his attempt is to locate in that literature 'a coherent and significant *figura*'.[4] Nemoianu finds it in the German notion of the Biedermeier, a classification that he extends to all European literature of the period. The title of Nemoianu's book, *The Taming of Romanticism*, condenses his argument into a phrase. In the 1820s and 30s 'the sheer energy of the romantic breakthrough is captured and tamed in a long phase of late romanticism that has a configuration of its own'

(28). There is much in this with which I am happy to agree. In some of the chapters that follow I will trace the taming of the isolated heretic into the dutiful member of the congregation; of the revolutionary into the citizen; of the guilty raptures of the Romantic brother and sister sexually consummating their love for each other into the wedded bliss of Victorian first cousins whose wedding meets with beaming family approval. Nevertheless, I remain suspicious of Nemoianu's enterprise. First, it relies on a definition of Romanticism so narrow that it excludes all but a tiny proportion of the writing produced between 1790 and 1824. The Biedermeier is left with a double duty to perform. It labels the writing that appeared after Byron's death, but it also names all the writing before then that will not fit with Nemoianu's rigorous notion of the Romantic. For Nemoianu, for example, Scott, Austen, and Crabbe are representative Biedermeier writers, even though they began their literary careers at almost the same time as Wordsworth and Coleridge. Second, Nemoianu only shakily establishes the coherence of the literary period that he discusses. Is it persuasive, for example, to describe Cobbett as 'a social ideologist equally opposed to the relentless growth of capitalism and to the messianic notes of radicalism' (70), or Beddoes as a poet who 'tones down the Gothic impulse' (72)? But in the end, I suspect, my differences with Nemoianu have less to do with matters of interpretation than with a difference of temperament. 'Can we then assert with confidence that there is an English Biedermeier?', Nemoianu asks, and replies, 'Let us say, guardedly, that it seems difficult to write on the history of English literature in the first half of the nineteenth century without postulating one' (75). I am afraid that I do not feel the difficulty. In fact, for me, one of the pleasures of writing this book has been the opportunity my chosen period has given me of evading 'Romanticism' and 'Victorianism', the lumbering reifications that guard its borders. Hence the absence from this book, regretted by a sympathetic and intelligent reader of my manuscript, of any 'period-defining theory'.

   But this is not to say that I prefer to read texts 'in themselves', whatever that might mean. On the contrary, my primary interest in the chapters that follow is in the relationships between texts. In particular, I am interested in the manner in which writers remember their predecessors, which is to say I am interested as much by what they forget as by what they remember. 'Close thy Byron, open thy Goethe', Carlyle recommends in *Sartor Resartus*, and his advice has a general application. It may be that we are what history makes of us, and that all writers are produced by their predecessors, but it is equally true that history is what we make of it, and that writers produce the writers who produce them. This book takes some of those who began to write in the years following Byron's death, and asks which books they chose to open, and which books they chose to close. But it is just as interested in how they read the books that they chose to open. In my final chapter, for example, I consider the young Henry Alford, opening a copy of Shelley's *The Revolt of Islam*, and writing on the fly leaf a poem before presenting the volume to his young bride. Alford was twenty-three, and newly installed as vicar of the country parish of Wymeswold. It was the beginning of a distinguished career. He was to become Dean of Canterbury Cathedral, and to win scholarly fame as editor of the Greek Testament. Alford's mother had died at his birth, and he had been raised in the family of his uncle. His bride, just twenty years old, was his cousin, his uncle's daughter, and the two had been brought up together as brother and sister. The question that interests me is how Alford contrived to read Shelley's epic of revolution and incestuous love in a manner that made it seem a suitable gift for a young clergyman to present to his young wife. All literary history, of course, is an attempt to answer such questions, but they seem to me particularly interesting in this period. The early Victorians established relations with their predecessors that were peculiarly fraught, and one of the reasons is that their predecessors were dead.

When Byron died at Missolonghi on April 19, 1824, the second generation of Romantic poets had, in little more than two years, been wiped out. It was not a thing that anyone could have known at the time, for the Romantic poets were not grouped under that label until much later in the nineteenth century – Taine seems to have been the first to use the term in 1863 – and it was still later, almost at the beginning of the twentieth century, that the label was generally assumed to refer to six poets neatly divided into two generations. But the death of Byron seemed to those who lived through it a shockingly abrupt ending. Tennyson was just fourteen. For him, it was 'a day when the whole world seemed darkened'. In a little hollow near Somersby, his family home, he carved on a rock the words 'Byron is dead'.[5] Hazlitt was at work on a tart summary of Byron's poetic career for *The Spirit of the Age*, and he marks the news of his death by a blank space after which his 'strain of somewhat peevish invective' swells into eulogy: 'Lord Byron is dead: he also died a martyr to his zeal in the cause of freedom, for the last, best hopes of man. Let this be his excuse and his epitaph!'. His loss, Disraeli tells us in *Vivian Grey* 'can never be retrieved'. The death of Shelley had made nothing like such a stir, and the death of Keats had attracted little notice. But very soon Browning happened on Benbow's pirated edition of Shelley's poems, and not long afterwards Maurice was celebrating Shelley in the *Athenaeum*, and Maurice's Cambridge admirers, led by Hallam and Milnes, appeared at the Oxford Union to argue, to the astonishment of their Oxford contemporaries, that Shelley was a greater poet than Byron. Keats's fame grew more slowly, but before the mid-century he had become a dominant influence on English poetry. By 1824, then, the poets who were to exert the most powerful influence on their nineteenth-century successors were all of them dead, with the single exception of Wordsworth, and he, as Harold Bloom colourfully puts it, was undergoing for the last thirty years of his life 'the longest dying of a major poetic genius in history'.[6]

Andrew Bennett has argued that Romantic poets are distinctive in that they address their audiences as if posthumously. They speak from the grave to readers who are not yet born.[7] Romantic poems are written as if their authors were already dead. But for their successors the important point was that by 1824 the Romantic ambition had been realised. The children of living parents find it hard enough to establish a sensible relationship with them: the task is much harder for the children of parents who are dead. The ellipsis in Hazlitt's essay on Byron makes the point as well as anything. Up to that point, Hazlitt has been reading a contemporary: after it he contemplates a poet who has undergone the 'natural canonization' of death. Death, he robustly insists, 'cancels everything but truth', but, he goes on to admit, although death is powerless to obliterate truth, it transforms its nature. It 'strips a man of everything but genius and virtue'; at its touch 'the drossy particles fall off, the irritable, the personal, the gross, and mingle with the dust – the finer and more ethereal part mounts with the winged spirit to watch over our latest memory, and protect our bones from insult.'

Keats, Shelley and Byron were canonised prematurely, when they were still young men. They never lived to become the older contemporaries of the young Victorians. Disraeli's novel *Venetia* seems driven by a nostalgia for this frustrated possibility. His Shelley, Marmion Herbert, is drowned only in his late middle-age, when he has become a stooping, grey-haired, mellow man who looks back with benign amusement at his youthful extremism, and offers counsel to the youthful poet, Lord Cadurcis, that is suffused with the wisdom of age. Cadurcis is Disraeli's version of Byron, but at this point in the novel he serves to realize a dream that Disraeli could entertain only in fiction, the dream that his literary discipleship might be modulated by a social relationship. Disraeli is nostalgic for the lost possibility that he might have with Shelley the kind of conversations that Byron had with him when

> the swift thought,
> Winging itself with laughter, lingered not,
> But flew from brain to brain, – such glee was ours,
> Charged with light memories of remembered hours,
> None slow enough for sadness.
> *Julian and Maddalo*, 28–32

It is the same dream that suddenly infects Browning in 'Memorabilia':

> And did you once see Shelley plain,
> And did he stop and speak to you?
> And did you speak to him again?

But, for Browning, what strikes is the difficulty of imagining that any-one had ever actually spoken to Shelley. He is not saddened by Shelley's death so much as startled by the thought that he had ever been alive.

But lots of poets have died young. Three premature deaths would not have been enough in themselves to establish the sense that the early Victorians seem to have shared, that the death of Byron marked an epoch, and that the oddest thing about the era that it brought to a close was that it had been so brief. It seemed as if a century had been pressed into thirty years, which is why it seemed so strange to Browning to meet someone who had actually spoken to Shelley. The thing about Romanticism, as we now call it, was that it happened so fast that its end bumped into its beginning. 'Bliss was it in that dawn to be alive', writes Wordsworth, remembering his summer vacation of 1790, and metaphors of new births, of a world reborn, echo through English poetry for the next thirty years. But by 1826, when Mary Shelley pub-lished *The Last Man*, her baleful vision of the end of the world, the topic was widely criticized as hackneyed. A novel with the same title had been published in 1806, Byron had offered his own version in 'Darkness', and Hood's poem 'The Last Man' was published in the same year as Mary Shelley's novel.

The sense that history had gone through a period of crazy acceleration had its origin in political events, I think, and more particularly in events in Paris between 1789 and 1795, six years in which France underwent a process of political change that would have been rapid if it had been spread over a hundred. Nothing, not even the English Commonwealth, had prepared the witnesses of these events for evidence so dramatic that history might somehow slip the leash, and its stately pace turn into a mad gallop. The sense so hard to withstand, that the careers of the Romantic poets were oddly speeded up, so that Wordsworth, Byron, Shelley and Keats completed, in a decade, five years, or less, a process of poetic development that ought to have taken a lifetime, owes something to the fact that three of them died and the fourth outlived his talent, but it relies too, surely, on the impulse to credit to their careers the wild revolutionary energy of the six years of the Revolution. Napoleon, in Carlyle's account, in 1795, on the twelfth vendemiaire, gave the Paris mob his 'whiff of grapeshot', 'and the thing we specifically call *French Revolution* is blown into space by it, and become a thing that was! – ' (3, 320). It is not entirely fanciful to suggest that the death of Byron marked for the fourteen-year-old Tennyson almost as dramatically abrupt a conclusion. It was because so much had been pressed into so few years, and that it had all ended so suddenly, that the Revolution continued to occupy the English mind for much of the nineteenth century, and it was the same, I think, with the dead poets. Michael O'Neill has written on Beddoes's preoccupation with 'haunting', and shown how the ghosts of the dead Romantics, particularly Shelley, haunt his verse.[8] The interest is predictable in a poet hailed by Pound as 'prince of morticians', but it is an instance of a more general plight. Those who die too young, the stories say, are hard to lay to rest: they are very likely to haunt us.

I begin with biography, the most direct of all the ways in which living writers encounter the dead. Byron had generated huge biographical interest in his lifetime, and the process only accelerated after his death. Thomas Moore's authorized life of 1830 was swamped by its competitors. But it was not until 1848 that Monckton Milnes published the first full life of Keats, and later still, in 1858, that Thomas Jefferson Hogg published the first two volumes of his life of Shelley, the poet's father having forbidden any biography during his lifetime. In my first chapter, I find a common thread in these biographies, an impulse at once to summon the ghost of the dead poet and to lay it. In fact, the more strenuously the biographers attempt to summon the dead poet, the more elusive he seems to become. These biographers share an ideal, that the poet be allowed to tell the story of his life in his own words, but the more the biographer tries make himself invisible the more prominent his presence seems to become, until, in Hogg's life of Shelley, the biography of the poet is reduced to a series of fragmentary episodes in Hogg's autobiographical account of his own early years. The respect for the poet's own words itself proves oddly unstable, because the biographers are unsure as to whether the poet is more authentically revealed in his written or in his spoken communications. If the former, then the biographer is reduced to the humble task of transcription, copying out a selection of the poet's correspondence and journals. But writing is an indirect expression of the self. Hence the temptation, to which many of these biographers succumb, to reproduce the voice rather than simply the words of the dead poet, to represent him speaking rather than simply writing. The ambition is to render the likeness of the poet more lifelike, more authentic, except, of course, that the words that the poet speaks must be supplied by the biographer. The more complete the desire to render the poet in his full, living presence, the more completely he becomes a fictional character in someone else's novel.

In the second part of the chapter I turn to representations of Byron and Shelley in acknowledged fictions. Caroline Lamb's *Glenarvon* was published in 1816, but Mary Shelley's *The Last Man* and Disraeli's *Venetia* were written after Byron and Shelley had died. Lamb's novel is an act of revenge, Disraeli's and Shelley's are acts of homage. Disraeli, unlike Lamb and Shelley, had never met the poets he commemorates. Nevertheless, the evident differences between the novels are interesting chiefly because they make their similarities the more striking. In particular, all three novelists remove the poets from their own time, and all three make them characters more remarkable for their political than their literary activities. Caroline Lamb allows Byron to lead the Irish insurgents in the rebellion of 1798; Mary Shelley transports Byron and Shelley to the end of the twenty-first century, when each in turn becomes Lord Protector of England; and Disraeli makes Byron and Shelley eighteenth-century gentlemen, and Shelley the general chiefly responsible for America's victory in the War of Independence. It is a tactic, I argue, that allows the novelists at once to accept and to deny the notion that, as Hazlitt argued of Wordsworth, 'the political changes of day were the model on which [they] formed and conducted [their] poetical experiments'.

In this, I argue in the second chapter, the novelists were participating in a wider cultural project, of which the chief monument is Macaulay's *History of England*. Macaulay did not live to complete his work. He had planned to write a history of England from the Revolution of 1688 to the Reform Bill of 1832, from 'the Revolution which brought the Crown into harmony with the Parliament, and the Revolution which brought the Parliament into harmony with the nation'. It is a story that is designed expressly to deny the notion that another Revolution, the one that occurred in France, had exerted any effect on the history of this island. In *The Last Man*, the plague disregards national boundaries. Even an ocean is no barrier against its progress. But, for Macaulay, the narrow stretch of water that separates England from France is wide enough to preserve the triumphant insularity of English history. His is a notion that had been powerfully challenged even before it had been advanced. In this chapter Carlyle figures, as he did in M.H. Abrams's *Natural Supernaturalism*, as the writer who most completely recapitulates Romanticism for a later generation, but for me he does so most power-fully in *The French Revolution*. For Carlyle, the Revolution is not an event that happened more than forty years ago in a foreign country, not an event that is over and over there, but an event through which we are all still living, and will be living for hundreds of years.

Chapter Three begins with the two most successful poets of the decade that followed the death of Byron: Felicia Hemans and Letitia Landon. Formally, neither poet was particularly innovative. Both wrote within the tradition of Scott and Byron. Nevertheless, between them, they effected a startling transformation of English poetry. In effect, they established femininity as the one possible vessel for the life of the affections, and hence as the only source of those values that poems enunciate. This will seem strange given that both poets, but especially Hemans, seem wedded to an entirely conventional ideal of masculinity. But in the work of Hemans and Landon masculinity becomes itself an ideal that can be articulated only by a feminine voice. The second part of the chapter considers two male contemporaries of Hemans and Landon who tried to establish their poetic careers in the age of 'woman's rule' that Hemans and Landon had instituted. George Darley and Thomas Lovell Beddoes were poets who lived uncomfortably with the bleak recognition that Beddoes ascribes to one of his characters in *Death's Jest Book*, 'O! it is nothing now to be a man'. The chapter ends with one male poet's brilliantly simple solution to the problem. Tennyson chose to write a number of his most successful early poems as a woman.

'Mrs Hemans' and 'L.E.L.' were brand names. The two women wrote in the tradition of Scott and Byron, because these were the precursors who had most successfully converted their authorship into a commod-ity. John Murray marketed Byron as the 'childe', the 'pilgrim'. The poems themselves became the centre of a merchandising industry – all the busts and engravings of the poet, the open-necked shirts, the cos-metics purchased in order to secure a designer pallor – in a manner that was not to be outdone until the 1960s. Scott – unlikely as it might seem, given the winning diffidence of the man – achieved the same feat twice: once as 'the minstrel', and afterwards as the author of the novels, 'the great unknown'. The commodification of culture is a topic much like the rise of the middle classes: as soon as it is identified it begins a retrogressive journey through the years. It has currently reached the beginning of the eighteenth century. But it was in this period that writers first began to flaunt the status of their productions as commodities. Literature, writes Disraeli, is 'the mere creature of our imaginary wealth ... Consols at 100 were the origin of all book societies'. It is a remark that he makes in *Vivian Grey*, the first pure example of silver fork fiction, the first true fashionable novel. These were the novels that dominated the fiction market in the late 1820s and 1830s. They are novels about commodities – watches from Brequet, coats from Stultz, ices from Clark's – but they are also commodities themselves. They were the first novels that are more usefully identified by their publisher than by their authors, and they provide the subject for my fourth chapter.

Almost all the fashionable novels were published by Henry Colburn, and almost all were published anonymously. Colburn seems to have grasped very early the lesson that the 'Scotch novels' had given on the commercial power of anonymity. He also understood, perhaps following the example of John Murray in his proprietorship of the *Quarterly*, the advantage for a publisher of books of also owning reviews. He set up the *Literary Gazette*, the *New Monthly Magazine*, and then, when he lost control of the *Gazette*, bought a controlling interest in the *Athenaeum*, explaining to the *Gazette*'s editor, William Jerdan, that he had done so 'in consequence of the injustice done to my authors generally (who are on the liberal side) by the "Literary Gazette".'[9] Thus equipped, Colburn was able to cultivate the art now known as hype, but then called 'puffing'. His reviews advertised his novels, often hinting that they were written by some unnameable person of extraordinary eminence in the fashionable world (which was only very rarely the case), and the novels themselves, much more clearly than any fiction before them, were informed by the manner in which they were marketed. They were novels about fashionable items that were themselves fashionable items. They were recklessly contemporary, written not for all time, not even for the age, but for the season, the brief few months in which a particular cut of waistcoat was modish. Everything that they represented was anathema to another writer of the time. These were novels that flamboyantly tied themselves to a fleeting present, but for Carlyle a 'true Book' is not likely to appear more than once in two centuries, and a 'true Work of Art' is distinct from 'a Daub of Artifice' because in it one can see 'Eternity looking through time; the Godlike rendered visible'. But Carlyle found nowhere to publish *Sartor Resartus* except *Fraser's*

*Magazine*, with the result that the medium of publication implicated the work with the commodified writing that it denounced so violently. Carlyle's oddly ambivalent negotiations with the fashionable novel provide the second focus for this chapter.

Fashionable novels construed their readers as consumers. In Chapter Five I turn to a quite different kind of writing, a kind that attempts to enfranchise its readers and address them as fellow citizens. For the first generation of Romantics the ideal of citizenship was irremediably contaminated by its association with the French Revolutionaries, and their successors had failed to reinstate it. For them, there remained only a Byronic celebration of an individuality that was authentic precisely in so far as it was inexpressible within any possible social relationship, or the apparently contradictory ideal, often favoured by Shelley, that required the individual to surrender any sense of a separate self by triumphantly merging the self with all humankind. In his early poems, a poet such as Browning swithers uncomfortably between these possibilities. Sordello alternates between fierce boasts of his irreducible individuality and touchingly naïve aspirations to melt into the crowd: 'Mankind and he were really fused'. I begin with Tennyson and his Cambridge friends attempting to free themselves from the politics of their predecessors by re-living their revolutionary enthusiasms, before turning to the 'awfully radical' writings of Browning in the 1830s. I end in 1851, with Elizabeth Barrett Browning's *Casa Guidi Windows*, the poem that explicates most fully the notion of citizenship, less an ideal than a practice, that came to dominate the nineteenth century.

Chapter Five concerns relationship between people, and in Chapter Six I turn to relationships with things, in particular with landscapes. It is a chapter that traces the movement from the landscapes of a poem such as *Alastor* to the landscapes celebrated by Browning's painter in *Fra Lippo Lippi*, the movement from landscape celebrated as a picture of the mind of its beholder, to landscape celebrated as separate from the observer, and, if a picture of any mind, then a picture only of the mind of God. But this chapter too is concerned with enfranchisement, the enfranchisement not of a readership but of an individual writer, the poet, John Clare. It was Clare himself who claimed, 'I found the poems in the fields / And only wrote them down'. None of Clare's recent critics is willing to accept so simple an account of his compositional methods, and yet one still very often detects a desire to preserve Clare's special place amongst the English poets by insisting that Clare's perceptions of the natural world are mediated, if they are mediated at all, only though the community to which Clare belonged, the village of Helpston, and the particular dialect that this community shared. There is a widespread unwillingness to accept the literariness of Clare's poems. And yet he was a great reader, and in many of his poems he responds to the poems of his contemporaries. One of my purposes in this chapter is not just to assert the fact that Clare responded in his own poems to the work of poets such as Wordsworth, Coleridge and Keats, but to insist on the intelligence of that response, and on its representative character. In particular, Clare turns against the Romantic notion that art might ever free itself from the material conditions out of which it was produced, that it might ever succeed in becoming 'unbodied', and in doing so he became the unacknowledged and unknown precursor of much Victorian poetry.

Chapter Seven turns to Victorian piety, but a particular kind of Victorian piety. *In Memoriam*, for example, was very widely understood as a pious poem and a Christian poem, despite the difficulty of locating in it a single statement that might confidently be identified as an orthodox expression of Christian dogma. In fact, the poem's theology seems to be put together largely in response to a single desire – that death might not separate us from those we love. Though movingly human, it is an ambition that seems to have no secure foundation at all in Christian belief. The poem is remarkable for two manoeuvres. First, scepticism is presented not as the opposite of faith, but as faith's most authentic expression: 'There lives more faith in honest doubt, / Believe me, than in half the creeds.' Second, the poem drives not so much towards a newly confident religious belief as towards a regained sense of the self as a member of a social community. I trace both these manoeuvres in early poems by Tennyson, 'Supposed Confessions' and 'The Two Voices', and in a rather later poem by Browning, *Christmas-Eve*. All three poems bear the imprint of Coleridge, and the last two echo one of Coleridge's poems, *The Ancient Mariner*. At the end of that poem the mariner confides that he finds it sweeter to 'walk together to the kirk / With a goodly company' than to attend marriage feasts. It is a strange moment, because it seems at once to admit and to deny the joy of human society, so that the mariner's liking for 'goodly company' fails somehow to impinge at all on his unassuaged loneliness. That loneliness, which is also the isolation to which the Romantic poet is at once elected and doomed, is what Tennyson and Browning seem most determined to escape, and they do so by becoming members of a church. These are poems that find the solution to religious doubt not in an experience of conversion, but in a decision to join a community of believers. They are poems about 'Church Going', but for Browning and Tennyson, unlike Larkin, churches are not best visited when they are empty, but when they are

# 1
# Memorializing Romanticism

They had problems with Romantic memorials. Keats instructed his own epitaph. He remembered, as he was dying, some lines from Beaumont and Fletcher's *Philaster*, 'all your better deeds / Shall be in water writ, but this in marble' (5.iii.81–2), and asked Severn to arrange that his grave be nameless, marked only by the words, 'Here lies one whose name was writ in water'. Severn attended to Keats's wishes, and, when he was buried in the Protestant Cemetery in Rome, he arranged for the epitaph that Keats himself had chosen to be carved on the stone. But he added a broken lyre of his own devising, and, after consulting with another of Keats's friends, Charles Brown, added, too, an explanation of the epitaph, 'This grave contains all that was mortal of a young English poet, who, on his death-bed, in the bitterness of his heart, at the malicious power of his enemies, desired these words to be engraved on his tombstone'. Brown later repented of his decision, but it was too late. The myth that Keats himself repudiated, of the poet killed by criticism, snuffed out by an article, had been stamped on Keats's grave. Shelley seized on the paradox – writing that leaves no trace made permanent in stone, a durable monument to the ephemeral – and produced an epigram:

'Here lieth One whose name was writ on water.'
But, ere the breath that could erase it blew,
Death in remorse for that fell slaughter,
Death, the immortalizing winter, flew
Athwart the stream, – and time's printless torrent grew
A scroll of crystal, blazoning the name
Of Adonais!

As the fragment indicates, it was the tombstone that gave Shelley the clue for his own memorial to Keats. *Adonais* was to direct the way in which Keats's poems were received for a century. His Victorian reputation had its origin in the well-intentioned failure of two friends to attend to Keats's wishes.[1]

The case of Byron's memorial was more tangled. His friend, John Cam Hobhouse, had been outraged by the refusal to allow Byron's body, after its return to England, to be interred in Westminster Abbey, and in 1826 he set up a committee to commission a memorial statue, determined that the poet's monument, if not his body, should be allowed a place in Poet's Corner. It was a distinguished committee, chaired by Byron's schoolfriend, Lord Clare, and including Sir Francis Burdett, the Duke of Devonshire, and Byron's fellow poets, Scott, Moore, Rogers, and Campbell. Even Goethe later agreed to become a member. Moore's suggestion that a place be found for Jackson, the boxer who had schooled Byron in the art, was indignantly rejected. But the project dragged. In 1829 Sir Francis Chantrey refused the commission, and the committee turned to Thorwaldsen, the Danish sculptor who was resident in Rome, and had sculpted the bust of Byron that Hobhouse himself now owned. The statue was completed, and arrived in England, but only to be deposited in a Customs House. Hobhouse was waiting for Dean Ireland, who had vetoed Byron's burial in Westminster Abbey, to die, and unfortunately he lived until 1842, dying just a few days before his eighty-first birthday. Hobhouse immediately renewed his petition to the Abbey authorities, and this time he was able to bring to bear the influence of the Prime Minister himself, Sir Robert Peel, another schoolfriend of the poet's. But, Peel reported, it was to no avail. The Abbey was intransigent. Hobhouse wrote a splenetic pamphlet to protest against the decision, and in 1844 at last agreed that the statue might be installed in the library of Trinity College, Cambridge.[2]

There can be few who regret that Onslow Ford's cloying memorial to Shelley was not erected as had been planned on Shelley's grave in the Protestant Cemetery at Rome. It would have clashed alarmingly with the monument to Caius Cestius, the 'keen pyramid with wedge sublime', that Shelley admires in *Adonais*. Installed in 1893 in its specially designed chamber in University College, Oxford, it has served as a fitting act of revenge on the institution that had, some eighty years before, expelled Shelley for atheism. Edward Trelawny had bought the plot in Rome in which Shelley's ashes were interred, and, as he had wished, his own ashes were buried there next to those of his friend. His daughter refused Lady Jane Shelley permission to place the statue on her father's plot. The grave remains as it was in 1822, when the simple stone with its inscription by Leigh Hunt was erected. On it is carved a simple tribute, 'Cor Cordium', heart of hearts.[3] Mary Shelley must have approved Hunt's choice – variations on the phrase are threaded through the novel in which she raised one of her own memorials to her husband, *The Last Man*.[4] But it is hard to credit Hunt's and Mary Shelley's failure to register the epitaph's grotesque irony. Shelley's body was badly decomposed when it was washed up on shore near Lerici and was burned on the beach, but one part of it at least contributed nothing to the ashes that were carefully collected for burial in Rome, the heart. Trelawny snatched that from the fire before it was consumed. There followed an undignified tussle in which Hunt unsuccessfully tried to resist Mary Shelley's proper claim to the relic. 'What does Hunt want with it?' Byron said, 'He'll only put it in a glass case and make sonnets on it'.[5] When Mary returned to England she took it with her, and, enclosed in an ornate box, it formed the centre of the shrine that Lady Jane Shelley made for her father-in-law at Field Place, the Shelley family's Sussex seat. Later in the century it seems to have been mislaid. Hunt's epigraph risks calling attention not to the presence in the grave of Shelley's ashes, but to the absence of his heart.

These are just anecdotes, of course, and yet for me they have an allegorical value. They figure the difficulty that I hope to explore throughout this book. How do writers build fitting monuments to their dead fellows? I want to suggest that for early Victorian writers the question was an especially difficult one, because the writers that they wished to memorialize seemed at once very close and very far away. Browning's 'Memorabilia', was prompted, it seems, by Browning's shock when, in the summer of 1852, he met by chance in a London bookshop a man who claimed to have known Shelley personally.[6]

> And did you once see Shelley plain,
>   And did he stop and speak to you?
> And did you speak to him again?
>   How strange it seems, and new!

It seems, on the face of it, an excessive response to an unsurprising encounter. Shelley, after all, had been only nineteen when Browning was born, expelled from Oxford just eighteen months since, the youthful husband of the still more youthful Harriet Westbrook. Had he lived, he would have been fifty-nine in the summer of 1852, an elderly man, grey-haired or bald no doubt, but scarcely ancient. In the year that

Browning was born, Shelley had himself learned that he had been wrong to enrol the name of William Godwin 'on the list of the honorable dead', and that the philosopher was, in fact, a fifty-five year old bookseller living in London in Skinner Street.[7] It is always a little surprising when a name on a title page becomes attached to a living human being, a surprise akin to passing a well-known television personality in the street, but the jolt is trivial enough, not the kind of shock that Browning records in his poem. Browning stared in astonishment at the man who had known Shelley not because it seemed surprising that Shelley could have been alive so recently, but, surely, because Browning was shocked by the casual display of evidence that he had ever been alive at all.

Between 1821 and 1824 the second generation of English Romantic poets died, and became at once creatures out of myth, people the harder to believe in the more closely they were looked at. Peacock gives a dry account of the process when comparing Medwin's and Hogg's accounts of the master at Sion House Academy, Shelley's first school, a man so hateful, according to Medwin, that neither he nor Shelley could ever bring themselves to speak of him in later life, and, according to Hogg, someone of whom Shelley spoke 'not without respect, saying, "he was a hard-headed Scotchman, and a man of rather liberal opinion"'. As Peacock notes, 'Between these two accounts the Doctor and his character seem reduced to a myth',[8] which establishes, Peacock suggests, the Doctor's right to preside over the early education of a poet whose life would resist biography precisely because so many of the events in it would 'resolve themselves into the same mythical character'.

Byron's foot is a more telling example of the process. The most vivid description of the poet's limbs is offered by Trelawny, who, arriving at Missolonghi on the day after Byron's death, devised a ruse for sending Fletcher, Byron's servant, from the room, and seized the opportunity to inspect the corpse:

> I uncovered the Pilgrim's feet, and was answered – the great mystery was solved. Both his feet were clubbed, and his legs were withered to the knee – the form and features of an Apollo, with the feet and legs of a sylvan satyr.[9]

Byron is revealed as Hyperion above and a satyr below. The poet's body is itself an allegory, a compact emblem both of the work and of the man who produced it. Unfortunately, Trelawny may, in fact, never have seen Byron's body at all. There is evidence that he arrived at Missolonghi only after the preserved corpse had been sealed in its coffin.[10] His description has the vividness not of memory but of myth. Trelawny, as Byron quickly recognized, was an incorrigible liar, but even scrupulous witnesses found that when they thought of the foot it doggedly failed to materialize. Lady Blessington undramatically describes Byron as 'slightly lame, and the deformity of the foot is so little remarkable that I am not now aware which foot it is'.[11] This seems candid, but, as Lady Blessington knew, her uncertainty was by the time she wrote itself an element of the Byron myth. Moore, in a footnote at the very end of his *Life*, reports the curious fact that Byron's closest friends were equally divided as to whether he was lame in the left or right foot.[12]

Moore ends his book curiously, by transcribing a brief selection of Byron's detached thoughts before hurrying to a perfunctory conclusion. It was one thought in particular, I suspect, that made this seem a proper way to end: 'Let any man try at the end of *ten* years to bring before him the features, or the mind, or the sayings, or the habits of his best friend … and he will be surprised by the extreme confusion of his ideas' (653). It is as if Moore were anxious that, in the last words that he quotes from his dead friend, Byron himself should offer an excuse for the deficiencies of all biographers, no matter how well-qualified for their task. But it was a problem that the biographers of the Romantic poets seemed to find more intractable than most.

## II

In the ten years following his death, Byron's status as a biographical subject was exceeded only by Napoleon's. There were book-length accounts by Anne Louise Belloc, George Clinton, Thomas Medwin, R.C. Dallas, John Galt, Leigh Hunt, William Parry, James Kennedy, J.W. Simmons, Moore, and the Countess of Blessington.[13] All deaths leave a gap, and the more famous the dead person the greater the volume of writing needed to fill it. But the mass of writings on Byron did not succeed in filling the hole, they served only to define it. The interest of the prurient reader, into which category all readers of biographies fall, centred of course on the reasons for the breakdown of Byron's marriage, and on this all the biographers are perversely, even infuriatingly, reticent, far more reticent than commentators had been while Byron was alive. Moore's discussion of the event represents it as predictable, because poets of genius are peculiarly ill-fitted for marriage; as humdrum, resulting from those trivial irritations impossible to avoid when marriage reveals a 'general incompatibity' between the married pair; but also as 'unexampled', in that husband and wife seemed to be on the best of terms at the point at which the separation took place (296). He complains that Lady Byron's determined silence left a space which was filled by 'dark hints and vague insinuations, of which the fancy of every hearer was left to fill up the outline as he pleased' (297), but contrives, in a discussion of several thousand words, to leave the space as empty as he found it. As Peacock remarks:

> In the points about which the public were most curious, what was before mystery, is still mystery. It remains, like Bottom's dream, in the repositories of the incommunicable.[14]

Shelley's marital difficulties, though less widely broadcast than Byron's, were also, during his lifetime, public property. His biographers, since silence was impossible, preferred to compress the whole painful episode into a phrase or two in which concern for fact surrenders to the requirement of blandness. So, Leigh Hunt tells us, Shelley and Harriet 'separated by mutual consent, after the birth of two children'.[15] These are, of course, sensitive matters, and Moore's reticence and Hunt's dishonesty are understandable. But there is a tendency at all critical moments in these biographies, not just the sensitive ones, for the biographer unaccountably to avert his eyes. Take, for example. Leigh Hunt's account of his reunion with Shelley at Leghorn in June 1822. It was the first time that Hunt had seen Shelley, that 'heart of hearts', for almost four years. 'I will not dwell upon the moment', he writes. Nor does he dwell on the week that the two spent together before Shelley embarked on the fatal voyage back to Lerici. Instead, he describes Leghorn and Byron's house in Pisa, the Casa Lanfranchi, and comments on his wife's state of health, recommends a healthy diet and exercise as the best defences against consumption, finds the Italian custom by which servants kiss the hands of their master on his returning home from a journey 'agreeable' but too expressive of social distinctions, and at last records that he and Shelley, on the day before Shelley's death, spent a 'delightful afternoon' at Pisa, and visited the cathedral (13–18). Peacock, a much less egotistical man than Hunt, last saw Shelley on March 10, 1818, three days before Shelley sailed for Italy, when they went together to a performance of 'The Barber of Seville'. Peacock remembers the cast, and then takes the opportunity to reflect on the decline in the standards of opera performance: 'Two acts of opera, a divertissement, and a ballet, seem very ill replaced by four or five acts of opera, with little or no dancing' (115). It seems an odd way to record his final farewell to his friend.

It seems odder still if one reflects that throughout the nineteenth century biographers aspired to an impossible ideal of invisibility. The commonest kind of biography consisted of a chronological arrangement of the subject's correspondence, the letters linked by a commentary that claimed only to supply the information that could not be transmitted in its most appropriate form, in the subject's own words. Unable to disappear as they would have wished, biographers contrive to be as unobtrusive as possible. Monckton Milnes weighs the awesome responsibility that falls on him as Keats's first biographer, and is driven to the conclusion that his one proper recourse is 'to act simply as editor of the Life which was, as it were, already written' in Keats's poems and his letters.[16] Milnes had never met Keats, and felt perhaps that he had no alternative, but Thomas Moore was a close friend of Byron's. Nevertheless, he repeatedly affirms that Byron is himself his own best biographer. His years at Harrow are described in excerpts gathered together from Byron's notebooks: 'Coming, as they do, from his own pen, it is needless to add, that they afford the liveliest and best records of this period that can be furnished' (20). It is an ideal, of course, that limits the right to engage in the profitable business of biography to those who have access to the subject's manuscripts and correspondence. This was no doubt one of the reasons for the appearance of a rival ideal of biography, though another reason, just as powerful, was the pre-eminent place amongst biographers accorded by almost everyone to Boswell.

This kind of biography centres not on correspondence but conversation. Moore, Trelawny believes, gives 'no idea of the individuality of the man', because Moore, who had seen Byron only 'in society', as Trelawny falsely asserted, knew nothing of his private conversation, and because Moore assumed that Byron's letters offered direct access to his mind, whereas in fact the letters to himself and to Murray, which Moore had relied on, 'were written carefully, expressly to be shown about'. They were written, so to speak, for publication, and hence should have been printed 'with his prose works' (209–11). Trelawny was, of course, an interested witness. He did not have many of Byron's letters in his possession, since Byron did not often write to him. His strong claim to represent 'the individuality of the man' more truly than Moore must rest, then, not on his transcription of a few brief letters, but on his reproduction of lengthy conversations.

Of the early biographers of Byron and Shelley, Medwin, Kennedy, Trelawny, the Countess of Blessington, and Hunt all base their claims to authenticity on conversation rather than correspondence. It seems at first sight odd that this biographical mode should have been favoured by those whose biographical subjects were writers. Writers, one might think, are, more than most people, better represented by their writing than their speech. But, in fact, as Trelawny indicates, it is the professional expertise that in itself places the writing under suspicion. Writers write 'carefully', and hence it is in their spoken rather than their written words that they are likely unwittingly to reveal themselves.

The suspicion of writing is compounded rather than allayed by the recognition that these were writers unusually concerned with self-characterization. As Peacock says of Byron, 'Whatever figures filled up the middle and back ground of his pictures, the fore-ground was invariably consecrated to his own'.[17] He took the public into his confidence, but 'his confidences were only half-confidences', and hence more likely to deceive than a habit of reticence. Leigh Hunt offers Byron's apparently magnanimous parting lyric to his wife, 'Fare Thee Well', as evidence that he had never loved her. Byron 'set out to *imagine* what a husband might say who had truly loved his wife', and what proves that the love is only imaginary is that 'he said it so well' (111).

There is a widespread feeling that these poets had transmuted themselves into their own fictional characters, and no-one felt it more strongly than Byron himself, for he had been the first and most spectacular victim of the tendency. His wife's ploy of insisting that she had reasons for separation from him too dark to be divulged relied for its persuasiveness on the extent to which the man had been subsumed into the character of his own heroes – Lara, for instance, who hides a secret known only to those 'too discreetly wise' to do more than 'hint' at its true nature (1, 151–2). It is as if these poets had written their own lives in their fictions, fictions too powerful to be displaced by the factual lives that the biographers attempted to recover. Peacock found it impossible to resolve the contradictory accounts he had heard of Shelley's schooldays in part because Shelley himself, in his Dedication to *Laon and Cythna* for example, makes of his schooldays a myth too potent to be dispelled by fact, a young boy weeping as a May morning dawns, and dedicating himself at that moment to a lifetime struggle against the tyranny of the 'selfish and the strong'. Even his closest friends, I suspect, could not remember on which side Byron limped because in a fiction such as *The Deformed Transformed* Byron had transformed so completely his own disability into myth. Byron made repeated efforts to deny his own fictionality. 'My poesy is one thing. I am another' (74), Trelawny records him as saying. But his protestations are futile. If he avoids disappearing into his earlier poems, he succeeds only in melting into his later manner: 'In company Byron talked in Don Juan's vein' (Trelawny, 89). The quotation with which Milnes ends his life of Keats is oddly revealing:

> The world of thought must remain apart from the world of action; for, if they once coincided, the problem of Life would be solved, and the hope, which we call heaven, would be realised on earth. And therefore men
>
>> Are cradled into poetry by wrong:
>> They learn in suffering what they teach in song.

He ends with a quotation from *Julian and Maddalo*, with words that Shelley, who figures himself in the poem as Julian, gives to Maddalo, his fictional version of Byron. It seems somehow appropriate that the biography of a Romantic poet should end in an aphorism spoken by a poet who is himself a fiction in another poet's poem.

This is one reason, I think, that Byron and Shelley lend themselves to conversational biography. The mode in itself bends biography towards the novel, because, before the invention of the tape recorder, the memorialist is obliged to reconstruct conversations, remembering perhaps their gist, but relying for the impression of authenticity on the techniques of the novelist. A spoken rather than a written syntax must be used, and the character stamped with individuality by the regular appearance of a number of speech mannerisms. So, Trelawny's Byron speaks in staccato sentences, avoiding conjunctions. His conversation has the laboured liveliness so characteristic of second-rate novels. When this Byron looks at the sky, he is apt to say, 'Where is the green your friend the Laker talks such fustian about?' (73), a sentence in which 'your friend the Laker' is preferred to 'Coleridge' in the naïve belief that it approximates more nearly to the manner of sprightly conversation. Lady Blessington's Byron is far more dandiacal. Like Trelawny, her renderings of Byron's conversation become more persuasive with practice. At the beginning of her account, she relies far too heavily on having Byron sprinkle his conversation with French phrases to establish him as a denizen of the beau monde, nine in a single conversational outburst, from the acceptably common 'ennuyeux' to the bizarrely affected 'espièglerie' (38–9).

Trelawny and Blessington make use of the techniques of the novelist as a way of lending their subjects the plasticity of fiction, and they need to do this in order to accommodate apparently conflicting representations of them. In particular, the conversational mode proves more supple for writers anxious to represent the poets at once as heroes and as butts. It is a tendency only mutedly present in Moore's *Life*, in the slight jar between his habitual, somewhat obsequious references to 'the noble poet' and the passages in which he surveys those aspects of Byron's character of which he affects to disapprove, his religious scepticism, for example, with a lofty tolerance that verges on the condescending. But Moore's is on the whole a heroic portrait of Byron. Leigh Hunt's Byron, in his *Lord Byron and Some of his Contemporaries* is a butt, asking in innocent vanity what Hunt's wife had thought of a particular portrait of him by Harlowe, and utterly discomforted to learn that Mrs Hunt had not responded respectfully to the expression of contemptuous, melancholic reserve that the painter had caught. To her, 'it resembled a great schoolboy, who had a plain bun given him, instead of a plum one' (27). More often, as in Blessington's *Conversations*, both impulses are evident.

Blessington's Byron is repeatedly put out of countenance by her sharp rejoinders, as when she refuses to listen to his malicious gossip about a friend (122), points out to him that those most sensitive to a vice in others, in this case vanity, are often prone to it themselves (44–5), or writes him a poem rebuking his willingness to display his most private affairs to all and sundry:

> And canst thou bare thy breast to vulgar eyes?
>   And canst thou show the wounds that rankle there?
> Methought in noble hearts that sorrow lies
>   Too deep to suffer coarser minds to share.
>
> (34)

And yet Blessington at other times projects herself into Byron so completely that he becomes the mouthpiece for her own opinions. Her husband, we are told, was so completely a paragon that he 'shook Byron's scepticism in perfect goodness' (167). Her protegé, John Galt, is confessed by Byron to be 'as amiable a man as his recent works prove him to be a clever and intelligent author', and if he had not taken to Galt when they met, the fault was entirely his: 'to say the truth, his manner had not deference enough for my then aristocratical taste' (146). Such examples are transparent enough to be comical, but the whole book repeatedly suggests a much more radical self-identification with Byron. His most frequent topic of conversation is the rankling bitterness inspired in him by the social ostracism that he suffered after his separation from his wife, and whenever he speaks on the matter his voice merges with Lady Blessington's. She had become a Countess only after a tangled career in which she had been passed around from man to man before being bought for £10,000 by Lord Blessington from a Captain Jenkins. When Blessington married her, her ambition was to be accepted into the social circles of the Whig aristocrats, and predictably she met with stinging rebuffs. All her own accumulated bitterness finds expression in Byron's repeated denunciations of English cant.

In these lives the poet is by turns admired and despised, reduced to sulky silence by a sharp rejoinder, or commandeered as a convenient medium for the expression of the biographer's own opinions. The poet is, in fact, treated very like a wife, and there is nothing on which these biographers are more generally agreed than the womanliness of their subjects. 'He is as impulsive and jealous as a woman, and may be as changeable', Trelawny reports Shelley saying of Byron (74), and says himself to Shelley, 'Byron is as perverse as a woman' (100). But Shelley himself was as ignorant of the 'working-day world' as 'a girl at a board-ing-school' (127). Lady Blessington saw glimpses in Byron of 'a delicacy and tenderness resembling the nature of woman more than that of man' (72). Hunt found him 'as acute as a woman' in detecting those who did not think highly of him (27). Byron, Moore tells us, had no capacity for 'consecutive ratiocination':

> In this, indeed, as in many other peculiarities, – his caprices, fits of weeping, sudden affections and dislikes, – may be observed striking traces of a feminine cast of character; – it being observable that the discursive faculty is rarely exercised by women; but that nevertheless, by the mere instinct of truth (as was the case with Lord Byron), they are often enabled at once to light upon the very conclusion to which man, through all the forms of reasoning, is, in the mean time, puz-zling, and, perhaps, losing his way.
>
> (600)

The poets become women in order for the biographers to become their husbands, arrogating to themselves the husband's duty to speak on behalf of a wife unfitted by her gender to speak for herself.

Biographies, it might seem, are written memorials, extended epitaphs that fix in print all that happened in between the two simple dates that are inscribed on the tombstone. They are attempts to preserve in writ-ing the living quality of the person who has died. But the biographies of these poets seem oddly despairing that they can achieve any such thing. How, Peacock asks of Shelley, can one write the biography of a poet the events of whose life, try as one might to sift the evidence, per-sist in resolving themselves into a 'mythical character'? How, Moore implies, can one write the life of a poet who himself acknowledged that the lapse of ten years is enough to throw our memory of 'the features' and 'the mind' and 'the sayings' and 'the habits' even of our best friend into 'extreme confusion'? Amongst Byron's biographers the impossibility of adequate biography is an unlikely but common theme, a consequence of the extreme 'mobility' that all his biographers recognize in him, and also of another of his traits, his delight in 'mystification'. Blessington's Byron admits 'that it amuses him to *hoax* people, and that when each person, at some future day, will give their different statements of him, they will be so contradictory, that *all* will be doubted, – an idea that gratifies him exceedingly' (47). Mystification for Byron was, it seems, a social game: in Shelley it resulted from his vulnerability to self-serving delusions. Hogg and Peacock describe many such incidents. Shelley once explained to Peacock a sudden decision to move house by saying that he had just returned from a walk on which he had encountered a man who had warned him of a plot against him. Noticing that Shelley was carrying Peacock's hat rather than his own, Peacock asked him to put the hat on: 'it went over his face' (101). So it is that these biographers come to grief, torn between two contradictory beliefs; that their subjects are best represented in their own words, and that these same words are utterly unreliable.

Perversely, these biographies seem less adept at summoning the presence of the dead poet than in revealing his absence. The biographies become memorials to their own omissions. Moore's *Life of Byron* is haunted throughout its length by an omission that Moore confesses only in its final pages, the absence of Byron's own memoir with which he had entrusted Moore, who was to publish it after Byron's death, and which Moore, goaded by Hobhouse, had reluctantly agreed should be burned. For two decades after his death Byron remained the most biographized man in Britain, but every book about him served only to bring more sharply into view that missing manuscript, Byron's account of himself. Shelley, though the biographical notices of him in the period are much fewer, became not long after his death himself the object of a very wide curiosity, and again the written accounts are haunted by an absence, in this case a book unwritten rather than destroyed, the biography of her husband that Mary Shelley was forbidden by the poet's father to write. The first attempt at a full biography of Shelley did not appear until 1858, when Thomas Jefferson Hogg published the first two of the four volumes of his life of Shelley. It is somehow appropriate that the third and the fourth volumes were never written, so extreme was Shelley's daughter-in-law's disapproval of the earlier volumes. Shelley's career is traced up to that interesting moment when he is about to elope with Mary, and at that point the biography breaks off, so that it comes to a close with two letters to Hogg from Charles Grove, the brother of Harriet Grove, the cousin to whom Shelley had formed a youthful attachment, in which Grove recalls that though he had often been with Shelley in London, he cannot 'recapitulate the conversations' (2, 555).

Hogg's is the masterpiece of this kind of biography, if only because it seems so curiously conscious of its own duplicities. Like Moore's life of Byron, Hogg's is a hybrid biography, at once an arrangement of Shelley's correspondence and an account of a personal acquaintance, but in both of its aspects it is curiously exaggerated. Milnes assures the reader that he had conscientiously sought out Keats's surviving friends and asked them for information about the poet while preparing his biography. Moore did the same. But Hogg, with a strange excess of scrupulosity, prints the letters that he or his wife, the former Jane Williams, received in response to their enquiries, refusing to omit even admissions of helplessness, as when an Eton contemporary of Shelley's writes, 'I am only sorry that I have no anecdotes, or letters, of that period to furnish' (1, 45). Hogg mimes a classical scholar's concern for accuracy. He is 'unwilling to state' a fact from memory, if he has no documentary confirmation of it. It is to him a matter of moment whether Shelley's first wife, Harriet, spelt her name with double 't' at the end, and from the evidence of her letters both to himself and to others he is able to refute the charge (2, 205). One of his qualifications for his task is that he has 'occupied the same dingy chambers in the Temple for some fifty years', and, since he has never thrown away a single document, 'every letter, every scrap of paper, although thickly covered with dust and soot, must remain' where it had been put away, in 'locked drawers, desks, and closets'. But Hogg makes this claim only as a preface to his confession that he is 'unable at present to lay [his] hand' on many of these papers: 'Hereafter doubtless they will turn up. The inconvenience is only temporary…' (2, 203–6). But they never do. His, then, is a documentary biography that makes room for the surprising confession that the bulk of the documentation on which Hogg had planned to rely is missing.

Hogg's is also a conversational biography, and like all others of its kind its manner is novelistic, but again Hogg's bent is extreme, even in comparison with Trelawny. It is not just that Hogg confidently records lengthy conversations that he had taken part in almost fifty years before. More than any of his fellows he uses the techniques of the novelist. Hogg is the Thackeray of Romantic biographers, not so gifted perhaps, but with quite as much capacity for acerbic malevolence. Harriet

and, being short of time, had supplied ten of these pieces by offering extracts from his unpublished novel. It is as if Hogg is covertly confessing his own readiness to merge fact with fiction. Ostensibly, of course, he is put in mind of his own novel-writing experience, by the fragmentary novel written by Shelley himself. This is an epistolary novel, written in the tradition of *Werther* and *La Nouvelle Heloise*, but Hogg does not much admire it: it lacks 'the warmth, the tenderness, of Goethe and Rousseau'; the 'tone is rather that of the novels of William Godwin or Holcroft; it is cold, bald, didactic, declamatory, frigid, rigid.' But in fact the 'fragment of a novel' that Hogg has just quoted (2, 490–7) is not an attempt at fiction at all, but a transcription of a letter from Shelley to Hogg in which Shelley upbraids Hogg for his attempt to seduce Harriet, Shelley's wife.[18] Hogg re-classifies the letter as fiction, no doubt, to preserve his own reputation, but also, surely, as a tart indication that the letter in which Hogg is repeatedly berated for 'sophistry', 'self-deception' and 'insincerity' is itself the production of a poet constitutionally unable to distinguish between his life and his imaginative productions, a poet who writes letters as a way of transforming lived experiences into fiction.

To Hogg, Shelley is even more extravagantly a hero than Byron is to Moore, 'the divine poet' rather than 'the noble poet', and he is also extravagantly caricatured as a sort of poetical Mr Bean. In Hogg's biography more clearly than any other the adulatory and contemptuous impulses are revealed as intimately connected. One of Shelley's eccentricities, for example, was that nothing he said could be relied upon: 'He was altogether incapable of rendering an account of any transaction whatsoever, according to the strict and precise truth', so that 'had he written to ten individuals the history of some proceeding in which he was himself a party, each of his ten reports would have varied from the rest in essential and important circumstances'. But this is not at all evidence of 'an addiction to falsehood, which he cordially detested, but because he was the creature, the unsuspecting and unresisting victim, of his irresistible imagination' (2, 68). So, Shelley's untrustworthiness becomes a confirmation of his poetic genius, of the power of his imagination, or, to reverse the proposition, the power of a poetic imagination is defined by its ability to free itself from any reference to fact.

Fact and fiction are represented in these biographies as mutually exclusive, so that the poet, whose business is with fictions, is professionally removed from the factual world that the rest of us inhabit, and the more complete the removal the more complete the demonstration of the poet's professional qualifications. Biographies are written in prose, and prose, it seems, retains an obligation to the world that it represents from which the poet, the supreme fiction-maker, is exempt. Hence, Hogg is appalled at the confusion produced by a text such as Shelley's *Queen Mab*, in which the poem is accompanied by notes. It is a practice that implies a connection between fiction and fact, or between poetry and philosophy, and hence will mislead all but the most careful reader, able to understand, like Hogg, that the verse and the prose are quite unconnected, and present in fact 'a strong and strange contrast' to each other, for the poem is 'excessively spiritual, 'replete with imaginary, unearthly creations', whereas the notes promulgate 'violent opinions', 'so-called philosophical' in their nature, which threaten 'to give a meaning to the poem itself which does not in reality belong to it' (2, 347–8). Indeed, no meaning could truly 'belong' to a poem, because the poetic has been defined as that which escapes meaning.

And as for poems, so too for the poets who composed them. Their true life is lived in the imagination, which is the premise on which all these biographers, in their different ways, seem agreed. But it is a rather odd premise from which to write literary biography, which on the face of it is committed to the view that fact and fiction, lived experience and imagined poems, are not independent of one another but mutually illuminating. It is the clash between the premise and the enterprise that produces the oddity shared in different measure by all these biographies. In several of them, in the writings of Lady Blessington, Trelawny, and Leigh Hunt, it produces an odd tendency for the biographer to usurp the place of the biographical subject, so that the biography of the poet tends to be reduced to an episode in the autobiography of the biographer. Hogg is unusual only in that in him the tactic is both exaggerated and explicit. Hogg's is the *Don Juan* of Romantic biographies, the adventures of its hero never more than a thread on which to hang the digressions of its narrator. A brief anecdote of a dinner given by the Duke of Norfolk at which Shelley had been seated next to the Earl of Oxford, is followed by a much more elaborate anecdote of a dinner party attended not by Shelley but by Hogg. The Countess of Oxford had been much entertained by his 'sallies'. For example, the conversation turning on where each of the guests would wish to be buried, Hogg had set the table in a roar by declaring his preference for a grave 'under the kerb-stone, before the door of the most fashionable milliner of London', a position that would allow him to look forward to an eternity of being stepped over by 'the prettiest feet and ankles in the world'. At this point Hogg reminds himself, 'I am not writing the history of my own life and times, but the biography of a Divine Poet, to the illustration of whose remarkable character alone every word should tend', and at once embarks on an episode remarkable for its lack of any connection with Shelley: a coach on which he was once travelling stopped at Stratford-on-Avon for breakfast, Hogg took the opportunity to see Shakespeare's house, so that it was not until the coach arrived at Birmingham that he was able to get anything to eat (2, 271–5). In another excursus of several pages Hogg describes the tedium of life as a provincial lawyer's clerk, the irredeemable vulgarity of conveyancers, his own devotion to classical scholarship, the benefits to be gained from lengthy walks, life at the Inns of Court, and the mutation of Sir Francis Burdett from canting Radical to 'fine old English gentleman' (2, 159–65). On this occasion he excuses himself on the ground that it is sometimes necessary 'briefly to tell the simple story of my own life, in order to follow the tangled thread of the Divine Poet's multiform and ever varying existence', but he fails to establish the explanatory value of the casually assembled anecdotes of himself that follow.

Much of the joy of reading Hogg comes from witnessing his duty as a biographer crumble before his egotism. His biography is a fine comedy of self-exposure, but it is a self-conscious comedy:

Shelley was fugitive, volatile; he evaporated like ether, his nature being etherial; he suddenly escaped, like some fragrant essence; evanescent as a quintessence. He was a lovely, a graceful image, vanishing speedily from our sight, being portrayed in flying colours. He was a climber, a creeper, an elegant, beautiful, odoriferous, parasitical plant; he could not support himself; he must be tied up fast to something of a firmer texture, harder and more rigid than his own, pliant, yielding structure; to some person of a less flexible formation; he always required a prop. In order to write the history of his fragile, unconnected, interrupted life, it is necessary to describe that of some ordinary every day person with whom he was familiar, and to introduce the real subject of the history, whenever a transitory glimpse of him can be caught.

(2, 46)

So Hogg writes the history of his own life and opinions, confident that only so sturdy a topic can hope to contain those 'transitory glimpses' of the poet which is all that the poetic nature allows.

So it is that Hogg allows Shelley to haunt his biography rather in the manner that the scholar gipsy haunts Matthew Arnold's Oxford, ever-present but never seen except out of the corner of the eye, and the likeness is not accidental, for Matthew Arnold inherited a notion of the poet that had been established not only or perhaps even principally by his Romantic precursors but by their interpreters, that is, by their biographers.

It is the habit of these biographers to stress their difference from their subjects; Lady Blessington serenely happy in her marriage to her saintly lord and a Byron unremittingly tormented by his separation from his wife; Trelawny, the man of action, and Byron and Shelley who live through their imaginations. Hogg, as usual, takes the tactic to extremes:

> I was of the earth, earthy; he was of the heavens, heavenly; – I was a worldling; he had already returned to nature, or rather he had never quitted her.
>
> (2, 294)

Shelley would forget to eat unless reminded, Hogg never loses an opportunity to comment on the quality of his dinner. Shelley is a visionary radical, Hogg a worldly Tory. Hogg is a man of fact, Shelley a creature of fiction. Hogg is prose to Shelley's poetry. But the assertion of difference alternates with a contrary tendency in which biographer and subject merge, so that Byron can be credited with opinions that transparently belong to Lady Blessington rather than himself. Leigh Hunt believes that Byron's admirers found in the poet only a mirror in which they could admire their 'flattering self-reflection'. The mirror may have been shattered by scandal, but they were content to gaze adoringly into such fragments as remained, until the 'mirror was pieced at Missolonghi, and then they could expatiate at large on the noble lord's image and their own' (63). But it is a tendency from which, in a perverse form, Hunt seems himself to suffer. He is never more Skimpole-like than in *Lord Byron and Some of His Contemporaries*, himself a very child in matters to do with money, but happy to acknowledge the virtue of those who supply his needs with a proper delicacy. Byron failed the test, and Hunt credits him with a vulgar, grasping obsession with cash that seems to derive not so much from Byron as from himself.

Hogg is again remarkable because he seems half-conscious of the tendency. In one of his apparently inconsequential digressions he argues that 'two people...who appear to be the most unlike of mankind' might nevertheless exhibit 'in many respects the strongest similarity' (2, 359). Hogg even claims that he was repeatedly mistaken for Shelley:

> Not that we were at all like one another, but persons who knew who we were, who knew the two friends, but did not know which was

which, frequently addressed me for him, persons of both sexes; and this occurred during the whole period of our intimacy.

(2, 355)

He goes on to make some rather uncomfortable innuendoes about occasions when women mistook him for his friend, but the passage serves at least to point to the oddity of a man who had attempted to seduce Shelley's first wife, unsuccessfully proposed to his second, and finally took to live with him the Jane Williams who had been the last object of Shelley's capricious devotion.

The early biographies of the second generation of Romantic poets are interesting in themselves, and interesting for the light that they shed on the development of biography as a kind, but it is another kind of interest that I want to point to. These books reveal with peculiar clarity the operation of a series of stratagems that characterize not just the procedures of the biographers but the manner in which the Romantic poets were accommodated by their successors. First, the poets are firmly placed in a realm of the imagination, the boundaries of which are closed by a definition of the imaginative as the opposite of the real, the factual or the historical. A critic of the mid-twentieth century anxious to secure a similar end would have pressed an emphatic distinction between poet and poem, denying that the work of art should be considered in its relation to the life of the artist. That is not a tactic available, of course, to literary biographers, nor was it at all favoured in the period in which these biographers wrote. Their procedure is more extraordinary: they insist that the works of poets are continuous with their lives, but rather than assimilate the work within the life, the life melts into the work, so that the life of the poet becomes simply the most characteristic of the poet's fictions. Second, and consequently, there is an unusually emphatic distinction between poetry and prose, beauty being allowed to the one and meaning to the other. It is an aspect of this stratagem that the poets are so consistently feminized. No doubt, as has been commonly pointed out, this was a tactic attractive to those who wanted to admire Romantic poems without assenting to the opinions that they express and without condoning the irregular lives of the poets who wrote them, but its effect is more far-reaching. It defines the poetic precisely as that which cannot be understood in relation to anything other than itself. It is unsurprising that poetry of this kind might either provoke admiration or contempt, but the peculiarity here is that the admiration tends to soar to a height precisely corresponding to the depth of the contempt. This is predictable because the two emotions share a single origin in the insistence that the imagination is the more powerful the more completely it dispenses with reality. Finally, and again consequently, the biographers prompt in their readers an impulse at once to identify themselves with the poets with unusual intensity, and to distinguish themselves from them with unusual emphasis. Several of them make use of the techniques of the novelist, but it is still more important that they adopt themselves and encourage in their readers a relationship to their subjects of a kind more like the relationship we have with fictional characters than with real people. Given this, it is unsurprising that some writers chose to represent the Romantic poets not through biographical accounts of them but in confessed fictions, in novels. I shall discuss just three of them; Caroline Lamb's *Glenarvon* (1816), Mary Shelley's *The Last Man* (1826), and Disraeli's *Venetia* (1837).

## III

*Glenarvon* is, according to Lord David Cecil, 'a deplorable production: an incoherent cross between a novel of fashionable life and a fantastic tale of terror', but, he adds, 'it has its interest'.[19] Its immediate success was ensured by its status as a roman à clef, a novel in which Caroline Lamb represents herself as Lady Calantha Delaval, her husband, William Lamb, as Lord Avondale, and Byron as Lord Glenarvon. There is even a tiny role for the woman that Byron married. 'Miss Monmouth' seems to represent Miss Milbanke, refusing Glenarvon's first proposal as Annabella had Byron's out of 'fear of his principles' (3, 53).[20] Cecil finds it deplorable, presumably, because the motives for its composition are so transparently personal. The novel is at once an apologia and a denunciation. At a time when the scandal of her affair with Byron was still fresh in the public mind, Caroline Lamb published her novel as a way of soliciting forgiveness for her own behaviour and outright condemnation of Byron's. Nothing seems further from *The Last Man*, a novel that Mary Shelley wrote while her grief for the death of her husband, drowned in 1822, was still fresh. As she worked on it, she wrote in her diary, 'The Last Man! Yes I may well describe that solitary being's feelings, feeling myself as the last relic of a beloved race, my companions extinct before me.'[21] Both novels, it seems, were therapeutic for their writers, but Caroline Lamb writes as a way of ridding herself finally of Byron, whereas Mary Shelley seems to write in obedience to two jarring impulses. The first is to escape, like the novel's 'editor', who finds relief from her 'real sorrows and endless regrets, by clothing these fictitious ones in that ideality, which takes the mortal sting from pain'.[22] The second is to memorialize the past and in doing so restore to those she has loved a frail illusion of life, like her narrator Lionel Verney, who tells the story of his life and the great plague that has left him, he fears, the sole survivor of the human race as a way of pretending to himself that his friends are still alive. Caroline Lamb writes to fix in print all the whispered slanders that had attached themselves to Byron since his separation from his wife, and Shelley is intent on freeing her husband from the insinuations of his detractors. Verney is the only character in her novel who is an author. His books are 'unpretending', but their character is significant: 'they were confined to the biography of favourite, historical characters, especially those whom I believed to have been traduced, or about whom clung obscurity and doubt' (157). *The Last Man* is a similar kind of book. The account of Adrian's drowning, his boat capsized by a sudden squall, for example, is a bitter revision of all the narratives in newspapers and journals in which Shelley's death was presented as a demonstration of God's judgement on the atheist poet.[23] *Venetia* seems quite different from either Lamb's or Shelley's novels: it celebrates the two poets that Disraeli most admired, Byron and Shelley, but he did not know them personally. That the three novels were written from such different motives makes it the more significant that they have so much in common.

First, and least surprisingly, all three play on the threshold that separates fact from fiction. Glenarvon's letter of farewell to Lady Calantha Delaval is a transcription of a letter from Byron to Lady Caroline Lamb.[24] *The Last Man* begins when the editor visits the cave of the Cumaean Sybil in the bay of Baiae in the company of her 'selected and matchless companion', and the date of the visit, December 8, 1818, corresponds precisely with the date that Shelley had visited the same place with her husband. Byron died when she was at work on the novel, and the tribute that she pays Raymond at his death overflows the fiction to embrace her friend: 'Now his death has crowned his life, and to the end of time it will be remembered, that he devoted himself, a willing victim, to the glory of Greece' (204). In *Venetia*, Disraeli points out the connection between his fictional Lord Cadurcis and the real Lord Byron still more transparently, by plagiarizing. When Cadurcis and Herbert speak together their conversation is assembled from bits and pieces from Byron's correspondence and Shelley's recently published essays. Herbert, for example, quotes from the 'Essay on Love': 'Love, on the contrary, is an universal thirst for a communion, not merely of the senses, but of our whole nature, intellectual, imaginative, and sensitive'.[25] In his comment on the scandal that persuades Cadurcis to leave England, Disraeli even appropriates the best known sentence from Macaulay's review of Moore's *Life*, 'It has been well observed that no spectacle is so ridiculous as the British public in one of its periodical fits of morality' (320).[26]

Second, there is a tendency for Byron and Shelley to be represented as allegorical figures rather than realistic characters. Calantha is torn between her admiration for her husband, and her passion for her lover, but, as the names of the two men reveal, her good and her bad angels are of one essence. 'Glenarvon' is simply a Celtic translation of 'Avondale', so that the contrast between the two men comes to represent not so much the evident enough differences between William Lamb and Byron as the war within Calantha between the two opposed sides of her nature.[27] On the one hand there is the calm, upright and reasonable self that she associates with England, and that finds its fit mate in Avondale, and on the other there is the wild, passionate, violent self that she associates with Ireland and with Italy, and that responds passionately to Glenarvon. Mary Shelley characterizes Adrian and Raymond as antithetical types, a device that through Moore and Hunt was to become conventional in biographical treatments of Byron and Shelley. 'Adrian felt he made part of a great whole' (45), whereas for Raymond all things exist only in relation to himself. Raymond is the man of power, who aspires to be another Napoleon (56), Adrian the man of knowledge, content with his books. Raymond demands to rule others, but cannot rule himself, whereas Adrian, even though he is the heir of a King, has no political ambitions.

Because the characters tend towards abstractions, the link that binds them to their historical counterparts is loosened. So, in addition to representing Byron as Glenarvon, Lamb introduces a cousin of Calantha's called Buchanan. His mother has made up her mind that he must marry Calantha in order to guarantee his succession to the family dukedom, but Buchanan is only ever a reluctant, coarse and half-hearted suitor. His Scottish name, and its shape, 'B – – – n', give the clue that he, too, is a version of Byron, the version that allows Caroline Lamb to incorporate within the novel her uncomfortable sense that Byron's relationship with her was for him scarcely more than an irksome and embarrassing episode in which his desire to cut a dash in society briefly outweighed his consistent preference for full-breasted women. Buchanan is Byron reduced to a Regency rake. Mary Shelley similarly divides her responses to Shelley between Adrian and Raymond. Raymond's wife, Perdita, when she believes that he has been killed, bitterly repents that she had emotionally withdrawn from him after she had learned of his involvement with another woman. It is an episode so feelingly represented that it is hard not to read it as confessional. Disraeli employs a similar device far more extravagantly when he attributes Byron's marital history and his Italian mistress not to Lord Cadurcis but to Marmion Herbert, his version of Shelley.

Third, all three novels oddly exaggerate the political importance of their central characters. Lamb's Glenarvon is a poet, but much more importantly he is a revolutionary. The publication of Glenarvon's that makes him 'a rage, a fashion' (2, 7) is his address to the United Irishmen, not a poem like *Childe Harold*. He leads an armed insurrection designed to free Ireland from English rule and establish an Irish Republic modelled on the French. Glenarvon lends his support to the 'more violent' of the rebels, whose 'real object' is 'the equalization of property, and the destruction of rank and titles', though he differs so far 'in practice from his principles' that he insists that all his followers address him as 'my lord' (2, 79–80). This is the odder because *Glenarvon* was written long before Byron's active involvement with the Italian carbinari or the Greek nationalists. Byron had, it is true, taken his seat in the House of Lords in 1812, and made a handful of speeches, evidently in an attempt to establish himself as a Foxite Whig, a glamorous new addition to the Holland House set, but his interest seems rather quickly to have petered out. Mary Shelley is even more extravagant. Her Byron, Count Raymond, establishes himself as leader of the monarchical party, and defeats Ryland, an unflattering caricature of Cobbett, to become Lord Protector of England (England has been declared a Republic in 2073). Her Shelley, Adrian, is the son of the deposed King, and rejects a political career for a life of scholarly retirement, but when the plague has devastated the country he, in his turn, agrees to accept the Lord Protectorship. Disraeli's Shelley, Marmion Herbert, unlike Mary Shelley's is a poet. But he is also a man who fought with Washington in the American War of Independence, and hence cannot return to Britain where he has been proscribed as a traitor: 'To his exertions the successful result of the struggle was, in a great measure, attributed; and he received the thanks of Congress, of which he became a member' (223). All three novelists seem oddly determined to translate literary into political power, as if in an effort to ensure that the role of poets as the legislators of the world should no longer go unacknowledged.

Nevertheless, in all three novels politics is subordinated to love. Glenarvon proves a traitor to the Irish cause, but this is presented as no more than an echo of a more important act of treachery, his

betrayal of Calantha's love. Plague, as Mary Shelley knew, had functioned for decades as the most pervasive of all political metaphors, simply because it appealed to every political faction. In her husband's
poetry it is endemic: tyranny is a pestilence that fatally infects the
body politic, as is radical reform in the political rhetoric of his opponents. Mary Shelley literalizes the metaphor, and when she does so the
effect, as Verney tellingly puts it, is that political debate 'dwindles to
insignificance' (223). The only value that the plague leaves intact is the
reality of human love. In *Venetia*, Shelley's politics, his religious scepticism, and his hostility to marriage are given to Marmion Herbert and
allowed to infect Lord Cadurcis when he reads Herbert's poems, but
they are safely contained within a novel that centres on Cadurcis's
extended courtship of Venetia, Herbert's daughter. By tracing the
course of their love Disraeli even contrives to reconcile Marmion, who
gives over his Italian mistress, with Lady Annabel Herbert, thus reunit-
ing Byron with his wife. By the end of the novel Herbert, now a stooping figure, his hair streaked with grey, looks back on his youthful career,
and feels serenely detached from its fierce struggles. His thoughts, he
finds, on politics, religion, and marriage are 'very much modified',
which is after all only to be expected, because 'a man at fifty' cannot
even claim to be 'the same material being that he is at five-and-twenty'
(417). The poems that Herbert now writes simply celebrate his new
found domestic happiness. He has made himself into a minor poet,
and a poet of a distinctively Victorian kind.

Finally, and most strangely, though the novels are all dated with a
care that seems incongruous with the extravagance of their subject matter, the effect of the dating in each case is to transport Byron and Shelley
out of their own historical period, and set them down at some other
time. *Glenarvon* is carefully set in 1798, during the short and savagely
repressed Irish rebellion of that year. Admiral Buchanan, for example,
Lady Margaret's brother, but, unlike her, a staunch, soldierly man, is
given a Parliamentary vote of thanks for his 'distinguished conduct and
assistance on the memorable 4th of June' (2, 97). June 4 remains a memorable day in Irish history, the day of the Irish Republic, when, in 1798,
the historian of that year tells us, 'the French Revolution' seemed to
have 'spread to Ireland'. Wexford had fallen to the rebels, and Napoleon
had set sail from Toulon with his armada, intent, it was fondly believed,
on supporting the revolution. In Wexford the republic was proclaimed,
but on the very next day it was overthrown after a desperately close-run
battle in which the loyalist forces were led not by Admiral Buchanan,
but by General Johnson.[28] Byron knew the events of the 1790s well. For

him, they constituted a heroic period, but a period in which, inevitably, he had played no part. On March 8, 1814, for example, he dined with Rogers, where Sheridan was one of the company, and noted the conversation in his journal: 'Much of old times – Horne Tooke – the Trials – evidence of Sheridan, and anecdotes of those times, when *I* alas! was an infant'. He added: 'If I had been a man, I would have made an English Lord Edward Fitzgerald'.[29] In *Glenarvon* Caroline Lamb mischievously fulfils his ambition, but she makes him an inauthentic version of the Citizen Lord.[30] Like Lord Edward, Glenarvon leads an Irish rebellion. Both are aristocratic revolutionaries, their leadership at least as dependent on their aristocratic lineage as their devotion to the rights of man. Like Lord Edward, Glenarvon begins his career as an officer in the British forces, and like Lord Edward, too, he is at once an active rebel and an intimate in the great houses of the Irish aristocracy. But Caroline Lamb gives Byron his wish, makes him Lord Edward Fitzgerald, only to point how far he fell below his hero. Lord Edward died in the cause, whereas Glenarvon betrays it. At the last he makes his accommodation with England, and in return for the restoration of his titles and the command of a ship publicly states his 'entire disapprobation of the lawless measures which had been recently adopted by the disaffected' (3, 203). The time shift seems to be just another device allowing Caroline Lamb to traduce her ex-lover. But similar shifts occur in all three novels.

*The Last Man* is set between the years 2073, when England becomes a Republic, and January 1, 2100, the date that Lionel Verney, apparently the last survivor of the plague that has devastated the human race, carves on the topmost stone of St Peter's before he leaves Rome to set sail around the world in a forlorn attempt to discover a fellow survivor. It is a novel set, then, in the distant future, but it has its origin, we are told, in an unimaginably distant past. The novel transcribes the account of his life written by Lionel Verney in the last year of the twenty-first century, but it is an account that is found written on leaves in the cave of the Cumaean Sybil, a prophecy that has its origin in a legendary past, at a time before history began. It is a story written at once in the fantastic past and in the fantastic future, and it is also an exactly contemporary novel. It was on December 8, 1818, the unnamed editor tells us, that he or she first discovered the cave, and began to collect the leaves on which the story was recorded, and it was some years later that she fashioned from these 'scattered and unconnected' writings a continuous narrative. *The Last Man* was published in 1826.

Disraeli's *Venetia* begins in 1765, 'some ten years before the revolt of our American colonies', at which point Herbert is a grown man who has already separated from his wife, and Cadurcis is a young boy. On the outbreak of that revolt Cadurcis becomes 'a most violent partisan' of 'that national party who opposed themselves to the disorganizing opinions then afloat' (166). He sides, that is, with the ministry led by North which fought a war in an attempt to resist American claims to independence. Herbert, meanwhile, has travelled to America and raised a regiment to fight for Washington. For Cadurcis, as for Lady Annabel, Herbert's action aggravates his existing offences, making him a 'man whose name is synonymous with infamy', 'a traitor to his king, and an apostate from his God' (201). But some years later Cadurcis is introduced to Herbert's writings, and becomes as enthusiastic an admirer as he had once been a detractor. He is also inspired by Herbert's example to attempt poetry himself. By the beginning of the novel's fourth book, Cadurcis and his poetry are the talk of London. Again, the time is precisely dated, 'during the period immediately subsequent to the Coalition Ministry', that is, the Fox–North coalition that ended in December, 1783. It is presumably, then, in 1784 that the public's fit of moral indignation forces Cadurcis abroad, where he travels widely through Europe and the Near East, as Byron had between 1809 and 1811. By chance he puts in at Leghorn where he meets Herbert and is reunited with Venetia. His third proposal to her is accepted before he embarks with Herbert on their fatal voyage. The date is not given, but it is at 'the commencement of autumn' (462), and the year can be no later that 1787, which means that Cadurcis dies at least a few months before January 22, 1788, the date on which Byron was born.[31]

It is easiest to begin an explanation of these time shifts with *Venetia*. It is a novel impelled by two motives. One impulse distances Disraeli from Byron and Shelley by taking events of the recent past, events that occurred within twenty years of Disraeli writing his novel, and pushing them back to a time more than half a century ago. The other moves the novel in the opposite direction, beckoning Byron and Shelley out of the Regency and re-making them as Victorians before their time. The dual effect is clearest, perhaps, in Disraeli's handling of the dangerous politics of Byron and Shelley. On the one hand, he exaggerates their revolutionary character. When Herbert raises a regiment and fights for Washington, he becomes out of high principle a traitor to the Crown. Neither Byron nor Shelley contrived anything so dramatic. Disraeli had in mind, no doubt, the army of Suliotes that Byron raised when he joined the Greek war of independence, but the cases are quite different. Byron, when his body was returned to Britain, was received like a hero: Herbert cannot return because he would risk execution.

And yet by 1837 the American War had long lost its controversial character: Herbert was a traitor to a cause in which no-one any longer believed. Disraeli sets his novel in the eighteenth century precisely because it allows him to represent the issues that so fiercely divide his characters as lapsed or long ago resolved. In particular, he excludes the French Revolution, the event that determined the character of Byron's and Shelley's politics, just as it did the politics of all their contemporaries.

This seems quite untrue of *Glenarvon*, which is set in 1798, the year in which the French Revolution obtruded itself most forcefully on the imaginations of the British. And yet there is something odd about Lamb's representation of that year. She contrives throughout the novel to avoid any mention of events in France. There is no landing of French troops to support the rebels. Glenarvon arrives from Italy to take his place as the leader of the rebellion, whereas his real life counterpart, Edward Fitzgerald, arrived from Paris, where he had lodged with Tom Paine. When Glenarvon proves a turncoat and takes command of a British ship, the naval action in which he takes part is a battle against the Dutch. Presumably, the allusion is to the Battle of Camperdown of October, 1797, but there is no reference to the fact that since 1795 the United Provinces had become the Batavian Republic, a satellite state of France. The effect is paradoxical. Caroline Lamb exaggerates Byron's political importance while at the same time exorcising the novel's politics of their most distinctive characteristic. She offers a picture of Ireland in 1798 which makes not a single reference to the French Revolution.

Like Disraeli, but much more extravagantly, Mary Shelley at once pushes her story back into the past, when it was written on sybilline leaves, and transports it into the future, the twenty-first century, and, as with Disraeli, the effect is to draw from the novel's politics any sharp contemporary sting. The French Revolution is represented, but only in baleful parody. When Adrian gathers together the last remnants of the English nation and conducts them into France, the survivors converge on Paris, and there they act out the Revolution. Adrian's authority is challenged by an 'impostor prophet', the leader of a new religion whose adherents, he claims, are immune from the plague. Adrian takes up his residence at Versailles, the prophet at the Tuileries. When the prophet and his followers march against Adrian, they mimic the march of the women of Paris to Versailles in October of 1789, but the prophet himself seems to parody Robespierre. He rules by Terror, and preserves the myth of his followers' immunity from the plague much as Robespierre preserved the purity of the Revolution, by murdering any who show signs of sickness. At the last, when he is exposed, he shoots himself, but more efficiently than Robespierre, who survived his attempted suicide long enough to be guillotined. The Revolution is acted out again, but diminished to a grim puppet show in which the foolish and the desperate are seduced into rebellion by a criminal lunatic.

The central fiction of the novel, the plague itself, works as a powerful depoliticizing agent. All human differences seem utterly inconsequential in the face of a plague that inexorably eliminates the human race until Verney is left alone. This is particularly the case with political differences. England in the late twenty-first century is divided between three political parties, the aristocrats, the monarchists and the democrats, a division that corresponds fairly closely to that between the Whigs, Tories and Radicals in the England to which Mary Shelley returned in 1823, but also looks back to the great debate of the 1790s. It seems to be the radical side of the debate that is satirized, particularly in its millenarian aspect,[32] which is articulated by Adrian in a manner that seems deliberately to parody Percy Shelley:

> The choice is with us; let us will it, and our habitation becomes a paradise. For the will of man is omnipotent, blunting the arrows of death, soothing the bed of disease, and wiping away the tears of agony.
>
> (76)

A scientist, Merrival, is introduced apparently in order to mock the pseudo-scientific foundation that Shelley's father and husband both claimed for their optimism: ' "The pole of the earth will coincide with the pole of the ecliptic," continued the astronomer, "an universal spring will be produced, and earth become a paradise' " (220).[33] In comparison, the several quotations from Burke's *Reflections* seem weighted with a sober recognition of the reality of the human condition. Mary Shelley might seem to have transferred her affection from the tree of liberty to 'the British oak', the growth of centuries, in the shade of which Burke imagined the nation grazing like great cattle. But, in fact, the plague functions as a satire on Burke no less effectively than on Godwin and P.B. Shelley. Burke may celebrate 'the mode of existence decreed to a permanent body', which 'in a condition of unchanging constancy, moves on through the varied tenour of perpetual decay, fall, renovation, and progression' (228), but the plague eliminates the variety on which Burke's ideal of permanence rests. Burke's vision of 'the great mysterious incorporation of the human race', which is always composed at once of the young, the middle-aged and the old, is rigorously demystified by a plague which makes no distinction between ages, but kills everyone indiscriminately. The plague annuls politics because it annuls history. Differences of political principle, between monarchists and republicans, for example, dwindle into insignificance in an era in which 'Plague had become Queen of the World' (346).[34]

All the devices shared by the three novels serve the same purpose. They allow Byron and Shelley at once to be remembered and forgotten. It is not hard to understand why Mary Shelley should wish to do both. It is one of the humdrum paradoxes of grief. Caroline Lamb, when Byron ended their affair, grieved, too, after her fashion. But when Disraeli's novel shares so many of the same characteristics one begins to think that they are participating in a wider cultural project. It is a project that I will explore throughout the remaining chapters of this book, but one aspect of it emerges from the novels with unusual clarity. The novels at once exaggerate and minimize the political importance of the poets. Caroline Lamb makes Byron the leader of the United Irishmen, Mary Shelley makes first Byron and then Shelley Lord Protectors of England, and Disraeli makes Shelley an American war hero and a Congressman. And yet Glenarvon, it emerges, is a revolutionary not out of principle but out of pique. When his title and estates are restored to him, he at once makes his peace with the crown. Raymond and Adrian live to learn that political differences dwindle into insignificance in the face of the plague. The ambition of Ryland, the leader of the Republican party, was to establish a nation in which 'the name and title of Englishman was the sole patent of nobility' (222). But his plans are forestalled by the arrival in Britain of a leveller more furious and determined than he is:

> We were all equal now; but near at hand was an equality still more levelling, a state where beauty and strength, and wisdom, would be as vain as riches and birth. The grave yawned beneath us all ...
>
> (317)

The plague offers a stinging satire on democrats, but it is a true leveller and satirizes reformers and monarchists equally. Disraeli's eighteenth-century setting works more gently to the same effect. It encourages the reader to look back on Byron's and Shelley's politics as at the contentions of a bygone age, in the same way, in fact, in which Herbert at the age of fifty recollects them himself.

*Venetia* is, to use Nemoianu's term, a perfect example of the Biedermeier: it is a novel in which 'the sheer energy of the romantic breakthrough is captured and tamed'.[35] It seems unusual only because it pursues its task so literally, allowing the fiercely unaccommodating Shelley to grow into the mellow, mild-mannered old man he never had the opportunity to become. But *Venetia*, when it was published in 1837, did not make much of a stir. Readers and reviewers were much more struck by a very different book that was published in the same year. Carlyle's *The French Revolution* seemed no tamer to its first readers than it did to its author, who described it as a 'wild, savage book'. I turn to it next in part because it so forcefully contests Nemoianu's characterization of the period.

# 2
# Historicizing Romanticism

In *Glenarvon*, *The Last Man* and *Venetia* the literary power of Byron and Shelley is translated into political power, and the paradoxical effect is to depoliticize the poets that the novels commemorate. It is a paradox that depends on a single manoeuvre: the poets are displaced from their own historical period, and the effect is to dissociate the poets from the one event that makes their politics intelligible. There is, then, a certain appropriateness in the publication of *Venetia*, the latest written of these novels, in 1837, the same year that Carlyle published the three volumes of his *The French Revolution*, because Carlyle's history confronted his readers with a vivid account of precisely the events that Disraeli seems most anxious to exclude from his novel.

It is eccentric of Disraeli to have transformed Byron and Shelley into eighteenth-century gentlemen, but it was at least a representative eccentricity. After the success of *Pelham* in 1828, Edward Bulwer turned back to the eighteenth century to provide the setting for *The Disowned* and *Devereux* (1829), *Paul Clifford* (1830), and *Eugene Aram* (1832). Nostalgia for a bygone age is, perhaps, too common amongst novelists then and since to require comment, but it may be that in these years it answered a more pressing need. By turning back to the eighteenth century, the novelists quietly asserted their continuity with the past. Carlyle's history is important in its emphatic denial of any such comforting notion, but it is also exceptional. This becomes clear enough if it is compared with the most representative of Victorian histories, Macaulay's *History of England*, the first two volumes of which were published in 1849, though it remained unfinished in 1859 when Macaulay died. In fact, Carlyle's *History* can be read as a pre-emptive satire on Macaulay's.[1]

Macaulay had planned to continue his history to the 'death of George IV', which would, he believed, be 'the best halting-place':

> The History would then be an entire view of all the transactions which took place, between the Revolution which brought the Crown into harmony with the Parliament [that is, the Revolution of 1688, represented as the final resolution of the Civil War], and the Revolution which brought the Parliament into harmony with the nation [that is, the passing of the Great Reform Bill in 1832].[2]

His history is celebratory, end-stopped and insular. It celebrates a constitutional development, which, in the course of almost two hundred years, has secured England's liberty, prosperity and stability. The 1832 reform is represented as concluding that process of constitutional development, so that Macaulay can commandingly survey a history that has ended. English history is celebrated because in the seventeenth century England successfully resisted a system of absolute monarchy that was triumphant throughout the rest of Europe, and because in the nineteenth century it accommodated peaceably the just demands of the educated to be represented in Parliament. In the rest of Europe similar demands had provoked violent revolutions. 'Whig history,' writes Hugh Trevor-Roper 'is insular history',[3] a fact of which Macaulay himself was proudly conscious.

Macaulay's prose style is precisely adapted to his programme. In its balanced periods, and its preference for antithesis, it enacts the presiding virtue that Macaulay finds in his nation, the recognition that 'the truth lies between two absurd extremes'.[4] Just as important, it establishes Macaulay as writing in an unbroken tradition of English prose that extends from writers such as Sir William Temple, through Addison, to him. It is a style that establishes the English republic of letters as having been spared, like the English state, the upheaval of violent revolution. Lastly, Macaulay addresses a unified readership. There are eruptions, from time to time, of individual prejudice. The calumnies directed at William Penn, for example, irritated Quakers, as they were bound to do. But, by and large, Macaulay is much less polemical as a historian than he is as an essayist, and this is essential to his rhetorical strategy. He writes from a retrospect that frees him from partisanship, that enables him to see that the Tories were as essential an ingredient in the historical process that he celebrates as his own party, the Whigs, and he needs to do so, because his is a celebration in which all of his readers, all of his fellow countrymen, are expected to join. It is this that gives point to J.W. Burrow's observation that 'the final act of the projected *History* is the History itself'.[5] Macaulay celebrates an English-ness which is the product of a lengthy tradition supposed to be held in common by him and his readers. It is a tradition into which his readers are inducted by the act of reading his *History*.

Carlyle's *History of the French Revolution* dissents emphatically from each of these positions; in its style, in its content, and, not least, in itself. The French Revolution dominates Macaulay's book, but only by its absence (for once the modish cliché seems appropriate). The virtue of England and the English constitution is implicitly guaranteed by the simple fact that the French Revolution did not happen there, but in France.[6] The crucial effect of Carlyle's *History* is to tunnel under the channel that for Macaulay preserves the happy insularity of English history. Through his prose as much as anything else Carlyle undoes any such simple opposition between the foreign and the English.

It is a book that seemed to its first readers as difficult to categorize as the events that it recorded. Its first reviewers were, predictably, sharply divided as to its value. John Stuart Mill insists that 'no work of greater genius, either historical or poetical, has been produced in this country for many years', whereas Lady Sydney Morgan found the book 'alto-gether unworthy of criticism'. They were even divided as to whether a book on the French Revolution was wanted. Lady Morgan asks, 'What need have we of a new *History of the French Revolution*?', and the reviewer for *The Christian Examiner* concludes that 'the chasm which existed in English literature, the want of a just history of the first French Revolu-tion, is now filled in a manner to prevent all competition'. More striking is the manner in which the reviewers disagreed as to the book's mean-ing. Christopher North in *Blackwood's* seems confident that Carlyle is 'hand in glove with the men of blood' and refers the reader for a correc-tive to Burke, for whom 'Thomas Carlisle [sic] seems to care little', whereas Thackeray in *The Times* suggests that the 'hottest Radical in England' could not maintain the ardour of his principles after reading it. Lady Morgan convicts Carlyle of the belief that the Revolution had its origin in Enlightenment 'philosophism'. Carlyle fails to recognize that it was the consequence of 'want, and misery, and oppression in the lower classes'. Merivale, on the other hand, protests in *The Edinburgh Review* against 'the theory implied throughout his pages, which makes hunger the one great mover of revolution'. Reviewers even disagreed about the manner in which Carlyle tells his story. *The Christian Examiner* admires Carlyle's detachment from the events he records: 'he beholds calmly like a god the fury of the nation', and *The Monthly Repository* praises a narra-tive that invites the reader to 'go through the Revolution with feelings analogous to those who suffered in it, who wept in it, who hoped in it'. Several reviewers were perplexed, like the reviewer in *The Literary Gazette*, by the book's tone: 'we cannot tell whether the author is in earnest or in jest'. Taken together the reviews express a collective bewilderment, and it is in this that they offer an index not only of the character of Carlyle's book but of its importance.[7]

The book repelled Christopher North because it failed to express a proper horror of events like the September Massacres and the Revolutionary Terror. Carlyle 'understands *intus et in cute* [inside out] each cutthroat as he tramps by on his vocation with tucked-up shirt sleeves, and looks after him with a philosophic smile'.[8] He deplores Carlyle's failure to imitate what Carlyle calls the 'shriek' with which the British had responded to the Terror, a response that for Carlyle trivialized the events that provoked it by allowing them to be understood as 'mere "Horrors of the Revolution"'.[9] Such shrieks had infiltrated literature, in John Sterling's novel, *Arthur Coningsby* (1833),[10] for example, in which a young woman is forced to drink the blood of a murdered aristocrat in order to win the life of her brother. Carlyle himself repeats the story, which is recorded by Dulaure, but finds it believable only 'if universal Rumour can be credited' (3, 30). It is a condition strong enough to stifle any shrieking in favour of a quietly lifted eyebrow. Elsewhere Carlyle deals more roughly with the shriekers, as when he coolly counts the victims of the Terror, 'the frightfulest thing ever born of Time', and arrives at the number 'Two thousand, all but a few', 'a horrible sum of human lives', 'not far from the two-hundredth part of what perished in the entire Seven-Years War'. These are grim ironies, all preparing for the startling assertion that 'there is no period to be met with, in which the general Twenty-five Millions of France suffered *less* than in this period which they name Reign of Terror', an oddity that Carlyle finds easy of explanation. It was the victims of the Terror who had the power to name the event, 'the Speaking Thousands, and Hundreds, and Units; who shrieked and published', not 'the Dumb Millions' (3, 311–12).

Carlyle refuses to shriek, just as he refuses to view the Revolution through either of the moral lenses that had been manufactured during the forty years that separated Carlyle from the events that he records. Merivale distinguishes 'one mode' of discussing the Revolution 'very satisfactory from its simplicity' from another that seems to him equally inept.[11] Some historians simply apply conventional moral standards to those who acted in it and assign them a moral ranking on that basis. Merivale may have in mind Scott, whose *Life of Napoleon* (1827) applies at great length to Bonaparte standards drawn from Scott's own notion of gentlemanly conduct, and finds him wanting. The alternative is a historical mode that confines itself wholly to 'abstractions' and hence allows enthusiasm for the revolutionary project to be sustained uncompromised by any sympathy with human sufferers. If, as seems possible, Merivale has in mind here Hazlitt's *Life of Napoleon* (1828), this seems unfair, though in discussing matters such as the kidnapping and killing of the Duc d'Enghien, Hazlitt is alarmingly brusque in his dismissal of principled objections to Napoleon's behaviour. In comparison with Scott and Hazlitt, Carlyle impresses by the fine unpredictability of his judgements. Marie Antoinette, Mirabeau, Danton, Camille Desmoulins, Charlotte Corday, and Madame Roland are all of them established in his personal pantheon, as are stalwart soldiers such as the counter-revolutionary, Bouillé, and the young 'olive-complexioned' artillery officer from Corsica, Napoleon himself.

It is this unpredictability that persuaded *The Monthly Review* that Carlyle's book was quite without 'an intelligible system of political ethics'. Mill makes the same point more charitably: if one asks 'is he Tory, Whig, or Democrat, he is none of these', but he has 'appropriated and made part of his own frame of thought, nearly all that is good in all of these several modes of thinking'.[12] This seems too willing to assume a stable frame within which Carlyle's judgements are placed. Carlyle is himself a better guide, when, for example, he recounts the death of Mirabeau, and then asks how he should be remembered:

> As he, for his part, had swallowed all formulas, what Formula is there, never so comprehensive, that will express truly the *plus* and the *minus* of him, give us the accurate net-result of him? There is hitherto none such. Moralities not a few must shriek condemnatory over this Mirabeau; the Morality by which he could be judged has not yet got uttered in the speech of men.
>
> (2, 145)

Throughout the book Carlyle judges, but his judgements are confessedly provisional, even erratic, because they are made in the knowledge that the events he records have themselves removed the foundations on which judgement could once depend for its stability. The judgements of the Revolutionaries were themselves notoriously erratic. The body of Mirabeau himself was installed in the Pantheon, its first resident, and then, when he was found to have been in negotiation with the Court, ignominiously ejected. Carlyle's judgements preserve a similar quality: he administers, as it were, a benevolent counterpart to Revolutionary justice. It is important that it is a benevolent counterpart – even Robespierre, when he dies, is embraced by Carlyle's pity – but equally important that it is a counterpart: Carlyle's judgements remain Revolutionary in their character, because they are made in the knowledge that the morality on which his judgement might be founded 'has not yet got uttered in the speech of men'.

'It is a wild, savage book,' Carlyle wrote to Sterling, 'itself a kind of French Revolution'.[13] His revolutionary heroes are those like Mirabeau, who have abandoned 'all formulas', and he emulates them in writing a book, that, as he told his brother John, he wrote 'tumbling head foremost through all manner of established rules' (*Letters*, 8, 326–7). A Revolution, for Carlyle, is defined by its 'velocity', and in his favourite figure he compares Revolution with fire. His ambition was to write a book as fiery and as speedy as its subject: 'I mean to write with the force of fire till that consummation [the conclusion of the volume on which he is working]; above all with the speed of fire' (*Letters*, 9, 122). He self-consciously allows his book to be contaminated by the frenzy of the Revolutionary mob. He becomes the historian as sansculotte. But not always so. There is also a quite contrary tendency to view the Revolution as from a great distance, from a perspective in which, for all the apparent chaos of events, a single very clearly defined story emerges. Mill accurately condenses it into a single sentence: 'Mr Carlyle's view of the Revolution is briefly this: That it was the breaking down of a great Imposture: which had not always been an Imposture, but had been becoming such for several centuries'.[14]

Carlyle develops a narrative method that swings violently between the two viewpoints.[15] A present tense places the reader at the elbow of one of the actors: the view is partial, sometimes obscured, the outcome unknown. At such moments Carlyle becomes an anti-historian, who holds that the truth of an event is a function of its presence, always hidden to retrospect: 'For indeed it is a most lying thing that Past Tense always' (3, 81). Elsewhere, Carlyle departs to an immeasurable distance from his characters, a perspective from which the present dwindles to the brief gleam that separates two eternities, 'in the intersection of primeval Light with the everlasting Dark' (3, 43).

Carlyle's narrative swings violently between extremes, consistent only in its refusal of that still point from which Macaulay was to write, the point from which the fierce conflicts of history can be calmly recalled in the secure knowledge that the bitter antagonisms that once divided people to the death have been long since assuaged.[16] 'It was the best of times, it was the worst of times', writes Dickens, in a sentence that at once imitates and contradicts the violent transitions that mark Carlyle's narrative.[17] The quiet confidence of the antithesis disables the fierce contradictions that the sentence invokes. It establishes a perspective that Carlyle, too, can occasionally adopt, as when he represents himself and his readers 'standing wistfully on the safe shore' (3, 120), contemplating a tempestuous sea from which they are separated. But much more frequently that safety is denied. Carlyle closes his history in 1795, on October 5, the 13th Vendemiaire, when Napoleon's artillery scatters the Paris mob, and the Revolution is over, 'blown into space by it, and become a thing that was!' (3, 320). But, as Carlyle at once adds, history 'does not conclude, but merely ceases' (3, 321), and, from another point of view, the Revolution was not ended by Napoleon, and will not be ended for hundreds of years. May 4, 1789, the day of the opening of the Estates-General is 'the baptism-day of Democracy', the 'extreme-unction day' of the 'Feudalism' that had been the organizing principle of society for a thousand years. It is a day that set in motion a chain of events that did not come to an end in 1795 – 'Battles and bloodshed, September Massacres, Bridges of Lodi, retreats of Moscow, Waterloos, Peterloos, Tenpound Franchises, Tarbarrels and Guillotines': 'and from this present date, if one might prophesy, some two centuries of it still to fight! Two centuries; hardly less' (1, 133). Sansculottism is not something scattered by Napoleon's cannon shot on October 5, 1795, but 'the crowning Phenomenon of our Modern Time' (1, 212). The old rule, founded on the command *'Thou shalt'* has been overthrown by the new commandment, *'I will'*, (2, 106) and Carlyle recognizes that he still lives in this new dispensation. Macaulay writes as the historian of a history that has ended, Carlyle as a man trying to describe a battle by peering through the gunsmoke.

When Carlyle speaks of 'the safe shore', he invokes at once a temporal and a spatial distance. He is separated by forty years from the events that he records, but also by salt water. The English Channel lies between him and the volatile Paris sections. 'God bless the narrow sea which keeps [France] off', as Tennyson was to write in *The Princess* (1847, 'Conclusion', 51). Carlyle often presents the Revolution as a geographical event, an event that took the form it did because it was an expression of the French national character. The French, like the Teutons, are a fiery race, but theirs is 'a fire comparable to the burning of dry-jungle and grass; most sudden, high-blazing'. Teutonic fire, on the other hand, 'we liken to the burning of coal, or even of anthracite'. French fire produced 'innumerable Voltaires, Racines, Laplaces', whereas the Teutonic anthracite is to be seen in 'Luthers, Leibnitzes, Shakespeares'

(3, 297–8). The English, it seems, are preserved by the solidity of their national character from the violent extremes of French politics. Englishness itself constitutes 'a safe shore' from which to view the doings in France. Carlyle can echo the school of British commentators, later to be headed by Macaulay, who valued the French Revolution largely as a pretext for self-congratulation. The defects of the French character ensured that a reform movement was compressed into a few years that might have 'spread itself over generations', and the consequence was that the necessary process of reform involved a 'torture-death' rather than a 'quiet euthanasia' (2, 232–3). More often, the Revolution is presented as a warning to Britain rather than as a sop to its complacency. If a widow gathers nettles for her children's dinner, there is 'a perfumed Seigneur', who will claim from her 'every third leaf':

> Such an arrangement must end. Ought it not? But, O most fearful is *such* an ending! Let those, to whom God, in his great mercy, has granted time and space, prepare another and milder one.
>
> (1, 229)

But far more often and more emphatically Carlyle describes the Revolution as an event in 'World-History' rather than the history of France, and Sanculottism as a global rather than merely French phenomenon. It is not just in France that 'Faith is gone out: Scepticism is come in' (1, 14), nor only in France that one can find 'a Society grown obsolete, cracked asunder, dissolving into rubbish and primary atoms' (2, 34). The Revolution initiated 'the New Era' (1, 179), which is the Era of Britain just as much as of France, and from this perspective the Revolution is not an event in the history of another country, but the defining moment of the historical process through which Carlyle and his readers are living.

It is characteristic of Carlyle that his history should embrace contradictory perspectives. *The French Revolution* is, after all, the successor to *Sartor Resartus*, in which Carlyle explores most fully his dualistic understanding of human experience.[18] Professor Diogenes Teufelsdröckh, whose philosophy of clothes the book explicates, is, as his name, 'God-born Devil's-dung', indicates, the living embodiment of Carlyle's recognition that man is a 'biped-quadruped' (*The French Revolution*, 2, 204). Teufelsdröckh is as extreme in his 'descendentalism' as in his 'transcendentalism', and so is Carlyle as historian. As Merivale objected, he represents the Revolution as a direct consequence of the price and scarcity of bread, 'scanty, ill-baked loaves, more like baked Bath bricks, – which produce an effect on the intestines!' (1, 243). The Revolution is explained with reference to the digestive tracts of the French people: quite literally Carlyle offers as an account of the Revolution a history of dung. But it is just as true, as Lady Sydney Morgan complained, that Carlyle's is a philosophical history that locates the Revolution in the moment at which the French people came to recognize no authority except the authority of their own wills, the moment at which the authority of the Scriptures was abandoned in favour of Rousseau, 'the Gospel according to Jean-Jacques'. Again, the appropriate contrast is with Macaulay, because, whether he is writing in descendentalist or transcendentalist mode, Carlyle is consistent in his rejection of the kind of history written by Macaulay and the Whig historians who were his predecessors. They wrote political history: history for them is made in Parliaments and in Cabinets. For Carlyle, politics is rarely more than a comic pretence to supervise forces that are not subject to political control, and not at all likely to be swayed by an oratorical flourish in a Parliamentary debate.

It is perfectly proper, of course, to point to Carlyle's habit of self-contradiction as marking what is most distinctive in his rhetoric or habit of mind. But in *The French Revolution* it becomes, also and perhaps more importantly, the primary means by which Carlyle persuades his reader to experience the Revolution while reading about it. The book forces its reader to live through the fierce ideological conflicts that it records. Mill is accurate but inadequate when he points out that Carlyle is neither 'Tory, Whig, or Democrat', and still further from the mark when he claims that Carlyle has appropriated 'nearly all that is good in all of these several modes of thinking'. Mill is engaged here in fostering the illusion on which Macaulay depends, the notion that there is some vantage point available to the imaginative person, the historian, the poet or the novelist, from which the differences that divide the unimaginative somehow dissolve or are reconciled. Carlyle entertains this notion just once, when he describes the dying Mirabeau's negotiations with Marie-Antoinette: 'One can say that, had Mirabeau lived, the history of France and of the World had been different...Had Mirabeau lived another year!'. But even here Carlyle shies away from Mill's dream of some Tory–Whig–Democrat consensus. Whatever arrangement Mirabeau had contrived it would have been 'a result you could have loved, a result you could have hated', but not one to which anyone could be indifferent. In any case, Carlyle does not accept that Mirabeau's death was an accident, for 'men's years are numbered':

> Wert thou saving French Monarchies; wert thou blacking shoes on the Pont Neuf! The most important of men cannot stay; did the

World's History depend on an hour, that hour is not to be given. Whereby, indeed, it comes that these *would-have-beens* are mostly a vanity; and the World's History could never in the least be what it would, or might, or should, by any manner of potentiality, but simply and altogether what it is.

(2, 138–9)

That last phrase might imply that Carlyle entertains the notion that history might free itself from values and achieve a pure objectivity, and indeed he occasionally writes as if this were possible, as if his duty as a historian were simply to '*look* honestly' (3, 204). Mill makes a similar claim when he praises Carlyle for preserving a clear distinction between 'the thing' and 'his opinion' of it: 'the thing is there, and any reader might find a totally different set of propositions in it if he can; as he might in reality, if *that* had been before him'. It is hard to imagine a more misleading impression of Carlyle's manner, in which, as John Holloway has shown, opinion permeates description so completely that it becomes difficult to identify a single phrase that does not also imply a judgement.[19] Carlyle's is a history that constantly takes sides: its distinctive characteristic is that it jumps erratically from one side to the other.

Thackeray calls this habit 'impartiality': 'He sees with equal eyes Madame Roland or Marie Antoinette – bullying Brunswick on the frontier, or Marat at his butcher's work or in his cellar – he metes to each of them justice, and no more, finding good even in butcher Marat or bullying Brunswick, and recording what he finds'. But Thackeray immediately feels the need to make a distinction. Carlyle's is 'a far loftier and nobler impartiality' than Thiers's, the impartiality of whose history is ensured by his 'never drawing a single moral' from any event, 'or seeking to tell aught beyond it'. It is also a much stranger kind of impartiality, because it is produced by the fervour of Carlyle's partisanship. His is a history that far outdoes Hazlitt's in its Sansculottism and Scott's in its Royalism. It reserves its most consistent disdain for those who attempted to mediate between the two extremes, in particular, for the Girondins, who dreamed of 'a respectable Republic for the Middle Classes' (3, 115). It is a method that secures two effects. First, it impels its readers to act out the Revolutionary conflict, by showing events through the eyes of a Jacobin and Royalist in quick succession. Second, it establishes the book as a sustained assault on the view of the Revolution that had very quickly established dominance in Britain, and that achieves its finest expression in Macaulay. The Revolution was understood as a clinching counter-example proving the virtue of British constitutional monarchy, and its capacity to countenance and to regulate reform. The Revolution became a disastrous but conclusive experiment that had been conducted in another country, an event at once over and over there, finished and foreign. Carlyle's history challenges both notions.

Macaulay's prose, like his narrative, is remarkably clear. Trevor-Roper pays proper tribute to 'the absolute clarity of his views and his style'.[20] Reviewers pointed out, some cuttingly, others embarrassedly, that Carlyle's history is not at all remarkable for the clarity of its narrative. *The Monthly Review* describes it as 'unintelligible to anyone who has not previously made himself acquainted, and minutely too, with the records of the period here embraced, and meant to be depicted'. The reviewer in *The Monthly Repository* agrees that the book 'should not have been called a "History": for it cannot be said to tell the story to those who are unacquainted with it'. Even Mill admits that 'Mr Carlyle's book is less fitted for those who know nothing about the subject, than for those who already know a little', and welcomes a forthcoming translation of Thiers, because 'Whoever has read Thiers first, will be the better fitted both to enjoy and to understand Carlyle'.[21] Embarking on his account of the storming of the Bastille, Carlyle exclaims, 'Could one but, after infinite reading, get to understand so much as the plan of the building!'. He seems anxious to place the reader of his volumes in a similar plight. His history is a sequence of great set pieces like the march of the women to Versailles and the feast of the Champ de Mars. It includes episodes that seem self-contained, like 'the History of Charlotte Corday; most definite, most complete; angelic–daemonic: like a Star!' (3, 172). But the connecting narrative is often absent or cloudy. Even within individual episodes Carlyle has a habit of referring to characters as if they were wholly familiar to his readers, who are here mentioned for the first time and are never to reappear. As the siege of the Bastille begins, we are told, 'Half-pay Elie is home for a suit of regimentals; no one would heed him in coloured clothes: half-pay Hulin is haranguing Gardes Francaises in the Place de Grève.' It is one or the other of them – 'men do not agree on it' – who promises quarter to the Swiss guards if they surrender, 'Foi d'officier, On the word of an officer'. And then they exit the history, Elie marching 'with the capitulation-paper on his sword's point' and Hulin following, until he 'sinks exhausted on a heap of stones' (1, 191–6). They are names summoned briefly into spectral but oddly vivid life, and then allowed to vanish, and there are hundreds of such names in *The French Revolution*. It is a self-conscious technique – Carlyle repeatedly calls attention to it by dismissing one of these characters from the narrative with a wry, oddly elegiac farewell – 'and history knows him no more' – and it secures another of the dominant paradoxes of the book. Carlyle is at once a more commanding presence than any historian before him, a writer who surveys events from a prophetic height, and he is also a writer who repeatedly calls attention to the randomness of 'foolish History', that takes as its subject 'mere sin and misery', contrives no more than a 'written epitomised synopsis of Rumour', and has nothing to say of all those things that truly make the world what it is, the 'kind harvests, the hand of the craftsman, the mind of the thinker' (1, 28). Carlyle offers three first-hand accounts of the September massacres, but he ends by summoning the ghosts of all those who left no record:

> Thus they three, in wondrous trilogy, or triple soliloquy; uttering simultaneously, through the dread night-watches, their Night-thoughts – grown audible to us! They Three are become audible, but the other 'Thousand and Eighty-nine, of whom Two-hundred and two were Priests,' who also had Night-thoughts, remain inaudible; choked for ever in black Death.
>
> (3, 38)

It is a sounding sentence, as so many of Carlyle's sentences are, but it surrounds a silence. So indeed does the whole of Carlyle's history, which never for long forgets that for all the multitude of names that the history records, names even of little half-pay officers like Elie and Hulin, the great mass, the 'dumb millions', of the French nation remain unnamed and silent, as do most even of that small band, 'Two thousand all but a few', who died in the Terror:

> Jourdan one names, the other Hundreds are not named. Alas, they, like confused fagots lie massed together for us; counted by the cart-load: and yet not an individual fagot-twig of them but had a Life and History; and was cut, not without pangs as when a Kaiser dies!
>
> (3, 215–16)

History, for Carlyle, is a kind of naming, which is why it is false, for a true history would remember all those whose names are forgotten. It is a history that he aspires to write, but cannot, of course, because it is impossible. It is just one instance of a more general impossibility. History is an attempt to do 'what Father Adam began life by doing: strive to *name* the new Things it sees of Nature's producing – often helplessly enough.' For the historian of the French Revolution the task is peculiarly difficult:

> But what if history were to admit, for once, that all the Names and Theorems yet known to her fall short? That this grand Project of

Nature was even grand, and new, in that it came not to range itself under old recorded Laws of Nature at all, but to disclose new ones? In that case, History, renouncing the pretension to *name* it at present, will *look* honestly at it, and name what she can of it! Any approximation to the right Name has value: were the right Name itself once here, the Thing is known henceforth; the Thing is then ours and can be dealt with.

(3, 204)

Carlyle, of course, does not just explain his predicament, he acts it out, and he does so by developing the prose style that Sterling was shortly to name 'Carlylism', which is distinguished by its use of a vocabulary gathered promiscuously from 'English, Scotch, German, Greek, Latin, French, Technical, Slang, American, or Lunar, or altogether superlunar, transcendental, and drawn from the eternal Nowhere, – he uses it with a courage that might blast an academy of lexicographers into a Hades, void even of vocables'.[22] By naming this style 'Carlylism' Sterling, like most of Carlyle's admiring critics, makes it the index of Carlyle's irreducible individuality, but it is at least worth suggesting, as John Forster did, that the style may have its origin not just in the personality of the writer but in his subject. For Forster it is 'the very language of the season and the men': its peculiarities are a direct product of the events that Carlyle describes.[23]

New events, according to Carlyle, demand new names, and Revolutions demand of their historian a style so new that it is itself Revolutionary. Carlyle, as he wrote, was anxious: 'The style! Ah, the style!', he wrote in his journal, but, in a letter to his brother John, he offered a robust self-defence: 'If one has thoughts not hitherto uttered in English books, I see nothing for it but you must use words *not* found there, must *make* words'.[24] Carlyle makes hundreds. There are facetious nonce words. Lafayette's struggle to impose habits of civic obedience on the Paris mob becomes, for example, a battle between Patriotism and 'Patrollotism'. One of the ways in which Carlyle establishes the Revolution as the crucible for the production of a chaos of competing ideologies is to coin new isms; 'aristocratism', anticivism', 'courtierism', 'attorneyism', 'clubbism', 'scoundrelism', sansculottism' and its antithesis 'culottism'. Carlyle has a fondness for extreme metonymic coinages: 'oeil-de-boeuf', the name given to a small vestibule in Versailles, itself a metonym derived from the single window that lit it, becomes a word for the Royal Court; Carlyle draws from Italian his word for the rentier class, 'the agio', and the single word, 'gigs', stands for the complete code of middle-class respectability. It is an appropriate figure for a history of a period in which the whole issue of representation, of how and by what title a part might stand for a whole, was violently contested. The diction may be comically inflated: those who jump for joy 'tripudiate', loud noises are 'fremescent', and the greedy are given to 'gulosity'. But just as often the diction deflates: the assembly of the people becomes 'the National Palaver', and mobs dispersed by grapeshot have been 'whiffed'. It is a diction that flagrantly refuses to confine itself within acceptable limits, and refuses to maintain distinctions between the high and the low, and in this, too, it is a Revolutionary diction. The reviewer of *The Literary Gazette* is accurate, if disapproving when he points out that, in addition to the French Revolution, Carlyle's history represents 'the Revolution of the English language'.[25]

Reviewers, as Carlyle anticipated, objected to the 'multitudes of new-coined words and concocted phrases', and Carlyle's 'unintelligible jargon and adulterated English'.[26] Carlyle reproduced for these readers the experience of listening on May 3, 1798, to the proceedings of the Parlement of Paris, 'Dissonant hubbub there is; jargon as of Babel' (1, 100). But in both cases the 'jargon' has the same origin: it is the inevitable consequence when new things are spoken of, things for which no existing names are available. The language of the National Assembly was to become still more Babel-like, because foreign Deputies were elected, amongst them, Tom Paine and Anacharsis Clootz, self-proclaimed 'Orator of the Human Race'. The Revolution did not admit national boundaries, and nor does Carlyle who borrows words and modes of word formation from a number of languages, most obviously German. It is this that particularly offended Lady Sydney Morgan:

> With respect to language, in particular, every nation must be permitted to 'speak for itself'; and the pedantry of engrafting on any language foreign modes of expression, is unmitigated folly. Words may successfully be naturalized when they express new ideas; but foreign grammatical idioms are ever ill-assorted patches, which disfigure, and cannot adorn, the cloth to which they are appended.

*The Monthly Review*, too, fears for the consequences 'if such quaint, deformed, whimsically affected, and bastard modes of expression should become fashionable amongst our sober-minded countrymen'. The reviewer asks whether 'anyone can be so ignorant as to suppose' that the English tongue 'is too poor and destitute of signs for the most subtle or exalted thoughts as to require … monstrous coinages' such as Carlyle's.

it was a rejection of the manner of the eighteenth-century historians, Hume, Robertson, and Gibbon, in which history becomes a matter of 'abstractions', in favour of the method of Shakespeare and of Schiller (Merivale properly adds Scott) which is concerned not so much with detailing historical events as in imagining what it felt like to take part in them. The result will, as Thackeray notes, outrage all those who 'love history as it gracefully runs in Hume, or struts pompously in Gibbon'. The reviewers agreed that Carlyle achieves his literary revolution by breaking down the barriers between 'prose and verse', that is, between discursive and imaginative literature, and they agreed too on the genre to which *The French Revolution* best approximates. It is, according to Mill, 'not so much a history, as an epic poem; and notwithstanding, or even in consequence of this, the truest of histories', for *The American Biblical Repository* it is 'a prose epic', for *The Boston Quarterly Review* 'an Epic Poem'.[29] The reviewers are repetitive, but on the best of authority, Carlyle's own, for he clearly offers his book as the kind of epic the modern world demands, a prose epic, based on fact, for 'all Delineation, in these ages, were it never so epic, "speaking itself and not singing itself", must either found on Belief and provable Fact, or have no foundation at all' (3, 31). Of modern critics A.J. LaValley has most thoroughly defended the epic claims of the book. He notes Carlyle's several references to Homer, Virgil, Dante and Milton, compares Carlyle's repeated epithets – Robespierre as 'the sea-green incorruptible', Lafayette as 'the Hero of Two Worlds' – with the stock heroic epithets of epic, and identifies Carlyle's third volume as a visit to the underworld, here located not in space but in the nether regions of the human psyche, where is to be found the 'fulginous confused Kingdom of Dis, with thy Tantalus-Ixion toils' (2, 242).[30] For LaValley Carlyle repeats Wordsworth's discovery that within 'the Mind of Man' there are heights to which 'the heaven of heavens is but a veil' and depths deeper than the 'darkest pit of lowest Erebus'. The French revolution is, for Carlyle, an epic plot that has no need of 'Epical Machinery' other than the passions of the French people (1, 127). But LaValley adds that Carlyle is more interested in the 'difference between his book and all previous epics' than the similarities, and he points out that it is at least as easy to class *The French Revolution* as mock-epic rather than epic proper. It is an epic in which the epic action is reversed, the Olympians of Versailles are overthrown by the Titanic mob of Paris, an epic in which 'light dies' before the 'uncreating word' of the dumb millions of France. Mark Cumming goes further, because for him *The French Revolution* is 'a disimprisoned epic', an epic freed, that is, from generic constraints. It is a work that 'depends on the fundamental principle of generic transgression', and hence can itself be described as an epic only by an extreme paradox.[31] *The French Revolution* is, after all, like the *Vanity Fair* of Carlyle's admirer, Thackeray, an epic without a hero. Mirabeau comes closest, but he dies mid-way through Carlyle' second volume, and at the last Carlyle writes of him, 'This brother man, if not Epic for us, is Tragic; if not great, is large' (2, 147). If there is a true hero in this epic it is the French people, 'this Typhon of Anarchy, Political, Religious; sprawling hundred-headed, say with Twenty-five million heads; wide as the area of France; fierce as Frenzy; strong in very Hunger', (2, 137).[32] But it is an odd kind of epic hero that is defined by its dumb anonymity.

In 1836, just a year before the publication of *The French Revolution* Disraeli published his own attempt at an epic of the Revolution.[33] His failure is total, but instructive. In his preface he acknowledges four predecessors: Homer who in the *Iliad* wrote the 'Heroic Epick'; Virgil who took as his theme 'the consolidation of the most superb of Empires'; and wrote the 'Political Epick'; Dante who 'presented us in the Divine Comedy with a National Epick'; and Milton whose *Paradise Lost* is the 'Religious Epick'. Wandering over the plains of Troy, Disraeli thought, 'And the sprit of my Time, shall it alone be uncelebrated?'. The 'Revolution of France' seemed to him as important an event as the siege of Troy, Napoleon no less 'interesting' than Achilles', and he discovered his mission, 'For me remains the Revolutionary Epick'. Disraeli's is a visionary epic, modelled on poems by Southey and Shelley, in particular *The Revolt of Islam*. Two 'Genii' appear before the throne of Demogorgon, each appealing for judgement in his favour. In the first book Magros, 'the Genius of Feudalism' makes his case, which is drawn directly from Burke. Magros commends 'Prejudice, at which fools scoff, unknowing / The precious fruit that husky rind enfolds' (33). At least once, Burke is quoted directly, 'Art is man's Nature' (38), but still the orotund diction, the flat blank verse, and the remorselessly allegoric mode (two beautiful brothers serve as Magros's pages and their names are 'Faith' and 'Fealty') deprive Burke's argument of all its transgressive, polemical vitality. In the second book Magros is countered by 'Lyridion', who represents what Disraeli calls 'Federalism', but also names 'Equality'. Lyridion is as transparently a version of Shelley as Magros is of Burke, but the parody is slightly more successful. In America, Washington makes each man 'Lord of himself' (89): 'None tremble where none frown; and none will fawn / Where none can trample' (90). The whole passage is drawn directly from the reports on the regenerated world given by the Sprits of the Earth and the Hour in *Prometheus* its disruption of all generic decorum: 'In startling transitions, in colours all intensated, the sublime, the ludicrous, the horrible, succeed one another; or rather, in crowding tumult, accompany one another' (3, 106–7). Inevitably, it is generically closest to the genre that can only be defined by its refusal of generic constraints, it is closest to the novel. Carlyle's use of stock epithet, for example – Lafayette as 'the Hero of Two Worlds' – is surely much further from 'pius Aeneas' than it is from Mr Turveydrop, 'the Master of Deportment'. Like the novel, Carlyle's *History* has an inbuilt disposition towards comedy. In the third volume, the Terror is 'a sable ground' on which the ludicrous 'paints itself': in the first two volumes it is the ludicrous that supplies the ground. *The French Revolution* for most of its length gives voice to what Carlyle calls 'one boundless inarticulate Ha-Ha; – *transcendent* World-Laughter' (1, 288). At times the laughter tightens into a smirk, into 'mocking tehees' (1, 45), as when the members of the 'Tennis-Court Club' arrange to commemorate their oath with a 'far-gleaming Brass-plate' which will act 'as a deathless memorial, for some years' (2, 51). But more often the laughter is less sardonic, heartier, as when Mrs Momoro, the wife of a book-seller, is chosen to personate the Goddess of Reason and carried in solemn precession to Notre Dame. All agree that Mrs Momoro 'made one of the best Goddesses of Reason; though her teeth were a little defective'. Carlyle is left tantalized by one great mystery, wondering what 'articulate words poor Mrs Momoro uttered; when she had become ungoddessed again, and the Bibliopolist and she sat quiet at home, at supper' (2, 229).

It is the wild comedy of the book, almost as much as its style, that perplexed its reviewers. *The Literary Gazette* could not tell 'whether the author is in earnest or in jest':

> with Mr Carlyle, not only life, but death, is a standing jest; not only murder, but fusillades, noyades, and massacres, the merries of jocular descriptions. The very titles of his chapters are like grinning and hideous laughs at mortality, and mortal suffering.

Mill offers a fine defence of Carlyle's manner in which 'passages of grave drollery ... not inferior to the best in Mr Peacock's novels' are terminated by 'a soft note as of dirge music, or solemn choral song of old Greek tragedy, which makes the heart too full for endurance, and forces you to close the book and rest for a while'. For Mill the manner is justified because 'this mixture and confused entanglement of the great and the contemptible' is 'precisely what we meet with in nature'.[34]

He defends Carlyle in almost the same way that Dickens defends his own manner in *Oliver Twist*, a novel that began to appear in 1837, the very same year in which Carlyle's work was published. Dickens points out that 'in all good murderous melodramas', 'the tragic and the comic scenes' are presented 'in as regular alternation as the layers of red and white in a side of streaky bacon', and that although this may be 'condemned as outrageous and preposterous' it is 'less unnatural' than it seems, for 'the transitions in real life' are 'not a whit less startling' (Chapter 17). It seems odd, but is, I think, significant that Dickens is much less like Carlyle in the novel that draws most directly on the history.

It was more than twenty years later, in 1859, that Dickens published *A Tale of Two Cities*, a novel heavily indebted, as Dickens fully acknowledged, to *The French Revolution*.[35] But Dickens admits, too, that 'the main idea' of his story came to him not when he was reading Carlyle, but when he was acting the part of Richard Wardour in Wilkie Collins's melodrama, *The Frozen Deep*.[36] According to Collins, Dickens 'surpassed himself' in the role: 'He literally electrified the audience'. At the centre of the play is an example of heroic self-sacrifice. Wardour is cut off in the Arctic wastes in the company of the man, Frank Aldersley, who is engaged to the woman he believes has jilted him. He is tempted by the opportunity he has been given to murder his rival, but, in the event, he preserves Aldersley's life at the expense of his own. Wardour gave Dickens the clue for Sydney Carton's act of self-sacrificing heroism which brings *A Tale of Two Cities* to its conclusion. Collins, in other words, showed Dickens how he might make use of the material that he gathered from Carlyle by subsuming it within the formal shape of a melodrama. *The French Revolution* is so different from the novel because it refuses to 'name' the genre to which it conforms: 'were the right Name itself once here, the Thing is known henceforth; the Thing is then ours and can be dealt with' (3, 204), but Carlyle writes without knowing 'the right Name', and it is from that ignorance that all the monstrous, anarchic vitality of his book derives.

*The Boston Quarterly Review* boldly insists that *The French Revolution* establishes Carlyle as 'emphatically the English poet of our epoch': 'is he not Shelley and Wordsworth combined, and greater than either?'. It would have been proper to add the name of Byron, not only because the reviewers disturbed by the 'grinning and hideous' laughter with which Carlyle surveys the events he describes rehearse the outrage voiced by many of the early readers of episodes such as the shipwreck in *Don Juan*, but because Byron was at least as aware as Shelley and Wordsworth that it was the French Revolution that provided the central plot of his age and of its poetry. In 1821, he wrote to Murray that his plan for Don Juan was to 'take him the tour of Europe, with a proper mixture of siege, battle, and adventure, and to make him finish as *Anacharsis Cloots* in the French revolution'.[37] Clootz went to his death on March 24, 1794, preserving to the end, Carlyle tells us, 'an air of polished sarcasm' (3, 258).

But it is not Byron that Carlyle puts J.S. Mill in mind of. He ends his review instead by comparing Carlyle with Wordsworth and Coleridge. Both men entered Carlyle's thoughts as he was working on his history. He met Wordsworth, a 'genuine kind of man, but intrinsically and extrinsically a *small* one, let them sing or say what they will', and he read *Yarrow Revisited and Other Poems* when it was first published in 1835, but in all the volume he found only 'A Wren's Nest' to admire. He read Coleridge's *Table Talk*, too: 'Never did I see such apparatus got ready for thinking, and so little thought'.[38] But Mill does not claim that Carlyle recognizes Wordsworth and Coleridge as congenial, but rather that there is a radical similarity between *The French Revolution* and *Lyrical Ballads*. Both are expressions of 'one of the most conspicuous new elements that have sprung up in the European mind' in the years that separate the two publications, 'an insatiable demand for realities, come of conventionalities and formalities what may'. Carlyle's rejection of the manner of eighteenth-century historians, his violent dismantling of 'the whole structure of our Johnsonian English', seemed to Mill equivalent to Wordsworth's repudiation of eighteenth-century poetic diction. Mill had read *The Spirit of the Age* (1825), and probably remembered Hazlitt's account of *Lyrical Ballads*:

> It is one of the innovations of the time. It partakes of, and is carried along with, the revolutionary movement of our age: the political changes of the day were the model on which he formed and conducted his poetical experiments. His muse (it cannot be denied, and without this we cannot explain its character at all) is a levelling one. It proceeds on a principle of equality, and strives to reduce all things to the same standard.

Hazlitt sees in Wordsworth the poet as sansculotte, and Mill sees in Carlyle the historian in the same character.

Like M.H. Abrams, though for quite different reasons, Mill finds in Carlyle the most direct conduit through which High Romanticism passes into the Victorian age, and it is a thought that helps to explain the authority that, throughout those years, Carlyle's works were accorded.

But although *The French Revolution* made Carlyle's reputation, it did not make his fortune. It was not just that he was unlucky in his dealings with the literary marketplace, it was rather that the mere thought that any such marketplace existed provoked in him 'a feeling mild and charitable as that of a starved hyena'.[39] Not all his contemporaries were so fastidious. In my next two chapters I turn to writers who wrote rather successfully for the marketplace. First, I turn to Felicia Hemans and Letitia Landon. Carlyle was, of all the great Victorians, commonly perceived as the most 'manly', whereas the success of Hemans and Landon depended on the manner in which they projected their femininity. In the 1820s and 1830s, I shall argue, femininity became a marketable commodity. Then, in the following chapter, I shall turn to a group of writers, many of them women, who not only supplied literary commodities for the market, but took commodities as the chief topic of their fiction, the fashionable novelists.

and have begun the task of re-writing literary history in order to accommodate it.[3] But their work, too, is not free from embarrassment. Curran, for example, boldly identifies Hemans as the 'major figure' in the forging of the bourgeois or liberal literary culture that was to dominate Victorian England, but he cannot control his impatience with Hemans's sentimentality and her celebration of domesticity. For him, Hemans is, 'above all, the creator and enforcer of ideological control masking itself as praise for feminine instinct and female duty' (190). It seems almost churlish to insist that Hemans be accorded her rightful place in literary history only to lambast her for having chosen to occupy it. The problem is that Hemans, as Mellor points out, 'constructed her self and poetry as the icon of female domesticity', and it is not an icon that many modern critics are prepared to reverence. The common response is to argue that Hemans in fact subverts the values that she seems to celebrate. So, Mellor finds that 'having accepted her culture's hegemonic inscription of the woman within the domestic sphere, Hemans's poetry subtly and painfully explored the ways in which that construction of gender finally collapses upon itself, bringing nothing but suffering, and the void of nothingness, to both men and women' (142). Wolfson agrees that the presiding theme of Hemans's most popular volume, *Records of Woman*, is 'the failure of domestic ideals, in whatever cultural variety, to sustain and fulfil women's lives' (145), and Leighton, in an admirably balanced account of Hemans, still manages, by drawing her metaphors from 'The Chamois Hunter's Love', to identify Hemans's proper place as neither in the 'family home' in the valley nor on the mountain-tops in the 'wild loneliness of "rocks and storms"', but rather in a 'hut' 'edgily between' the two, where she exists 'lonely and forsaken' (25–6).[4] The problem here is obvious enough. Mellor, Wolfson and Leighton rescue Hemans from Curran's disparaging description of her work, but only by making the fact of her enormous popularity either inexplicable or the product of a grotesque misreading. Is it really credible that Hemans could have contrived to win her place as the most successful poet in Britain by the production of poems that expose the destructive hollowness of the values that her readers held most dear?[5]

Such critical contortions are produced by a desire to reclaim the work of a poet whose poems seem, on the face of it, to celebrate an ideology that most modern critics, for perfectly good reasons, find distasteful. Hemans celebrates both domesticity and heroism; she pays her devotion, as her memorialist and daughter, Harriet Owen, notes, at once to 'the chivalrous and the tender',[6] and modern critics are no happier with her cult of heroism than they are with her cult of domesticity. Her most famous poem, 'The boy stood on the burning deck' or 'Casabianca', celebrates the staunchness of a boy who will not abandon a burning ship, because his father is unconscious below deck, and so unable to respond to the boy's pleas that he be permitted to leave his station. It is impossible for a reader now not to respond queasily to the boy's increasingly panicky appeals to his father before he and the ship are blown to smithereens, and the poem reaches its conclusion:

> But the noblest thing that perished there,
> Was that young faithful heart.
>
> $(39-40)^7$

Nevertheless, when Armstong offers the poem as 'a violent elegy about the way phallic law destroys itself', or Mellor insists that the boy's 'filial fidelity' is shown to be 'not only futile but counter-productive' and that the ' "noblest thing which perished there" was perhaps not Casabianca's "young faithful heart" so much as the domestic values to which that heart foolishly adhered', then, surely, the poem is reclaimed only by being wilfully misread.[8] The boy's conduct is represented as heroic rather than foolish, and the readership that made the poem famous, we must assume, found that heroism underscored rather than undermined by the manner in which his appeals to his father invite the reader to register the full pathos of his situation.

But modern critics, one suspects, are not simply responding to ideological pressures. Hemans's poems present to the reader a glassy surface that seems to offer no crevice to which the critical intelligence can cling. Jerome McGann, in a characteristically independent intervention in Hemans studies, points out how her poetry 'covets an undisturbed appearance', that it registers 'no apparent divorce between form and content', and that it was precisely this characteristic of poems that are 'finished throughout with an exquisite delicacy, and even serenity of execution' that Jeffrey admired and that makes them seem to modern readers merely 'bland'.[9] It is, of course, discrepancies between form and content, between the formal characteristics and the expressive qualities of a poem, on which all critics educated under the auspices of New Criticism have been trained to focus. Hemans characteristically offers no such discrepancies, and the critical response has been to locate an ideological complexity that can stand in for the complex relationship between form and content that is felt to be disablingly absent. If, as Paula Feldman suggests, Hemans's poetry 'undercuts, even while it reinforces, conventional views of women',[10] then the critic is freed to trace a complex relationship, not between form and content, but between text and sub-text, so that the critical argument, even though it may lack the substance, can comfortably retain the structure of the kind of argument that New Criticism represented as distinguishing literary studies.

It is significant, perhaps, that both Ross and Mellor centre their discussions of Hemans on a poem that lacks the glassiness, 'the serenity of expression', that characterizes Hemans's best known work. *The Siege of Valencia* is a heroic tragedy modelled on the dramas of Joanna Baillie that Hemans admired, though it claims even loftier precedents. When Elmina leans over the body of Ximena, her daughter, the echo of Lear gazing at the body of the dead Cordelia is clear enough:

> Hush! Doth she move? –
> One light lock seemed to tremble on her brow,
> As a pulse throbbed beneath ...
>
> (3, viii, 154–6; 113)

Valencia, besieged by the Moors, is governed by Alvar Gonzalez. By the time that Gonzalez's two sons are captured by the Moors, it seems impossible that the city can hold out for more than a few days. The Moorish general, Abdullah, promises to spare them if Gonzalez will yield the city, and, when Gonzalez proudly refuses the offer, his wife Elmina goes in disguise to the Moorish camp, and promises to give Abdullah's army passage into the city. Later, she repents her decision, and reveals what she has done to her husband in time for him to repel the Moorish forces. But then Gonzalez is forced to witness helplessly the execution of his elder son. An attempt to rescue the younger son fails, and he too dies, but not before the father has received his death wound in the attempt to save him. At last, a relief force arrives, but by this time Elmina alone of the family is alive: even her daughter, Ximena, is dead.

For Ross, the play traces the history of how Elmina learns to recognize her error. She betrays the state, 'and, as she later realizes, in betraying the state, she also betrays her own domestic obligations, her own wifely and maternal affections'. For Mellor, on the contrary, the play offers 'a powerful critique of the patriarchal code of heroism' by showing that 'when the public sphere takes control of the private, both realms are destroyed'.[11] *The Siege of Valencia* is an atypical example of Hemans's work because it does invite contrary readings. The action of the play is instigated by a debate. Elmina begs her husband to submit to Abdullah's blackmail and save their sons. When he refuses, she passionately denounces both him and the masculine code that he prizes more highly than the lives of his children:

> Oh, cold and hard of heart!
> Thou shouldst be born for empire, since thy soul
> Thus lightly from all human bonds can free
> Its haughty flight! – Men! Men! Too much is yours
> Of vantage: ye, that with a sound, a breath,
> A shadow, thus can fill the desolate space
> Of rooted up affections, o'er whose void
> Our yearning hearts must wither! So it is,
> Dominion must be won!
>
> (3, i, 273–81; 74)

She contrasts a mother's 'deep, strong, deathless love', with paternal love, which is always contaminated by self:

> It is but pride, wherewith
> To his fair son the father's eye doth turn,
> Watching his growth. Ay, on the boy he looks,
> The bright, glad creature springing on his path,
> But as the heir of his great name, the young
> And stately tree, whose rising strength ere long
> Shall bear his trophies well.
>
> (3, i, 435–41; 77)

But Gonzalez is implacable, responding to all his wife's accusations by re-stating his own code of masculine honour:

> Was the oath, whereby,
> On th'altar of my faith, I bound myself,
> With an unswerving spirit to maintain
> This free and Christian city for my God
> And for my king, a writing traced on sand?
> That passionate tears should wash it from the earth,
> Or e'en the life-drops of a bleeding heart
> Efface it, as a billow sweeps away
> The last light vessel's wake? – Then never more
> Let man's deep vow be trusted!
>
> (3, i, 290–9; 74–5)

Mellor and Ross respond to this scene by taking sides, different sides, but it seems to me that the scene works to express, as powerfully as

Hemans can, two irreconcilable points of view, neither of which can be rejected. No soldier like Gonzalez can sacrifice the lives of his troops in defence of his city, and then yield the city in order to save the lives of his sons. Equally, no mother can be required to assent to the murder of her children.

This is the play's tactic throughout. Elmina and her daughter, Ximena, are not only contrasting types of womanhood, but contrasting ideals of womanhood. Elmina is heroic when she dons male disguise and dares to make her way though enemy lines to deliver her appeal to Abdullah in person, and so is Ximena when she leads the reluctant citizens to battle carrying the banner of the Cid. The two sons are similarly characterized. The younger, Carlos, is given all Casabianca's sweet helplessness – all he wants is to 'see [his] mother's face / At morning when [he] wake[s]' (3, iv, 57-8; 90) – but the older is given all Casabianca's stalwart virtues, appealing at the moment of his execution to his father, who looks on helplessly from the city walls, to witness his bravery:

> But look upon me still! – I will not blench
> When the keen sabre flashes – Mark me well!
> Mine eyelids shall not quiver as it falls,
> So thou wilt look upon me!
> (3, vii, 62–5; 108)[12]

Both sons are ideal boys, but contrasting and irreconcilable ideals.

In this play, as throughout her work, Hemans shows herself, in Leighton's words, 'obsessed by gender',[13] but gender crosses sexual boundaries, so that Elmina is a feminine and Ximena a masculine ideal of womanhood, Carlos a feminine and Alphonso a masculine ideal of boyhood. For Mellor the tragedy is produced by the subordination of the feminine to the masculine ideal. The play exposes the inadequacy of the masculine code, she claims, most eloquently in its characterization of Hernandez, a frighteningly sociopathic monk. Hernandez took vows after his son had fallen in love with a Moorish woman, and converted to Islam in order to marry her. Later, in battle against the Moors, Hernandez unwittingly kills him. The lesson he has derived from this experience is the folly of parents who fasten their affections on their children. Hence the consolation he offers Elmina when she confronts the threat to her sons:

> Let them die!
> Let them die *now*, thy children! So thy heart
> Shall wear their beautiful image all undimmed
> Within it, to the last! Nor shalt thou learn

> The bitter lesson of what worthless dust
> Are framed the idols, whose false glory binds
> Earth's fetter on our souls!
>
> (3, ii, 289–95; 84)

This goes beyond tactlessness: it is insane, and so by implication is the ethic that it supports, that public duty is incompatible with private affection. Unsurprisingly, the citizens of Valencia disappoint him:

> These men have earthly ties
> And bondage on their natures! – To the cause
> Of God and Spain's revenge, they bring but half
> Their energies and hopes. But he whom Heaven
> Hath called to be the awakener of a land,
> Should have his soul's affections all absorbed
> In that majestic purpose, and press on
> To its fulfilment, as a mountain-born
> And mighty stream, with all its vassal-rills,
> Sweeps proudly to the ocean, pausing not
> To dally with the flowers.
>
> (3, ii, 115–25; 81)

So far Mellor is right. The difficulty is that she shares the priest's analysis, so that her understanding of the events of the play remains the mirror image of Hernandez's. Both agree that earthly, feminine ties are incompatible with masculine public duties: they differ only over which should give way to the other. The play presents either possibility as beyond tragedy, as nihilistic, and it figures that possibility most powerfully in the breakdown of a marriage, the marriage of Elmina and Gonzalez.

When Gonzalez refuses to yield the city and save his sons, Elmina curses him to experience a life devoid of any human affection, comforted only by the empty possession of fame:

> May you live
> To be alone, when loneliness doth seem
> Most heavy to sustain!
>
> (3, i, 469–71; 78)

She loses her love for her husband, and when she does so she becomes a ghastly echo of Hernandez:

> Ay! They that fix
> Affection's perfect trust on aught of earth,
> Have many a dream to start from!
>
> (3, v, 165–7; 97)

When Elmina betrays the city to the Moors, Gonzalez similarly loses his love for her, and in doing so he loses his humanity: for him 'the nobleness/Henceforth is blotted from all human brows', and he can no longer bear even to look Ximena, his faithful daughter, in the face – ''tis too like hers!' (3, v, 272–3, 292; 100). The play is tragic because at its close only Elmina survives, but the catastrophe of nihilism is averted, and it can be averted because, although sex is immutable, in this play and throughout Hemans's work, gender can be blurred. When Elmina assumes male disguise and makes her way through the lines, she shows, as Abdullah notes, more than masculine courage, and when Gonzalez stands helplessly to watch his son be killed he displays a more than feminine capacity for suffering endurance. So it is that at the very last Elmina and Gonzalez can rediscover their love for one another. It is because she recognizes her love for her husband that, at the moment of Gonzalez's death, Elmina can say, 'Now is my life uprooted, – and 'tis well'. (3, ix, 202; 121)

Mellor judges *The Siege of Valencia* Hemans's 'finest literary work'. It may be so – it is true at least that it offers the most comprehensive treatment of the themes that recur in all her poems – but it remains uncharacteristic, and it was not the poem on which her fame rested. By 1823, when the play was published, Hemans had already sustained her literary career for fifteen years. Her first volume had been published in 1808, when she was only fifteen. It was a career that began, then, just a year after Byron's and pre-dated Shelley's and Keats's. Early poems such as *The Restoration of the Works of Art to Italy* (1816) and the prize-winning 'The Meeting of Wallace and Bruce on the Banks of the Carron' (1819) had secured her a solid reputation, but in a review of her work in 1819 the *Edinburgh Magazine* notes that she has few readers, and asks 'Why are they so few?'.[14] It was only with the publication of *The Forest Sanctuary*, and *Lays of Many Lands* both in 1825, *Records of Woman* in 1828, and *Songs of the Affections* in 1830 that she secured her place as the pre-eminent British poet, and it was in these volumes that she developed the poetic form with which she was always most closely associated, her own version of the lyrical ballad.

The *Edinburgh Magazine* had in fact identified her failure to offer the public the narrative poems that they craved as the principal reason for her lack of popularity, but it is a want that in her later poems she amply supplies. The poems may tighten towards the lyric, though still retaining a narrative character, or they may expand towards the romance, while still preserving their concentration on states of feeling rather than patterns of event. The states of feeling deployed are most commonly melancholic, and the response insistently demanded of the reader is sympathetic pity. In other words, the poems are characteristically sentimental. The poems are rhymed: couplets and quatrains are the commonest schemes, but there is great variety, Spenserian stanzas, for example, in *The Forest Sanctuary*. Metrically, there is even greater diversity – iambs and anapaests, pentameter lines and stanzas in common measure, even experiments in classical metre – but in all cases the intonations of the speaking voice are subordinated to the flow of the metre. Angela Leighton is right to point out that in some of the *Records of Woman* the movement of the couplets is more fluid, but even in 'Properzia Rossi', where the fluidity is at its most extreme, and more than half the poem's iambic pentameter couplets are enjambed, the couplet form continues to superimpose itself on Properzia's voice in a manner far removed from Browning's in a poem like 'My Last Duchess'. The diction is chastely ornate. Neologism and archaism are avoided, and the vocabulary selected from a stock of words that had been familiar in poetry for many years.

Jeffrey offers the most exact description of this style, which 'would strike us, perhaps, as more impassioned and exalted, if it were not regulated and harmonized by the most beautiful taste':

> It is infinitely sweet, elegant, and tender – touching, perhaps, and contemplative, rather than vehement and overpowering; and not only finished throughout with an exquisite delicacy, and even serenity of execution, but informed with a purity and loftiness of feeling, and a certain sober and humble tone of indulgence and piety, which must satisfy all judgements, and allay the apprehensions of those who are most afraid of the passionate exaggerations of poetry.

Jeffrey is equally exact in defining the dominant characteristic of such a style: it is 'feminine', and establishes Hemans's work as 'a fine exemplification of Female Poetry'. Jeffrey makes this seem not only a modest achievement, but an achievement of modesty. Hemans's poems are as 'perfect' as they are because she accepts rather than rebels against the limitations of her gender: 'the delicacy of [women's] habits, and the still more disabling delicacy which pervades their conceptions and feelings', which prevent them from delineating 'the fierce and sullen passions of men', and limit them to representations of that area of life which is woman's proper concern, 'the practical regulation of the private life in all its bearings, affections, and concerns'. It is significant that this ideally feminine style was not developed by Hemans until she was in her thirties. In 1819, reviewing her prize poem on Wallace, the *Edinburgh Magazine* could still describe her poetry as 'by far the most *manly* which ever came from a female pen'.[15] Two oddities remain. First, there is an odd discrepancy between the modesty of the achievement that Jeffrey describes and the power that he attributes to it: it has forced from 'its place of pride' even 'the blazing star of Byron himself'. There is an equally odd discrepancy between Jeffrey's insistence that women writers must confine themselves to the private life, and the content of the poems themselves. It is easier to address the second point first.

Hemans's poems range further from home both in time and in space than those of any of her male predecessors with the possible exception of Southey. She outdoes even Baillie's *Plays of the Passions*, that she so much admired, in appropriating all human history and the whole of the known world to provide the subject matter for her poems. She speaks as Sappho in the sixth century BC, as the wife of Hasdrubal at the end of the third, as the wife of Rudolph von Wart in the fourteenth century, the wife of Charles V in the sixteenth, and as Arabella Stuart in the seventeenth. The geographical range is equally wide, from American Indians to those of the sub-continent, from the Russia of 'Ivan the Czar' to the tropical island home that the exile dreams of in 'The Palm Tree'. Jeffrey does not neglect this characteristic of her poems, but singles it out for praise. She has taken her themes 'from the legends of different nations, and the most opposite states of society; and has contrived to retain much of what is interesting and peculiar in each of them, without adopting along with it, any of the revolting or extravagant excesses which may characterise the taste or manners of the people or the age from which it has been derived'. She shares with Southey an imperial imagination,[16] but for Jeffrey she can do so without compromising her femininity, which requires her to restrict her sphere to 'private life' and not to venture on 'affairs of moment as they are conducted in the great theatre of the world'. Her ingenious solution, as Tricia Lootens shows, is to expand the domestic sphere, the sphere of private life, until it becomes co-extensive with the globe. In one of her most popular poems, 'The Graves of a Household', she seems to mourn a family that, even in death, is dispersed around the world. The children over whom the 'same fond mother bent' each night now lie in distant graves, one in America, another committed to the sea, one in Spain, a soldier presumably who fell in the Peninsular War, and the last, a daughter who perhaps suffered from consumption, in an Italian grave. The poem apparently mourns their dispersal, and yet it is infused too with a proud sense that the most intimate of domestic spaces, the English country churchyard, has become as wide as the world. As she puts it in another poem: 'Wave may not foam, nor wild wind sweep, / Where rest not England's dead' ('England's Dead').

Jeffrey insists that Hemans's verse shows an 'exquisite delicacy', which seems to be at once a delicacy of execution and a delicacy of sentiment, and he praises her tenderness and her purity. He has in mind, one assumes, a poem such as 'The Memorial Pillar' which celebrates the piety of the Countess of Pembroke who erected the pillar in 1656 at the place where she had last parted from her mother more than forty years before:

> Can I, while yet these tokens wear
>   The impress of the dead,
> Think of the love embodied there,
>   As of a vision fled?
>
> (49–52; 307)

The answer of course is no, and the poem ends by imagining the reunion of mother and child in Heaven: 'Surely your hearts have met at last!'. 'Edith, A Tale of the Woods' tells the story of a young woman who is left alone in the wilds of America when her whole party, including her young husband, are slaughtered. Edith is fostered by an old Indian and his wife, who have lost their own daughter. Cared for by them, she recovers, and gradually leads the Indians towards Christ until 'their prayers were one'. She feels then that her work is done, and the poem closes when the old warrior sings over her dying body a tender but pious lament.

Jeffrey's description perfectly accommodates both poems. But there are an equally large number of poems by Hemans that seem on the face of it neither delicate, nor tender, nor, at any rate from a Christian point of view, edifying. A substantial group of poems, for example, commemorates women whose passions erupt into suicidal and/or murderous violence. As early as 1819 in *Tales and Historic Scenes*, there is 'The Wife of Asdrubal', in which the wife bitterly denounces her husband's ignoble capitulation to the Romans before stabbing her children to death and throwing herself into the flames of the burning citadel, and 'The Widow of Crescentius' who disguises herself as a minstrel boy in order to poison the Emperor Otho, avenging his execution of her husband. As she watches Otho expire in agony a 'feverish glow of triumph dyed' her cheek. In *Lays of Many Lands*, 'The Suliote Mother' hurls herself and her children from a precipice rather than be taken captive. In

*Records of Woman,* Maimuna avenges the murder of her son by raising a
Muslim army to burn to the ground 'The Indian City' of her son's killers
after putting its inhabitants to the sword; and the 'Indian Woman's
Death Song' is sung as she paddles her canoe towards the cataract over
which she and her baby will plunge to their deaths. She has been
deserted by her husband, but as she paddles 'upon her Indian brow / Sat
a strange gladness, and her dark hair wav'd / As if triumphantly' (9–11;
293). It is the same triumph with which Sappho throws herself from
the cliff in 'The Last Song of Sappho'.

Jeffrey quite fails to register a recognition that Hemans's poems are
divided in their character, and he is, I think, right. Edith and Maimuna
are violently contrasting types of womanhood, but they are accommodated within poems that very clearly share a style, and it is Hemans's
style that acts for Jeffrey as the guarantee of her tenderness and delicacy,
of her femininity. This remains the case almost without reference to the
content of the poems. It is what gives Hemans's mature verse the quality that W.M. Rossetti tartly describes as 'the monotone of mere sex',[17]
but it is the construction of that monotone that is her most powerful
achievement. Jeffrey alludes, I think, to the same quality, when he refers
to her 'serenity of expression', a serenity that remains quite undisturbed
by even the most sensational and violent subject matter. Both Jeffrey
and Rossetti recognize that serenity as the badge of her femininity, but
it works to project femininity as something both theatrical and, for all
its sentimentality, incongruously cold. Hemans was a much sought after
contributor to the annuals that began to dominate the poetry market in
the later 1820s, and was, unlike Landon, powerful enough to dictate her
own terms. She was not reduced, like Landon, to the composition of
hasty verses to accompany whatever plates the publisher had selected
for the volume. But from the mid-1820s her own poems become
increasingly pictorial, so that to read one of her volumes is like being
conducted through a gallery of pictures, pictures most often of women
who are placed in a rich variety of postures that have in common a certain extravagance and theatricality. The reader is invited to respond sen-
timentally to these pictures, but also coolly, rather as the Soul walks
through her gallery in Tennyson's 'The Palace of Art':

> Nor these alone, but every landscape fair,
>   As fit for every mood of mind,
> Or gay, or grave, or sweet, or stern, was there
>   Not less than truth designed.
>
> (89–92)

As I shall argue, this is not a coincidence, for Hemans and L.E.L. were
two of the principal, if largely unacknowledged, influences on the early
Tennyson.

It is Hemans's unfaltering 'serenity of expression' that persuades her
contemporaries that her poems remain properly enclosed within the
feminine sphere of private, domestic affections, and that continues to
persuade many of her modern readers of the same thing. Marlon Ross,
for example, is a careful reader of Hemans, and yet he offers her essay
on Goethe's *Tasso* as an exploration of the irreconcilablity of 'the realm
of the romantic, of sentiment and affection' and the masculine world,
'the outer struggle for worldly quest and conquest',[18] and he does this
despite Hemans's italicized insistence that Tasso, one of the major figures in her own pantheon, was at once a poet and a warrior, '*superior
with the sword and the pen to all men*', and despite her vigorous translation of Goethe's lines:

> Not steel to steel
> Is bound more closely by the magnet's power
> Than the same striving after lofty things
> Doth bind the Bard and Warrior.

In fact, the narratives to which Hemans consistently turns are those in
which the domestic and the chivalrous, the inner world of the affections and the outer world of conquest, the feminine and the masculine, are brought together.

Her demonic women erupt into masculine violence, even if often
their violence is directed only against themselves and their children.
Her angelic women are given to frequenting battlefields, most often in
search of a lover's body. 'Woman on the Field of Battle' is for Hemans a
defining icon, though in the poem of that name, the woman, who has
followed her lover to the wars, is herself among the slain:

> Why camest thou here?
>
> Why? – ask the true heart why
> Women hath been
> Ever where brave men die,
> Unshrinking seen?
> (36–40; 338–9)

Edith sits by her young husband as he dies 'and vainly bound / With
her torn robe and hair the streaming wound'. In 'Joan of Arc, in

Rheims', roles are reversed. It is Joan's moment of triumph as she stands helmeted in the cathedral, carrying the banner of France that is witnessed by her menfolk, her father and her two brothers, and it is the woman whose thoughts are recalled to the domestic paradise that she has left. 'Marguerite of France' compacts within herself both the masculine and feminine ideals when she rallies the cowardly troops by threatening to don armour and herself attack the besieging Muslims, carrying her infant son in her arms:

> And I will gird my woman's form,
> And on the ramparts die!
> And the boy whom I have borne for woe,
> But never for disgrace,
> Shall go within mine arms to death
> Meet for his royal race.
>
> (89–96; 495)

But more often it is femininity itself that is transformed into armour, as when in *The Siege of Valencia* Gonzalo praises his daughter:

> She hath put on
> Courage, and faith, and generous constancy
> E'en as a breastplate.
>
> (3, i, 382–4; 76)

Or in *The Forest Sanctuary*, when a young woman goes valiantly to her death strengthened by her love for her brother, 'The perfect image of affection pressed / Like armour to [her] bosom' (355–6; 225).

  Far from segregating it from the masculine sphere, Hemans consistently suggests that it is only in its relationship with the masculine that the feminine is defined or valorized. Her representative women are those like 'Gertrude' who sits by her husband, wiping his brow, as he suffers his last ordeal, being broken on the wheel, or, in a less ghastly manifestation of the type, 'The Switzer's Wife', who sends her husband from home to fight for his nation's freedom with her blessing:

> 'I know what thou wouldst do, – and be it done!
> Thy soul is darken'd with its fears for me,
> Trust me to Heaven, my husband, – this, thy son,
> The Babe whom I have borne thee, must be free!
> And the sweet memory of our pleasant hearth

May well give strength – if aught be strong on earth.'

(79–84; 275)

Here, as in almost all her poems, Hemans reinforces conventional notions that woman finds her best fulfilment in selfless service of a man, and of the masculine values that he represents. Her willingness to do so is, of course, one of the grounds of her huge popularity. The patriotic Swiss is named in the poem as Werner, and in Hemans's headnote identified as Werner Stauffacher, but the woman is identified only as his wife – appropriately, it might seem, because her virtue is that she finds her only being in him. But this is to ignore the fact that his masculinity finds its only expression through her. The code of values that defines him as a man can only be articulated by a woman. The same is true in all Hemans's mature poems, for, whether or not they give voice to a woman character, the sentiments of the poems are the expression of a voice that is the product of Hemans's style, a style that Jeffrey correctly read as definitively feminine. Angela Leighton, in a fine reading of 'The Chamois Hunter's Love', points out that the chamois hunter, who loves the perilous, stormy heights, is almost a metonym for the Byronic, that is, the Romantic Byron of *Manfred*.[19] The young woman who loves him must abandon for him her 'blessed home' in the valley, and she anticipates that her married life will be 'mournful', a life spent waiting fearfully for her husband to return from one of his perilous expeditions. Leighton is right to point out that she repudiates her own life in a gesture that is at once dutiful and exhilarated, but it is even more significant that the male Romanticism to which she surrenders her independence is itself the product of her own voice. She at once subordinates herself to it, and fully accommodates it within herself. Landon creates a somewhat similar effect in *The Improvisatrice*. Lorenzo, the object of the improvisatrice's passion is described at the moment that she first sees him, with his 'dark and flashing eye' that yet betrayed an 'almost female softness', his pale cheek, 'raven curls', 'high and haughty brow' as white as the mountain snow, and his heart-stopping eloquence (422–39; 29–30).[20] We learn later that he has 'thick-clustering curls' and a 'smile which past like lightning o'er/The curved lip' (438–41; 63). It is a description that, as all of her early readers would have recognized, is derived directly from the idealized prints of Byron's portraits that were so popular in the years immediately following his death. The improvisatrice is utterly in thrall to the dark charms of her Byronic hero, and yet the poem, from another point of view, quite disempowers him, reduces him to the status of a character in a poem by L.E.L., a prop in a feminine fantasy.

Hemans, like Landon, found in Scott the most powerful model for her own poems, although, again like Landon, Scott's influence is often mediated through that of Byron. But Scott's manner, and, to a large extent, his values, are transformed when she mimics them in her own voice, or rather in the voice that she developed in the mid-1820s, when her literary career was already far into its second decade. Ross scarcely overstates the case when he claims that 'Hemans sees her goal as the feminization of culture at large'.[21] At least one part of that goal she achieved. When, late in her life, she visited Scott at Abbotsford, she was pleased with her reception, and, as a farewell gift, left Scott a poem. She insists emphatically on Scott's masculinity, his voice is

> Like a chieftain's gathering-cry;
> While its deep master-tones hold sway
> As a king's o'er every breast...
> (12–14; 481)

But by 1829, when Hemans wrote this poem, 'deep master-tones' already seemed both odd and antiquated, and it was Hemans who, more than anyone, had made them seem so. L.E.L. was her chief assistant in the work, and it is significant that at the time of her death Landon was working on a study of Scott's female characters, as though her project was to appropriate for women not only Scott's poetic manner but even his robustly masculine novels.

The two women never met, and yet it might be argued that each produced the other. Both women, as Mellor points out, constructed themselves as icons, and, since there were only two niches available, the choice one made in large part determined the choice of the other. The names under which they published are themselves indicative. After 1812, when she married, Felicia Browne became 'Mrs Hemans', and retained that style long after her death, in the many editions of her poems throughout the nineteenth century. She presented her work to her readers as the poetry of a wife and mother, despite the fact that, in 1818, after she had borne him four sons and was pregnant with a fifth, Captain Hemans departed for Italy and never saw his wife again. Her most successful predecessor, Charlotte Smith, had made from a similar predicament the signature tune of all her poems, in which a domestic calamity, though never explained, is alluded to repeatedly. Hemans seems to have turned her misfortune to social advantage – Wordsworth admired her 'above all, for her delicate and irreproachable conduct during her long separation from an unfeeling husband'[22] – but she allows no trace of her domestic circumstances to seep into poems which maintain her privacy quite intact. So too did her way of life. Until the death of her mother she lived in Wales, moving to Wavertree near Liverpool in 1828, thus avoiding by her choice of residence any role within the London literary scene. She remained for almost all her readers a name on a title page, and the name she chose, 'Mrs Hemans', she donned in the same way that Ximena dons her virtues, as 'a breastplate', as a hard, protective surface that allows no chink through which the reader's prying gaze can penetrate.

Landon, who lived her whole life in London and was so enamoured of society that she insisted, as her one-time friend Rosina Bulwer records, on going to a ball even when ill with the flu, published under the three letters, L.E.L.[23] The tactic may first have been suggested by her mentor, William Jerdan, her next-door neighbour and the astute editor of *The Literary Gazette*, who first ushered her into fame by making her the most regular contributor of 'Original Poetry' to his journal. Bulwer remembered the effect on him and his fellow undergraduates at Cambridge:

> At that time, poetry was not yet out of fashion, at least with us of the cloister; and there was always, in the Reading Room of the Union, a rush every Saturday afternoon for "The Literary Gazette", and an impatient anxiety to hasten at once to that corner of the sheet which contained the three magical letters of "L.E.L.". And all of us praised the verse, and all of us guessed at the author. We soon learned it was a female, and our admiration was doubled, and our conjectures tripled. Was she young? Was she pretty? and – for there were some embryo fortune-hunters among us – was she rich?[24]

'L.E.L.' was a device that from the first invited the reader to decode the poem and reveal the poet, to pry beneath the text, which is conceived as a somewhat diaphanous material scarcely obscuring the warm and palpitating body of the woman who wrote it. All the six volumes of Landon's poetry can be read as a large expansion of the invitation compressed into the 'three magical letters of "L.E.L."'.

Hemans was interested in the figure of the woman poet, whose verses won her fame, but who found at last that this was no compensation for her failure in love. Madame de Stael's *Corinne, or Italy* was, in many ways, the founding text of nineteenth-century women's poetry. 'C'est moi', Hemans wrote in the margin, and Landon contributed the verse to the 1833 translation.[25] Hemans explores the topic in poems such as 'Corinne at the Capitol', 'The Last Song of Sappho', and, most powerfully in the monologue, 'Properzia Rossi' in *Records of Woman*. But for Hemans the Corinne figure is just one of her large gallery of female types: for Landon she is the controlling figure of all her poetry. It is a theme that she addresses directly in 'Corinna' from her first volume, *The Fate of Adelaide and Other Poems*, in the title poem of the second volume that made her famous, *The Improvisatrice and Other Poems*, in 'Erinna' from *The Golden Violet and Other Poems*, and in 'A History of the Lyre' from *The Venetian Bracelet*, Landon's finest poem, in which she tells the story of a second Italian improvisatrice, Eulalia. But it is a story implicit in all Landon's major poems.

At the end of *The Golden Violet* she turns, as she several times does at the conclusion of her longer poems, to address the reader directly. 'My power', she writes 'is but a woman's power' (3525).[26] This is at once a confession, and a quotation, from her own *The Improvisatrice*, where it is the character rather than her creator who concedes 'My power was but a woman's power' (25; 3). The quotation reveals belatedly, as it were, that the Italian woman poet of *The Improvisatrice* was only ever a mask for L.E.L. herself, except that it is not really a revelation because her readers had never doubted it. *The Literary Magnet* was entirely conventional when it described *The Troubadour* as an 'elegant volume from the pen of the charming Improvisatrice' (1826).

Landon offers the subjects of her poems as the evidence that hers is only a woman's power. She writes almost exclusively of love:

> If that I know myself what keys
> Yield to my hand their sympathies,
> I should say it is those whose tone
> Is woman's love and sorrow's own ...
>     (*Golden Violet*, 3529–32; 238)

She knew herself very well, as does her character, 'Erinna', whose topics are indistinguishable from Landon's:

> I have told passionate tales of breaking hearts,
> Of young cheeks fading even before the rose;
> My songs have been the mournful history
> Of woman's tenderness and woman's tears ...
>     ('Erinna', 375–8, *Golden Violet*; 266–7)

Landon's poems tell over and over again the same story. A young woman is loved, returns the love, is abandoned, and dies. The abandonment may be by betrayal or by accident, the errant lover may never come back in which case the lady will die of grief, but even if he should return it will only be in time to catch the woman's body as she falls. In *The Troubadour* the framing tale is of exactly this kind, and embedded within it are a variety of smaller narratives which almost without exception repeat the same story. In 'Rosalie' she compresses into just three lines the story that, expanded and repeated, fills all six volumes of her verse:

> Alas! Alas! Hers is a common tale: –
> She trusted, – as youth ever has believed; –
> She heard Love's vows – confided – was deceived!
> (Improvisatrice, 136–8; 118)

In 'St George's Hospital' she reduces it still further, 'She had loved, / Trusted, and been betrayed'. But these are not really stories about the sorrows of love. The women in them function simply as surrogates of the poet, and that is why they have to be abandoned. Mutual love, fulfilled love, is for Landon an impossible topic, as she several times recognizes, for example in *The Troubadour*:

> But what has minstrel left to tell
> When love has not an obstacle?
> My lute is hush'd, and mute its chords,
> The heart and happiness have no words![27]

Or earlier, and with a more charming brusqueness, in 'A Legend of the Rhine':

> They loved; – they were beloved. Oh, happiness!
> I have said all that can be said of bliss
> In saying that they loved.
> (Improvisatrice, 93–5; 35)

Happiness in love is a heresy against Landon's 'woman's creed of suffering' (*Golden Violet*, 367; 25), but, much more importantly, it allows an intrusive interloper into the relationship that remains central in all of Landon's poems, the relationship between herself and her reader. These are stories of 'woman's tears', and tears, for Landon, dissolve the distinction between poet and character. Her characters weep, and she represents the verse that records their tears as itself a kind of weeping.

Poetry came to her, she tells us, just as it came to Erinna for whom 'song came gushing, like the natural tears, / To check whose current does not rest with us' ('Erinna', 121–2, *Golden Violet*, 250). The weeping woman, the woman abandoned and fast dwindling into death, exerts over the reader a powerful sentimental appeal, but her true function within the poems is to figure the appeal that the poems themselves make to their reader, who is himself the chivalrous man who, by reading Landon's poems, rescues her from her desolate loneliness. It is very knowingly done.

Landon's style is at once utterly natural and extremely artificial.[28] She represents poetry as a spontaneous overflow of emotional fluid, as tears. She weeps onto paper, like the aged mother of 'The Sailor':

> The Bible lay
> Open beside, but blistered were the leaves
> With two or three large tears, which had dried in.
> > (*Improvisatrice*, 99–101; 226)

But here the tears are realized with an awkward precision that sharpens melancholy into pain, an effect that Landon is usually anxious to avoid. Hence her reliance on a narrow and cosseted diction, much of which is merely conventional – the roses, stars, violets and nightingales, the pale cheeks over which blushes come and go, the miraculously white hands – but which is nevertheless stamped with her own mark. If a tree is to be rested under, it is likely to be a chestnut, often 'chesnut'; if there is a dance it will probably be the saraband; the conventional roses, lilies and violets are variegated by flowers that seem personal favourites, the tulip and the laburnum; women are like flowers, and flowers are like women; verbs are active, especially when they are describing plants, which are much given to flinging. So, the 'wilding broom' of 'Gladesmuir' 'gracefully / Flings its long tresses like a maiden's hair / Waving in yellow beauty' (14–16, *Improvisatrice*; 194). The landscapes that this style is peculiarly adapted to describe are like those of *The Golden Violet*, where the poems on the first day are spoken in a 'spacious hall' that shuttles between being an outdoors and an indoors place:

> The dome above like a glory shone
> Or a cloud which the sunset lingers upon,
> While the tinted pane seem'd the bright resort,
> Where Iris' self held her minstrel court...
> > (*Golden Violet*, 317–20; 21)

On the second day the contest moves outside into the gardens, but the gardens offer a 'carpet meet' of flowers, and the mossy tree on which the Countess takes her seat accommodates her like a chaise longue:

> And at her feet, as if from air
> A purple cloud had fallen there,
> Grew thousand violets, whose sighs
> Breathed forth an Eastern sacrifice...
> (*Golden Violet*, 2505–8; 164–5)[29]

It is peculiarly appropriate that the prize for which the poets compete, the golden violet, is itself insecurely placed, seeming sometimes a flower and sometimes a jewel.

That odd union of the natural and the artificial is Landon's special mark, and it seeps into her representation of human relationships. Her verse is a natural outpouring which is also and always self-consciously poetic. She presents it as unpremeditated song, and yet there is always implicit in it a sidelong glance at the reader. Her women characters, too, are at once unselfconscious, and tremblingly sensitive to the presence of young men. Hence, she is particularly fond of representing her women at moments when they are conscious of someone looking at them:

> There was a blush, as if she knew
> Whose look was fixed on her...
> (*Improvisatrice*, 62–3; 5)

It is an often repeated moment. When the Improvisatrice arrives at the costumed ball dressed as 'a Hindoo girl', the thought of Lorenzo's eyes on her makes her blush:

> For well my conscious cheek betrayed
> Whose eye was gazing on me too.
> (*Improvisatrice*, 755–6; 50)

The power of these moments is in the precision with which they echo that distinctive relationship with the reader that is Landon's special mark. Her poems, more often than they are tears, are the blush, the rush of blood to the face with which she like her heroines signals her consciousness of the beloved, who is for her not Lorenzo but the reader.

Landon writes about love in poems the real subject of which is her own poetry. Hence the association she repeatedly insists on between love and poetry. When the Improvisatrice paints Sappho it as at the moment when she takes farewell of 'lyre, life, and love' (10). Life, as it is represented by Landon, is only constituted by poetry and love, and the two are scarcely distinguishable, as in *The Troubadour*:

> I know not whether love can fling
> A deeper witchery from his wing
> Than falls sweet Power of Song from thine.
> (10–11)

The central character of the poem, Raymond, a man more errant than knightly, is enraged by the caprices of his mistress, and loses in his anger the complexion proper to all Landon's heroes and heroines:

> Not his the paleness that may streak
> The lover's or the minstrel's cheek.
> (108)

But in the end it is love that figures poetry, rather than vice versa. The unhappy love careers that she so consistently ascribes to her heroines are moulded to echo her understanding of the poet's career, a career that she repeatedly charts. First, there is the youthful poet's dizzy rise to fame, a period in the poet's career which is exactly analogous to the first rapture of young love. Raymond is an unlikely poet, but Landon makes him one, it seems, only so that she can allow him to enjoy

> The loveliest part
> Of the young poet's life, when first,
> In solitude and silence nurst,
> His genius rises like a spring...
> (10)

Erinna triumphs in her first success:

> I felt immortal, for my brain
> Was drunk with its first draught of fame.
> (*Golden Violet*, 42–3; 245)

Even the still more mournful Eulalia joyfully remembers her poetic youth:

> The flowers were full of song: – upon the rose
> I read the crimson annals of true love;

> The violet flung me back an old romance...
> ('The History of the Lyre', 211–13)[30]

First poems are like first love. It is impossible to tell:

> What the young minstrel feels, when first the song
> Has been rewarded by the thrilling praise
> Of one too partial, but whose lightest word
> Can bid the heart beat quick with happiness.
> (231–4)[31]

The triumphant peak of the poet's career is the supreme moment of erotic consummation, the moment when 'Corinna' stands crowned on the Capitol, and responds to her coronation with a triumphant blush 'Such as young Psyche wore, when love first taught/His own sweet language' (*Fate of Adelaide*, 27–8; 98). Afterwards, as for all Landon's women, comes abandonment, not by a lover, not even by her readers (though that may be the concealed fear), but the poet loses her pleasure in the fame that she has won. Raymond is warned that though his 'songs be on every tongue,/And wealth and honours round him flung', he will at the last own that his fame has been 'dearly bought'. Erinna casts aside her lyre in disillusion, and Eulalia, too, acknowledges that the exercise of her talents has not compensated her for her loneliness. In the poem in which she memorializes Hemans, Landon asks 'Was not this [her fame] purchased all too dearly'.[32] In 'A History of the Lyre' in particular the familiar story has a deeper resonance. The poem is marked by the sad self-knowledge of a poet who had to make a living, and hence had to make a compromise with 'worldliness', not being able to afford the idealism of the unknown poet (Landon, I suspect, is thinking of Keats) who is commemorated by the Countess of *The Golden Violet*. He 'fondly woos/The world without that worldliness/Which wanting, there is no success' (247–7; 17). Eulalia's complaint seems to figure Landon's sense that she has not fulfilled her talent, and that her failure is in part a consequence of having to write for an inadequate readership, winning praise that a 'passing moment might light up my cheek,/But haunted not my solitude' (*Golden Violet*, 352–3; 109). But in the earlier poems, the trajectory of the poet's career seems not so much a product of self-knowledge, still less a surrender to the view that a woman's proper role is as wife and mother rather than as poet, but more a kind of flirtation. It is a career that enables her to assume the position of her own abandoned women, making an identical claim on the chivalrous, protective instincts of her reader. The technique is at its most transparent at the conclusion of *The Troubadour*, when, after thanking the reviewers for their kind treatment of her, she ends the poem by paying a heartfelt tribute to her father. It was a very widely admired passage. As she writes, she tells us, her 'page is wet with bitter tears', for no success, however triumphant, can console her for the loss of her father:

> But never will thy name depart
> Until thy orphan girl may share
> The grave where her best feelings are.
> Never, dear father, love can be,
> Like the dear love I had for thee!
>
>          (*Troubadour*, 254)

The self-presentation as an 'orphan girl' may be the most flagrant bid for a sympathetic reading that any poet has ever dared: it is a very knowing passage, and yet also, one feels, entirely sincere.

Landon consistently represents the poet as both subject and object, as seeing eye and as object of another, always male, gaze. Her attempt is to dissolve the distinction between poet and poem, so that she becomes herself the object of the reader's admiring attention. Again her lovelorn women echo her. In abandonment, and in death, their bodies petrify until they become statues of themselves, 'like to marble, when the sculptor's skill / Has trac'd each charm of beauty, save the blush' ('Fragment', 'Is not this grove', 59–60, *Fate of Adelaide*, 152). The Queen of Cyprus appals her heartless husband by dropping dead in front of him:

>       The brow was set
> In its last mould; that marble cheek,
> Fair as if death were loth to break
> Its spell of beauty...
>
>       (*Golden Violet*, 1893–6; 123–4)

Mirza, on being abandoned, is transformed even before she dies: 'your sculptors never wrought / A form in monumental stone / So cold, so pale' (*Golden Violet*, 3326–8; 224). Leila, who is rash enough to fall for Raymond, is found dead by a pool, gazing at her own reflection. She is transformed into a garden statue, and the red light of the setting sun eerily preserves in the reflection the tints of living flesh that have drained from her skin:

> 'Twas strange to look upon her face,
> Then turn and see its shadowy trace

> Within the fountain; one like stone,
> So cold, so colourless, so lone, –
> A statue nymph, placed there to show
> How far the sculptor's art could go.
> The other, and that too the shade,
> In light and crimson warmth array'd ...
>
> (*Troubadour*, 205)

The melancholy of these moments does not quite efface their triumphant quality, which celebrates a woman's release from transient flesh into enduring marble, and from the painful subjectivity of experience into the cold objectivity of art. Once again, the dead lovers are sculpted only as figures of the dead poets. Poets, of course, have traditionally claimed the power to bestow immortality, so that to be celebrated in a poem is to be granted a memorial that will outlive marble and gilded monuments, but Landon's distinction is that her poet frankly confesses that the monument she builds is a monument to herself. It is a gesture performed most extravagantly by Eulalia, when, very shortly before her death, she takes her visiting English friends into the garden, and poses for them beside a statue of herself:

> And in the midst
> A large old cypress stood, beneath whose shade
> There was a sculptured form; the feet were placed
> Upon a finely-carved rose wreath; the arms
> Were raised to Heaven, as if to clasp the stars
> Eulalia leant beside; 'twas hard to say
> Which was the actual marble ...
>
> ('A History of the Lyre', 430–6, *Venetian Bracelet*; 114)

Eulalia identifies the statue as her 'emblem', and within a few months she dies, finally eliminating the distinction between herself and the sculptured form she so closely resembles.

All of Landon's poetry returns obsessively to a tightly bunched arrangement of a small group of motifs, all of them already deployed in the poem that first made her famous, *The Improvisatrice*. This is the figure, the Italian woman who wins fame through her talent at poetic improvisation, that Landon found in *Corinne*, and that underlies all her poems. It suffced her so completely because it allowed the most complete possible identification between poet and poem, both because the Italian woman could be understood, and was always understood by her contemporaries, as a transparent mask for L.E.L. herself, and because improvisation is a performance in which the poet and the poem are equally and indistinguishably the object of the audience's regard.

The verse form that she employs here, and in most of her poems not written in blank verse, had been developed by Hemans, but Landon's use of it is distinctive. Couplets are interrupted at irregular intervals by quatrains, but, unlike Hemans, Landon prefers quatrains in which the first and third lines are unrhymed, allowing her verse to seem far less controlled, more spontaneously improvised than Hemans's. Again as with Hemans, the iambic beat is interspersed with anapaests, but far more unpredictably, so that one often has to correct a misconception of a line's metre as one reads. Hemans's verse is remarkable for its technical assurance, Landon's for a technical uncertainty so marked that metre and syntax are likely at any time to collapse. Both seem to founder in lines describing Petrarch as first glimpsed by Laura:

> Pale, dark-eyed, beautiful, and young
> Such as he had shone o'er my slumbers.
> (*Improvisatrice*, 53–4; 4)

This is the Improvisatrice's first painting. Petrarch is depicted standing in a 'gorgeous hall', the accoutrements of which are even more awkwardly described:

> Censers of roses, vases of light
> Like what the moon sheds on a summer night.
> (*Improvisatrice*, 45–6; 4)

Such lines are indications, I suppose, that the poem was written at high speed – Landon claimed to have completed it in a month – but they are also curiously functional. First, they lend the verse its improvisational quality, and second, and more importantly, they foster in the sympathetic reader an anxious tenderness for the poet, working almost like the heart-stopping wobble that the accomplished tight-rope artist builds into her performance. They create the illusion that one is not reading a poem but listening to a live performance, an improvisation, and the illusion is more powerful, of course, in a poem that centres on descriptions of exactly such performances. The improviser is so potent a figure for Landon precisely because she is a performer, in intimate contact with an audience, and it is a similar intimacy that Landon's poetry works towards, so that the poem becomes 'a sweet and breathing bond / Between me and my kind' ('Erinna', 71–2, *Golden Violet*; 247).

The story of the poem is quickly told, and closely based on *Corinne*. Lorenzo sees the improvisatrice in Florence, and at once loves her as she loves him. They meet in a flowery alcove, he presses one burning kiss upon her hand, and then he disappears. She next sees him in church, at his marriage ceremony. Years later he returns and explains that he had been from childhood betrothed to Ianthe, a young orphan adopted by his father and brought up with him. He 'loved her as a brother loves / His favourite sister' (1387–8), and felt unable to break off the engagement. Ianthe was a delicate consumptive woman, and despite Lorenzo's tender care of her, she has died, freeing him to return to Florence and the improvisatrice. But it is too late. She is herself about to die of a broken heart. As usual, echoing tales are woven into the narrative – a Moorish woman helps the Christian captive that she has fallen for to escape, but both are drowned at sea; Ida administers a love potion to Julian in a desperate attempt to revive the love he once felt for her, and inadvertently poisons him; an Indian bride joins her young groom on his funeral pyre. After Lorenzo abandons her the improvisatrice can only sing songs that reflect her own predicament:

> And lays which only told of love
> In all its varied sorrowing,
> The echoes of the broken heart,
> Were all the songs I now could sing.
> (1067–70; 71)

But all the previous examples given of her work are similar. It is the same with her paintings. After she has witnessed Lorenzo's marriage she paints herself as Ariadne deserted by Theseus in the hope that, after she has died, Lorenzo 'might these tints behold, / And find my grief; – think – see – feel all / I felt, in this memorial' (1346–8; 90). But before ever she had met Lorenzo she had painted Sappho abandoned by Phaon and taking her last farewell of 'lyre, life, and love'. The impulse that drives the whole poem is not the improvisatrice's desire for Lorenzo, but her desire to become herself a work of art, to transform herself into her own painting of Ariadne:

> I drew her on a rocky shore: –
> Her black hair loose, and sprinkled o'er
> With white sea-foam; – her arms were bare,
> Flung upwards in their last despair.
> Her naked feet the pebbles prest;

> The tempest-wind sang in her vest:
> A wild stare in her glassy eyes;
> White lips, as parched by their hot sighs;
> And cheek more pallid than the spray,
> Which cold and colourless on it lay: –
>                                         (1325–34)

Which is why Lorenzo's return works only to precipitate her death. At the end of the poem Lorenzo has become a man prematurely aged with grief, living alone in a 'stately hall' amongst his pictures and statues amongst which there is one, 'the brightest of all there', showing the improvisatrice playing at her harp, apotheosized, seeming like Sappho or the Pythian priestess, beside which is placed her funeral urn (104–5).

   This is alarming, as if the fate of Browning's 'My Last Duchess' should be represented not as a consequence of the Duke's monstrous perversity, but as the goal to which the Duchess all her life aspired. Landon, like Hemans, self-consciously transforms herself into a cultural icon of womanhood. She constructs herself as the icon of feminine vulnerability just as self-consciously as Hemans constructed herself as the icon of rooted, feminine domesticity. Neither icon is likely to find modern favour, but it is at least as important to recognize the power that they once exerted, a power that enabled two women, for the first and only time in the history of English poetry, quite to eclipse in popularity and prestige the work of their male contemporaries. Hemans, by making women the guardians and the mouthpieces of masculine values, transformed masculinity into an idea that depended on women for its stability and its articulation. Landon's achievement is odder. Much more insistently than Hemans she insists on her own vulnerability. She does not, like Hemans, negotiate energetically between genders, but seems content to remain 'A woman in her woman's sphere / Of joy and grief, of hope and fear' (*Troubadour*, 195). She insists, or seems to, on a woman's utter dependence on and vulnerability to a man, and yet, when she insists on women's capacity to love with an utter selflessness that is unknown to men, the word she chooses to describe that quality is odd, 'self devotedness' (*Troubadour*, 116), a phrase in which the complete devotedness of the self seems insecurely distinguished from a complete devotion to the self.[33] It is the second, disguised meaning that dominates a body of work in which a rhetoric that seems wholly designed to figure the vulnerability of a woman to a man, and of a poet to a reader, work in which feminine vulnerability is extended from a social posture until it becomes a poetic style, can nevertheless drive repeatedly towards a vision in which victimhood becomes apotheosis, in which abandonment frees a woman from the flesh, transforming her into a marble monument that commands the male gaze, but remains itself as coolly impervious to the existence of its male worshippers as is the improvisatrice to Lorenzo, when he is reduced to musing 'his weary life away', gazing forlornly on a woman who, because she has become a painting, is forever removed from him. Landon writes a poetry that seems to exhibit throughout a servile dependence on its readership that is presented as a guarantee of its authentic femininity, and yet the poems drive towards climaxes in which the woman frees herself from dependence on her male lover, and the poet frees herself from dependence on the reader. These are moments in which the poet disappears into the poem, but the poem is itself only a representation of the poet. The distinction between the two disappears, and they are fused together in a gesture that is mournful, because it always signals the poet's death, and yet triumphant, because in death the poet can at last celebrate the autonomy of her art.

## II

Marlon Ross describes Felicia Hemans as 'a rare female voice' speaking 'simultaneously with a blustering male choir'.[34] That may have been true when she began her career in 1808, but, by the time she reached her poetic maturity in the mid-1820s, it was almost the reverse of the case. The age of what Landon calls 'a lady's rule' (*Golden Violet*, 36; 3) in poetry had begun. One obvious cause of this was the new dominance of women in the audience for poetry, a dominance that was already irritating Byron and Keats by 1819. Throughout the years of its composition Byron conceived of *Don Juan* as a bold masculine gesture of defiance, an acerbic demonstration of his refusal to 'make "Ladies Books" al dilettar le femine e la plebe'[35] [to please women and the mob], and he believed that he suffered the full commercial consequences of his decision. The first volume of *Don Juan*, he wrote to Hopper 'has *not sold well*, so Murray says'.[36] Murray encouraged him to write 'a poem in the old way to interest the women', but, he insisted, 'I shall attempt of that kind nothing further'.[37] He repudiated the 'false, stilted, trashy style' of his own early poems in part because he thought that it had been borrowed by male poets that he considered effeminate, such as the 'mannikin' Keats, and by the leading woman poet that it amused him to call 'Mrs. Heman', and who would do better to 'knit blue stockings instead of wearing them'.[38] He seems to have understood Murray's tepid response to *Don Juan* as an indication of his publisher's surrender to the new commercial power of the woman reader. *Don Juan* sold poorly because 'there has been an eleventh commandment to the women not to read it – and what is still more extraordinary they seem not to have broken it'.[39] His letters to Murray begin to include increasingly tart comments on books by women; 'if you prefer the bookmaking of women', 'a *She* book'.[40] The women readers closest to him, his sister Augusta and Teresa Guiccioli, were at one in their disapproval of his poem, and he quickly developed a theory to account for their dislike: 'the women hate everything which strips off the tinsel of *Sentiment*', and 'D.J. strips off this illusion'.[41] For the last five years of his life Byron conceived of himself as an embattled male poet, an Orpheus thrown amongst sentimental maenads.

Byron despised Keats's poems (except, belatedly, *Hyperion*), and dislike of Byron became in his last years one of the ruling passions of Keats's life, but on this matter they were unlikely allies. Woodhouse wrote anxiously to Keats's publisher, Taylor, about revisions that Keats proposed to 'The Eve of Saint Agnes' that made more explicit the erotic consummation enjoyed by Madeline and Porphyro:

> tho' profanely speaking, the Interest on the reader's imagination is greatly heightened, yet I do apprehend it will render the poem unfit for ladies & indeed scarcely to be mentioned by them among the 'things that are'. He says he does not want ladies to read his poetry: that he writes for men ... [42]

Taylor responded robustly in a letter in which concern for moral propriety struggles for the upper hand against Taylor's sharp publisher's sense that Keats was ruining any prospects that his book might sell. 'I will not be accessory', Taylor writes, '(I can answer also for H. [Hessey] I think) towards publishing any thing which can only be read by Men ... Had he known truly what the Society and what the Suffrages of Women are worth, he would never have thought of depriving himself of them'. He ends with an ultimatum: 'if he will not so far concede to my Wishes as to leave the passage as it originally stood, I must be content to admire his poems with some other Imprint'.[43] Shortly before leaving England to die in Rome, Keats heard depressing reports of the sale of his 1820 volume, even though he had acceded to Taylor's demands, and he was inclined to blame the women:

> The sale of my book is very slow, though it has been very highly rated. One of the causes, I understand from different quarters, of the

unpopularity of this new book, and the others also, is the offence that ladies take at me.[44]

There is a dry comedy here, because Byron was convinced that Keats's poems were written in the 'false, stilted trashy style' that he had once favoured himself, and that he thought peculiarly designed to appeal to women, whereas Keats thought Byron's *Don Juan*, in its aristocratic insouciance, a display of exactly the kind of lordly masculinity that women found seductive, but they agree at least that it was women readers who now determined a poet's commercial success.

They controlled a market that was, at least from the mid-1820s dramatically shrinking, in part because the sale of individual volumes of poetry was severely affected by the popularity of the new annuals, in which poems were attached to engravings, most commonly of landscapes and of glamorous, aristocratic women.[45] Hemans and L.E.L. were the two most sought after contributors to these annuals, some of which Landon edited. It may be significant that the years in which women poets were dominant coincided fairly precisely with the years in which the sale for poetry collapsed. Towards the end of her life, Landon turned from poetry to the novel, and it may be that men intent on making a literary career anticipated her decision. It nevertheless remains the case that in the late 1820s and early 1830s the women poets held out against the market trend far more successfully than the men. The 'blustering male choir' was reduced to a stammer.

The point is best made by considering the fates of two of Hemans's and Landon's chief male rivals in the 1820s, both poets of great talent, George Darley and Thomas Lovell Beddoes. They shared a predicament, each unable to carve out a space between the 'literary market-place' and 'the impossibly private spiritual domain' in which they located the poetic impulse.[46] First Darley, because his stammer was cruelly literal, so severe that it left him unable to enjoy a normal social life: 'I can only enjoy society as a picture drawn in my mind, the thing itself is to me a punishment' (xi).[47] Darley made his bid for fame in 1825, when he published *Sylvia, or, The May Queen : A Pastoral Drama*.[48] The poem won the admiration of Coleridge, Lamb, Mitford, Cary, the translator of Dante, Sir Henry Taylor, and Elizabeth Barrett, but it failed, and Darley's career stalled. In 1840 and 1841 he published two historical plays, *Thomas A Beckett* and *Ethelstan*, neither of which made any impact. After the publication of the first he wrote despairingly to a friend, 'Why have a score of years not established my title with the world? Why did not 'Sylvia', with all it faults, ten years since?'[49] Six years earlier, in 1835 he had published his most ambitious poem, *Nepenthe*, but it is a fragment, printed by himself and intended only for private circulation. *Sylvia* was the one wholehearted attempt by Darley to secure public recognition as a poet.[50]

To describe the plot of the drama as Disney-like would be to exaggerate its sophistication. The play is set in a secluded valley the rule of which is divided between two hostile powers, Morgana, Queen of the Fairies, and Ararach, King of the Fiends. The fairy side of the valley is a rural paradise, the fiend side darkened by 'Fen-pampered clouds that blot the skies, / And from their sooty bosoms pour / A blue and pestilential shower' (1. iv. 2–4; 95). The boundary between the two zones is marked by a 'running landmark', 'By sad and sun-green grasses made / A boundary of light and shade'. (2. ii. 3–5; 108) The inhabitants of the fairy side of the valley can cross this boundary at will, but not the fiends, ''tis thinner than blown soap, / Yet strong as adamant to smoky natures' (2. iii. 19–20; 109). There is a romantic plot – Sylvia, the shepherdess and the may queen, is courted by an upright youth who has wandered into the valley, and is appropriately called Romanzo – and there is a romance plot tracing Ararach's attempt to conquer Morgana's kingdom and take Sylvia as his queen – a series of botched attempts ends with the kidnap of Romanzo by Ararach, but then the fiends are routed by the fairy army, and Romanzo is freed to wed Sylvia. There are comically evil elves, winsomely charming fairies, and rustics given to malapropism. The play seems to take place in a poetic realm as remote from the realities of the 1820s as is the secluded valley from the England that surrounds it.

Darley delights, as Richard Dadd would later, in the miniature.[51] Floretta, the fairy charged with the care of the flowers, will spread her wing 'Between the driving rain-drop and the rose', and risk 'Drowning amid the fields to save a daisy' (1. ii. 143, 5; 90). The couriers of the fairy army 'scour from wing to wing / On a soft ambling jennet-fly' (5. vii. 6–7; 192). Darley offers a miniaturized echo of the heroic Romantic tradition, an echo in which the conflict between God and Satan, or between Jupiter and Prometheus, is diminished to a contest between an elf and a fairy. The charm of the poem relies on an utter disproportion between its means and its ends, between the virtuoso talent displayed in its vigorous Elizabethan prose, and its variety of delicate lyrical forms, some of which seem modelled on the lyrics of *Prometheus Unbound*, and the apparent triviality of its content. But it is always an uneasy charm, because the poem never seems quite at ease with itself. The division of the valley, for example, clearly echoes, and is intended to echo, the divisions of England, between the ever smokier, newly industrialized cities, and an idyllically conceived countryside, and between a woman's realm of tender mutuality and a male realm devoted to power and to conquest. So, an elf tempts Romanzo's comical servant to cross the boundary into the fiend's kingdom by masquerading as a drinking fountain, a cast iron statue holding a bowl, exactly the kind of grotesque object that was by the 1820s being mass produced and sold as garden ornament. Andrea asks: 'what have we here? A noddling mandarin-cup-bearer! A Hottentot Granny-maid! – if it be not rather a newly-cast chandelier walking abroad from the foundery!' (2. iii; 115). The foundry intrudes almost shockingly into the magical valley, and so does the issue of parliamentary reform. In order to win Roselle's hand Andrea promises to reform himself, to learn temperance and fidelity:

> Reform, sir! Reform! – it is the order of the day, and I shall be radical in my constitution. I have determined to remedy all abuses, redress all grievances, root out all old prejudices, customs, and inveterate habits, which have so long made a borough of my body...
>
> (5. ix; 204)

The poem seems always in danger of overstepping its prescribed limits, just as its characters are sometimes tricked into crossing the boundary into the kingdom of Ararach.

Darley very evidently addresses the poem specifically to the women readers who will determine, as he recognises, his chances of success. One of his innovations is to introduce each scene with an extended stage direction in octosyllabic couplets, most of which are delightful, but at the beginning of Act 5, scene 3, as he describes Romanzo sitting with Sylvia under a tree, his arm around her waist and his forehead almost touching hers, he imagines a young girl leaning over his shoulder, anxiously gazing at his page:

> The while my cheek delighted feels
> Thy rolling curls, like little wheels
> Course up and down that swarthy plain...
>
> (5. iii. 3–5; 172)

The incongruous brush of girlish curls on manly stubble is comically described, and it may just be a modern squeamishness that flinches at it, but when the poet goes on to look down the girl's dress, the effect is surely less charming than disturbing:

> Half-smiling Maiden! Whose pink breast
> Peeps like the ruddock's o'er its nest,

Or moss-bud from its peaked vest...
(5. iii. 27–9; 173)

The lines betray the male poet by exposing his discordance with his materials. The effect is more dramatic in the introduction to Act 5, scene 8 in which the poet apologises for not displaying the battle between the fairies and the fiends. Again the passage is comic. Only Milton who 'scorned all deeds to chronicle/Less than the wars of Heaven and Hell' would be fit for the task (11–12). But as it proceeds, celebrating Homer, Shakespeare and Milton as the supreme poets, 'Leagued in supreme tri-union' (80), the comedy yields to a wry acknowledgement that no poet can in these days seek to rival their achievement. Even Byron is dead, 'Last-favoured child of the fond Nine', a 'gloomy Thing indeed, who now/Lays in the dust his lordly brow' (30–1):

Not mine the same
High audience, nor a theme so high,
Nor oh! such passing minstrelsy.
(110–12; 194–6)[52]

Hemans and Landon also confessed the modesty of their achievements, but Darley expresses a bitterer sense of the humiliation of writing for an audience, and it has to do surely with his sense that in order to please such an audience the poet must now resign even the fragile, theatrical masculinity that the 'lordly' Byron maintained. *Sylvia* failed, one suspects, because for all its talent it exposed Darley's contempt for his own poem and for the audience to which he addressed it. The action of the play shows a matriarchal fairyland repelling an invasion led by the king of the fiends, but the narrative exposes the narrator as himself a male encroacher into the realm the purity of which he pretends to defend. The play failed because, in writing it, Darley was at cross-purposes with himself.

Darley condescended and failed: Beddoes remained intransigent, and failed still more dramatically. In 1822, when he was only 19, he published *The Bride's Tragedy*, a pastiche Jacobean drama even more accomplished than the fourteen-year-old Tennyson's, *The Devil and the Lady*, begun the following year possibly in emulation. In February 1829 he despatched to England from Germany, where he was a medical student, the manuscript of the play on which he had been working for five years, *Death's Jest Book*, and was told by all who read it that it was unpublishable. During the following nineteen years, until his suicide in 1848, Beddoes attempted to revise his play, but otherwise wrote little. The play was not finally published until 1850, under the title *Death's Jest Book, or the Fool's Tragedy*.

It is, as its title indicates, a play about death. It was a subject of obsessive interest to Beddoes, who exhibited suicidal tendencies throughout his adult life, and whose medical researches in Germany were an unavailing attempt to find physical evidence for the immortality of the soul. But it was also his theme because, more intensely than any other writer, Beddoes felt his own belatedness. The earth is a 'grave-paved star' (2, iv, 147):

> Under the green sod are your coffins packed,
> When scarce a lover, for his maiden's hair,
> Can pluck a stalk whose rose draws not its hue
> Out of a hate-filled heart.
>
> ...
>
>         Thou art old, world,
> A hoary atheistic murderous star:
> I wish that thou would'st die, or could'st be slain,
> Hell-hearted bastard of the sun.
>
>         (2, iii, 160–9)[53]

To create in such a world, to give birth to a poem, is a ghastly, incongruous exercise: it is an attempt to make 'earth's rooty, ruinous, grave-piled caverns / Throb with the pangs of birth' (3, iii, 265–6). In Beddoes' most ghastly figuration of his own cultural position, he sings as an aborted foetus, as if the modern poet were a creature dead before even he was born:

> Squats on a toad-stool under a tree
> A bodiless childfull of life in the gloom,
> Crying with frog voice, 'What shall I be?
> Poor unborn ghost, for my mother killed me
> Scarcely alive in her wicked womb.
>
>         (3, iii, 328–32)

In a letter to his most devoted admirer, T.F. Kelsall, Beddoes argues (incidentally, just before a compliment to Darley on his *Sylvia*) that the proper business of the modern dramatist is not to revive the Elizabethans, but to 'beget' something new. But even as he states the thought resurrectionist metaphors to do with ghosts, bodies removed from the grave, and vampires overpower the possibility of a new birth:

> I am convinced the man who is to awaken the drama must be a bold trampling fellow – no creeper into worm-holes – no reviser even – however good. These reanimations are vampire-cold. Such ghosts as Marlowe, Webster &c are better dramatists, better poets, I dare say, than any contemporary of ours – but they are ghosts – the worm is in their pages – & we want to see something that our great-grandsires did not know. With the greatest reverence for all the antiquities of the drama, I still think that we had better beget than revive – attempt to give the literature of this age an idiosyncrasy & spirit of its own & only raise a ghost to gaze on, not to live with – just now the drama is a haunted ruin.
>
> (*Works*, 595)

But *Death's Jest Book* hinges on the raising of a ghost, the ghost of Wolfram, killed by the Duke, his close friend, because both men love the same woman, and once raised from the dead Wolfram must be lived with until the moment the curtain falls, as Wolfram is leading the Duke into the grave.

For Beddoes, to write a play is an act of necromancy, because the literature that he admires is dead: it has 'the worm in its pages'. Repeatedly in *Death's Jest Book* Beddoes voices his contempt for the literature that has succeeded it. Death, says Mandrake, the play's second jester, is just an artful fiction, 'a cunning invention to avoid paying poor's rates and the reviewers''. (3, iii, 12–14). A lady advises the principal jester, Isbrand, that he should send his cap and bells 'to England for the bad poets and the critics who praise them' (2, iii, 116–17). The 'bad poets' targeted by Beddoes are plainly the sentimental poets, poets like Hemans and Landon.[54] It is Isbrand who sings the song of the aborted foetus, and when his companion praises it as a 'noble hymn', he replies:

> I fear you flatter: 'tis perhaps a little
> Too sweet and tender, but that is the fashion;
> Besides my failing is too much sentiment.
>
> (3, iii, 376–8)

*Death's Jest Book* is in its entirety a calculated and bitter affront to the fashion for sentimental verse. In Act 5, scene iii, for example, Sybilla gathers flowers with her ladies, and is told that man 'looks on nature as his supplement', and searches out 'likenesses' between natural objects and 'his own being':

> So he loves the rose
> For the cheek's sake, whose touch is the most grateful
> At night-fall to his lip.
>
> (17–19)

This, she is told, is 'the sacred source of poetry'. This lady is clearly a devoted reader of L.E.L. Sybilla, a woman of a more Beddoesian cast of mind, traces her love of flowers to the fact that they arise from the grave, like ghosts. Winter is an uncongenial season because the absence of flowers signals that, in the winter months, the dead do not walk, and human beings feel forlorn without their presence.

As one might expect, the world of *Death's Jest Book* is dominantly masculine. There are only two significant female characters, Sybilla and Amala, and their only function is to prompt men to kill each other in competition for their love. The Duke kills Wolfram, his rival for the affections of Sybilla, and Athulf, his son, stabs his brother Adalmar to death to prevent his marriage to Amala. Love is a pretext rather than a motive for murder, as the Duke realizes at the end of Act 3, scene i, when he acknowledges that the 'fascination, near to madness' that prompted him to kill his rival withered into 'coldness' the moment the deed was done. It is a masculine world, but a world unsustained by any coherent code of masculine values. The father of Isbrand and Wolfram was murdered by the Duke: Isbrand dedicates his life to the duty of revenge, and Wolfram becomes the Duke's closest friend. The responses seem equally arbitrary. Isbrand leads a successful rebellion against the Duke, but his fellow rebels conclude as soon as their victory is secure that Isbrand is likely to prove worse than his predecessor. A single conspirator, Mario, seems dedicated to the republican ideal of liberty that Beddoes himself had inherited from his father and from his favourite modern poet, Shelley, but Mario's idealism results only in absurdly haphazard conduct. After helping Isbrand overthrow the Duke, he stabs Isbrand and exits from the play inexplicably assuring himself, 'now my task is o'er'.

It is a male world, but the men who people it, are empty, devoid of any reasonable purpose, because their world seems not to admit the stable values that might give their actions point. There are moments of tenderness in the poem, most movingly there is the lovely epithalamium sung under Amala's window on the night before her wedding:

> We have bathed, where none have seen us,
> In the lake and in the fountain,

Underneath the charmed statue
Of the timid, bending Venus.
When the water nymphs were counting
In the waves the stars of night...

(4, iii, 165–70)

It is significant, I think, that this song is sung by 'female voices',[55] but it is equally significant that they are voices floating in the air, not the voices of any women in particular, and that the delicate beauty of the song is wholly incongruous with the event it celebrates. Amala is to marry Adalmar even though she prefers his brother, Athulf, and in any case the wedding will not take place, because, after failing in his attempt at suicide, Athulf decides to murder his brother instead.

When he believes himself to have taken a fatal dose of poison, Athulf exclaims, 'I am unsouled, dishumanised, uncreated' (4, iv, 364). In fact, the draught he has taken is harmless, and this is appropriate because the play's characters are 'dishumanised' already. It is much earlier in the play that Athulf describes himself as 'this deserted human engine' (2, iv, 166). The male body in this play is a machine that even the ghost has deserted, a 'flesh mechanism' (5, iv, 212). To lose the love of life is to suffer a merely mechanical breakdown: 'no more round blood-drops / Roll joyously along my pulseless veins' (3, iii, 672–3). These corpuscles are far less human than Keats's billiard balls, they are more like ball bearings. Beddoes does not just see the skull beneath the skin, he sees its emptiness, nowhere perhaps more eerily than in the metaphor with which Isbrand boasts of his ability to penetrate men's minds:

My spies, which are
Suspicion's creeping words, have stolen in,
And, with their eyed feelers, touched and sounded
The little hiding holes of cunning thought,
And each dark crack in which a reptile purpose
Hangs in its chrysalis unripe for birth.

(3, iii, 87–92)

His spies enter human skulls like insects intruding into an abandoned, empty house.

The world of the play is a masculine world, and a world without values, and by 1825 it is hard to see how it could be one without being the other, for Beddoes wrote within a culture that represented women as both the origin of values and their guarantors. The age of chivalry, as Burke proclaimed, had gone (Landon used the phrase as the epigraph to *The Troubadour*), and with it disappeared the last male-centred public code of values. Hemans and Landon disguise this by appearing to set their poems almost exclusively within chivalric settings, but in fact chivalry as they re-construct it is radically changed. It remains a code that takes woman as its idealized object, but woman is also represented as the code's originating subject. It becomes a code that makes men entirely peripheral. In the 1830s one principal business of male poets was to construct an alternative code to replace it. It was to be a code of values based on an ideal of citizenship, and Elizabeth Barrett Browning was to dispute the notion that this, like the code of chivalry, was an exclusively masculine ideal. But that is a matter for another chapter. At this point, it is enough to note that *Death's Jest Book* drives towards the conclusion that Isbrand reaches in Act 4, scene iv: 'O! it is nothing now to be a man' (175). *Death's Jest Book* is a play that explores with its 'eyed feelers' the idea of masculinity, and finds that it is vacuous, empty of all meaning. His friends were right that it was not a discovery at all likely to propel him into literary eminence.

## III

April 19, 1824 was for Tennyson 'a day when the whole world seemed to be darkened for me'. On a rock, close to his home, he carved the words 'Byron is dead'.[56] It was a momentous day for him as it had been for Darley, and not just because of the death of a great poet. The death of Byron marked in the poetic realm what the death of William IV was to mark in the national realm, the beginning of an era of 'woman's rule'. Tennyson's *Poems, Chiefly Lyrical* of 1830, and *Poems* of 1832 are most remarkable for a group of poems that concern enclosed or secluded women, poems such as 'Mariana', 'The Lady of Shalott', 'The Palace of Art', 'Oenone', 'Fatima', and 'The Sleeping Beauty'.[57] In an influential article Lionel Stevenson derived these enclosed maidens from Shelley's 'To a Skylark', in which the skylark is first compared to the 'poet hidden / In the light of thought', and is then said to be

> Like a high-born maiden
> In a palace tower,
> Soothing her love-laden
> Soul in secret hour
> With music sweet as love, which overflows her bower.
>
> (41–5)[58]

Stevenson concludes that for Tennyson the enclosed woman figures the poet, and in this group of poems Tennyson explores his own predicament as a poet isolated by his calling from the busy world around him. It is not just for ideological reasons that I share Carl Plasa's suspicion of a reading that so 'blithely turns the "she" of the text into the "he" of its poet'.[59] All of Tennyson's poems, even 'The Palace of Art' which immures a feminized 'Soul' rather than a woman, seem fraught with a distinctively female experience of a kind that never intrudes into Shelley's stanza. Stevenson's failure, and one that is replicated by all his successors, with the single exception of Herbert F. Tucker,[60] is that he does not attend to the poems that intervened between Tennyson and Shelley's ode, and in particular that he does not attend to the poems of Mrs Hemans and L.E.L., for if Tennyson's poems derive ultimately from Shelley it seems clear that he reads Shelley through poems written by the women poets who succeeded him.

Hemans treats the topic of the enclosed maiden in poems such as 'Arabella Stuart', spoken by Arabella in the prison cell in which she has been enclosed since her frustrated elopement with William Seymour. She speaks her poem to a lover, who, she fears, has already forgotten her, 'Dost thou forget me, Seymour?':

> My friend! My friend! Where art thou? Day by day,
> Gliding like some dark mournful stream away,
> My silent youth flows from me.

She is surely one of the prototypes of Tennyson's Mariana, as is Landon's *L'Improvisatrice*, when Lorenzo marries his betrothed and abandons her:

> He came not! Then the heart's decay
> Wasted her silently away.
>
>                                    (78)

Oenone resembles these women, too, abandoned by Paris, but by the end of the poem, when 'fiery thoughts' 'shape themselves' within her, and she leaves her valley bent on the vengeful destruction of Troy she has become like one of Hemans's more savage heroines, 'The Widow of Crescentius' or the mother who burns down 'The Indian City' in revenge for the killing of her sons. 'The Lady of Shalott' who gives up her art, 'left the web' and 'left the loom', and, enthralled by her vision of Lancelot, floats singing down the river into Camelot, is transformed by the end of her voyage from an artist into a work of art, a funeral sculpture of herself. It is the metamorphosis that L.E.L. treats in poem after poem. Landon, as Armstrong remarks, prefers to describe an action 'not *as* it happens, but when it is either just over or just about to happen'. 'How the pulses will beat, and the cheeks will be dyed', the *Improvisatrice* sings of 'The Indian Bride' (821; 55).[61] In 'Fatima' Tennyson, like Hemans and Landon before him, looks back to Sappho and writes a love song of erotic anticipation so complete that it seems to render it unnecessary that Fatima's lover should ever in person arrive. The Soul in *The Palace of Art* at the end of the poem abandons her gorgeous palace for a humble cottage in the vale, in a gesture that, not least in its ambivalence, closely echoes the self-abnegating eagerness with which Hemans and Landon imagine women poets such as 'Properzia Rossi' and Eulalia ready to surrender their fame for a life of humble, loving domesticity.

Landon writes, she tells us, out of 'her woman's sphere / Of joy and grief, of hope and fear' (*Troubadour*, 195). Darley encroaches into that sphere, but charily, with ruinous misgivings, and Beddoes brusquely repudiates it. Tennyson, in this group of poems, writes quite uninhibitedly as a woman. It is not to be imagined that he was unmoved by commercial considerations. Tennyson, unlike Browning, had no private income and no expectations. The market for poetry had collapsed, and Hemans and Landon were the two poets who had most conspicuously managed to resist the market trend. But I doubt if it was just this. Masculinity, as Beddoes reveals in *Death's Jest Book*, no longer seemed capable of housing the life of the affections. The male poet was an empty skull, his words escaping from a 'lipless grin',[62] from the grave with its 'earthy mouth' and 'nettle-bearded lips' (3, iii, 518–19). Tennyson turns away from this to a female experience that seems more vital even if, like Mariana's, it is an experience that is rich only in its atrophy.

These poems by Tennyson share another characteristic with the work of Hemans and Landon. Almost all of their poems are set in the long ago, the far away, or the never was, and that this should be so is a condition of their achievement. It is not true that Hemans, or indeed Landon, oppose, as Marlon Ross would have it, the inner female world and the external masculine world of power and conquest: the opposition is rather, as Hemans makes clear in her essay on Goethe's *Tasso*, between 'the spirit of poetry and the spirit of the world'.[63] Hemans and Landon can admit the male world of conquest into their poems, what they cannot admit is the world of money. The fiction that their poems cling to is that poetry escapes from the cash nexus, that it is not an item that has a market value, and they must protect this fiction so

# 4
# Fashioning Romanticism

## I

Felicia Hemans and Letitia Landon wrote for money – both had families to support – and this may in itself be one reason for the fervour with which they repudiated the notion that poetry might be a commodity. Their poems are placed within a world in which the poet is properly rewarded only by a prize that, however rare and costly, has no exchange value, such an object as Landon's 'golden violet'. Both grasped the paradox that in order to maintain the commercial value of their work, it was necessary to deny that the work, poetry, ought properly to be regarded as having any commercial value at all.[1] They maintained the conventional opposition between poets, and those that Keats calls 'ledger-men', those for whom 'red-lin'd accounts / Were sweeter than the songs of Grecian years'. It had become the first article of the creed to which all poets must publicly subscribe that, as Shelley puts it, 'Poetry, and the principle of Self, of which money is the visible incarnation, are the God and the Mammon of the world'.[2]

It was a creed from which the novelists had been granted exemption, though less out of generosity than contempt. Novelists were allowed to write for money, and, by a natural extension, this freed them to write about money. In the decade in which Mrs. Hemans and L.E.L. secured their position as the most successful poets in Britain, a new school of novelists dominated the market for fiction. They wrote 'fashionable novels' or 'silver fork fiction', novels about the tiny group of people, 'twice two thousand' in Byron's estimation, who, from February until July, occupied their London houses in the city's West End, and retired for the rest of the year to their country estates. These novels, most of which were published by a single publisher, Henry Colburn, were more energetically

marketed than any novels before them.[3] Colburn treated them frankly
as commodities, but they are also novels about commodities, and this is
why they offer so apt an opportunity to explore one of the more interesting aspects of the period from 1825 to 1840, the commodification of
culture.

Fashionable novels are of various kinds, but I will focus on just two
of them. One group of novels describes the adventures of young men
on the make. Disraeli's *Vivian Grey* (1826) and Bulwer's *Pelham* (1828)
are the definitive examples of the type. Another traces the fortunes of a
man who in middle age seeks to restore his jaded appetites by marrying
a teenage bride. In their plots these novels look back to *Tremaine* (1825),
which seems to have been recognized as the first fashionable novel
by the fashionable novelists themselves, but the examples I choose,
Catherine Gore's *Women As They Are, or The Manners of the Day* (1830)
and Mary Shelley's *Lodore* (1835), are stamped too by the influence of
Jane Austen and of Bulwer. In between I shall turn to the great anti-
fashionable novel of the period, Carlyle's *Sartor Resartus* (1833). But I
begin with Disraeli and Bulwer, or rather with the poet who exercised
the decisive influence on both of them, Byron.

## II

In the poems that made him famous Byron, like Hemans and Landon,
favoured exotic settings for his poems, and with the same effect. It
enabled him to free his characters from economic relations with one
another. Unlike his successors, the young Byron could afford to maintain not just in his fictions but in his practical life his independence
from economic pressures. Hence the quixotic generosity that allowed
him to offer as a gift to the ungrateful R.C. Dallas the manuscript of
the first two cantos of *Childe Harold*. But by the time that he moved to
Italy, as his correspondence with Murray shows, Byron had reconciled
himself to the notion that he should be paid for his work, and had
begun to insist on earnings commensurate with his sales. In his letters
Byron begins to mimic with some relish the language of the book trade,
as when he announces to Moore the contents of the seventh and eighth
cantos of *Don Juan*: 'There is a deal of war – a siege, and all that, in the
style, graphical and technical, of the shipwreck in Canto Second, which
"took", as they say in the Row.'[4] Byron still distinguished between himself, the poet, and his publisher John Murray, the tradesman, but the
distinction becomes increasingly tenuous. Publication was, after all, a
trading venture in which the two men co-operated, and the profits

from which were shared. It is predictable, though it may seem odd, that Byron's recognition that poetry was a commodity sharpened in his last years, as he felt that his popularity was waning. He was obliged to moderate his expectations, and declared to Murray that he was ready 'to make any allowance, in a *trade* point of view – which unpalatable speculations may render necessary to *your* advantage'.[5] Douglas Kinnaird was by then acting in a role that would only many years later be given a name, as Byron's literary agent. Financial matters, he told Murray, 'must be arranged with Mr Douglas K.':

> He is my trustee – and a man of honour. – To him you can state all your mercantile reasons, which you might not like to state to me personally – such as 'heavy season' – 'flat public' – 'don't go off' – 'Lordship writes too much – 'Won't take advice' – declining popularity – deductions for the trade – make very little – generally lose by him – pirated edition – foreign edition – 'severe criticisms', &c., with other hints and howls for an oration – which I leave Douglas who is an orator to answer.[6]

But it is only in the final three instalments of *Don Juan*, Cantos IX, X, and XI, published on August 29, 1823, Cantos XII, XIII, and XIV, published on December 17, 1823, and Cantos XV and XVI, published on March 26, 1824, that Byron allows this new sense of himself as manufacturer of a saleable commodity to seep into his poetry.

These are the cantos in which the poem, as Byron himself only threatened to do, returns to England, so that for the first time it shares a space with its readers. It was an England of which Byron had had no first-hand experience since the spring of 1816, an England remembered rather than recorded. When, for example, Juan is attacked by a highwayman on Shooter's Hill he is the victim of a crime that by 1823 was already thought of as belonging to the past, to the eighteenth century. But this should not blind us to the aggressive modernity of the English cantos. Juan travels to Moscow after participating in the Siege of Ismail in 1790. His position in the Russian court, where he serves as the empress's lover, seems short-lived, but when Catherine sends him to England he travels through time as well as space. He takes the coach from Dover and arrives in Regency London.

One crucial sign of this is that in the English cantos, for the first time in the poem, Juan needs cash, which fortunately has been amply provided by Catherine. The moment he disembarks, Juan is confronted by the Dover hotels and their 'long, long bills, whence nothing is deducted' (X, 69),[7] and in London he puts up at a hotel patronized only by those too rich to 'find a bill's small items costly' (XI, 31). He is widely travelled, but England is the first society he has visited in which the most important relations between people are economic. Even hats are an item of speculation for the milliners who offer credit to 'drapery Misses' in the hope that the bills will be paid 'ere the honeymoon's last kisses' (XI, 49). July, when the fashionable world leaves the town for its country seats, is an anxious time for London's tradesmen:

> Alas, to them of ready cash bereft,
> What hope remains? Of hope the full possession
> Or generous draft, conceded as a gift,
> At a long date till they can get a fresh one,
> Hawked about at a discount, small or large;
> Also the solace of an overcharge.
>
> (XIII, 45)

Byron quotes Scott's minstrel, 'Love rules the camp, the court, the grove', only to refute him:

> But if love don't, cash does, and cash alone.
> Cash rules the grove and fells it too besides.
> Without cash camps were thin, and courts were none.
> Without cash, Malthus tells you, 'take no brides'.
> So cash rules love the ruler, on his own
> High ground, as virgin Cynthia sways the tides.
>
> (XII, 14)

Marriage in England is a matter of 'speculation' (XII, 33) in the matrimonial 'sweepstakes' (XII, 36), and adultery is chiefly to be avoided on account of the 'damned damages' (XII, 65).

Satirical poetry, of course, very commonly excoriates a society that values only cash. But in the later cantos of *Don Juan* Byron flamboyantly implicates himself in the values of the society that he laughs at. The miser rapt in contemplation of his amassed wealth is 'your only poet' (XII, 8), and in these cantos the reverse is also true, the poet is a miser:

> How beauteous are rouleaus! How charming chests,
> Containing ingots, bags of dollars, coins ...
>
> (XII, 12)

*Don Juan* is notoriously a poem that displays its own workings, that makes a topic of the process by which it was composed, and the effect is to demystify the poet's craft – 'But that last simile was trite and stupid'. In the last cantos Byron takes the process of demystification further by exposing the status of his own poem as a commodity. The poet becomes a variety of tradesman, selling poems in much the same way that milliners sell hats, and, it may be, to the same people. The poet caters to the taste of the reading public, and to that extent his role is not far different from Lord Henry's cook, the 'mystery' of whose profession demands a Homer to pay it proper tribute (XV, 62).

As Andrew Bennett has shown, the Romantics evaded the indignity of writing for customers by addressing themselves instead to 'posterity'.[8] Byron mocks the practice: 'Why, I'm posterity and so are you; / And whom do we remember? Not a hundred.' (XII, 19). Poems once promised immortality to those they celebrated, but this is a role that has been usurped by the newspapers, where for example Lord Henry's and Lady Adeline's departure from London is recorded:

> A paragraph in every paper told
> Of their departure. Such is modern fame.
> 'Tis pity that it takes no further hold
> Than an advertisement, or much the same,
> When ere the ink be dry, the sound grows cold.
> (XIII, 51)

Poems seem scarcely to take firmer hold. Even the 'greatest living poet' has a tenure of only a decade: the title has passed in Byron's memory from Scott to Byron himself, and now rests, he supposes, with George Croly (XI, 55–7).

Poetry, it seems, is as subject to fashion as dress, so that the poets even of the recent past have proved as evanescent as the dandies: 'Where's Brummell? Dished. Where's Long Pole Wellesley? Diddled.' (XI, 78). Everything in these last cantos of Don Juan is subject to the law of change, and change has become increasingly, dizzyingly, rapid:

> Where is the world of eight years past? 'Twas there –
> I look for it – 'tis gone, a globe of glass,
> Cracked, shivered, vanished, scarcely gazed on, ere
> A silent change dissolves the glittering mass.
> (XI, 76)

In seven years Byron has seen changes that 'might suffice a moderate century' (XI, 82). He is sounding here the *ubi sunt* theme, but with a crucial difference. Previous poets had asked, where are the snows of yesteryear? They chose emblems of transience – snow, the rose, the violet – but made sure that, though the objects named were transient, their emblematic significance was permanent: snow melts, but it has always melted. Byron prefers emblems that are themselves transient. Who were 'Long Pole Wellesley', or 'the Lady Carolines and Franceses' (XI, 80)? Even the names of some of them have been forgotten:

> Where is Lord This? And where my Lady That?
> The Honourable Mistresses and Misses?
>
> (XI, 79)

It is the transience of the emblems of transience that qualifies the comedy of the passage with a fragile pathos which is the more affecting because it infiltrates the very texture of the poem. Throughout these cantos Byron's references and his diction are recklessly localized: they are bound by a particular time and a particular social space. This is poetry that does not pretend to be safely removed from the world in flux that it contemplates, but offers itself rather as a 'glittering mass' that is just as subject to dissolution as its subjects.

The cantos are exclusively set

> In the great world – which being interpreted
> Meaneth the West or worst end of city
> And about twice two thousand people bred
> By no means to be very wise or witty,
> But to sit up while others lie in bed,
> And look down on the universe with pity –
>
> (XI, 45)

The smallness of the 'world' is one of the standing jokes of the cantos.[9] When the season ends London empties: 'The world was gone / The twice two thousand, for whom earth was made'(XIII, 38). Nevertheless the cantos are completely worldly in a way in which the earlier cantos are not. In them a possibility was realized that nineteenth-century poetry spent much effort trying to reclaim. Hemans and Landon, Byron's immediate poetic successors, took as their model the earlier Byron of the Eastern tales, and reinforced the barrier separating the world of the poems from the world of their readers. One characteristic Victorian solution was to accept the barrier but to position it within the poem rather than between the world of the poem and the world of the reader. Tennyson embarks on his re-telling of the legend of Godiva from the platform at Coventry railway station, or Rossetti in 'The Burden of Nineveh' enters his vision of ancient Assyria by passing through the revolving doors of the British museum. But Byron's only important successor amongst the Victorian poets was Arthur Hugh Clough, especially in *Dipsychus*, the poem that he set in Venice, Byron's city. It was the novelists rather than the poets who continued *Don Juan*.

## III

In the *New Monthly Magazine* for April 1, 1826, Henry Colburn inserted a puff for his latest publication: 'A new novel to be named Vivian Grey is said to be a sort of Don Juan in prose, detailing the adventures of an ambitious, dashing and talented young man of high life'. Disraeli, followed very shortly by Bulwer, were the chief architects of the fashionable novel, and both were fervent Byronists. Disraeli seems to have persuaded his father to employ Byron's servant, Tita, and Bulwer occupied Byron's rooms in Albemarle Street for some years, after which Disraeli thought seriously of taking them. Bulwer took his discipleship to the unusual length of conducting an affair with Caroline Lamb.

*Vivian Grey* and *Pelham* are additional acts of homage. Both are sprinkled with references to Byron. One of Vivian's friends, Cleveland, had seen Byron in Pisa, and been shocked by his fatness, his bad teeth, greying hair, and the 'dandified' foreign style of his dress (2, 166),[10] but all the young men are agreed on his pre-eminence. His loss 'can never be retrieved. He was indeed a man – a real man, and when I say this, I award him, in my opinion, the most splendid character which human nature can aspire to' (2, 168). The admiration is clearly focused on the late Byron, and in particular the Byron of *Don Juan*. *The Corsair*, for example, would not prompt the thought that 'if one thing were more characteristic of Byron's mind than another, it was his strong, shrewd, common sense – his pure, unalloyed sagacity' (2, 164). In fact, Disraeli introduces into his novel an aristocratic poet named Lord Alhambra, who is either a version or an imitator of the early Byron. Vivian Grey picks out the following couplet as 'the most admirable lines' in his recently published poem:

> The Crescent warriors sipped their sherbet spiced,
> For Christian men the various wines were iced.
>
> (1, 198)

The mockery of the earlier Byron is as common as the praise of the later. In his 1835 preface to *Pelham* Bulwer explains that the melodramatically gloomy Reginald Granville was 'drawn purposely of the Byron School' in an attempt to 'put an end to the Satanic mania, – to turn the thoughts of young gentlemen without neckcloths, and young clerks who were sallow, from playing Corsair, and boasting that they were villains'.[11] But, of course, it was Byron himself who had already emerged in *Don Juan* as the most powerful mocker of the Byronic. The Duchesse de Perpignan may be laughed at for her inability to be 'excessively enamoured of any thing but an oyster paté and Lord Byron's Corsair',[12] but the mockery is broader of the unrefined taste that would 'prefer Bloomfield's poems to Byron's' (1, 78). Byron is the only modern who has the strength of the ancients (2, 50), and Lord Vincent, who has impeccable taste, recognizes only two giants in all of English literature, 'Shakespeare and Byron' (1, 209).

Like the last cantos of *Don Juan*, these novels are set in what Catherine Gore calls 'the world, the exclusive world, whose territories are so narrow of limit, and whose population is so easily resolved by the census of Debrett'[13] (1, 136). As Michael Sadleir notes, the sentimental novel of the late eighteenth and early nineteenth centuries characteristically chose its central characters from the aristocracy too, but for him 'fashionable novels' are distinguished from earlier novels about fashionable people by their concern for 'verisimilitude': the fashionable novel 'might be dull and silly, but it must appear correct'.[14] But it is a very particular kind of verisimilitude, and consists most importantly in references to real people, real clubs, real shops and real tradesmen. When Vivian Grey's father wishes to speak seriously to his son, he invites him to 'step into Clark's and take an ice' (1, 33). In *Pelham*, there is a meeting in Calais with Pelham's legendary predecessor, Beau Brummell (Pelham outdoes Brummell by employing three rather than two tailors to make his gloves), and the two discuss the relative merits of Staub, who tailors in Paris, and Stultz of London, agreeing that Stultz reveals 'a degree of aristocratic pretension in his stitches, which is vulgar to an appalling degree' (1, 288–9).

The novels often accommodate melodramatic plots – there is a rape and a murder in *Pelham*, an attempted murder and a fatal duel in *Vivian Grey*, a suicide in Lister's *Granby*, and in Gore's *Women As They Are* both a suicide and an averted incestuous relationship between a father and his natural child – and they most often incorporate a love story, but these are predominantly novels of conversation. Characters talk at their club, as they stroll through the gardens of a country house, as they endure a rainy day with no shooting, and they talk at dinner. Their conversation has no end other than itself, and for the reader its sole purpose is to identify a community of speakers. Vivian Grey, unlike Disraeli himself, is sent a.way to a public school, and startles his schoolfellows by the stylishness of his dress: 'What a knowing set out', one of them exclaims (1, 14). To choose a friend is to decide who one will 'crony with' (1, 34). The public school is a proper preparation for the fashionable world that Vivian will enter because its pupils are bound together by their possession of a shared language. In the fashionable world fast young women are 'dashers', one fears being a 'quiz', second sons are 'scorpions'. One of the pleasures that these novels offer their readers is initiation into the closed world of fashionable slang. But it is also revealing that the idioms of an English public school should be reproduced in *Vivian Grey* by a novelist who had never been to one.

Colburn did succeed in enlisting some genuine aristocrats – Constantine Henry Phipps, for example, the first son of the Earl of Mulgrave, and, even more exalted, Lady Charlotte Bury, the daughter of the Duke of Argyll – but their novels were far from the most successful of their kind. Colburn's most successful authors were not quite of the 'ton' whose doings they described. Disraeli was the son of a retiring Jewish scholar, Catherine Gore's father was a wine merchant, and, although Bulwer, as he always insisted, was of ancient family, it was, even at the time of his birth, a family in reduced circumstances, and he began writing novels only when he was disinherited and wholly reliant on his own earnings. Isaac D'Israeli was surprised to learn that his son's second novel was entitled *The Young Duke*: 'But what does Ben know of Dukes?'.[15] But in fact Ben's lack of first-hand acquaintance with the upper reaches of the aristocracy makes him a representative fashionable novelist. It was a position that allowed the novelists to mediate between the society inhabited by their characters and the more modest social milieu of the greater part of their readers. It encouraged the cultivation of a perspective at once within and outside, with the result that these novels characteristically satirize the world they celebrate, and celebrate the world that they satirize. It also lends their representations of the world of fashionable life a certain anthropological quality. Disraeli inspects the language of the English public school with a delighted curiosity that is prompted by his never having attended one, and the conversation at aristocratic dinner tables is recorded in much the same way. The effect that Byron gained by seeing the fashionable world through the eyes of the young Spaniard, Juan, is maintained in these novels by the social difference that divides the novelists from their characters.

In its insistent contemporaneity and in its concentration on the ephemeral, silver fork fiction is a reaction against the historical novel,

and in particular the novel as practised by Scott. And yet the fashionable novel cannot quite free itself from Scott's influence. The novelists
retain, but in a new form, the historical sense that Scott had made central to fiction. They become the historians of the contemporary. The
novels delight in slang and in fashions in dress precisely because slang
and fashion are so completely of their moment, vulnerable not just to
the passage of years but of months. These novels respond like Byron to
the pathos inherent in social forms that dissolve almost before they
have been noticed. For Catherine Gore, fashionable novels are 'the
amber which serves to preserve the ephemeral modes and caprices of
the day' (*Women As They Are*, 2, 235). She defends 'triflers', because,
'like a straw thrown up to determine the course of the wind, the triflers
of any epoch are an invaluable evidence of the bent of the public
mind'.[16] Triflers, here, seem to comprehend not only the characters of
the fashionable novel but their authors. Like Byron, these novelists
daringly refuse to address themselves to posterity. Their popularity
lasted for some fifteen years, from 1825 to 1840, but it is somehow fitting that by 1833 Bulwer could speak of 'the three-years' run of the
fashionable novels' as if it were already a phenomenon of purely historical interest.[17] The novels seem oddly aware of their own obsolescence. Even in *Pelham*, his first attempt of the kind, Bulwer imagines
the rapidity with which his novel will become antique: 'the novel
which exactly delineates the present age may seem strange and unfamiliar to the next' (1, 120). The rapidity with which the novels will
become obsolete is offered as a guarantee of their verisimilitude,
because the society that they represent is defined by the swiftness with
which it changes. It is an age in which, as Byron puts it, 'Change grows
too changeable' (XI, 82), and in such an age the conscientious novelist
must attempt to write novels as ephemeral as newspapers.

It is significant that newspapers are the reading matter to which these
novels refer more often than to any other kind except the fashionable
novel itself, and the novels recognize the similarity between the two
kinds. Catherine Gore's Lord Willersdale says of the 'English modern
novel, with its my Lord Dukes and Sir Harrys, and caricatures of the
beau monde', 'I hold its vulgarity and bad taste as secondary only to
that of the columns of your newspapers after a drawing room' (*Women
As They Are*, 2, 237). The column most eagerly scanned is 'Fashionable
Intelligence', in which the characters can read of the balls that they
attended, and their arrival in and departure from town. It is as if they
rely on the newspapers to authenticate their existence. But this gives
them a peculiarly ephemeral identity, which persists only for the hours

or days that a newspaper commands attention. The books that record their doings seem designed to last little longer. In *Vivian Grey* Disraeli solemnly regrets such a state of affairs: 'Amid the myriad of volumes which issued monthly from the press, what one was not written for the mere hour?' (2, 162). But these novels, and *Vivian Grey* more than most, seem gleefully to accept their own transience as the condition of faithfully representing a society that is fashionable precisely because its commodities so quickly become obsolete. In Lister's *Granby*, Trebeck, who is at the very centre of the fashionable world, 'quite one of the recherché few – the pet of the exclusives' (1, 281), abandons the dandyism of his youth, when he is 'seriously disgusted' at seeing a style of waistcoat that he had himself devised 'adorning the person of a natty apprentice' (1, 108). Literary modes, these novels seem to accept, are subject to the same rigorous law as fashions in clothing, in which the difference between the fashionable and the vulgar becomes a matter not of taste but of time, and the period of time that secures the difference becomes ever briefer, until it is reduced to a matter of weeks.

The novelists often describe their age as marked by an accelerated process of change. The best of them, *Vivian Grey*, *Pelham*, Theodore Hook's stories in the *Sayings and Doings* series, most of Catherine Gore's fashionable novels, move with an unusual rapidity, so that to turn to them after reading a novel by Scott is to experience an equivalent of the metrical acceleration that one notices when laying down *The Prelude* and picking up *Don Juan*. 'There never was a novel written at such a slapping pace', says R.H. Horne of Catherine Gore's *Cecil*.[18] It is a calculated effect. Gore suggests that 'the velocity of steam inventions seems to demand a corresponding rapidity of narrative, dialogue, and discourse' (*Women As They Are*, 3, 123–4), and that the 'accelerated velocity' of modern society demands a different kind of novel: 'The rapidity of the waltz offers no pause for soft ramblings; and the endless whirl of engagements supersedes the possibility of plots such as endangered Miss Harriet Byron and annihilated Miss Clarissa Harlowe' (*Women As They Are*, 1, 133).

Conventionally, the novel deplores societies that whirl like a waltzer, given up to a process of frenetic and purposeless change. In *Women As They Are*, Lord Willersdale is pained to see his teenage bride waltzing with fashionable young men, and the novelists often mimic his disapproval. Bulwer himself defended the fashionable novel as a variety of satire: 'Few writers ever produced so great an effect on the political spirit of their generation as some of these novelists, who, without any other merit, unconsciously exposed the falsehood, the hypocrisy, the arrogant and vulgar insolence of patrician life'.[19] But satire is itself a disguise for novelists who are as practised as their characters in 'the consummate dissimulation of bon ton' (*Pelham*, 2, 175), and what it disguises is the novelists' own delighted fascination with the fashionable world that they mock.

The fashionable novelists, supported by Colburn their publisher, daringly presented their books as commodities, as items for sale in a world inhabited by people like the characters of these novels, people who are defined by the character of their purchases. 'In fact', says Lister, 'fashion is not so aristocratic as you may imagine; it may be bought, like most other things' (*Granby*, 1, 257), or, as Vivian Grey explains to the Marquis of Carabas, 'Think you not, that intellect is as much a purchasable article as fine parks and fair castles?' (1, 95). The high-spirited cynicism of these novels is itself an expression of the glee with which the novelists confess that they are not, like Robert Plumer Ward in *Tremaine*, writing fictions that soberly protest against the 'wide spread of that luxury which is consequent on wealth' (iii), but rather themselves the purveyors of luxury items. Literature is not, for Disraeli, an index of the moral state of the nation, but of its economic prosperity: 'There is nothing like a fall of stock to affect what it is the fashion to style the literature of the present day'. Literature is 'the mere creature of our imaginary wealth...Consols at 100 were the origin of all book societies' (2, 160).

It is because fashionable novels are themselves fashionable items that they so frequently figure in the conversations that the novels record. These are novelists as self-conscious as Byron in *Don Juan*. In *Vivian Grey* Disraeli acknowledges only one precursor, but compensates by the frequency of his references to him, as for example when Grey is surprised by a country house library – 'I thought the third edition of Tremaine would be a very fair specimen of your ancient literature' (1, 149–50) – or when he replies to a young lady who asks him if he knows who wrote it: 'O! I'll tell you in a moment. It's either Mr. Ryder, or Mr. Spencer Percival, or Miss Dyson, or Mr. Bowles, or the Duke of Buckingham, or Mr. Ward, or a young Officer in the Guards, or an old Clergyman in the North of England, or a middle-aged Baronet on the Midland Circuit' (1, 153). Pelham's mother responds to his loss of his parliamentary seat by withdrawing to her bedroom where she 'shut herself up with Tremaine, and one China monster, for a whole week' (2, 89–90), and when he goes into Brooke's one evening Pelham recognizes the author himself: 'Mr. – – – – –, the author of T – – – – – – –, was conning the Courier in a corner' (2, 171–2). In Catherine Gore's *Women as They Are*, Bulwer himself becomes a topic of conversation, 'And Pelham! – with its sparkling conceits, that blind one, as though the pages were dried with diamond dust' (2, 235). But more often the self-consciousness is self-mocking, as when Pelham hurriedly leaves his uncle, going off 'with the rapidity of a novel upon "fashionable life"' (2, 5). Or the derision may be keener, and never more so than when challenging the claims of rival novelists to be truly familiar with the fashionable world that they represent.

Bulwer and Disraeli were to become friends, but Pelham seems to have Disraeli in mind when he winces at the use of the words, 'genteel' and 'dashing'. 'those two horrid words! low enough to suit even the author of " – – – – – – ".'(2, 20) Catherine Gore is apt to measure the fashionable qualifications of her characters by the number of French words that intrude into their conversation: her Lady Louisa apologizes for breaking into English: 'Il n'y a pas ici une âme qui vaille la peine d'une – flirtation! – thank heaven we have one Anglicism worth preserving' (*Women As They Are*, 3, 24). But it is a technique that Bulwer had already satirized. Pelham's mother, for example, offers him this advice when he is about to leave Paris, 'You will also be careful, in returning to England, to make very little use of French phrases; no vulgarity is more unpleasing'(1, 232). Most commonly of all, the novelists offer a mocking recipe for the production of fashionable novels. In *Vivian Grey* Disraeli invents

a Mr. Thomas Smith, a fashionable novelist; that is to say, a person who occasionally publishes three volumes, one half of which contain the adventures of a young gentleman in the country, and the other volume and a half the adventures of the same young gentleman in the metropolis; a sort of writer, whose constant tattle about beer and billiards, and eating soup, and the horribility of 'committing' puns, gives truly a most admirable and accurate idea of the conversation of the refined society of the refined metropolis of Great Britain.

(1, 74)

Bulwer includes in *Pelham* a discussion of the social ignorance of novelists who claim to be fashionable: 'Most of the writers upon our little, great world, have seen nothing of it: at most, they have been occasionally admitted into the routs of the B.'s and C.'s, of the second, or rather the third set' (3, 48). By 1828 Lord Normanby could include in his *Yes and No: A Tale of the Day*, a more precise description of the requirements of this kind of novel:

> Do you know the modern receipt for a finished picture of fashionable life? Let a gentleman*ly* man, with a gentleman*ly* style, take of foolscap paper a few quires, stuff them well with high-sounding titles – dukes and duchesses, lords and ladies, *ad libitum*. Then open the Peerage at random, pick a suppositious author out of one page of it, and fix the imaginary characters upon some of the rest; mix it all up with a quantum suff of puff, and the book is in the second edition before ninety-nine readers out of a hundred have found out that the one is as little likely to have written, as the others to have done, what is attributed to them.[20]

Normanby, as one of the few authentically aristocratic writers of fashionable novels, could afford the gibe, as could Lady Charlotte Bury, daughter of the Duke of Argyll, who included in *Journal of the Heart*, one of the three fashionable novels that she published in 1830,[21] a warning that many such novels are written by those who have had no opportunity 'even of seeing or mixing, at whatever distance, and under whatever circumstances, with those they intend to represent; and others again by persons who have only achieved their station among the race apart, and are not of that indigenous stock which alone enables anyone to write of the arcana of ton'.[22] But the novels of Lord Normanby and Lady Charlotte Bury have little other than the rank of their authors to recommend them. As Bulwer remarks 'gentlemen, who are not writers, are as bad as writers who are not gentlemen' (*Pelham*, 3, 49). Disraeli, in his scorn for the fictitious fashionable novelist Thomas Smith, is the significant figure, precisely because he is himself so vulnerable to the same charge. The best fashionable novelists, Disraeli, Bulwer, and Catherine Gore, have in common a gleeful effrontery. Their novels are enlivened by the impudence with which they claim intimacy with a world, 'the world', into which they were only grudgingly admitted.

*Vivian Grey* and *Pelham* are the most complete examples of the fashionable novel because their heroes so completely mimic the dashing effrontery of their writers. The story of young men in a hurry, young men intent on gaining recognition in the most exclusive society by an astute use of their only talents, impudence, and cleverness, is reproduced in novels which are themselves the means by which Disraeli and Bulwer made their triumphant assaults on the world of letters, and the fashionable world that literary success opened to them. 'To enter into high society,' says Vivian, 'a man must either have blood, a million, or a genius' (1, 50). He, like Disraeli, recognizes that he has only the third qualification, but, again like Disraeli, he is quite confident that it will suffice. Pelham, like Bulwer, is luckier – he has blood as well as genius – but he shares fully Vivian's reckless confidence in his own social skills, and in both cases the talents of the heroes are scarcely distinguishable from those of the novelists.

On his first entry into Parisian society Pelham considers what 'character' to assume, and decides that none is more likely to be so 'remarkable among men, and therefore pleasing to women, than an egregious coxcomb': 'accordingly I arranged my hair into ringlets, dressed myself with singular simplicity (a low person, by the bye, would have done just the contrary), and putting on an air of exceeding languor, made my maiden appearance at Lord Bennington's'. There he successfully discomforts a young man whose watch and chain from 'Brequet's' he is invited to admire by announcing that he can imagine 'nothing so plebeian' as wishing to know the time, and outrages all the other men present by recalling that on the only occasion on which he had ventured on the Parisian pavements 'à pied', he had stepped into a gutter, and been forced to stand still and scream for assistance. (1, 61–4) Compare Disraeli at Malta, flushed with the success of *Vivian Grey*, reporting an incident at the garrison when he had watched two young officers playing racquets:

> Yesterday at the racket court sitting in the gallery among strangers, the ball entered, slightly struck me, and fell at my feet. I picked it up, and observing a young rifleman excessively stiff, I humbly requested him to forward its passage into the court, as I really had never thrown a ball in my life. This incident has been the general subject of conversation at all the messes today![23]

There is a seamless transition from the novels to such letters.

Robert Blake has shown that the plot of *Vivian Grey*, which concerns Vivian's failed attempt to propel the doltish Marquess of Carabas into the premiership at the head of a new party, is closely modelled on Disraeli's similarly botched attempt to assist the publisher, John Murray, in setting up a Tory newspaper to be called 'The Representative'. Vivian's plan collapses when he fails to persuade the brilliant Cleveland to accept the leadership of the new party in the Commons, and Disraeli's plans were foiled when Lockhart declined to take on the editorship of the new paper.[24] Pelham, too, is foiled in his political ambitions when the party that he has helped to gain power breaks its promise to him.

Both heroes end their novels disillusioned with the world that they have so assiduously courted. Vivian Grey retreats to the continent, and Pelham into marriage with Ellen Glanville, whose 'pure and holy love could be at once [his] recompense and retreat' (3, 208). Their worldly ambitions are thwarted at the last in a manner that seems to counterpoint rather than echo the careers of their authors. *Pelham* and *Vivian Grey*, after all, made Bulwer and Disraeli famous. But the novels also made them extremely unpopular.

In this, too, both novels seem oddly self-conscious. They wantonly provoke their unsympathetic readers in a way that closely corresponds to Pelham's performance at Lord Bennington's Parisian soirée, which prompts one man to mutter to another, 'What a damnation puppy' (1, 64). Bulwer provoked a hostile campaign against him, led by *Fraser's*, unexampled for its ferocity and for the length of time that it was sustained, and Disraeli found himself described in *Blackwood's* as 'an obscure person for whom nobody cares a straw', who had written a 'paltry catchpenny' which had succeeded only by virtue of Colburn's 'shameful and shameless puffery'.[25] He also made a lifelong enemy of John Murray, the most powerful publisher in London, who thought himself lampooned in the person of the Marquess of Carabas. Both Disraeli and Bulwer were wounded by these attacks.[26] They came to think of the novels which charted the youthful indiscretions of their heroes as themselves constituting a youthful indiscretion. The brittle cynicism of the novels seemed inappropriate to the lofty literary and political careers that both men were anxious to pursue. The oddity is that this retrospective embarrassment infiltrates the novels even as they were being written. *Vivian Grey* ends mournfully, with Vivian in Germany, where he becomes 'addicted to field sports' and 'feared nothing so much as thought, and dreaded nothing so much as the solitude of his own chamber' (2, 233). When Disraeli continued the novel he transformed it into a solemn bildungsroman modelled on *Wilhelm Meister*. Pelham, even more than Grey, is aware throughout that, however adept he might be at acting the puppy, he preserves underneath this façade a quite different character which is evident to his more perceptive friends such as Lady Roseville: 'While you seem frivolous to the superficial, I know you to have a mind not only capable of the most solid and important affairs, but habituated to consider them' (3, 111). By the end of the first volume Pelham, under the tutelage of his uncle, Lord Glenmorris, is preparing studiously for his political career by studying utilitarianism, beginning with 'Mr. Mill, upon Government' (1, 334). They are odd novels in which the novelist seems at once anxious to appear before his readers as a 'damnation puppy', and to invite his readers to recognize, like Lady Roseville, a moral earnestness concealed beneath the frivolity. The contemporary who seems to come closest to recognizing this is, strangely, the Fraserian who made the most enduring of all attacks on the fashionable novel, Thomas Carlyle.

## IV

Andrew Elfenbein has argued that in *Sartor Resartus* Carlyle mimics the Byronism that he ends by repudiating.[27] Teufelsdröckh proclaims his new creed, 'Close thy Byron; open thy Goethe', but only after he has re-traced Byron's steps, becoming himself a Germanic Childe Harold, who 'quietly lifts his Pilgerstab (Pilgrim-staff)' and sets out on a 'perambulation and circumnavigation of the terraqueous Globe' (103). But *Sartor Resartus* is also a parody of the fashionable novel. It was first published in *Fraser's Magazine* (1833–4), and it continued the campaign against the fashionable novel in general and Bulwer in particular that preoccupied William Maginn, the editor of *Fraser's*, throughout the 1830s. It is only in the tenth chapter, 'The Dandiacal Body', that the attack on the fashionable novel is explicit, but it is implied throughout.

Most obviously, Carlyle parodies the style of the novels, 'apparently some broken Lingua-franca or English-French', by inventing a rival language of his own, broken between English and German. Second, Teufelsdröckh is designed as the antithesis of the fashionable hero. His English editor is obliged to admit that Teufelsdröckh's style often reveals his 'apparent want of intercourse with the higher classes' (29). He lives in scholarly squalor, and spends his evenings in coffee houses, reading periodicals and consuming huge tumblers of 'Gukguk' or beer, a way of life that acts in itself as a satire on such a hero as Pelham, who, in a Parisian café, is apt to choose a glass of lemonade, the most expensive drink available. Third, there is puffing. Fashionable novels, Maginn and others asserted, were wholly reliant for their success on their unscrupulous publisher's skill at puffing, and *Sartor Resartus* is presented by Carlyle as a single, monumental puff, an attempt by Teufelsdröckh's English editor to boost the sales of his hero Teufelsdröckh's massive volume 'Die Kleider, ihr Werden und Wirken (Clothes, their Origin and Influence)', by publishing 'Article after Article on this massive Volume, in such widely-circulating Critical Journals as the Editor might stand connected with, or by money or love procure access to' (17). The practice of puffing was the clearest evidence of a literature that was offered for sale like any other commodity.

Bulwer introduces into *Pelham* his own recognition that the novel should be a useful not just a luxury item. His hero, after all, abandons his self-indulgent life of gentlemanly leisure to study utilitarianism, but this would not have impressed Carlyle, because utilitarianism seemed to him itself simply a commodification of ethics. The whole of *Sartor Resartus* is written in earnest protest against the notion that 'the Past Forms of Society' may be destroyed and burnt except for 'the sounder Rags among them' which may be 'quilted together into one huge Irish watch-coat for the defence of the Body only!' (156). Teufelsdröckh's business is with the spirit, not the body. It is a choice that he can afford. His appointment at Weissnichtwo as 'Professor der Allerley-Wisschenschaft, or as we should say in English, "Professor of Things in General"' has given him a modest competence, freeing him from the literary marketplace to assume instead the vantage of the prophet, a 'wild Seer, shaggy, unkempt, like a Baptist living on locusts and wild honey' (29). But Carlyle's economic position was very different. In 1833, he was still painfully trying to earn enough to keep himself by offering his work to periodicals. To suppose that, in a piece of writing itself published in *Fraser's*, Carlyle could express an uncomplicated contempt for those like Bulwer who wrote for their living is to credit him with an improbable lack of self-awareness. His response to the fashionable novel in *Sartor Resartus* becomes interesting precisely to the extent that we recognize its ambivalence. Carlyle defines himself in opposition to the fashionable novelists, but he also recognizes himself in them. They are, in however distorted a manner, a reflection of himself.

Most obviously, he shares with them a recognition of the supreme importance of clothes. Man, for Teufelsdröckh is 'a Tool-using animal... of which truth Clothes are but one example' (35–6), and yet they are the crucial example, for it is clothes that gave us 'individuality, distinctions, social polity; Clothes have made Men of us' (35). It is a point that would have been quickly taken by Pelham, who devotes a chapter of ten pages to the description of a single meeting with his tailor, generalizing from the incident a brief dissertation on 'the greatest of all sciences – the science of dress' (2, 68). Teufelsdröckh comes close to quoting the sentence when he claims that 'the essence of all Science lies in the PHILOSOPHY OF CLOTHES' (56). But, of course, for him there remains a crucial difference. Clothes, having made us men, 'are threatening to make Clothes-screens of us', and, in the case of men such as Pelham, the threat has been realized. Pelham's attention is exclusively fixed on 'the minutiae of dress, such as the glove, the button, the boot, the shape of the hat, &c', and, for Teufelsdröckh this is a kind of fetishism, a worship of a sign independent of its significance. For Teufelsdröckh clothing is the supreme figure, because it figures figuration itself. It is only through figures that the infinite spirit that dwells in us can accommodate itself to the finite world in which we live, only by figuring itself in word or deed that thought can act upon the world, and all such figurings are regarded by Teufelsdröckh as varieties of clothing: 'The thing Visible, nay the thing Imagined, the thing in any way conceived as Visible, what is it but a Garment, a Clothing of the higher celestial Invisible, "unimaginable, formless, dark with excess of bright"?' (51). So, language is 'the Flesh-Garment, the Body of Thought'. Language is essentially metaphorical, for in metaphor thought finds the clothing that it needs in order to issue out into the world as language (55). For Teufelsdröckh clothes are the only guise in which the spiritual can gain entry into the world: 'must not the Imagination weave Garments, visible Bodies, wherein the else invisible creations and inspirations of our Reason are, like Spirits revealed, and first become all-powerful?' (55). Nothing seems further from Pelham in earnest discussion with his tailor. Pelham too chooses his clothing so carefully because it is the only guise in which he can gain entry into the world, but the world he has in mind is 'the World', the exclusive world of the twice two thousand. And yet in his obsessive concern with clothing Pelham offers not a contradiction but a compelling instance of the central tenet of Teufelsdröckh's philosophy, so that it cannot be understood as wholly ironic when the editor remarks: 'The all-importance of Clothes, which a German Professor of unequalled learning and acumen, writes his enormous Volume to demonstrate, has sprung up in the intellect of the Dandy, without effort, like an instinct of genius' (177).

When he hears of a new school of novelists distinguished by their deep interest in styles of dress, Teufelsdröckh eagerly searches out some examples of their work. Unfortunately, all his attempts to read them are frustrated:

> that tough faculty of reading, for which the world will not refuse me credit, was here for the first time foiled and set at naught. In vain that I summoned my whole energies (mich werdlich anstrengte), and did my very utmost; at the end of some short space, I was uniformly seized with not so much what I can call a drumming in my ears, as a kind of infinite, insufferable Jew's harping and scrannel-piping there; to which the frighfulest species of Magnetic Sleep soon supervened. And if I strove to shake this away, and absolutely would not yield, came a hitherto unfelt sensation, as of Delirium Tremens,

and a melting into total deliquium; till at last, by order of the Doctor, dreading ruin to my whole intellectual and bodily faculties, and a general breaking-up of the constitution, I reluctantly but determinedly forbore.

(179–80)

He is forced to rely for his knowledge of the novels on a torn sheet of *Fraser's* that had been used to wrap one of his parcels of books and happened to include the second of Maginn's furious attacks on Bulwer.[28] The alarming physical symptoms that attempts to read the novels induce in Teufelsdröckh seem wittily to continue Maginn's attack, but the joke is far from simple. It was, after all, Carlyle who, as he well knew, was pronounced unreadable by most of his contemporaries whereas *Pelham*, to quote the novel itself, 'went off like a fashionable novel'. The mockery of Bulwer in such passages is heavily tinged with self-mockery.

Both *Pelham* and *Sartor Resartus* are books about clothes, and both of them are bildungsromane, narratives which reveal, as Carlyle puts it, in 'the forged [lineaments] of fiction, a complete picture and genetical History of the Man and his spiritual Endeavour' (57). There is a literal connection in the early nineteenth century between books and clothing, which Carlyle explains: 'Despise not the rag from which man makes Paper' (55). For Teufelsdröckh this is a 'Ragfair of a World' (150), and these are 'rag-gathering and rag-burning days' (169), by which he means not only that it is an age that clings to outworn beliefs, but an age chiefly characterized by the production of paper, of print: 'is it not beautiful to see five million quintals of Rags picked annually from the Laystall; and annually, after being macerated, hot-pressed, printed on, and sold, – returned thither; filling so many hungry mouths by the way?' (38). When he visited London Teufelsdröckh found his religious instincts most deeply stirred by Monmouth Street, famous for its shops selling old clothes: there 'in motley vision, the whole Pageant of Existence passes awfully before us; with its wail and jubilee, mad loves and mad hatreds, church-bells and gallow-ropes, farce-tragedy, beast-godhood, – the Bedlam of Creation!' (160).[29] The Editor imagines that it may have been 'in Monmouth Street, at the bottom of our own English "ink-sea", that this remarkable Volume first took being, and shot forth its radiant point in his soul' (160). Writers such as Bulwer and Carlyle are interested in clothes, because clothes provide them, in more than one sense, with their raw material.

Because both are interested in clothes, both are interested, too, in fashion. *Pelham* was famous in part because its hero's preference for black rather than blue coats, and his hostility to padding, established a new style in men's clothing. To be fashionable a style of clothing must be new, but not only that. It must also have, inherent within it, its own obsolescence, for styles of clothing become fashionable by virtue of being copied, and become unfashionable the moment they have been copied too often. Teufelsdröckh too is a student of fashion: 'Thus is the Law of Progress secured; and in Clothes, as in all other external things whatsoever, no fashion will continue' (39). And he too aspires to set new fashions. Churches and religions are to him only suits of clothes, and the existing religion, Christianity, is a coat that is 'sorrowfully out at elbows'. His second volume, he promises, will treat 'the Wear, Destruction, and Re-Texture of Spiritual Tissues, or Garments' (144–5).

The chief difference between Pelham and Teufelsdröckh might seem to be political, and born out of class. Pelham, like Bulwer, is proud of his ancient family name, whereas Teufelsdröckh, like Carlyle, takes pride in his own peasant stock: 'Wouldst thou rather be a peasant's son that knew, were it never so rudely, there was a God in Heaven and in Man; or a duke's son that only knew there were two and thirty quarters on the family coach?' (74). Teufelsdröckh, his Editor sorrowfully admits, is in politics an arrant 'sansculotte', apt to set the coffee-house cheering by proposing a toast, 'Die Sache der Armen in Gottes und Teufels Namen (The Cause of the Poor in Heaven's Name and – – – – 's)!' (20). He enters into correspondence with the Saint-Simonians, and is rumoured, when he disappears from Weissnichtwo, to have gone to Paris, drawn there by the outbreak of the 1830 revolution, though the Editor guesses that he may rather have come to London (191–2). In 'The Dandiacal Body', Teulfelsdröckh begins by deducing from Chapter 7 of the second volume of *Pelham* the dandy's articles of faith, consisting of such precepts as 'The good sense of a gentleman is nowhere more finely developed than in his rings'. Then, Teufelsdröckh turns from the Dandies to the Drudges, the Irish poor, who 'imitate the Dandiacal Sect in their grand principle of wearing a peculiar Costume', but in their case it consists of patched rags tied with a straw belt. He gloomily prophesies a nation divided between two sects which are separated even now only by 'a foot-plank, a mere film of Land'. The two sects are stores of energy, like 'two World-Batteries', one positive and one negative, and when they come into contact one with another: 'What then? The Earth is but shivered into impalpable smoke by that Doom's-thunderpeal: the Sun misses one of his Planets in Space, and thenceforth there are no eclipses of the Moon' (184–5). At this point, as Teufelsdröckh predicts a revolutionary apocalypse, the Editor nervously breaks off his quotation, but the point is already made. The fashionable novel is a symptom of a society increasingly divided between the rich and a poverty-stricken underclass from which the rich, in their daily lives and in their preferred fictions, wish only to avert their eyes.

The chapter represents one of Carlyle's earlier pictures of a Britain divided between the rich and poor, a Britain that has become two nations. The phrase did not become current until 1844, when Disraeli published *Sybil*, and it may seem no more than a coincidence that it was given currency by a writer who was one of the chief architects of the fashionable novel. But *Sybil* itself begins as a fashionable novel. Charles Egremont, whose education into the social realities of class division the novel will trace, is introduced at a grand evening party, where conversation centres on the Derby which is to be run the following day, and languid wits like Mr. Mountchesney say, 'I rather like bad wine; one gets so bored with good wine'. It may be that the fashionable novel from the first contained the potential to reproduce the picture of Britain that Carlyle offers in 'The Dandiacal Body'.

By the 1830s the fashionable novel was losing popularity to a kind of novel that seems its opposite in its concentration on the low life of thieves and scoundrels. Harrison Ainsworth published *Rookwood* in 1833 and *Jack Sheppard* in 1839, and between them, in 1837–8, came *Oliver Twist*. It was a fashion that Bulwer himself instigated with his *Paul Clifford*, 1830, the tale of a highwayman, and *Eugene Aram*, 1832, which tells the story, loosely based on fact, of a murderer. But Bulwer's crucial innovation was to show how the fashionable novel and the Newgate novel might be combined. Already in *Pelham* the final episode of the novel shows Pelham procuring the witness who can prove his friend, Glanville, innocent of murder by assuming a disguise and gaining entry to a thieves' kitchen, where he practises the thieves' cant in which he has been carefully schooled. Similar abrupt transitions between high and low life occur in his next two novels, *The Disowned* and *Devereux* (both 1829).

From the first, from Byron's *Don Juan*, it seems that the fashionable novel had the potential to produce its own antithesis. Juan enters on his fashionable life in London only after a fatal encounter with a highwayman:

> Who in a row like Tom could lead the van,
> Booze in the ken, or at the spelken hustle?
> Who queer a flat? Who (spite of Bow-Street's ban)
> On the high toby-spice so flash the muzzle?

Who on a lark, with black-eyed Sal (his blowing)
So prime, so swell, so nutty, and so knowing!

(XI, 19)

Long before Carlyle recognized the Irish pauper as a grotesque parody
of the dandy, Byron recognized, like Bulwer in *Paul Clifford*, that the
highwayman parodied the man of fashion, that thieves' cant, for example, was precisely analogous to gentlemanly slang.[30] It was not an original perception, but it was crucial, for it made possible a kind of novel
that reproduced the picture of an England divided between the
Dandies and the Drudges that Carlyle offers in 'The Dandiacal Body', a
novel like *Sybil* that represents Britain as an island divided between two
nations. It is predictable that it should have been Bulwer, in a novel
such as *Paul Clifford*, who first realized this potential, because it offered
him what he most needed, the means to reconcile his avid social ambition with the principled political radicalism that he represents Pelham
as imbibing from his uncle, Lord Glenmorris, for whom 'the only real
triumph which art can achieve' is the 'happy faces' of his tenants
(1, 308). But in working out his own dilemma Bulwer happened on a
structural principle that was to inform the novel of social criticism
throughout much of the nineteenth century. A late Dickens novel *Our
Mutual Friend* (1864–5) begins with Rogue Riderhood drifting on the
oily surface of the Thames as he pulls aboard the boat a corpse that
seems a ghastly embodiment of the oozy, unseen depths of the river,
and the second chapter switches abruptly to the Veneerings' vulgarly
ostentatious dinner party, which is seen for much of the chapter as it is
reflected in the hard, silver, depthless glass of the 'great looking-glass
above the sideboard'. One reflective surface, the river, darkly parodies
the other. It is the structural device that informs a large number of
Victorian novels.

## V

Jane Austen might seem to have little enough in common with Byron,
and yet her influence, like his, is evident in the fashionable novel.
After all, the two share a worldliness that sets them apart from their
contemporaries, a willingness to accept that human nature is best displayed by tracing its social relations, and hence that a dinner party is a
more interesting setting than a mountain-top. Lister pays his own
back-handed tribute to Jane Austen's novels by allowing Lady Harriet
Duncan, a benign caricature of Caroline Lamb, to despise them: 'I hope

you like nothing of Miss Edgeworth's or Miss Austen's. They are full of commonplace people, that one recognizes at once' (*Granby*, 1, 148). In Catherine Gore's *Women As They Are*, Lord Willersdale comes to suspect that his youthful bride might not be the rather glum young woman that she seems when he overhears her laughing over 'a scene of Scribe, or one of Miss Austin's novels' (1, 26), and in her preface to *Pin Money*, Gore describes her novels as an 'attempt to transfer the familiar narrative of Miss Austin to a higher sphere of society'.[31] The influence is clear enough, in the sharp dialogue as well as in the sharply ironic narrative voice of Gore's novels. But in their plots the novels that I turn to now look back not to Jane Austen but to Robert Plumer Ward's *Tremaine*.

The first volume of *Tremaine* traces the afflictions to which the man of refinement makes himself vulnerable. When the novel opens Tremaine is 'approaching the middle of life' (1, 12) and alighting from his carriage with 'a jaded look' (1, 2). As a young man he had wisely deciding that the 'kind of Epicurean notion of the Deity' (1, 12–13) that he had acquired unfitted him for a career in the Church, and he could not bring himself to enter the law because of the vulgar company he would be required to keep. So he enters the army, but this too fails to satisfy him, and after a single campaign he resigns his commission. When he inherits a large estate, he embarks on a political career, but fails in that, too. He decides to retreat to his estate to live a life of scholarly retirement, but after an hour or two of reading he becomes bored. So, in his late thirties, he finds himself without an occupation, and also without a wife. One relationship foundered when, climbing a hill with the young woman, her garter slipped, and revealed itself as 'considerably the worse for wear' (1, 19), another when an apparently respectable young woman turned out to have read *Tom Jones*, and a more serious relationship with a very young woman he had encountered in France, and who had impressed him by her 'delicious naiveté' (1, 28), and her possession of a mind that was 'disposed to be the very echo of his own' (1, 29), fails to survive his discovery that she has entertained a former attachment: 'the virgin heart which had appeared so ready to bless him was no longer virgin' (1, 40). Feeling that he has been 'duped by baby sweetness' (1, 46), he returns to England and cultivates his misogyny, until he meets the daughter of his old college friend, Dr. Evelyn, and finds that 'what the most brilliant females of London and Paris had for years been unable to effect, was once again produced, in a few minutes, by a simple country girl' (1, 153). He survives a tricky moment when she reaches out her hand to shake his before he has offered it, an action that had long been 'almost a crime in his notion of the decencies between the sexes', but she performs the gesture 'in a manner so modest and yet so naïve' that he forgives her (1, 196), and at last proposes, only to be refused on the ground of his religious scepticism. In the second and third volumes of the novel he is tediously won round to proper piety, and is at last accepted.

In *Women As They Are* Catherine Gore takes this plot, but allows us access to the young woman's point of view, and, just as interestingly, focuses less on the courtship than the marriage. The novel begins by distinguishing three kinds of marriage: the 'bon mariage', which 'is generally understood to include the promise of a park in the country, and a mansion in town, a set of horses, a diamond necklace, and an opera box'; an 'excellent match' which 'affords a mere multiplication of these advantages'; and 'the mariage délicieux' which is entered into by the 'etherealized and sentimental' who maintain an 'obstinate prejudice in favour of blue eyes or brown, or the aerial perspective of a damp cottage covered with honeysuckles' (1, 1–3). The marriage of the novel's heroine, Helen Mordaunt, seems to be of the second kind. When she is eighteen she accepts the hand of Lord Willersdale, a Cabinet minister of forty, who had been a confirmed bachelor until, at dinner, his 'obdurate heart was won in the progress of half a cutlet, by a "yes – I believe so," uttered with the sweetest intonation in the world, aided by a rising blush' (1, 11). Before the country house party has broken up, Helen 'had pronounced the monosyllable so insisted on by her friends at large, and so fondly coveted by Willersdale himself' (1, 20), and her parents 'had the gratification of expelling their lovely daughter from her home, in order to secure "a good match" in their family; while one of the most estimable and distinguished members of London society provided himself with the blessing of a reluctant and ill-assorted bride' (1, 22).

Their early married life is predictably miserable. Helen, in attempting to assume the cool and reserved demeanour that she believes her husband expects, impresses him only as cold and unloving, and she is intimidated by the attempts at familiarity of a husband who thought of her as 'a piece of mechanism fashioned by the skill of the governess', and saw it as his husbandly task 'to ascertain the combination of springs and wheels by which its movements were secretly prompted' (1, 23). He retreats into his political business, and she throws herself into the London social scene, indulging in a dangerous flirtation with the rakish Captain Seymour. The marriage is saved only when Willersdale is seriously wounded in a foolish duel with a political opponent and his long convalescence in Ireland gives husband and wife the opportunity to discover each other's true character.

*Lodore* (1835), Mary Shelley's attempt at a fashionable novel, begins with a version of the same plot. As Mary Shelley recognized, *Lodore* represented a new departure for her as a novelist. Her reputation was as a writer of 'wild fictions',[32] but *Lodore* was to be both a thoroughly contemporary novel, 'a tale of the present time' as she described it in her preferred subtitle, and a novel that embraced all the 'dingy-visaged, dirty-handed realities' (200) that had been excluded from her earlier fiction. Foremost amongst these dingy realities is the reality of hard cash, the fact that even those staying in cheap suburban inns must go hungry if they do not have the wherewithal to pay for their dinner. *Lodore*, like her earlier novels, finds room for the 'tortures of passion', but here Shelley is prepared to allow that such tortures are rarely felt by those 'whose situation in life obliges them to earn their daily bread', and are suffered chiefly by the 'rich and great' who find in such tortures convenient 'resources against ennui and satiety' (58).

Shelley is interested in almost all her fiction in the point of contact between inner feeling and material fact, and between the workings of the spirit and the workings of society, but in *Lodore* that interest is expressed differently, and the difference is most easily explained by pointing to the influence of the fashionable novelists such as Disraeli and Catherine Gore, and, most importantly, Bulwer. There was no novelist whose work she read more avidly and looked forward to more eagerly. She asked Ollier to send her a copy of Bulwer's fourth novel, *Devereux* (1829), adding, 'I want it very much'. She was even more emphatic in asking for his sixth, 'Do not forget Eugene Aram – every day earlier that I get it will be a debt of gratitude to you'.[33] But it was the fifth novel that prompted her most emphatic tribute, in the journal entry for January 11, 1831:

> I have been reading with much encreased admiration Paul Clifford – It is a wonderful, a sublime book – What will Bulwer become? the first Author of the age? I do not doubt it – He is a magnificent writer.[34]

It is not surprising, then, that Bulwer's influence is so evident in *Lodore*.[35]

Most importantly, Shelley learned from Bulwer a new mode of characterization, which refused any conventional categorization of characters as either good or evil. This was one of the aspects of Bulwer's work that was most fiercely attacked. The objection is most amusingly formulated by Thackeray in his spoof of *Eugene Aram*, in which he identifies Bulwer as 'the father of a new "lusus naturae school"' of novelists.[36]

Thackeray, posing as Bulwer's grateful disciple, has been taught by *Eugene Aram* how 'to mix vice and virtue up together in such an inextricable confusion as to render it impossible that any preference should be given to either, or that the one, indeed, should be at all distinguishable from the other'. In particular, he has learned from Bulwer a novel technique of characterization that requires, if an adulterer is wanted, to look for him in 'the class of country curates', and 'being in search of a tender-hearted, generous, sentimental, high-minded hero of romance' to find him 'in the lists of men who have cut throats for money'. The position is more temperately stated in the *Edinburgh* in its 1832 composite review of Bulwer's first five novels,[37] but it is recognizably the same. The technique produces characters which seem to the reviewer to result in a 'moral anomaly', most strikingly evident in *Eugene Aram*, in which a notorious eighteenth-century murderer is represented 'in the romantic garb of a refined lover, of an enthusiastic scholar, living quite as much in the ideal as the actual world'. The novel asks us to believe that 'this romantic enthusiast is, after all, a murderer, and for money!' Compare that with the response to *Lodore* of a particularly interested reader, Claire Clairmont:

> Good God to think a person of your genius, whose moral tact ought to be proportionately exalted, should think it a task befitting its powers to gild and embellish and pass off as beautiful what was the merest compound of Vanity, folly, and every miserable weakness...[38]

Claire Clairmont was, of course, an interested witness in both senses – she believed, surely mistakenly, that the plot of *Lodore*, in which an infant daughter is removed from the mother by the father, alluded to her own and Allegra's treatment at the hands of Byron[39] – but her personal interest does not blunt her critical perception. For her, Shelley's Lord Lodore represented exactly the kind of moral anomaly that the *Edinburgh* found so distinctive of Bulwer's fiction, and she is surely right.

But again caution is needed, because both Thackeray and the *Edinburgh* reviewer are conscious that the construction of characters who embody moral anomalies is a characteristic of Bulwer's fiction that reveals its indebtedness to the Godwinian novel. 'Eugene Aram', Thackeray recognizes, 'has certainly many qualities in common with the Anglo-German style of Mr. Godwin's followers'. The *Edinburgh* insists on a distinction between Aram who murders for money, and a 'Falkland, goaded into assassination by a brutal and irreparable outrage to his honour, yet retaining his native chivalry of soul, his lofty demeanour and tenderness of heart'. But even this admits the kinship, and it is not clear how Falkland's chivalry can remain unbesmirched by his willingness to allow the Hawkinses, both father and son, to be executed for the crime that he had committed. In Falkland, in Victor Frankenstein, and in Beatrice Cenci, Godwin and his followers had shown their interest in producing characters designed to induce in their readers a 'restless and anatomizing casuistry'.[40] Bulwer's originality lies less in the nature of his characters than in that of the prose through which they are represented, and it is in its prose that *Lodore* most clearly reveals Bulwer's influence.

The prose of *Lodore* is very often marked by a pointed, unillusioned wit quite unlike anything to be found in the earlier novels. For example, on the death of his father Lodore returns to England and is prevailed upon by his devoted sister, Elizabeth, to stay on for a few weeks after the funeral before going back to his Continental mistress. As a consequence,

> Elizabeth had the happiness of seeing the top of his head as he leant over the desk in his library, from a little hillock in the garden, which she sought for the purpose of beholding that blessed vision.
>
> (34)

Or there is Lodore justifying to himself his decision to remove his daughter from her mother. He begins by reviewing 'impartially' the failings of his wife and mother-in-law, the mother-in-law's 'worldliness', the wife's 'frivolity and unfeeling nature', until 'almost against his will, his own many excellencies rose before him; – his lofty aspirations, his self-sacrifice for the good of others, the affectionateness of his disposition' (62). Just occasionally this prose manner is lent by the narrator to one of her characters, as for instance when Lord Lodore is trying to explain to his wife that he must flee the country immediately or be obliged to fight a duel against his own natural son. Lodore makes his confession, but couched in a declamatory sentimental rhetoric that effectively obscures all significant facts, and properly merits Lady Lodore's response, 'This sounds very like a German tragedy, being at once disagreeable and inexplicable' (56). But it would be hard to claim that Shelley writes this kind of prose as well as Disraeli or Bulwer or Catherine Gore.

More interesting are those passages in which two styles, the sentimental, and what I shall call, for want of a better term, the styptic, are brought together, to produce a prose that tends both towards the antithetical and the oxymoronic. A simple example is the sentence that

Mrs. Elizabeth's certainty that she is irredeemably wicked, to Ethel's husband's judgement that she is 'a worshipper of the world, a frivolous, unfeeling woman' (255), to the response of Horatio Saville, who is Edward's cousin and best friend, and is inspired by Lady Lodore to a lifelong devotion. Lodore's unhappy marriage is paralleled in the novel by the marriage of his old schoolfriend, Derham, and the characterization of Derham's wife, though much slighter than Lady Lodore's, is produced by the same principle. Lodore first hears of her in America, just before his death, when he learns from an Englishwoman that Derham has been rejected by his family because of a 'mès-alliance': he had married an 'unequal partner' who was 'illiterate and vulgar – coarse-minded, though good-natured' (78). The thought that his old friend is bound to such a woman fills Lodore with a tender sadness. It is not until much later in the novel that we meet Mrs. Derham, when Ethel takes lodgings with her in London, and she emerges as a kind, motherly woman with much practical good sense, 'a little, plump, well-preserved woman of fifty' (195), and a woman of whom her daughter Fanny can say, 'My mother...is the kindest-hearted woman in the world' (212).

The most complete characterization of this kind is of Lord Lodore. Lodore's courtship of Cornelia, and the history of their married life together is narrated in a style in which the styptic predominates. He returns to England at the age of thirty-two suffering, like Tremaine and Lord Willersdale before him, from a 'palled appetite'. Having tired of his mistress and apparently uninterested in his son by her, he becomes convinced that all is 'vanity' (37), and, feeling haughtily misanthropic, he retires to Wales. There he first meets Cornelia. She is just fifteen, and he sees her as 'a vision of white muslin' (37). Her extreme youth and the material of her frock prove a potent combination for Lodore, whose favourite metaphor for his 'ideal of a wife' is 'white paper to be written on at will' (41). Lodore's relationships with women have hitherto been complicated by the fact that he nurtured a high 'ideal of what he thought a woman ought to be', without much liking any of the women that he met: 'he had no high opinion of woman as he had usually found her' (45). This proves no barrier to his courtship of Cornelia, because he takes the precaution of not speaking to her much. They 'conversed little' (41) before he proposes. On his marriage he transports his wife and her mother to London, and introduces them to his own fashionable circles, only to find that his wife develops an irritating liking for evening parties, and that he cordially detests his mother-in-law. Cornelia, just turned seventeen, gives birth to a daughter, and Lodore is outraged by her failure to display proper maternal feelings.

He introduces her to his ex-mistress, and is rendered insanely jealous by the friendship that develops between his wife and his natural son, who is entirely ignorant that Lodore is his father. He insults the young man, strikes him, and is forced to flee abroad to escape the charge of cowardice that would result if he refused his son's challenge. He offers his wife the chance to join him in his exile, stipulating only that she must sever all relationship with her own mother, and, when she refuses, spirits her infant daughter from their house and emigrates with her to America, convinced in his own mind that he is motivated solely by a tender concern for the welfare of his child.

And yet, framing this acerbic novella, is the account of the years that father and daughter spend in the wilds of Illinois, an almost wholly sentimental narrative in which Lodore finds fulfilment in tenderly nurturing his child and comes to embody for Ethel an ideal of manhood that can only be supplemented, not effaced, by the man she eventually marries. There is no attempt to articulate a relationship between the two narratives, by, for example, representing the years in America as assisting Lodore in a passage towards self-knowledge. To the very last he remains as convinced that he has been ill-treated by his wife, as is Cornelia that she has been cruelly used by him. Nor is he morally transformed. He dies in a duel which he had himself provoked, the desire to recover his reputation as a man of honour more precious to him than his responsibility to a fifteen-year-old daughter separated by two thousand miles from her kindred. Lodore remains to the end a man who properly merits Saville's revulsion at 'the inexcusable cruelty of his conduct' (120), and yet he is also and equally the refined and tender father who merits his daughter's exalted and idealizing love.

In *Lodore* Shelley produces her most extreme version of the kind of character that Bulwer invented, the character that embodies, as the *Edinburgh* reviewer put it, a 'moral anomaly', and in doing so she escaped, like Bulwer, from one of the more inhibiting conventional constraints of the novel, its placing of its characters within a single hierarchy of moral judgement. We are not asked to choose whether Lodore is a cruel or a loving man, high-minded or self-deceived, but to accept that he is all these things, and that it is in the acceptance of such anomalies that we are brought into a proper confrontation with the 'singular machinery' of human nature in which 'contradictions' may 'accord' (98).

I have already suggested that Bulwer's fiction marks a significant point in the development of the Victorian novel, but in one respect Shelley is the more prescient of the two. She recognizes that the new technique opens a new subject matter for the novel: it allows the novel of courtship, in the 1830s still the commonest of all kinds of novel, to develop into the kind of novel practised by the great Victorians, the novel of marriage, and more particularly, of unhappy marriage. *Lodore* is importantly a marriage novel, a novel which places at its centre not political, but 'domestic revolutions' (119). The courtship of Ethel and Villiers is only a necessary prelude to the account of their married life together, and the history of their relationship, though central, functions only to bind together the more vivid accounts of other marriages, of the Derhams, of Saville and Clorinda, and most importantly of Lord and Lady Lodore. The hybrid style lends itself to the marriage novel in part because marriage is itself a hybrid, both a sentimental state, and an institution that is embedded in social and economic practices. Ethel and Edward are all in all to each other, finding each the only happiness in the other's arms, so much so that when they set up house in London, 'they were always satisfied with one or two parties in the evening. Nay, once or twice in the week they usually remained at home' (176). It is a style, then, that can accommodate marriage in both its aspects. But, much more importantly, it is a style that can accommodate contradictory perspectives, and hence can admit the truth that only happy marriages admit stable description, for the reality of a marriage is only constituted by the manner in which the marriage is experienced by the two people joined in it, and in an unhappy marriage the experience of the two people will be, of necessity, inconsistent and incommensurate. The Lodores' marriage is not either a relationship in which the man suffers his conjunction with an unfeeling, worldly woman, or a relationship in which a woman suffers the tyrannical abuse of her husband, but both of these, for every unhappy marriage is, as Shelley would say, a 'strange riddle' in which 'contradictions accord'.

Finally, Shelley found in Bulwer's kind of novel the possibility of a new authorial stance, a manner of surveying people and their doings sharply different from anything to be found in her mother's work, or her father's, or her husband's. Take, for example, the elaborate comparison between Ethel's and Fanny Derham's upbringing (217–19). Both have been educated exclusively by their fathers. Lodore offers Ethel very much the kind of education that Rousseau gave to Sophie. Hers is, we are told, 'a sexual education': her father moulds her into conformity with 'his ideal of what a woman ought to be', that is, 'yielding', devoted to her male protector, and obedient. Fanny, on the other hand, is educated to be 'complete in herself', 'independent and self-sufficing'. There is very little doubt as to which educational system

Shelley prefers – she remains her mother's daughter – but she restrains herself from pressing her preference. We are allowed to smile at Ethel's inability to understand money, and her utter reliance on her father and her husband, but we smile, too, at the 'platonic notions of the supremacy of mind' (284) that Fanny has imbibed from her father. Shelley is content to admire both women, despite the difference of their education, and despite the very different personalities that their education has produced, with a kind of amused equanimity.

In *Lodore* Shelley develops a narrative manner that is always alert to difference, always sharp in its discriminations, but reluctant to pass final judgement. Her development of Bulwer's fictional manner issues in the end in a large and calm tolerance, which is the more persuasive because it is arrived at not by ignoring but by examining the human capacity for self-deception, for inconsistency, and most of all by recognizing the irremediable egotism that for all of us makes 'the ideas of our own minds … more forcibly present, than any notions we can form of the feelings of others' (129). This is not much like Mary Wollstonecraft, or Godwin, or Percy Shelley, but it does prefigure the work of another writer. In *Lodore* Shelley can sound oddly like George Eliot. Both writers interrogate the metaphor by which a just perception of the real is compared to a mirror's faithful reflection, George Eliot by offering in Chapter 27 of *Middlemarch* the 'parable' in which the random scratches in a mirror are arranged by a lighted candle into 'the flattering illusion of a concentric arrangement', and Shelley by pointing out that no mirror is true, that no two mirrors are alike, and that all mirrors, like prisms, refract the light that they reflect:

> Our several minds, in reflecting to our judgements the occurrences of life, are like mirrors of various shapes and hues, so that we none of us perceive passing objects with exactly similar optics.
>
> (L 62)

In Chapter 5 of *Amos Barton* George Eliot turns to confront the reader who finds her central character 'palpably and unmistakably commonplace', and Shelley anticipates her by rebuking those who would rather 'embark on the wild ocean of romance' than suffer the novelist 'to describe scenes of common-place and debasing interest' (201–2), but the commitment of both novelists to 'dingy-visaged, dirty-handed realities' is moderated by a lingering attachment to the ideal. Shelley trusts to the 'youth and feminine tenderness' of her heroine, Ethel, to irradiate the coarse realties of her poverty by shedding 'light and holiness around her', and Amos's wife, Milly, performs an exactly similar function in *Amos Barton*. It is the compromise that George Eliot announces in her review of Goethe's *Wilhelm Meister*, in which she insists that the right of the novelist to treat 'every aspect of human life' has its 'legitimate limits', and that only those truths are fit to be represented that are redeemed by the presence of 'some twist of love, or endurance, or helplessness to call forth our best sympathies'.[41] These resemblances are not accidental, nor simply the result of a shared interest of the kind that might prompt one to compare the final paragraphs of *Valperga* and *Middlemarch*, which both end with an elegy for a heroic woman whose name has escaped public record. In *Lodore* Mary Shelley is already moving towards a narrative stance that aspires to a wise, restrained disinterestedness. A willingness to recognize that such disinterestedness is difficult of attainment and that most of us see the world refracted through the prism of our own egotism, and a commitment to realism that is always tempered by a sentimental attachment to the ideal are the distinguishing characteristics of one kind of Victorian novel, the kind of which George Eliot is the most accomplished practitioner. The fashionable novels of the 1830s are no longer much read, and yet they have at least a historical importance. It is through them that we can most easily trace a line that joins Byron and Jane Austen with the major Victorian novelists, with Dickens and with George Eliot.

My first four chapters have been linked by a shared concern with genre. I have tried to describe the generic innovations that seem to me most characteristic of the period from 1824 to 1840. I end this section with the fashionable novel both because it is the genre that best defines the period, and because it exposes with peculiar clarity the manner in which a literary history that focuses on questions of genre demands an attention to the question of how literary works were produced and consumed. But even generic history cannot evade questions of content. The marriage novel, for example, may be the product of particular prose mannerisms and a particular narrative mode, but it is also a kind of novel distinguished by a particular subject matter. In the second half of the book I will turn directly to content. I will ask what it was that writers in this period chose to write about. Or rather, I will take the four topics that are conventionally thought of as preoccupying writers in the Romantic period, and ask how their successors treated them differently. First I will consider politics, then landscape, then religion, and then sex.

# 5
# Civilizing Romanticism

## I

In the space of a few years, from the late 1820s, a series of events changed, and changed radically, the relationship of the citizen to the state. The London University was founded in 1826 (students were first admitted two years later). Before then, there were only two English universities, both of them closed to students who were not members of the Church of England.[1] Robert Browning, for example, was brought up as a non-conformist, but in 1828 he was able to attend courses at the new university. In the same year the Test and Corporation Acts were repealed, extending full civil rights to Dissenters, and in 1829 the Catholic Relief Bill carried Catholic emancipation. Finally, in 1832 the Great Reform Act was passed, increasing from roughly 5 to roughly 10 per cent the proportion of adult males entitled to vote in Parliamentary elections. It is the last of these events that was best remembered. George Eliot, for example, chose the period of agitation leading up to the Bill as the setting for both *Felix Holt* (1866) and *Middlemarch* (1871–2). Although *Felix Holt*, in particular, seems implicitly concerned with the debate preceding the Reform Act of 1867, the fact that the novel is set in the early 1830s in itself registers George Eliot's recognition that the formation of the idea that both novels explore had its origin in the earlier period. It was an idea of which the four events I have described were both a cause and an effect, the idea that membership of civil society at once conferred rights and imposed duties, the idea, in short, of citizenship.

In March, 1845, Aubrey de Vere visited Wordsworth at Rydal Mount, and read to him two of Tennyson's poems, 'You ask me why, though ill at ease', and 'Of old sat Freedom on the heights'. Wordsworth listened with 'a gradually deepening attention, and 'after a pause he answered,

"I must acknowledge that these two poems are very solid and noble in thought. Their diction also seems singularly stately"'.[2] In 1833 Tennyson had written a group of poems inspired by the 'civic Muse' ('Hail Britons!', 169).[3] They are poems in which he accommodates the Reform Bill within a Burkean vision of a land:

> Where Freedom slowly broadens down
> From precedent to precedent.
> ('You ask me, why,
> though ill at ease', 11–12)

But, as Wordsworth would have recognized, it is a Burkean vision refracted through Coleridge.

At Rydal Mount, it seems, De Vere witnessed a graceful gesture in which Wordsworth recognized Tennyson as the poet who was to succeed him not only as Laureate, but as the spokesman for a distinctively English ideal of citizenship. But, in fact, the word 'citizen' was, throughout the years in which Wordsworth wrote his greatest poetry, tainted for him, a translation of a French term, '*citoyen(ne)*', the dead hollowness of which struck him with an intensity precisely proportionate to the thrilling resonance that it had once possessed. In the sonnet, 'Jones! as from Calais southward you and I', he recalls, as he walks the same road, the tour of France that he had undertaken with his college friend, Robert Jones, in the summer of 1790. But, in 1802, during the brief interruption of the war between Britain and France, he is conscious only of the difference:

> And now, sole register that these things were,
> Two solitary greetings have I heard,
> 'Good morrow, Citizen!' a hollow word,
> As if a dead man spake it!'
> ('Composed near Calais,
> on the Road to Ardres, August 7, 1802)

From 1798 both Wordsworth and Coleridge were concerned to rescue the ideal of freedom by releasing it from any connection with the idea of citizenship. Coleridge's 'France: an Ode' may end with an address to Liberty, but it is a liberty that is discovered in a solitary communion with the natural world, not in a new political dispensation:

> Thou speedest on thy subtle pinions,
> The guide of homeless winds, and playmate of the waves!

And there I felt thee! – on that sea-cliff's verge'
   Whose pines, scarce travelled by the breeze above,
Had made one murmur with the distant surge!
Yes, while I stood and gazed, my temples bare,
And shot my being through earth, sea and air,
   Possessing all things with intensest love.
O Liberty! My spirit felt thee there.

                                              (97–105)

One understands the puzzlement of a reviewer: 'What does Mr. Coleridge mean by liberty in this passage? or what connection has it with the subject of civil freedom?'.[4]

In the war years the idea of citizenship was usurped, as one would expect, by the idea of patriotism. Scott's minstrel asserts his devotion to his 'own his native land' quite independently of the political settlement that obtains there, and the Spanish in Wordsworth's *The Convention of Cintra* fight heroically not for a constitution but for Spain. Indeed, it seemed to both men in these years that interest in the constitution was itself unpatriotic, an expression of the diseased mania for constitution-making that characterized the French. The second generation of Romantics disowned the politics of their predecessors, but were unable to recover the ideal of citizenship that Blake, Wordsworth, Southey and Coleridge had shared in their youth. In *Childe Harold* Byron instituted the manner that was to dominate the immediate post-war years, a manner that offered as the one guarantee of an individual's authenticity his withdrawal from civil society. Shelley, more than any of his contemporaries, tried to retain a communal ideal, 'Man, oh, not men! a chain of linked thought' (*Prometheus Unbound*, IV, 394), and in a few poems, notably *The Mask of Anarchy*, he went some way towards imagining the kind of political reform that such a notion would necessitate, but, as Shelley reveals in his unfinished essay 'A Philosophical View of Reform', he had no clear view as to how such a reform might be brought about.[5]

The founding of a secular university, the repeal of the Test and Corporation Acts, the granting of Catholic emancipation, and the very limited electoral reform accepted in the Bill of 1832 worked together to resuscitate the idea of citizenship, which became, in very different ways, a key concern of all three of the most important early Victorian poets, Tennyson, Elizabeth Barrett Browning, and Robert Browning. It is best to start with Tennyson, whose closest friend, Arthur Hallam, organized the petition signed by Oxford men who opposed the passage of the Reform Bill, and witnessed the opening of the first reformed Parliament in 1832 with deep foreboding: 'Yesterday I saw (perhaps) the last king of England go down to open the first assembly of delegates from a sovereign people'.[6]

It was a foreboding that Hallam shared with Coleridge, not by coincidence, but because by 1832 Hallam's political views were closely modelled on Coleridge's as he had expressed them in his last publication, *Of the Constitution of Church and State* (1830), a book that is plainly written, despite Coleridge's characteristic shufflings, against the repeal of the Test and Corporation Acts, against Catholic emancipation, against the cause of Parliamentary reform, and against the foundation of the University of London. The last position may seem particularly odd in a book that lays such stress on the importance of education, but it follows directly from Coleridge's recognition that the University of London was established under the auspices of utilitarian thought. As a utilitarian institution, the university was dedicated not to 'education', but to 'instruction'. Coleridge's distinction became famous, but in *On the Constitution of Church and State* it serves a polemical purpose, identifying the University of London as the first of what he fears will be a growing number of institutions which are properly 'lecture-bazaars' masquerading 'under the absurd name of universities' (69). Dissenters and Catholics should not be accorded full civil rights because they do not recognize the King as the head of the national church, and Catholics should additionally be excluded because they recognize the authority of a foreign sovereign, the Pope. Coleridge does present a powerful argument in favour of Parliamentary reform. The health of the constitution depends on the maintenance of a proper balance between the force of 'permanence', which Coleridge locates in the landed interest, and the force of 'progression' that he locates in the manufacturing, trading and professional classes. That balance has been lost because of the undue preponderance in both Houses of Parliament of the landed interest, and hence of the resistance to change that the landed interest quite properly offers. Parliamentary reform is necessary, it seems, to redress the balance, until Coleridge goes on to argue that, in fact, the proper balance has been preserved by the growing importance of a new extra-parliamentary power that naturally lends itself to progression, the power of public opinion.

It seems only irritating, in the manner so characteristic of Coleridge, that he should preface his outright attack on the Catholic Relief Bill of 1829 by asking, 'is it true that I am unfriendly to, what is called, Catholic Emancipation?', and answering emphatically, 'No! the contrary is the truth' (6). But, however irritating, it is a manoeuvre somehow appropriate in a book that, despite its hostility to all the measures that co-operated to invest the idea of citizenship with a new power at precisely this time, still contrives to celebrate the civic ideal. Much of the book is concerned with the explication of the proper function of the 'national church' and its 'clerisy'. The 'clerisy' comprehends 'the learned of all denominations', but in particular parsons, schoolteachers and dons, and its crucial task is 'national education'. The clerisy embodies 'the shaping, and informing spirit, which *educing*, i.e. eliciting, the latent *man* in all the natives of the soil, *trains them up* to be citizens of the country, free subjects of the realm' (48). Surprising as it may seem given the bent of its arguments, *Of the Constitution of Church and State* is the book in which Coleridge at last frees the word, citizen, from the hollow ring that it had produced for him ever since 1798, and allows it to stand once again as the word that best expresses man in his proper condition as a member of the social order.

## II

By 1832 Hallam could glumly witness the state opening of the reformed Parliament without losing his faith in the idea of citizenship because he had read his Coleridge, but to understand fully his emotions it is necessary to give some account of the curious shifts that had marked his and Tennyson's political allegiances in recent years. The two men, although they were both undergraduates at Trinity, do not seem to have met until the spring of 1829, at about the same time that Hallam joined the exclusive Cambridge society known as the Apostles. Tennyson himself did not join until October, and his membership lasted only four months. He resigned on 13 February, 1820, after failing to fulfil the obligation that all members should read a paper to the society, but until he left Cambridge he continued to attend meetings informally. By the time that Hallam and Tennyson joined it, the character of the society was decisively marked by the influence of two former members, F.D. Maurice and John Sterling. Both had left Cambridge for London in 1827, and had become co-editors of the *Athenaeum*, but they retained close contacts there. Hallam wrote reverentially of Maurice to Gladstone, a close friend from Eton:

> I do not myself know Maurice, but I know well many whom he has known, and whom he has moulded like a second Nature, and these too men eminent for intellectual power, to whom the presence of a

commanding spirit would in all other cases be a signal rather for rivalry than reverential acknowledgement. The effect which he has produced on the mind of many at Cambridge by the single creation of that society, the Apostles (for the spirit thought not the form was created by him) is far greater than I dare to calculate, and will be felt both directly and indirectly in the age that is before us.[7]

One of the effects that Maurice had on the minds of many at Cambridge was to re-direct their literary taste. In a series of articles that appeared in the *Athenaeum* from 16 January to 30 July 1828, Maurice offered a rather full survey of contemporary letters, including essays on Jeffrey, Southey, Cobbett, Wordsworth, Moore, Brougham, Shelley, Scott, Mackintosh, Maria Edgeworth, Byron, James Mill, and Crabbe. His literary principles clearly owe much to Coleridge, but they are distinctively developed. First, literature is important for its effect: its value depends on whether its influence be 'for good or for evil'.[8] Scott, for example, falls below the first rank of writers because 'his works do scarcely anything towards making men wiser or better' (218). This might seem to indicate a utilitarian bent in Maurice, but, in fact, nothing is more consistent in these essays than their hostility to utilitarianism. Jeffrey is castigated for having 'recourse for the elements of human virtue...to subtle calculations of consequences' (49). The public life of Sir James Mackintosh, a man of right impulse, has not added to the common good, because his 'philosophy' is at odds with his 'benevolence': he remains 'one of the "Utilitarians"' (249–50). Maurice's concern for effect is distinguished from the depraved utilitarian habit of calculating consequences by his emphasis on the internal. Wordsworth's genius is to redeem us from 'the actual and outward' (114). Shelley teaches us that we must look for improvement not to 'outward circumstances' but to our 'inward powers' (194). But it would be quite wrong to suppose from this that Maurice was inattentive to social evils:

> We make speeches in favour of steam-engines and commercial competition, for without these sources of happiness and virtue, where shall we get our comforts and splendours? But we shut our ears to the gasping of decrepit children in the stifling atmosphere of cotton-mills, and turn away with carelessness from the flood of debasement and misery which rolls along our streets, and overflows into our prisons.
>
> (218)

Poets such as Wordsworth by addressing the 'inward being' open our ears to the wheezing of the children in the cotton mills. Maurice admires 'general and good-humoured benevolence' (218, of Scott) wherever he finds it. Southey's opinions are no more to his taste than Scott's, but still he admires in the poetry its 'feeling of brotherhood with all mankind' (64). Cobbett seems to him a man given up to political hatreds, and yet he must be allowed 'one great merit' – 'the strongest feeling for the welfare of the people' (98). The antithesis of benevolence is selfishness, a quality that the utilitarians accepted as the one efficient motive of all human behaviour. Its chief literary exemplar is Byron, whose concern is always to 'wrap himself up in his own selfishness', and whose poetry encourages a similar disposition in his readers (351–2).

The essays include the elements of what will become Maurice's Christian Socialism, but these elements are as yet scarcely harmonized. He attempts to maintain a liberal politics, a politics committed to social reform, while repudiating in its entirety the system of thought, empirical and utilitarian, that gave liberalism its intellectual basis. The rather odd result is this series of essays from which the two great heroes of modern letters emerge as Wordsworth and Shelley. Maurice wants a liberalism grounded on a direct appeal to the human heart. He recognizes Wordsworth as the great contemporary exponent of such appeals, the poet who, more powerfully than any other, makes us feel that 'we have all of us one human heart', but he could scarcely claim that Wordsworth had for the past decade put this perception to the service of a liberal politics. Wordsworth, then, had to be supplemented by Shelley, and the evident enough differences between the two poets suppressed or denied.

The Apostles' other chief mentor, John Sterling, has left no equivalent account of his literary creed, but, like Maurice, he admired both Wordsworth and Shelley. Unlike Maurice, he had been a youthful Cambridge radical. Monckton Milnes first encountered him at a Union debate on Catholic emancipation, and recalled that 'a Mr Sterling told us we were going to have a revolution, and he didn't care if his hand should be the first to lead the way'.[9] But almost as soon as he left Cambridge in 1828 his opinions began to change. He fell increasingly under the influence of Coleridge, whom he visited regularly. It was a time when, according to Carlyle, his democratic radicalism co-existed uneasily with the pious transcendentalism – or, as Carlyle terms it, 'transcendental moonshine' – that he was imbibing at Highgate.[10] At this time the coupling of Wordsworth and Shelley must have served much the same purpose for him that it did for Maurice: it was a means by which he held together his discordant ideals. Sterling and Maurice together inspired the Apostles of Hallam and Tennyson's generation with an enthusiasm for Shelley and Wordsworth not so much as two very different poets but as one imaginary compound poet, a chimera invented by Maurice and Sterling as necessary to their own imaginative requirements.

Late in his life, Monckton Milnes used to tell the story of how he had obtained the *exeat* for himself and his Apostolic friends to travel to Oxford and speak to the proposition that Shelley was a greater poet than Byron by allowing the Master of Trinity, Christopher Wordsworth, to gather the impression that the Cambridge men were to speak on behalf of his brother.[11] If he had substituted the name of Wordsworth for that of Shelley it would have been an understandable slip. At the Cambridge Union the Apostles instigated debates about the merits of both, and seem to have thought of the two debates as successive stages in a single campaign. A letter from Hallam, visiting Scotland, to Milnes is revealing: 'I tried to convert the nicest woman on earth to Wordsworth and failed. En revanche, I made a convert to Shelley on the Glasgow steamboat, and presented him with a copy of Adonais as a badge of proselytism'.[12]

The most direct result of this conflation was the composition of a number of poems in which the influences of Wordsworth and Shelley rather uncomfortably jostle against one another. Hallam's entry for the Chancellor's Gold Medal, which was won by Tennyson, is a typical example. The poem has an epigraph from Wordsworth's 'Yarrow Unvisited', and, of many Wordsworthian echoes, Hallam acknowledges a line borrowed from 'Tintern Abbey'. The poem echoes Shelley just as often, acknowledging a quotation from *Alastor*. But it is not just in his diction that Hallam owns two masters. He sometimes presents Timbuctoo as a Shelleyan kingdom of the just, like, say, the Temple of the Spirit in *The Revolt of Islam*. At these moments its function is to sustain faith in the ideal even when the ideal seems to have been obliterated from the actual world. The character of Hallam's lost kingdom seems equally Shelleyan:

> Methought I saw a nation which did heark
> To Justice and to truth: their ways were strait,
> And the dread shadow, Tyranny, did lurk
> Nowhere about them: not to scorn or hate
> A living thing was their sweet nature's bond:
> So every soul moved free in kingly state.
> (*Timbuctoo*, 148–53)[13]

Whenever he represents his ideal country 'decked in the bright colours of the thing to be', Hallam is Shelley's disciple. But the discovery of the lost city also figures for Hallam the contradictory and characteristically Wordsworthian truth that disillusion inevitably terminates all dreams of an ideal world, which is why he chose as its epigraph lines in which Wordsworth wryly acknowledges that Yarrow can remain a type of ideal beauty only for so long as he neglects to visit it. Of several similar poems by Tennyson the most revealing is 'The Poet'. The Shelleyan character of the poem has been widely recognized,[14] and seems unmistakable. The poet awakens 'Freedom', and when he does so 'rites and forms before his burning eyes / Melted like snow' (36–40). But Tennyson's Freedom has a fiery word inscribed on her hem,[15] 'Wisdom', and this is the quality in which, the Apostles followed Maurice in believing, Wordsworth was pre-eminent amongst all modern poets. The word establishes Tennyson's poet as the familiar compound ghost who seems to haunt all Apostolic poems of this period.

Richard Chenevix Trench was the most thoroughgoing Wordsworthian amongst the Apostolic poets, but it is in a poem by Trench, 'Atlantis', first published by Maurice and Sterling in the *Athenaeum* in April, 1829, that Shelley is most fully liberated from the Wordsworthian monitor that tempers his influence in more characteristic Apostolic poems.[16] Atlantis, like Hallam's Timbuctoo, is a lost utopia, and in the poem it is summoned to appear again. The poem is transparently Shelleyan, in its stanza form, which derives from lyrics in *Prometheus Unbound*, Act IV, in its diction, and in its sentiment. It ends:

> Oh, appear! appear!
> Not as when with spear
> Thou didst rule to the broad Egean,
> But in love's own might,
> And in Freedom's right,
> Till the nations uplift their paean,
>
> Who now watch and weep,
> And their vigil keep,
> Till they faint for expectation;
> Till their dim eyes shape
> Temple, tower, and cape,
> From the cloud and the exhalation.

The watchers keeping their vigil would have been easily identified by readers of the *Athenaeum*. For some years a steady trickle of Spanish refugees had been arriving in Britain in flight from Spain's Bourbon monarch, Ferdinand. Early in 1829 Maurice and Sterling had begun a campaign in the *Athenaeum*, which eventually won the support of *The Times*, to secure private and public funds for the relief of the refugees. Trench's poem is the earliest evidence of the Apostles' interest in the Spanish cause. Its publication marks the beginning of an episode in which their admiration of Shelley led the Apostles to extend their activities from the writing of Shelleyan poems to active participation in revolutionary politics.

The leader of the refugee Spanish liberals in London was General Torrijos, and Sterling became his chief English agent in a plot to overthrow Ferdinand and restore the liberal constitution of 1814. On his restoration to the throne Ferdinand had pledged to retain the existing constitution, but in 1823, as soon as he felt himself strong enough, he reneged on his promise, and invested himself with absolute powers. The Constitutionalists were forced into exile. By July 1830 Torrijos was at Gibraltar preparing to lead an invasion of the Spanish mainland. Trench, together with John Kemble, a fellow-Apostle, son of the great actor and sister of Fanny Kemble, and Robert Boyd, a cousin of Sterling's, who had used his whole fortune to finance the expedition, was with him. Tennyson and Hallam were on their way to the Pyrenees with money and despatches for another Constitutionalist leader, General Ojeda, who was to time his march from the North to coincide with Torrijos's attack from the South.

Hallam and Tennyson were back in England by September, Hallam still bubbling with excitement at his exploit. He scarcely concealed his irritation with Tennyson's brother, Charles, for being so little impressed by his adventure, and he complained that his father did 'not seem to understand that after helping to revolutionise kingdoms, one is still less inclined to trouble one's head about scholarships, degrees, and such gear'. He gives the continental news like an old hand at international agitation: 'Twas a very pretty little revolution in Saxony, and a respectable one at Brunswick'. Even in November he was still excited enough to strike uncharacteristically juvenile postures. He wondered whether a letter to his fellow-Apostle William Bodham Donne would find him at home: 'indeed in these days the presumption is always in favour of one's friends being far away, sucked into the race of some revolutionary Maelstrom'. [17]

As Hallam wrote this letter, Trench and Kemble were still in Gibraltar, intent on taking their part with Torrijos in an armed insurrection that they already recognized was bound to fail. They were far from sharing Hallam's theatrical enthusiasm. In fact, they were expecting to die. Trench was acting out the final stanza of 'Atlantis', his days spent gazing across at the Spanish mainland, looking for the beacon that was to signal that Torrijos's supporters had secured a landing place for the invasion force. The experience is recorded, or, if Trench's dating is to be believed, anticipated, in one of the two sonnets he addressed to 'The Constitutional Exiles of 1827':

> Like nightly watchers from a palace tower,
> In love and faith and patience strong to wait
> The beacon on the hills, which should relate
> How some fenced city of deceit and power
> Had fallen – ye have stood for many an hour,
> Till your first hope's high movements must be dead.[18]

Twice, Kemble and Trench set sail with Torrijos for the short voyage to the mainland. On the second occasion they succeeded in landing near Algerciras but were met by Government forces and withdrew. In February, 1831, Trench finally accepted that the cause was hopeless, and left for England. In May, Kemble followed him. Robert Boyd, who had sunk his whole fortune in the enterprise, stayed on. He had nothing to come home to. It was not until late November that Torrijos finally made his suicidal attempt. He landed near Malaga with 52 followers. No-one rallied to his cause. He was surrounded, he surrendered, and on December 11, 1831, all 49 insurrectionaries (four of those who landed with Torrijos seem to have been government spies), including Torrijos and Boyd, were executed by firing squad. The news reached England early in 1832. Sterling felt to the full his responsibility for 'the miserable event which has terminated the career of my friend Torrijos and my victim Boyd'. He added: 'I hear the sound of that musketry: it is as if the bullets were tearing my brain'.[19] Sterling's friends understood that for the rest of his life the matter was never to be mentioned before him.

The story is well enough known.[20] Carlyle's account remains the best, because Carlyle is more acutely aware than other commentators of the oddity of it all. Sterling was seized by his revolutionary enthusiasm not when it might have been expected, when he was a fiery young radical, but when his radicalism was all but spent, when he had given up Bentham for Coleridge, and was about to give up politics for religion. It was, as Carlyle puts it, 'while Radicalism was tottering for him and threatening to crumble', destabilized by the doses of 'Coleridgean moonshine' in which Sterling was bathing, that there 'came suddenly the grand consummation and explosion of Radicalism in his life;

whereby, all at once, Radicalism exhausted and ended itself, and appeared no more there'.[21] Kemble's case was similar. His youthful radicalism was underpinned by his utilitarianism, to which he clung, or so it seemed to Trench, with perverse stubbornness. He went to Gibraltar only after he had given it up.[22] The cases of Trench, Tennyson, and Hallam are even odder, for the political journey they were making from 1828 to 1832 was not a journey away from a fiery radicalism but from an enthusiastic but moderate liberalism towards a conservative distrust of any but the most gradual change. They were revolutionaries for three months in the summer and autumn of 1830, and their opinions in these months have scarcely any relation with their opinions either before or afterwards.

Hallam's letter to Trench of December 2, 1830 begins by sensibly advising Trench to come home. He still describes the Spanish Venture as 'the noble cause', but when he turns to speak of the condition of England the lack of any connection between his waning enthusiasm for revolution in Spain and his thoughts on English politics becomes startlingly apparent. It was the time of Captain Swing and the rick-burnings and of agitation for Parliamentary reform. Hallam trusts to the 'intelligent part of the community' and to energetic ministerial action to avert the danger of revolution.[23] Trench's case is just as remarkable. In 1829 he had shared the Apostolic enthusiasm for Catholic Emancipation but by the early 1830s he had become a convinced defender of the Protestant supremacy in Ireland, an attitude in which he never subsequently wavered – he was to end his life as Archbishop of Dublin, fighting a desperate and losing battle to avert the disestablishment of the Irish church.[24] His letters from Gibraltar show him as at best a strangely unenthusiastic revolutionary, feeling 'neither enthusiasm, nor hope, nor fear, nor exultation', and when he returned to England he had not just become disillusioned, he had changed sides:

> You do not know, you unfortunately, have never been in frequent contact with, the merest *lamina* of humanity, a Southern Liberal, who turns to France and its philosophy and its politics, as Caliban to Trinculo: 'I prithee be my god; thou bearest celestial liquor; let me kiss thy feet.' There is no line short enough to fathom the depth of his shallowness. Far, far superior to him in the dignity of humanity is the Spanish Royalist, who, with all his superstition, possesses two ideas – those of his King and his God.[25]

Within months of their return from Spain the Apostles found again a common cause, but this time 'the good cause', as Hallam calls it,[26] was opposition to the Reform Bill. The Apostles were active in collecting a petition of Oxford men protesting against this dangerously radical measure. Trench was honest enough to acknowledge that the two positions were not entirely consistent. In a letter of December 6, 1831, he wrote, 'To me it seems that the political vantage-ground which we lately occupied must now be abandoned'.[27] Hallam daringly denied any change of political principle. A poem addressed to Tennyson begins:

> Oh, falsely they blaspheme us, honoured friend,
> Who say the faith of liberty is gone
> Out of our bosoms ...[28]

It is true that he and Tennyson are implacable opponents of constitutional reform:

> True, we have leagued to keep a watch and ward
> O'er the deposit of our forefathers,
> The chartered rights, the links of age with age,
> The ancientries of sovereign Parliament,
> And law-created pomp of English Kings.

But still they are devotees of liberty, and the proof is that they side with the Poles in their nationalist revolt against Poland's Russian rulers. Support for the Poles helped him to glide comfortably between two quite different notions of liberty, the one associated with Shelley, the other with Burke.[29]

The idea of nationhood had become central to Apostolic politics, and it was a Burkean idea, filtered, for the Apostles, through Coleridge's *On the Constitution of the Church and State*. Trench defines the new notion eloquently:

> Unless there is something in a country not embraced by the birth and death of the fleeting generation which at any moment may compose it, you may have a horde, you may have a sovereign people, but you cannot have a nation. If it be a nation, it must look before and after. This, as of an individual, is its highest humanity.[30]

Shelley's phrase, 'look before and after' ('To a Skylark, line 86, though Shelley is himself remembering *Hamlet*), preserved like a fossil in the new Burkean landscape of Trench's politics is revealing, for the Apostles were at one in associating those mad months in 1830, months in which as if in an act of collective hallucination they persuaded themselves that they were bold revolutionaries, with Shelley.

Trench is typically forthright. He wrote to Kemble, when they were both safely back in England, and announced his change of opinion: 'I have given over despairing and reading Shelley, and am beginning to acquiesce in things just as they are going on'.[31] Hallam was comically cautious in making the same announcement to Tennyson. Early in 1832 a group of Saint-Simonians arrived in England, and Hallam asked Tennyson what he thought of them: 'The resemblance of their opinions in many points to those of Shelley is very striking: but they are much more practical'. He was not yet ready to share his view that the Saint-Simonians were 'prophets of a false Future, to be built on the annihilation of the Past in the confusion of the Present'.[32] He need not have worried. Tennyson had already identified Saint-Simonism as 'at once a proof of the immense map of evil that is existent in the 19th century and a focus which gathers all its rays'.[33] By the end of 1832, in a letter to Leigh Hunt acknowledging Hunt's gift of a copy of his edition of *The Masque of Anarchy*, Hallam recalled the time when he and his friends had formed themselves into 'a sort of sect, in behalf of [Shelley's] character and genius', but even though he was anxious to persuade Hunt to review Tennyson's new volume, he felt obliged to add that he had since 'somewhat tempered' his enthusiasm for Shelley 'in so far as it extended to some of his peculiar opinions'.[34] He had arrived at the position that John Sterling had reached rather earlier:

> I shd be still more reluctant to say anything about Shelley for though I deem as highly as ever of his genius his whole thinking seems to me to have been founded on a mistake, and I believe he has in his time done many of us a good deal of harm.[35]

The oddest thing about this letter is its date, November 25, 1829, the day before the debate at Oxford on whether Shelley or Byron were the greater poet, and more than two years before Robert Boyd was shot on the esplanade at Malaga. Trench's case was similar. In a letter written from Southampton just before embarking for Spain, Trench writes that Sterling reminds him of Shelley's Prince Athanase, 'labouring for his kind in grief' and infected at the heart with a 'core of despair'. Trench, too, despairs of his age, and particularly its poetry:

> After one or two revolutions in thought and opinion, all our boasted poetry, all, or nearly all, of Keats and Shelley and Wordsworth and

Byron, will become unintelligible. When except in our times did men seek to build up their poetry on their own individual experiences, instead of some objective foundations common to all men? Even we, who inhabit their own age, suffer by their error. Their poems are unintelligible to us, till we have gone through that very state of feeling to which they appeal; as, for instance, none can entirely comprehend 'Alastor' who has not been laid waste by the unslaked thirst for female sympathies, and so with the rest.[36]

Trench seems to understand, even before he has embarked on the venture, that his going to Spain is a literary exercise, a necessary exercise because he must live through Shelley's states of feeling before he can comprehend his poems. Before, one is almost inclined to say, he can fully comprehend their error. He did not, it seems, involve himself with the Spanish Constitutionalists, and then become disillusioned with their cause. It was rather that he involved himself in order to become disillusioned. In this, Trench seems to speak for all the Apostles, differing from them only in his self-knowledge.

One can only speculate, of course, that he spoke for Tennyson, because Tennyson, characteristically, preserves an all but perfect reticence as to his own involvement in the affair. Hallam Tennyson relates just one short but telling anecdote, in which Tennyson recalls the meeting in the Pyrenees between himself, Hallam, and the guerrilla leader, General Ojeda. Ojeda told the young Cambridge men of his desire to '"couper la gorge à tous les curés," then clapping his hand on his heart murmured "mais vous connaissez mon coeur" – "and a pretty black one it is," thought my father.'[37] Hallam and Tennyson's kind of liberalism, best displayed in their support for Catholic Emancipation, comes face to face with a quite different 'liberal' tradition, French in its origin, fiercely anti-clerical in its content, and violent in its methods. It was clearly a discomforting experience.

His other memory was pleasanter, of the Pyrenean landscape, and especially the Valley of Cauteretz with its 'stream that flashest white', through which he had walked with Hallam.[38] It is a landscape also represented in 'Oenone', part of which, Hallam Tennyson records, was written in the valley.[39] Herbert Tucker has described 'Oenone' as Tennyson's 'most important poem since 'Timbuctoo'.[40] It is certainly the poem over which he seems to have taken most trouble. After beginning it in 1830, in the Pyrenees, he seems to have continued working on it until shortly before the publication of the *Poems* of 1832, and then revised it more extensively than any other poem for its republication in the *Poems* of 1842.[41] It is also the poem that explores most fully, though also with rich indirectness, the experiences that he and his fellow Apostles shared in the years of its first composition.[42]

These were the years in which Tennyson and his contemporaries left Cambridge, and were faced with the problem of finding a place for themselves in the public world, the years in which they passed the threshold from youth to adulthood, and 'Oenone', like several other poems that Tennyson wrote at this time, like 'The Palace of Art' and 'The Lady of Shalott', is a threshold poem. The valley in which Oenone sits making her lament slopes towards Troy, and the whole poem is built around the opposition between the pastoral valley and the doomed city. Oenone recalls how her husband, Paris, was summoned to judge which of the three goddesses was fairest. At the time of the judgement Paris was still a shepherd, but his judgement marks the point at which he must resume his birthright, for he can claim Helen, the reward Aphrodite offers him, only as a prince of Troy. The poem ends when Oenone herself decides to cross the threshold and go 'Down into Troy'.

To cross a threshold is not simply to move from one place to another, it is to be transformed. Paris emerges from a life of pastoral ease into a world of power: he is transformed from a shepherd into a prince. But it is Oenone's poem, and it is her transformation that is the more startling. Her valley is a place of watery nostalgia. Oenone reclines there, and sings the kind of song appropriate to the daughter of a river-god, a song in which her tears blend with the 'loud glenriver' (1832) or the 'long brook' (1842), and, in the later version, blend too with the 'swimming vapour' that creeps all through the valley. But the poem ends only when her tearful memories become 'fiery thoughts', when nostalgia gives way to prophecy, and when the damp landscape of the valley explodes into an inferno: 'All earth and air seem only burning fire'. Her song begins as a monument to her sorrow:

> Hear me, for I will speak, and build up all
> My sorrow with my song, as yonder walls
> Rose slowly to a music slowly breathed,
> A cloud that gathered shape.
>
> (38–41)

Troy is the epic poem, the product of prophetic song, and Oenone's sweet pastoral elegy seems at first no more than its humble counterpart. But by the end of the poem Oenone sings apocalypse, the uncreating song that will undo Apollo's work.

Troy and the valley of Ida seem at first the twin poles of the poem, but by the end the poles have collapsed together, and the world of the poem has imploded. Trojans enter the valley and destroy it, hacking down its 'tall, dark pines', and Oenone takes her decision to go down into Troy and summon up the conflagration that will destroy the city. Oenone begins the song as Cassandra's opposite. She is the poet of memory, preserving in song her sense of her own betrayal. Cassandra's gaze is on the future, and if prophecy for her is as painful as memory for Oenone, it is as a consequence of her own treachery, for she accepted the gift of Apollo, and refused the price he asked. But the poem ends when Oenone decides that she will merge her song with Cassandra's, for she glimpses a 'far-off doubtful purpose, as a mother/Conjectures of the features of a child' (247–8). The checked, arrested rhythms of her song, with its refrain, its repetitions of word and vowel, its syntax turning back upon itself, become urgent with the onrush of events,

> Whereof I catch the issue, as I hear
> Dead sounds at night come from the inmost hills,
> Like footsteps upon wool.
>
> (244–6)

At the beginning of her poem Oenone's concern is to make a music that will arrest time: she ends with her ears pricked for the approach of the future, hearing it tiptoe towards her like a thief in the night, or a muffled army advancing for a surprise attack.

The account of the judgement of Paris has seemed to some readers a disruptive intrusion into Oenone's lament,[43] but it is Oenone's account of the judgement that impels her to transform herself and her poem. An immediate problem is that the Paris of 1832 is significantly different from the Paris of 1842, and so are the goddesses that he meets. In 1842 Paris is an innocent, proud that he has been chosen to judge of gods, and anxious that Oenone should witness his triumph. In 1832 Paris's pride in his appointment had been qualified by a gloomy sense of himself as a victim of his election. He knows that, whatever he decides, he will bring about

> Deep evilwilledness of heaven, and sere
> Heartbuning toward hallowed Ilion;
> And all the colour of my afterlife
> Will be the shadow of today.
>
> (72–5)

His election as umpire has already forced him into perplexities out of tune with the sweet simplicity of life in the pastoral valley. Oenone, safely hidden in the grotto, can witness all that takes place, but remain herself unimplicated: 'Thou unbeholden mayst behold, unheard / Hear all and see thy Paris judge of Gods' (87–8). The 1832 poem has at this point a pathos that the later version lacks. The threshold has narrowed from the long Idalian valley to the mouth of a small grotto, and Paris and Oenone, only a few feet apart, are separated irrevocably. Inside the cave, Oenone can still enjoy a life of pastoral ease, but Paris has been forced to take his stand in a world of choice, where choices, once made, must be lived by forever. His lot is hard, but neither is Oenone's position enviable, for she is married to Paris, and to be separated from him is to be separated from a part of herself.

It is the 1832 Paris who more directly reflects the experience of Tennyson and his friends, so many of whom found it difficult to cross the threshold between a university life in which all decisions were provisional, a life in which everything was potential and nothing was fixed, into a harsher public life in which decisions once made must be lived by. 'Oenone' was written out of this communal crisis. Oenone, bewilderedly watching her husband as he betrays her, seeing everything but powerless to influence it, is like a younger self impotently watching an older self forced to act within a world in which any action will be a betrayal, because the world does not accommodate actions that will express undistorted the ideal aspirations of youth. Young men dream of escaping from a world of thought, a student world, into a world of action. Trench saw his Spanish escapade as an exhilarating escape from a college world of talk: 'It is action, action, action that we want, and I would willingly go did I only find in the enterprise a pledge of my own earnestness'.[44] He very quickly realized that things were not so simple.

'Oenone' had its origin in the Spanish enterprise, and as soon as this is recognized the speeches by Here and Pallas no longer appear the rival collections of classical commonplaces that they may have seemed. Here tempts Paris with 'Proffer of royal power, ample rule / Unquestioned' (109–10). Pallas offers him the opportunity to 'live by law / Acting the law we live by' (145–6). The choice is between absolutist and constitutional government, between Ferdinand and Torrijos, and Oenone finds it as little perplexing as did the youthful Apostles: 'O Paris / Give it to Pallas' (165–6). Her interjection, commentators tell us, is designed to direct the reader's responses, and perhaps it is, but it directs only those who hear Oenone's exclamation with its impulsive spontaneity, its carelessness of the gauche chime of 'Paris' with 'Pallas',

as evidence of a trustworthy innocence. It is easier to respond like this
to the 1842 poem. In 1832 Here's and Pallas's speeches are more difficult, their drift harder to follow, and Oenone's response, though
charming, is likely to strike the reader as naïve.

Here seems to offer Paris the pleasure of unchecked tyranny, Pallas the
sober satisfaction of a life lived in obedience to the law, but in 1832 the
speeches fail to maintain this simple opposition. Here offers Paris power:

> Power fitted to the season, measured by
> The height of the general feeling, wisdomborn
> And throned of wisdom.
>
> (121–3)

The confidently expansive rhythm suggests that her purpose is to
embellish her gift, to underline for Paris the amplitude of the power that
she offers him. But if our attention strays from her tone to her meaning,
the power that she offers seems rather strictly limited. Paris will be free
to do whatever he likes, provided that it is neither unseasonable, nor
unpopular, nor unwise. It is hard to imagine a monarchical authority
more trammelled. Power, Here tells us, 'in all action is the end of all'
(120), and by the end of her speech there are grounds to interpret her
maxim quite literally, for the power that she offers Paris is a power that
best reveals itself in doing nothing. She offers him the chance to win
'Rest in a happy place', and enjoy the 'changeless calm of undisputed
right' (129, 133), which stops just short of implying that such power
will remain undisputed only for so long as it consents to changeless-
ness, only for so long as it agrees not to change anything.

Like Here, Pallas begins confidently:

> Self-reverence, self-knowledge, self-control
> Are the three hinges of the gates of Life,
> That open into power, everyway
> Without horizon, bound, or shadow, or cloud.
>
> (142–5)

The gates of life open to reveal a power that can properly be regarded
as infinite because it is internal. Pallas's is a very Apostolic speech, and
its opening is best glossed by the opinions of the Apostles' chief mentor, Maurice, with reference to his praise of Shelley for example:

> He teaches us to look for our improvement not to the outward cir-
> cumstances over which our control must always be limited, and

which can return no substantial happiness, but to those inward means which are beyond the reach of change or chance, to the improvement of which there is no bound assigned, and which furnish us from within with ample means for our satisfaction.[45]

Pallas is Apostolic, too, in her scorn of utilitarianism, in her insistence that to follow right 'Were wisdom in the scorn of consequence' (148), and in all this she seems calmly authoritative. But, as her speech goes on, Pallas loses her composure. She starts to wrestle with the problem of how to distinguish the concentration on self that she recommends from a self-interested self-absorption that she deprecates, and with the further problem of how a condition of earnest self-scrutiny will necessarily result in a life given over to benevolent activity. Her anxiety is neurotic because, within the terms of her own argument, it cannot be allayed:

> Good for selfgood doth half destroy selfgood.
> The means and end, like two coiled snakes, infect
> Each other, bound in one with hateful love.
> So both into the fountain and the stream
> A drop of poison falls.
>
> (153–7)

We can find happiness only by following the right, but if we recognize that we follow the right in order to secure happiness, then both our happiness, our selfgood, and the right to which we gave our allegiance are contaminated. In other words, self-reverence can be secured only by the exercise of a self-control so unremitting that it successfully eliminates self-knowledge. The difficult, self-involved similes with which Pallas ends her speech map out a programme to accomplish this:

> look upon me and consider me
> So shalt thou find me fairest, so endurance,
> Like to an athlete's arm, shall still become
> Sinewed with motion, till thine active will
> (As the dark body of the Sun robed round
> With his own ever-emanating lights)
> Be flooded o'er with her own effluences,
> And thereby grow to freedom.
>
> (159–65)

This seems to mean no more than that the habitual exercise of virtue makes virtuous action feel spontaneous or instinctive rather than willed, an ordinary thought, but expressed here so tortuously that it reveals the speaker's anxiety more clearly than her meaning.

Here's and Pallas's speeches begin in the world of the debating chamber, the Cambridge Union, with its easy moral certainties. Here offers Paris the chance to become king over men; Pallas holds up to him the loftier, Shelleyan ambition of becoming king over himself. Paris's duty seems as clear as the Apostles' choice to lend their support to constitutional government as represented by Torrijos, and oppose the absolutist rule assumed by Ferdinand. But even in 1830 that choice had been possible only by virtue of a collective decision to repress a recognition of complex political realities. Trench had travelled in Spain in 1829, and his letters home reveal a cool grasp of Spanish politics: 'Ferdinand has at present a difficult card to play, with the Liberals on one side, and on the other the Church praying for the re-establishment of the Inquisition and secretly abetting his brother Carlos'.[46] A year later his desire to escape from a life spent in scrupulous vigilance over his own moral state and lived in impotent detachment from the public world of power had become so insistent that he was prepared to throw up everything and risk death for the Liberal cause. But the speeches of Here and Pallas reveal that no such escape from the burden of thought is possible. Pallas may hold out to Paris the possibility of transforming himself into a muscled arm mindlessly performing the task it is trained for, but her tangled argument encourages in the listener exactly that state of painful self-consciousness from which her figure promises relief.[47] Oenone hears the two speeches and at once makes her choice: 'O Paris / Give it to Pallas.' But Paris only 'pondered', and our sympathies, surely, should be with him.

Immediately Aphrodite makes her ravishing approach and effortlessly takes the prize. It is hers by right, because all readers of folk tales know that when three choices are offered it is the third that must be accepted. But it is still worth noting the precise terms of her offer, because, however much her words are infected by the gorgeous sensuality of her presence, they scarcely confirm the general critical response that, in choosing Aphrodite, Paris's reason is unhinged by lust. In his review of *Poems*, 1832, Croker marked the oddity by italicizing it.[48] Aphrodite promises Paris 'the fairest *wife* in Greece', not mentioning that the wife she has in mind is someone else's. She offers Paris a life of adulterous excitement heavily disguised as a life of domestic bliss, and it is the domestic disguise rather than the adulterous substance that tempts. The domestic ideal pressed strongly on many of those involved in the Spanish fiasco, partly perhaps because marriage appealed to them as an alternative career, and a career that offered the possibility of escaping the perplexity and the guilt that seemed to attend their more dramatic attempts to emerge into the public world. Shortly after returning from Spain, Trench announced to William Bodham Donne his discovery that 'our only hope of lightening the burden and solving the mystery ... reposed in women's love'.[49]

But Paris's choice of Aphrodite does not lighten his burden. He succeeds only in betraying Oenone, and bringing upon Troy a war that will end only with his own death and the destruction of the city. 'Oenone' is a song of sorrow punctuated by a story of choice. In this, the central section of the poem, Oenone is relegated from her role as protagonist and becomes a helpless witness. Critics have pointed to this shift as the source of the structural failure of the poem, and from one point of view they are right. But only by writing a poem with two protagonists, a poem that offers within the song of the betrayed the story of her betrayer, is Tennyson able to accommodate within 'Oenone' the history of 1830, of those months during which Tennyson and his friends passed from a heady, perhaps factitious state of revolutionary excitement to a bewildered sense that, out of what had seemed the best of motives, they had acted in such a way as to betray themselves and betray each other. Sterling felt it most keenly. He was reduced by the news of the execution of Torrijos and Boyd to a bitter self-lacerating irony: 'I have the comfort of knowing that the whole is my doing'.[50] Trench, too, lapsed into depression. Hallam wrote to comfort him, to alleviate, if he could, Trench's 'backward yearnings of mind'.[51] I can think of no phrase that better expresses the lyrical impulse of 'Oenone'.

Only a few months after their return from Spain, Hallam and Tennyson were again actively engaged in politics. On December 3, 1830, they joined a band of undergraduates who armed themselves with cudgels and kept watch all night, intent on doing battle with an insurrectionary mob of agricultural labourers, followers of the mythical Captain Swing, that they believed to be marching on the town.[52] Confronted with what they naïvely assumed to be the possibility of revolution not in Spain but in England, the Apostles found that their political sympathies underwent an abrupt change. Two of them, Henry Lushington and George Venables wrote a light-hearted poem about the affair in which they record that Tennyson was a particularly staunch anti-revolutionary:

> Unto the poet wise we spoke,
> 'Is any law of battle broke,
> 'By pouring from afar

> 'Water or oil, or melted lead?'
> The poet raised his massive head –
> 'Confound the laws of war'.

Lushington and Venables admit that they and their friends are remarkable for their curiously divided principles:

> But doubtful in our dazzling prime,
> We watched the struggle of the time,
> The war of new and old;
> We loved the past with Tory love,
> Yet more than Radicals we strove
> For coming years of gold.[53]

But it was from that self-divided embarrassment that Tennyson recoiled to the calm Burkean periods that Wordsworth admired in the political poems of 1833.

## III

Isobel Armstrong has persuasively presented Tennyson and Browning as the chief representatives of the two major schools of Victorian poetry; the one Coleridgean and conservative, the other utilitarian and radical.[54] But in the 1830s the distinction between the two was less clear than Armstrong suggests. If F.D. Maurice was the figure whose thought most strongly influenced the youthful Tennyson, Browning recognized as his own literary godfather the unitarian minister and radical editor of the *Monthly Repository*, W.J. Fox. Browning identified himself as a member of the group of utilitarian radicals to which Fox's journal and the *Westminster Review* were addressed, and when he published *Paracelsus* he wrote frankly to Fox asking for the group's support: 'there are precious bold bits here & there, & the drift & scope are awfully radical – I am "off" for ever with the other side, but must by all means be "on" with yours ... therefore a certain writer [presumably Mill] ... must be benignant or supercilious as he shall choose, but in no case an idle spectator' (April 16, 1835).[55] Browning was most obviously 'awfully radical' in his devotion to Shelley, but Shelley, after all, had been championed almost as strongly by Maurice and by the younger Apostles who were under his influence. The following year Browning, encouraged by Macready, wrote his first tragedy, *Strafford*, which was finally produced at Covent Garden on May 1, 1837, and published by Longman on the same day.

It may seem odd to compare *Strafford*, which is written in a blank verse so fractured as to be often indistinguishable from prose,[56] with *Oenone*, and yet the play and the poem are similarly preoccupied with betrayal.

Browning was doubly occupied by Strafford in 1836, working on his play and at the same time assisting John Forster with the life of Strafford that he published that year.[57] The life insists on the consistency of Strafford's conduct and character. His ruling bent was his devotion to power, and he formed from the first the view that power was properly vested not in Parliament but in the person of the King. If, in the Parliament of 1628, he sided with the Opposition, and supported the Petition of Right that sought to limit the King's authority, this was simply a tactic designed to impress Charles I with a due sense of the value of his services. He knew from the first the truth Vivian Grey learned by hard experience, that 'no one is petted so much as a political apostate'. After the death of his enemy, Buckingham, he quickly made his composition with the King, and thereafter dedicated all of his enormous ability to the task of making the king's power absolute. In Ireland he succeeded, and was able to conclude a summary of his services by declaring, 'so now I can say the king is as absolute here as any prince in the whole world can be' (161). In England he was foiled, first by the violent response of the Scots Presbyterians to the attempt to impose on them the English prayer book, and finally when the Commons passed its Bill of Attainder, and the King signed the warrant for Strafford's execution. His trial, in which the prosecution was led by Pym as 'the chosen champion of the people of England' (242), was 'not the trial of an individual, but the solemn arbitration of an issue between the two great antagonist principles, liberty and despotism' (243), and its result is solemnly celebrated. Charles's betrayal of Strafford, teaching him the lesson that he stated so memorably, 'Put not your trust in princes, nor in the sons of men, for in them there is no salvation', was 'incredibly monstrous' (272), and yet the sentence itself is represented as just, for in Strafford 'Despotism' had found its most accomplished 'instrument' (278), and the Commonwealth could not safely spare him if it hoped to survive. For the people and their leaders in the Commons, Strafford was, in the words of Lord Digby, 'that grand apostate to the commonwealth, who must not expect to be pardoned in this world till he be dispatched to the other' (265). He is the man who had sought to destroy the power of Parliament that he had once defended. But this charge, the life tells us, is false, for it is not possible to 'discern one false step in Strafford's public conduct, one instance of a dereliction of the law of his being', namely, his allegiance to 'Despotism' (278).

The same charge is more elaborately refuted in a passage that no-one has disputed was written by Browning: 'Infinitely and distinctly various as appear the shifting hues of our common nature when subjected to the prism of CIRCUMSTANCE, each ray into which it is broken is no less in itself a primitive colour, susceptible, indeed, of vast modification, but incapable of further division' (61).[58] Characters, once formed, are fixed, and 'the long list of apostates with which history furnishes us' has been produced by historians who have overlooked this truth. It is an odd argument in itself, because apostates stand accused not of changing their characters but their allegiance, and particularly odd coming from Browning, who was a few years later to make of Wordsworth the best known apostate in all English poetry:

> Just for a handful of silver he left us,
> Just for a riband to stick in his coat ...[59]

It is a matter more feelingly explored in the play than in the prose life.

C.H. Firth complains in his introduction to the *Life* that 'Strafford is judged too much by the standards of 1832, and too little by the standards of 1632' (xv). In choosing the later date he acknowledges that the crucial issue raised by the life of Strafford is one of representation; whether the will of the people is more appropriately embodied in the King or the Parliament. That is the crucial issue in the play, too. In his final confrontation with Strafford, Pym claims authority as the spokesman for England, the country that he serves 'with disregard/To [his] own heart' (V ii 269–70). But Strafford is equally sincere when he retorts, 'I have loved England too' (V ii 304). The difference between them is simply that Strafford expresses his love of England through his devotion to its King, and Pym through his devotion to its Parliament. So, when Strafford thinks to begin a 'new life, founded in a new belief/In Charles', the Parliamentarian Hollis corrects him, 'In Charles? Rather believe in Pym!' (IV ii 102–3). It is a choice seemingly as simple as that Paris is offered between Here and Pallas, but in the play, as in the poem, it is complicated by its refraction within a tale of ill-requited love, a tale that itself involves questions of true and false representation. Lady Carlisle is briefly introduced in the *Life* as a mistress of Strafford's who passed, after his death, to Pym. In the play she is a central character, impelled throughout by a love of Strafford that he recognizes only as he is about to die. He does not understand her when she explains her plight:

> Could you but know what 'tis to bear, my friend,
> One image stamped within you, turning blank

> The else imperial brilliance of your mind, –
> A weakness, but most precious, – like a flaw
> I'the diamond which should shape forth some sweet face
> Yet to create, and meanwhile treasured there
> Lest nature lose her gracious thought for ever!
>
> (II ii 132–8)

Such love is precious precisely because of the inadequacy of its object, and Strafford perfectly well understands her point, if not its application, for it is just such a love he feels for Charles. In this, Browning develops a brief quotation from one of Strafford's letters quoted in the *Life*, in which Strafford confesses that he will 'be satisfied with nothing short of the dignity of becoming "the king's mistress, to be cherished and courted by none but himself"' (59). In the play Strafford is impelled throughout by a romantic love for Charles that is sustained rather than diminished by his recognition that Charles is weak, treacherous, and so far from requiting his love that, if ever Strafford should 'reach this heart' he would 'find Vane there!' (II ii 88–9). Strafford no longer has at heart the abstract ideal of kingship, but one 'sweet face', the face of the 'man with the mild voice and mournful eyes' (II ii 193). For this, Strafford is content to allow the King credit for all the good that his administration achieves, and take to himself all the odium provoked by his harshness, and because she loves and understands him Lady Carlisle abets him. As she points out, 'Prove the King faithless, and I take away / All Strafford cares to live for' (IV ii 136–7). So, both lovingly conspire to misrepresent the King that they serve. The last, and the most surprising of the play's unrequited lovers is Pym himself. The play develops the early friendship, mentioned in the *Life*, that Pym may have enjoyed with Strafford, into an intense attachment: 'I never loved but one man – David not / More Jonathan!' He demands Strafford's life before Parliament, speaking

> Of England, and her great reward, as all
> I look for there; but in my inmost heart,
> Believe, I think of stealing quite away
> To walk once more with Wentworth – my youth's friend.
>
> (V ii 295–8)

In the *Life* Pym is the voice of England, but in the play he assumes that voice only by painfully repressing the quite different voice that he hears in his 'inmost heart'.

The *Life* offers a radically simplified political landscape in which the choice is between despotism and a notion of citizenship embodied in the rule of a Parliament which is representative of the people. But in the play that landscape is misted over by what Tennyson in 'Oenone' calls 'sere Heartburning', and in this it is the play, not the life, that is characteristic of Browning's poetry in the 1830s. The play is typical, too, in its insistence on 'backward yearnings of mind'. Pym yearns for the time when Wentworth was his 'youth's friend', and Strafford, too, is haunted by the memory of Sir John Eliot, the dead Parliamentarian with whom he had worked in the Parliament of 1828, and who represents for both Pym and Strafford a simple, uncompromised integrity that they can neither recover nor forget. Strafford can only dream that he might cure

> All bitterness one day, be proud again
> And young again, care for the sunshine too,
> And never think of Eliot any more.
>
> (II ii 84–6)

One of the reasons that Browning chose this subject for his first play was surely that he wished to pay homage to the poet whose play *Charles the First* remained incomplete.[60] Shelley's play itself alludes to his poetic predecessors. When Pym, Cromwell and the other Parliamentary leaders think of emigrating to America, Archy, the court fool, is anachronistically reminded of Coleridge and Southey's plan to settle on the Susquehanna – 'they think to found / A commonwealth like Gonzalo's in the play, / Gynaecocoenic and pantisocratic' (II ii 360–2). But Browning's dealings with his own predecessors are a good deal less insouciant.

For Browning, as for Tennyson and his fellow-Apostles in 1829 and 1830, Shelley himself is the major precursor. His first surviving poem, *Pauline* (1833), ends with an address to Shelley in which Browning extravagantly proclaims his discipleship and his dependence:

> Sun-treader, I believe in God and truth
> And love; and as one just escaped from death
> Would bind himself in bands of friends to feel
> He lives indeed – so, I would lean on thee!
> Thou must be ever with me ...
>
> (1020–4)

But this provides an odd conclusion to a poem that carefully charts a youthful discipleship that did not survive the attempt to apply Shelley's 'theories to 'real life' (441–2). As soon as the poet does so, he awakes as if from a dream: 'I said, 'twas beautiful, / Yet but a dream, and so adieu to it' (449–50). Shelley's own heroes, the hero of *Alastor*, for example, regularly awaken from ecstatic dreams into the 'cold white light of morning' (*Alastor*, 193), but in Shelley's imaginative economy the discrepancy between what might be and what is empowers rather than disillusions the dreamer. It directs his attention outwards to the world 'to arrest the faintest shadow of that without the possession of which there is no rest nor respite to the heart' (*Essay on Love*). In *Pauline*, by contrast, the speaker responds by giving up his 'hopes of perfecting mankind / And faith in them – then freedom in itself, / And virtue in itself' (458–60), and he finds that, as soon as he abandons his Shelleyan ideals, he discovers 'new powers' such as 'wit, mockery', and a new confidence in his own mastery. The confidence does not last, but there is no indication that the Shelleyan faith returns, only a strange passage in which we are encouraged to escape the 'curse' of seeing 'our idols perish' by stoutly refusing to admit that we no longer admire certain painters or poets so much as we once did (543–59). By the time of *Sordello* Browning represents the confidence to write poems as dependent on Shelley agreeing to absent himself from the poet's mind:

> thou, spirit, come not near
> Now – not this time desert thy cloudy place
> To scare me, thus employed, with that pure face!
> I need not fear this audience, I make free
> With them, but then this is no place for thee!
> (1, 60–4)

For Browning as for the Apostles the example of Shelley brought into sharp focus the question of how poetry might and ought to act on the real world. Shelley himself only precariously maintained his faith that verse might have an incantatory power to realize the poet's imaginings, and his successors found it difficult to emulate even that fragile confidence. And yet their readers and reviewers insisted more stridently than Shelley's that poetry should exert a beneficial effect on society. The utilitarian thinkers with whom Browning sided predictably demanded that poets demonstrate their social utility, but even the anti-utilitarian Maurice is insistent that the value of poetry rests in its moral effect. Neither Browning nor Tennyson responded comfortably to these demands, but Browning's discomfort was the more extreme, and all his work of the 1830s addresses it. For him, it presented a difficulty that was compounded by, and entangled with an anxious relationship with his audience from which Tennyson was largely spared.[61] Moxon, according to Browning, justified his decision not to publish *Paracelsus* by pointing to the poor sales of his other poets, including Tennyson, whose 'poetry is "popular at Cambridge," and yet of 800 copies that were printed of his last [*Poems*, 1832], some 300 only have gone off'.[62] But Tennyson could at least find confidence in his Cambridge popularity. Browning, instead of the Apostles, had his 'set', the group of friends all of whom lived in and around Camberwell, and who functioned for him, as the Apostles did for Tennyson, as his first appreciative audience. But there remains a wide difference between the intellectual élites of Camberwell and Cambridge, not so much a difference in ability as in the social and cultural confidence that they possessed and that they had the power to bestow.[63]

Browning's anxiety betrays itself in *Pauline* in the contrast that so offended Mill between the confessional poem addressed to Pauline that the reader is only allowed to overhear, and the subscription, 'Richmond: October 22, 1832': 'this transition from speaking to Pauline to writing a letter to the public with *place & date* is quite horrible'. Browning explained that the subscription commemorates the performance by Kean of *Richard III* that he had witnessed, and points out that he makes a veiled allusion to Kean in lines 669–75 of the poem. But this serves to confirm rather than answer Mill's objection, first by admitting a sudden transition from a confessional lyric to its generic opposite, a theatrical performance, and second by alerting us to the special nature of the performance that Browning had attended. By late October 1832 Kean was dying, and the audience gathered to watch him were spectators of two tragedies: one was performed before them, but they were the voyeurs of the other. A few months later, on May 25, 1833, Browning attended Kean's funeral. The anxiety is evident too in the curiously divergent paths that Browning pursued in the 1830s. On the one hand he attempted to write for the stage, to write a poetry that would make an immediate appeal to the promiscuous audience of a London theatre, and on the other he occupied himself in the composition of three narrative poems, *Pauline*, *Paracelsus*, and *Sordello*, each of them hermetic, and the third so armed against easy comprehension that it dealt a blow to Browning's reputation from which he did not recover for almost twenty years. But it is an anxiety that is not only revealed by the poems, it is explored within them.

In *Paracelsus* Browning seems to take as his theme the disastrous consequences of severing knowledge from love. Paracelsus devotes his life to the quest for perfect knowledge, and in the second book he meets his counterpart, the poet Aprile. Paracelsus introduces himself as the 'mortal who aspired to KNOW' and Aprile responds, 'I would LOVE infinitely, and be loved' (2, 384–5). Paracelsus seems to draw the appropriate conclusion:

> Are we not halves of one dissevered world,
> Whom this strange chance unites once more? part? never!
> Till thou, the lover, know; and I, the knower,
> Love.
>
> (2, 634–5)

But in fact the two mirror rather than complement one another. The differences between them that make of each the counterpart of the other dissolve almost as soon as they are established.[64] For example, Aprile is a poet, Paracelsus a natural philosopher, but the difference between scientific and imaginative method disappears when Aprile addresses Paracelsus as 'Master, Poet' (2, 572). Both are suspicious that the other is the successor who will secure the triumph that eludes the predecessor. In meeting Aprile, Paracelsus encounters a version of himself, and in Aprile's fate he sees his own predicted, an experience so disturbing that when Aprile tries to embrace him he replies, 'Clasp me not thus' (2, 609). Aprile assures Paracelsus that he is different, that he, unlike Aprile, will not fail to secure his 'mighty Aim' (2, 488) by refusing 'the means so limited, the tools so rude', which are all that are given us to 'execute our purpose' (2, 499–500). But Paracelsus recognizes that he, just as much as Aprile, has 'gazed upon that End / Till [his] own powers for compassing the bliss / Were blind with glory' (2, 491–3). Aprile is the poet who cannot express his imaginative vision, and in the poem's third part Paracelsus is revealed as the wise man who cannot communicate his knowledge.

When he is awarded a professorship at Basel and enters the lecture theatre, Paracelsus for the first time directly encounters an audience, and finds the experience perplexing. Up till then he has lived in a world of thought, seeking the truth, but when he attempts to communicate the truth that he has so painstakingly acquired,

> *then* I first discovered
> Such teaching was an art requiring cares
> And qualities peculiar to itself; –
> That to possess was one thing ... to display
> Another. I had never dreamed of this.
>
> (3, 651–5)

He offers his innocence as a mark of his indifference to 'popular praise' (3, 656), but, as he also freely admits, it might equally be termed a contempt of his audience. When he lowered himself to display in the lecture theatre 'all the marvels of [his] art –/Fantastic gambols leading to no end', he was applauded, but when he began to feel not just a 'kindness' for his audience, but a 'trust in them and a respect' and began to 'teach them' rather than simply 'amaze them', they quickly fell away until he was left with 'a clear class-room' and 'a quiet leer' from those who had so recently admired him. In the end he is dismissed (4, 83–130). This is a poet's as much as it is a professor's story, and it raises the dilemma that was to preoccupy Browning for many years: how is it possible at once to respect and to retain one's audience? It is also a story that tellingly predicts the trajectory of Browning's own career. *Paracelsus* was to prove a critical if not a popular success, and *Strafford* was respectfully received by the reviewers and applauded at least by Browning's admirers in the audience, but *Sordello* all but emptied his class-room.

Paracelsus understands that to teach is not to communicate knowledge, but 'to impart/The spirit which should instigate the search/Of truth' (4, 94–6). He even suggests that he indulged in quackery as a way of encouraging his students to see through his antics, and learn a proper scepticism of intellectual authority. This is the sense in which Browning was right to claim that 'the drift and the scope' of the poem 'are awfully radical'. Paracelsus is a radical hero not because, when he saves the life of a prince, he takes little satisfaction in having spared him to 'plague his people some few years to come' (3, 427), but because he seeks to enfranchise his students as citizens in an intellectual commonwealth. He attempts to institute, as the frequent references to contemporaries such as Luther and Zwingli indicate, an intellectual reformation. He fails because his audience proves inadequate to the demands that he makes of them, and because he is unable to escape his own contradictions. In the poem's first part he admits that he longs 'to trample on yet save mankind at once' (1, 461), and it is only on his death bed that he is able to reconcile the impulses.[65] But it is also true that Browning fails him. When in the poem's final part Paracelsus delivers his last lecture, he insists that throughout his life he has been impelled by a proper ambition to act as midwife to the birth of mankind, for the infancy of mankind only begins when 'all mankind alike is perfected,/Equal in full-blown powers' (5, 750–1). His mistake was to imagine that 'one day, one moment's space' might 'change man's condition' (5, 821–2), and hence to despise rather than look tenderly on human weakness and imperfection. But in this last lecture Paracelsus delivers his truths to a reader who is invited passively to receive them, and in this it provides an appropriate conclusion to a poem which throughout gainsays its content in its form. The poem is obedient to an organicist aesthetic. It traces the growth of Paracelsus's mind. Paracelsus may stumble over the gap between a thought and its expression in the poem's narrative, but no equivalent recognition is allowed to intrude into the poem's style. In consequence it remains a poem committed at once to an ideal of active citizenship, and a poem that invites the reader's mute admiration. It is a contradiction that drove Browning on to the brilliant and disastrous experiment of *Sordello*.

Like *Paracelsus*, *Sordello* explores the relation between the poet's oblig-ations to his art and his duties as a citizen. Dante had established Sor-dello as the type of the citizen poet. When he recognizes Virgil he prostrates himself before a greater poet (*Purgatorio*, 7, 13–15), but he had earlier, when he learned that Virgil too was a Mantuan, embraced him as his fellow citizen ('al cittadin suo', 6, 81), and it is this embrace that prompts Dante to a vehement denunciation of an Italy that has lost its civic virtues. *Sordello* begins in Verona where Sordello has come with Palma to meet with Taurello Salinguerra, the Guelf warlord, but the first three books of the poem are taken up with a long retrospective. Sordello's retired boyhood in Goito is decribed, his journey to Mantua, his triumphant recognition as a poet, and his painful apprenticeship to his craft. Only in Book IV does the poem circle back to its beginning. Ferrara has been devastated in the brutal war between Guelf and Ghi-belline in which each side seems as bad as the other, but Sordello rec-ognizes that it would be irresponsible to withdraw from the conflict in pious horror. He accepts the utilitarian obligation to choose that course of action which promises the greatest happiness to the greatest num-ber, and concludes that at this historical moment, 1224, that end is best secured by siding with the Ghibellines and the Pope, and oppos-ing the Guelfs who support the power of the Emperor. Sordello makes his passionate appeal to Taurello, now revealed as his father, to aban-don his allegiance to the Guelfs, but Taurello scarcely pays attention. He is caught up in a grandiose scheme to marry Sordello to Palma and wage a war that will establish their rule over all Italy. When Sordello recognizes that the poetic imagination is powerless to influence Tau-rello, his dream of reconciling in his own person the poetic ideal and the ideal of citizenship collapses, and he dies. His failure seems more complete even than Paracelsus's, who retains at least a fragile confi-dence that in after-ages his achievement will be justly measured. But it is in the form of *Sordello*, not in its narrative, that Browning tries to realize his ideal.[66]

In *Paracelsus* it was the poem's hero who presented himself before his students as a quack. In *Sordello* it is the poet himself:

> Your setters-forth of unexampled themes,
> Makers of quite new men, producing them,
> Would best chalk broadly on each vesture's hem
> The wearer's quality; or take their stand
> Motley on back and pointing-pole in hand,
> Beside him.
>
> (1, 26–31)

This is the poet reduced to shabby impresario, part showman and part clown, drumming up readers for the poem.[67] 'Appears / Verona' first in Book 1, line 10, but in line 99 its appearance is announced again, and, still more dramatically, in line 175 Verona is again invited to appear. This poet has to wait on his own lumbering stage machinery, nervously gabbling the while to hold the attention of his impatient audience. The shift from the blank verse of *Pauline* and *Paracelsus* to the couplets of *Sordello* itself serves as a constant reminder of the poem's artifice. The poem never allows its readers to forget in their enjoyment of the illusion the painful effort with which the illusion has been constructed.[68] Browning conjures into existence the Italy of the thirteenth century, but he is quite deliberately an inexpert conjurer, and that is because he does not want to astonish his readership into admiration but to invite them to inspect the workings of his poem, 'Remark this tooth's spring, wonder what that valve's / Fall bodes' (3, 846–7). Poets, 'Makers-see', as Browning calls them, are not mysterious figures in this poem. They manufacture their poems, they 'ply the pullies' (3, 932), and then hand over the products to their readers to be inspected:

> And therefore have I moulded, made anew
> A Man, and give him to be turned and tried,
> Be angry with or pleased at.
>
> (3, 934–6)

In the end, their responsibility is not to any transcendent ideal of art, but, like the humblest of showmen, to their audience, who are quite entitled to 'bruise their lips and break their teeth' if they commit the one unpardonable sin of 'neglecting you' (3, 932, 934).

The tooth's spring and the valve in themselves indicate how fiercely Browning rejects in *Sordello* the organic model that the Romantics, Coleridge and Wordsworth in particular, had bequeathed to their successors. The human frame is an 'engine' (3, 849). Consciousness is a 'machine' to exercise the will (2, 427), or a 'Machine supplied by Thought / To compass self-perception with' (3, 25–6). It is not just that Browning rejects organicism for its Burkean implications, its conservative respect for the past, its reverence for a process of slow, unbroken development. The organic model fuses the form and content of the poem, and, in the Wordsworthian and Coleridgean versions, fuses both with the poet himself, with the result that the poem seems to have arrived at its final shape not by an act of will but in accordance with a natural law of growth, and as an inevitable expression of the personality of the poet. One can admire a tree, but scarcely question it. Browning's poet, dressed in motley and flourishing his pointing-stick, refuses to melt into his materials, and the poem's couplets loudly confess the arbitrariness of verse form. After his triumphant first appearance as a poet Sordello re-makes the language of poetry, but his is an anti-Wordsworthian reform of poetic diction. Sordello, Browning knew, had 'contributed to establishing the Italian language by happy and sagacious borrowings from the dialects of Cremona, Brescia and Verona, cities neighbouring on his native Mantua'.[69] For Browning, this is a kind of metalwork, work for a blacksmith:

> welding words into the crude
> Mass from the new speech round him, till a rude
> Armour was hammered out, in time to be
> Approved beyond the Roman panoply
> Melted to make it.
>
> (2, 574–8)

This is a language that does not claim any natural authority: it can only be culturally approved, and it is recommended by its superior usefulness. Sordello's stylistic revolution is clearly offered as a counterpart of Browning's own manufacture of a style which uses a vocabulary assembled piecemeal from Browning's extravagantly heterogeneous reading, linked by a syntax that exposes rather than seeks to disguise the robust hammer blows that weld clause to clause.

It is Eglamor, vanquished by Sordello in his first appearance as a poet, who writes organic poetry, for in songs such as Eglamor's 'you find alone / Completeness, judge the song and singer one' (3, 619–20), whereas Sordello always betrays his separateness from his poems, revealing to their readers that

> his lay was but an episode
> In the bard's life: which evidence you owed
> To some slight weariness, some looking-off
> Or start-away.
>
> (3, 629–32)

Such lapses are what signal that Sordello's are 'true works' (3, 622), and they introduce a lengthy passage in which Browning starts away from his poem, and admits his own weariness of it:

> I muse this on a ruined palace-step
> At Venice: why should I break off, nor sit
> Longer upon my step, exhaust the fit
> England gave birth to?
>
> (3, 676–9)

To read poetry such as Eglamor's is to be accommodated, like Eglamor himself, within a natural order, to feel oneself pleasurably absorbed into a wholeness that removes the painful sense of one's own irreducibly solitary individuality, and for that reason it is a poetry incompatible with the strenuous demands of citizenship. Browning writes instead the kind of poetry that Sordello aspires to, a poetry that absorbs neither its poet nor its reader, but rather is produced by an energetic common labour in which poet and reader share equally. As Sordello explains it, it is a language in which the poet and his readers talk to one another 'as brothers talk' who are able to communicate 'In half-words, call things by half-names' (5, 625–6). It is a language that makes extraordinary demands, 'speech where an accent's change gives each / The other's soul' (5, 636–7), but it is precisely by accepting those demands, by refusing to 'expand / Expatiate', that poet and reader can establish a relationship with one another as equals, as 'brothers' (5, 638–9).

Looked at in one way, Sordello's career mirrors that of Paracelsus. In his initial triumph he substitutes for his sense of himself as 'One of the many, one with hopes and cares / And interests nowise distinct from theirs' (2, 369–7), an ambition to force the world to bow to him 'in unexampled worship' (2, 214), and he must later learn how 'in the eagerness to rule' he had forgotten how it behoved him to 'think of men, and take their wants…as his own want' (4, 275, 266–8). Looked at in another, in the first three books the poem explores Sordello's duties as a poet, and in the final three his duties as a citizen, tracing his own ambition to become 'the complete Sordello, Man and Bard' (2, 690). But a third pattern imposes itself on both these, in which the action of the first three books is simply repeated in the second, Sordello's failure as a poet precisely paralleling his failure to persuade Taurello to act not in his own interest but in that of the many. Sordello speaks to Taurello in the full flush of his belief, Shelleyan and Carlylean, that the 'poet must be earth's essential king' (5, 506), but Taurello is a man of action, a man for whom 'thoughts were caprices in the course of deeds' (4, 855), and though he has high ambitions for Sordello as his son, and feels a tolerant kindliness towards poets, he is quite unwilling to entertain the bizarre notion that he might make his political decisions by reference to poetic visions. His response to Sordello's plea is perfectly prefigured at the end of Book II when Sordello fails to turn up to deliver the panegyrical poem that Taurello has been promised:

> The easy-natured soldier smiled assent,
> Settled his portly person, smoothed his chin,
> And nodded that the bull-bait might begin
> (2, 1014–16)

Sordello's failure as a poet is very similar. He is wildly popular with his audience, until he begins to make demands of them, until, that is, he begins to write verse like Browning's: 'painfully' his audience 'tacks / Thought to thought' (2, 596–7). In the person of Naddo, the all-purpose literary consumer, the representative nineteenth-century reviewer disguised as a thirteenth-century Mantuan, his audience demands that he supply them with a comfortingly abstract portrait of itself: 'there's nothing like / Appealing to our nature!' (2, 792–3). It is an audience wholly willing to elevate the poet over 'a host of warriors, statesmen' (2, 813), but only for so long as he furnishes a poetry safely confined within a purely aesthetic realm. Sordello's dream ever since his boyhood was to become Apollo, but by the end of Book II Apollo, who carries both a lyre and a bow, has come to represent a unity of 'Man and Bard', action and knowledge, politics and aesthetics, that Sordello's audience will not allow him to achieve. In the first three books Sordello tries to develop a political aesthetics and fails, in the final three he attempts to devise an aestheticized politics and fails again.

The failure of Sordello does not, of course, imply the failure of *Sordello*, for, unlike his hero, Browning does not despair of constructing a truly civic poetry, a poetry that neither instructs its audience from the heights nor servilely furnishes its readers with a flattering image of themselves. Both these modes, apparently antithetical but practically equivalent, are rejected in favour of a poetic manner that confines itself to 'half-words', 'half-names', a poetry, then, that comes into being only when it is completed by its reader, only when the reader supplies the 'accent' on which its meaning depends. In *Sordello* Browning devises a poetic style in which the poet and his readers communicate 'as brothers talk'. But he found no brothers: the commercial failure of the poem was complete. If, as Lee Erickson argues, the dramatic monologue is a genre that poets developed in order to express their sense of alienation from their audience,[70] then it was, one might argue, a fortunate failure. But it is better to leave the last word with the poem.

In the first flush of his enthusiastic belief that he can persuade Taurello to give his sword to the service of the multitude, Sordello feels that 'mankind and he were really fused' (4, 251). Like Oenone hidden in her cave – 'O Paris, give it to Pallas' – his naïvety is oddly touching. But at the end of the poem, when Browning looks for some saving evidence that Sordello's life was more than just a 'sorry farce' (6, 850), he finds it in a snatch of song sung by a child as he climbs a hillside near Asolo. The words of the song that the boy sings 'to beat the lark' are unintelligible, save for a brief snatch that Browning recognizes as a fragment of Sordello's 'Goito lay':

> the few fine locks
> Stained like pale honey oozed from topmost rocks
> Sun-blanched the livelong summer
>
> (6, 867–9)

This is the song with which Sordello first triumphed over Eglamor (2, 151–4), and it is the song that Palma repeats to Taurello in a last, forlorn attempt to persuade him to heed Sordello's words (5, 905–8). When it is sung, centuries later, by a boy climbing a hill Sordello has at last become 'really fused' with mankind. The words of the song flicker as they are repeated, but in the version sung by the boy its first couplet is also lopped from it:

> Some poor rhyme of 'Elys' hair
> And head that's sharp and perfect like a pear
> (5, 905–6)

Leaving out that first couplet, so awkward, so distinctive, smoothes the snatch of song, so that Sordello himself is bleached out of his lines.[71]

It becomes like one of Eglamor's songs, in which the poet melts into the poem. Even in the fragment that is all that survives of him, Sordello is somehow effaced.

## IV

In *Sordello* Browning is so preoccupied with the question of what a poetry of citizenship might be like that he scarcely attends to the question of what it might be for. Indeed, the decision to set his poem in thirteenth-century Italy effectively occluded the problem, and it was one that in his later career Browning only very indirectly returned to. [72] On political matters he was for the most part content, as he put it in 1860, to let his wife speak for him. It was, as Elizabeth Barrett Browning knew, an unusual disposition of responsibilities: 'So you and others upbraid me with having put myself out of my "natural place"', she wrote to a woman friend, 'What *is* one's natural place, I wonder?'.[73] In fact it was Barrett Browning, a woman, who, more vigorously than any of the major Victorian poets, not excepting Clough and Swinburne, developed a poetic manner that could appeal directly to the reader's sense of civic responsibility. It is typical that, far from seeking to redeem the word citizen from the 'hollow' resonance that it had been given by the Terror and the Napoleonic wars, she should have insisted that it was precisely in France that the civic ideal had its origin, and in France too under its new emperor, Louis Napoleon, the citizen king, rather than in the constitutional monarchy of Britain, that it found its strongest contemporary realization. In their election of him the people of France committed themselves once again to an ideal of citizenship that had been defeated in 1815. They chose that

> This man should renew the line
> Broken in a strain of fate
> And leagued kings at Waterloo,
> When the people's hands let go.
> ('Napoleon III in Italy', 7–10)

But this is a poem written only shortly before it was published in 1860. Barrett Browning was six years older than her husband and three years older than Tennyson, but the idea of citizenship did not preoccupy her as it did them in the 1830s.

From the very first Barrett Browning placed herself firmly within the tradition of liberal politics which had found, for her as for most of her contemporaries, its most glamorous spokesman in Byron, 'the Mont Blanc of intellect' (*An Essay on Mind* (1826), 70). In her very first published poem, *The Battle of Marathon* (1820), the fourteen-year-old girl was already commemorating a battle that, as all readers of Byron knew, sustained the dream 'that Greece might still be free'. It was the political stance to be expected in someone raised as she was in a non-conformist family,[74] and it informs several of her early poems. 'Lines on the Portrait of the Widow of Riego', for example, published with 'An Essay on Mind', celebrates the staunchness of a woman widowed when her patriot husband was executed after the failure of the Spanish Revolution of 1820. But in poems such as 'The Switzer's Wife' and 'Gertrude' Felicia Hemans had already made exhibitions of patriotic fortitude by women a popular poetic topic. It is more revealing to consider a poem that she did not write. In 1845 she was invited to write a poem for the Anti-Corn Law League, but was persuaded by her father, her closest male advisers, Kenyon and Chorley, and her brothers that it would be unbecoming in a woman poet to write on a controversial political issue.[75] It was not until 1846, when she escaped from Wimpole Street to Italy and from her father into marriage with Robert Browning, that she became free to cultivate the civic muse.

Elizabeth Barrett's domestic circumstances were famously peculiar, but nevertheless her story has a representative value. The four events which co-operated to direct the attention of Tennyson and Browning to the idea of citizenship in the early 1830s, the repeal of the Test and Corporation Acts, Catholic Emancipation, the founding of London University, and the Great Reform Bill, were all of them events that had an exclusive reference to men. If one were to identify events that had a similar significance for women one would find them much later in the century. One might begin, perhaps, with the Infant Custody Act of 1839, and add the founding of Girton College in 1869, the Married Women's Property Act of 1882, and the piecemeal recognition of the right of propertied women to vote in local elections by many local authorities in the last years of the century. It is predictable that women poets should have been slower than their male counterparts to begin to develop a civic poetry because such a poetry has as one of its conditions that its writers should at least entertain the prospect of exercising the responsibilities of citizens.

It is also true that Barrett Browning most often, like Byron, engages in the politics of nations other than her own. Her first important civic poem, 'The Cry of the Children' (1843), protested against the employment of children in British factories and mines, but *Casa Guidi Windows* (1851) and *Poems Before Congress* (1860), address themselves to Italian politics.[76] Byron had found in Italy and Greece the only arenas in which he could comfortably address himself to political realities because abroad, in pre-industrial, neo-feudal societies, he could assume his preferred political role as champion of the people without compromising his aristocratic status. Italy freed Barrett Browning to write political poetry for quite other reasons. For her, as for Hemans and Landon, *Corinne* was 'an immortal book' that 'deserves to be read three score and ten times – that is, once every year in the age of man'.[77] For her, as for her predecessors, the painful relationship between Corinne's identities as a woman and as an artist, and the conflict that disturbs Corinne between the desire for love and the desire for fame, provided the model through which she came to understand her own place as a woman poet in the nineteenth century. It is a theme that she explores most fully in *Aurora Leigh*. But *Corinne* is both a novel about a woman artist and about a country, both a romance and a travel book (even in long sections a travel guide), and, as its full title suggests, for de Stael the two aspects of the novel are indissoluble: it is *Corinne, ou l'Italie*, a title to which Romney Leigh pays his own unconscious tribute when he addresses Aurora as 'My Italy of women' (8, 358). Corinne's Italy is occupied and ruled by the French as Barrett Browning's was by Austria, and hence its people are deprived of citizenship in their own country. This is a sad truth that Corinne insistently presses on the Scottish aristocrat, Lord Nelvil. His pride, she tells him, is the product of the free institutions of his country, and he should look indulgently on Italians who 'have been denied the lot of being a nation'. In Italy, men are unlikely to 'acquire the dignity and pride characteristic of free, military nations', with the consequence that Italian 'men's characters have the gentleness and flexibility of women's'.[78] This is why it is a country that may appropriately be represented by Corinne, a woman, and it is also why her countrymen are so generously appreciative of her genius, so free from the prejudice, shared alike by Aurora Leigh's cousin Romney, and by many of Barrett Browning's reviewers, that women are by their gender barred from producing art of major importance:

> You give us doating mothers, and chaste wives,
> Sublime Madonnas, and enduring saints!
> We get no Christ from you, – and verily
> We shall not get a poet, in my mind.
>
> (*Auora Leigh*, 2, 222–5)

For Barrett Browning, then, residence in Italy was, as it had been for Mary Shelley, curiously empowering, curiously because it was a consequence of

living amongst a people disenfranchised by their nationality as definitively as Shelley and Barrett Browning were by their sex.

The absence of a civil society in Italy is, de Stael shows, in itself liber-
ating in so far as it frees Italians from the constrictive power of a commanding public opinion. Corinne attends Lord Nelvil on his sick bed,
and visits her country house alone with him, both of them actions that
would have compromised the reputation of an unmarried Englishwoman. It was the desire to enjoy such freedoms that attracted many
foreigners to Italy in the nineteenth century; people such as the friends
of the Shelleys, Lady Mountcashell and George Tighe, who, because
Lady Mountcashell was still legally married, found that they could live
together more comfortably in Italy, or the Brownings' friend, Harriet
Hosmer, the sculptor, who took a studio in Rome where it was easier
for a young woman to live alone and pursue her art without attracting
hurtful comment than it would have been in Britain or America. One
reason that Aurora takes Marian Erle and her infant son to Italy is her
desire to return to the country where she was born, but another is that
Italy offers a less rigid, a more yielding social space in which to establish a family consisting of a mother, a surrogate mother, and their
child, who has no father, and yet as Marian insists to Romney Leigh is
in spite of that not 'fatherless' (9, 414). Italy offers a place in which
you can 'be, as if you had not been till then, / And were then, simply
that you chose to be' (7, 1194–5) So, in the house overlooking Florence, Aurora can establish a new domestic economy in which she, a
woman, assumes the male role of provider, and yet is still woken each
morning by the kisses of Marian's child, his 'mouth and cheeks, the
whole child's face at once / Dissolved on mine' (7, 949–50). In the
house at Bellosguardo Aurora and Marian establish a small, enclosed
matriarchy, the domestic equivalent of the alternative civil society that
Mary Shelley placed in fourteenth-century Italy in *Valperga* (1823), the
hill-top fortress from which Euthanasia exercises a nurturing, uncoercive
maternal rule over her dependants.

For de Stael 'free' nations, civil societies, are also 'military' nations,
because, presumably, a nation devoid of military virtues would be
incapable of securing its freedoms. Britain is free because its citizens live
under a rule of law that secures their rights, but the rule of law can only
be itself secured by men such as Nelson and Wellington. It is a lesson
that Mary Shelley's Euthanasia learns when Valperga is attacked and
taken by the hero-villain of the novel, the warlord Castruccio Castra-
cani. In defending the tiny state over which she rules, Euthanasia is
obliged to appeal to the masculine heroic code that in her governance

of the state she repudiates. Unsurprisingly, when the warrior Castruccio forces her to meet him on his own terms, she is defeated, and left with the bitter reflection that she has betrayed the values by which she sought to govern by the very manner in which she was obliged to defend them:

> Euthanasia wept when she heard of the blood that had been spilt for her; and self-reproach, who is ever ready to thrust in his sharp sting, if he find that mailed conscience has one weak part, now tormented her that she had not yielded, before one human life had been lost in so unhappy a cause. 'Do not evil that good may come,' thought she. 'Are not those the words of the Teacher? I have done infinite evil, in spilling that blood whose each precious drop was of more worth than the jewels of a kingly crown; but my evil has borne its fitting fruit; its root in death, its produce poison.'[79]

The problem for Barrett Browning was less intractable, for she did not share Mary Shelley's absolute aversion to violence. But it remained severe. How could Italy achieve nationhood, and its people the dignity of citizenship, without submitting to a patriarchal rule of law that, as it was embodied in her father, Barrett Browning had fled to Italy to escape? Her solution is articulated in her poems, best of all, perhaps, in *Casa Guidi Windows*, and it is founded on a re-definition of citizenship not as a state but as a process. It is not an idea peculiar to Barrett Browning, and might, in fact, be claimed as the dominant Victorian idea of citizenship. It supposes that the individual is neither subsumed within the state nor distinct from it, but rather that the idea of citizenship is realized in an unending process of negotiation by means of which the individual defines and re-defines her place within the body politic. It is in this sense that all civil societies should be like Tennyson's Camelot, which is a city 'They are building still, seeing the city is built / To music, therefore never built at all, / And therefore built for ever' (*Gareth and Lynette* (1871), 272–4). Barrett Browning never condenses her civic ideal into so memorable a lyric cadence, but in *Casa Guidi Windows* she gives it more substance.[80]

Barrett Browning's poem takes as its subject the defeated Italian revolution of 1848. It is in two parts. The first, which records the Florentine celebration on September 12, 1847, of the restoration of their civil liberties is heady with enthusiasm: the second, which records the entry into Florence of an Austrian army of occupation on May 2, 1849, is heavy with disillusion. It is a poem in which Barrett Browning is much concerned with her own place in literary history, and hence it is appropriate that she should have borrowed this structure from the first major political poem in English written by a woman, Charlotte Smith's *The Emigrants* (1793), but it is still more important that the structure enables Barrett Browning to present her meditation on Italian nationalism dramatically. It is a structure that compels the reader at once to look with the speaker, to see events through her eyes, and to look at the speaker, to trace through her responses the universal truth that those who entertain excessive hopes leave themselves vulnerable to a correspondingly painful disillusionment. It is, then, an example of the 'double poem' that, as Isobel Armstrong has shown us, is the defining mode of Victorian poetry.[81] But male Victorian poets tend characteristically to establish an ironic relation between the two aspects of their poems, and one result of this is that an interest in politics is almost always subordinated to an interest in character. Clough's *Amours de Voyage* (1849), for example, describes the thwarted Roman revolution that immediately preceded the Florentine revolution of *Casa Guidi Windows*, but for Clough the Roman Republic functions most importantly as a means through which Claude, the English tourist, reveals and discovers his authentic or inauthentic selfhood. *Casa Guidi Windows*, too, is flecked with irony, but Barrett Browning never fixes the poem within an ironic mode, and in consequence the personality of the speaker never displaces the stumbling advance of Italy towards nationhood from the centre of the poem's concerns. The male poets use irony to dramatize their alienation from the social group, but Barrett Browning is interested in working out her relationship with the group. Hence the oddity that she, a disenfranchised woman, unlike her male contemporaries, finds an idiom that makes possible the writing of directly political poetry.

The poem's long opening movement defines the responsibilities of the civic poet by exploring two closely related questions: what language should civic poetry be written in, and what relationship should the civic poet assume with her literary tradition? Barrett Browning's insistence that the poet's responsibilties as an artist and her responsibilities as a citizen are inseparable informs the whole discussion. To select a metaphor is to make a political decision. For example, to describe Italy as the 'Niobe' of nations (1, 32) is to manufacture 'cadenced tears which burn not where they touch' (1, 35); it is to employ figurative language to disguise the pain that such language dishonestly claims to express. The poet has a responsibility not to 'sigh for Italy with some safe sigh / Cooped up in music 'twixt an oh and ah' (1, 163–4). *Casa Guidi Windows* is the first important poem that Barrett Browning wrote after

song, / If my dead masters had not taken heed / To help the heavens and earth to make me strong' (1, 432–4). Or, more originally, a poet's predecessors challenge her to re-make them in her own image, in order that history fulfil its proper function by serving the needs of the present. Barrett Browning re-creates Michelangelo and Dante as Mazzini's true predecessors, republicans who recognized only one authority, 'il popolo'.[83] In this, she was at least following Mazzini himself, but Savonarola is re-created in her own image, as a Protestant non-conformist, who 'tried the tank / Of old church-waters' and 'said they stank!' (1, 267–9).

The inconsistency is the point. The ambition entertained by some radical visionaries, the Jacobins and Shelley for example, to abolish the past, to consume it in a single apocalyptic conflagration to make way for an utterly new future, and the Burkean notion that the past must be allowed to hold the present forever in a dead man's grip, are for Barrett Browning both and equally refusals of the duty of citizenship, which requires that the relationship between past and present be unendingly re-negotiated. As with citizenship so with poetry. To write is to make delicate and always provisional accommodations with the poetry of the past. *Casa Guidi Windows* begins as a celebration of the Florentines' recovery of their citizenship, but it begins too by remembering a failure that saddened Barrett Browning throughout the rest of her life, the failure of her husband's poetry. The child's song, heard through the windows of Casa Guidi, recalls, as Barrett Browning's editors have noted, the song in *Pippa Passes* that transforms the lives of all who hear it when it sounds through their windows. But even more clearly it recalls the boy's song at the end of *Sordello*, which, like the song that Barrett Browning hears, mounts higher and higher until it leaves the 'lark, God's poet, swooning at his feet' (6, 866). *Sordello* was the climactic failure of Browning's career, and a failure that Barrett Browning in her two most important poems repairs. *Sordello* traces the failure of its central character to become 'the complete Sordello, man and bard', and Aurora Leigh is allowed to pursue the same enterprise to a rapturously happy conclusion. *Sordello* cannot find any means of bringing his poetic ideals to bear on the political world, so that his life amounts only to a 'solemn farce'. In *Casa Guidi Windows*, Barrett Browning seems to have no more success, and yet her poem ends smilingly confident that no human effort, neither the Italian revolutions of 1848 nor even *Sordello*, is ever wasted, for the 'world has no perdition, if some loss' (2, 780). She begins her poem with the song that ends *Sordello*, and yet hers is a quite different song, celebrating the beauty of liberty rather than the beauty of Elys' hair, and her poem founds its quite unironic confidence that 'God's in his heaven' and that all will be, even if patently it is not at present, 'right with the world' not in the joy of hopes realized but in the bitter experience of their failure. So her poem at once recognizes her husband's failure, denies it, and redeems it, and in this it offers a model for the manner in which both poets and citizens should conduct their dealings with the past.

Dorothy Mermin points out that in *Casa Guidi Windows* Barrett Browning 'defines herself explicitly ... as a woman',[84] but in fact the first part of the poem is as concerned to conceal her gender as the second part is to display it. Even when she describes visiting Vallombrosa with her husband, he is neutrally invoked as 'beloved companion' (1, 1130). In the preface to the poem she offers the 'discrepancy' between the two parts as a guarantee of her 'truthfulness'. She does not try to hide the fact that 'she believed, like a woman, some royal oaths, and lost sight of the consequence of some popular defects'. Here, her womanhood is presented as the sign of her credulousness, which makes it entirely appropriate that she should, throughout the first part of the poem, conceal it. It serves also to alert us to the fact that the rhetoric of the first part of the poem is carefully deployed in a not quite successful act of repression.[85] She has to blur her clear-sighted recognition of the folly of the widespread confidence that the Pope, Pius IX, would act the part of a benevolent liberal. Any such confidence, she insists, runs counter to the entire history of the papacy, is inconsistent with the character that a man must develop if he is ever to rise to the papal throne, and supposes that the Catholic Church might willingly embrace a contradiction that threatened its own existence, for free institutions are, she believes, a threatening affront to the claim to absolute authority on which the power of the papacy is founded. And yet, despite the overwhelming evidence to the contrary, she 'fain would grant the possibility / For *thy* sake, Pio Nono' (1, 867–8). All the objections to the likelihood of the Pope emerging as a hero of the liberal cause seem to apply equally to Florence's Grand Duke Leopold II, and yet, as she watches him acknowledge the people from the windows of the Pitti Palace, and present his children to them 'to suggest / *They*, too, should govern as the people willed' (1, 559–600), and especially when he is reported to have shed 'good warm human tears' (1, 563) on the occasion, she is eager to believe in his good intentions. 'I like his face', she writes, which is 'mild and sad', but the phrase itself conceals a warning in its echo of her husband's description of Charles I, who fixed himself in Strafford's heart as the 'man with the mild voice and mournful eyes' (II, ii, 193), and later signed the warrant for his execution.

Finally, in the poem's first part, as she watches the Florentine people walking in procession to the Pitti Palace, she successfully represses her knowledge of them as they are. She sees them walk along, all neatly divided into their orders, the magistrates, the lawyers, the priests, monks and friars, the artists, the trades, and last of all the 'populace, with flags and rights as good' (1, 497). And then there are the representatives of the other Italian states, marching behind their banners, Siena's she-wolf, Pisa's hare, and Arezzo's horse, and finally the delegation of foreigners

> Greeks, English, French – as to some parliament
> Of lovers of her Italy in ranks,
> Each bearing its land's symbol reverent.
>
> (1, 513–15)

For Barrett Browning, and for all like her who knew their Carlyle, such processions are a warning in themselves.[86] Descriptions of them punctuate Carlyle's *The French Revolution*. They constitute the great set pieces of his history, and always prompt his deep, fierce laughter, for what they offer is an idea of citizenship reduced to a mummery, an empty masquerade, and they command the belief only of those who cannot see the people marching in the procession for what they are, of those who can successfully repress any recognition of people in their gross, physical individuality. But in Part One of the poem, looking from Casa Guidi windows, Barrett Browning successfully sustains the illusion that the people who pass beneath the window, 'These oil-eaters, with large, live, mobile mouths / Agape for macaroni', as she so vigorously describes them earlier in the poem (1, 200–1), are transformed into an ideal citizenry rather than acting out a pantomime of citizenship.

After she had written the first part of the poem, and before she began to write the second, Barrett Browning became a mother, so that when the young boy singing who begins the poem is reflected at its end it can be in the form of Barrett Browning's 'own young Florentine' (2, 743), her son, Pen. Her motherhood informs the poem's second part throughout. When the Austrian troops enter Venice, her first thought is that the 'regular tramp' of their feet should not disturb her sleeping child (2, 288–98). It is her motherhood, too, that gives poignancy to her account of the death of Garibaldi's pregnant wife, who died as she was retreating with her husband and his army from Rome, and was hastily buried on the beach. She,

> at her husband's side, in scorn,
> Outfaced the whistling shot and hissing waves,

> Until she felt her little babe unborn
> Recoil, within her, from the violent staves
> And bloodhounds of the world: – at which, her life
> Dropt inwards from her eyes, and followed it
> Beyond the hunters. Garibaldi's wife
> And child died so. And now, the sea-weeds fit
> Her body like a proper shroud and coif,
> And murmurously the ebbing waters grit
> The little pebbles, while she lies interred
> In the sea-sand.
>
> (2, 678–89)

Hers is the death of the woman hero, and it seems, as Barrett Browning admits, to reinstate the image of Italy that in the first part of the poem she had so vigorously rejected, Italy as the woman beautiful in her grief, mourning her dead children, 'Still Niobe' (2, 726). The buoyant optimism of the poem's first part seems now only a symptom of womanly weakness, an inability to believe that even a Duke could lie when his children's kisses were warm on his face:

> And I, because I am a woman, I
> Who felt my own child's coming life before
> The prescience of my soul, and held faith high,
> I could not bear to think, whoever bore,
> That lips, so warmed, could shape so cold a lie.
>
> (2, 95–9)

She watches Duke Leopold return to Florence under the protection of the Austrian army, and knows that the Pope has already co-operated in the overthrow of Garibaldi's Roman Republic by entering into a league with Austria. The faith in Italy that she had so triumphantly expressed in the poem's first part stands revealed as not at all the prophetic utterance of the true poet, but just a woman's wishful thinking.

All the uncomfortable truths that had been repressed return. Leopold is revealed as a weak worthless man, and Pius IX as, after all, just a Pope, 'only the ninth Pius after eight' (1, 1033), who acted, quite predictably, as all the other Piuses had done. And the people had shown themselves quite unable to live up to the image of themselves as a noble, united citizenry that they had so flamboyantly presented as they marched in procession to the Pitti Palace on September 12, 1847. When Leopold fled from the city, its citizens 'set new café signs, to show / Where

patriots might sip ices in pure air / (Yet the fresh paint smelt somewhat)'
(2, 125–7). If they 'did not fight / Exactly', they at least fired their mus-
kets into the air (2, 154–5), and would have fought in earnest, had they
been willing to leave their 'piazzas, shops and farms / For the bare sake
of fighting' (1, 169–70). And at the last they had been quite happy to
invite Leopold back, and watch passively as he re-entered the city
under Austrian protection. This whole section of the poem is weighted
with a fierce, satirical Carlylean scorn for a people who had proclaimed
a 'true republic in the form of hats' (2, 131), and there is even a trace of
savage Carlylean satisfaction at the arrival of the Austrian army as a
brute fact to shatter play-acted republican flummery. It is as a sign that
she will no longer repress her grasp of unheroic actualities that Barrett
Browning does not write the second part of the poem in the person of
an abstract, ungendered poet, but rather from 'the faint heart of [her]
womanhood' (2, 406). She confesses her womanhood, then, as a signal
of her disillusionment, but the work of the poem's second part is to
locate in that same confession the ground of a renewed and strengthened optimism.

Most obviously her optimism is grounded on the fact of her child.
She presents herself in this part of the poem as an 'Italy of women',
and, if that is granted, then the fact of the child, Pen, grants Italy a
future, and frees the land from the sweet, sad nostalgia that benumbs it
when it is characterized as Niobe. More importantly, the manner in
which the mother looks at her child offers a model of the way we
should all look at our fellows, a maternal model. Women, the suggestion is, can at once see children as they are and see them lovingly. So,
Aurora Leigh can look smilingly at Marian's child in a temper. Marian
peels him a fig, but does not place it in his mouth, so that he

> Sucked at it
> With vehement lips across a gap of air
> As he stood opposite, face and curls a-flame
> With that last sun ray, crying, 'give me, give,'
> And stamping with imperious baby-feet.
>
> (8, 10–14)

This is a real child, a human child, but the hair that becomes an aure-
ole in the light of the setting sun reminds us that he is also divine. It is
the same image that ends *Casa Guidi Windows*. Pen shakes 'the glittering nimbus' of his hair, and in doing so he becomes the 'witness' that
'New springs of life are gushing everywhere' (2, 760–2).

In the poem's second part Barrett Browning looks at the Italian people and finds them cowardly in their failure to defend the revolution, vicious in the assassination of the Pope's minister, Count Rossi (2, 540–65), and fickle in their invitation to Duke Leopold who had fled from them to return as their ruler. But she can see all this without losing her faith in them, because she looks at them with the eyes of a woman and a mother, and in this poem the maternal gaze can look lovingly not despite but because of the individual's flawed humanity. It is repelled only by the sight of people who have surrendered their individuality to the group, and in doing have become inhuman, a nightmare vision that is realized when the Austrian troops march into Florence, staring straight ahead, 'not an eye deflect / To left or right' (2, 312–13), and every 'single man, dust-white from head to heel' (2, 305). *Casa Guidi Windows* acts out the recognition that Aurora Leigh expresses abstractly, that 'all society', all civil society.

> Howe'er unequal, monstrous, crazed, and cursed,
> Is but the expression of men's single lives,
> The loud sum of the silent units.
>
> (8, 876–8)

But, unlike *Aurora Leigh*, it remains a civic poem, because it acknowledges the importance of the sum as well as of the units, and of political as well as moral reformation. Neither does the poem try to fix the relationship between the two. It suggests instead that civil society comes into being, like the poem itself, in an unending process of negotiation between the claims of the individual and the claims of the state, which is why civil society is at once always building and never built.

As with the national, so with the international community. Other nations, but especially Britain and France, have a duty to support the Italians, because nations, like the individuals that make up those nations, have duties to each other, and in both cases that duty is confirmed rather than threatened by a recognition of difference. The Great Exhibition that was taking place in Hyde Park as Barrett Browning wrote is wittily offered as at once an expression and a parody of proper international relations. It has become a 'Fair-going world' (2, 578), and those who visit the Crystal Palace see arranged the products of every nation, all of them boasting their distinctive national character: 'These corals, will you please / To match against your oaks?' (2, 592–3). The Exhibition offers a model of an international community, except that it confines itself to objects rather than values, to goods rather than goodness.

All the events of the poem are seen through Casa Guidi windows. In her preface Barrett Browning presents the poem's title as a defensive stratagem:

> The poem contains the impressions of the writer upon events in Tuscany of which she was a witness. 'From a window,' the critic may demur. She bows to the objection in the very title of her work.

The windows acknowledge that she is separated from the events she describes both by her nationality and her gender. She looks at Italy through English eyes, and the business of men through the eyes of a woman. But, in the end, the poem suggests, her vision is the truer for it, because the poem repudiates equally an exclusive cultivation of our own 'single lives' and the kind of surrender of the single self to the state so powerfully figured in the Austrian soldiers, all of them rendered indistinguishable, 'dust-white from head to heel'. The windows secure the distinction between the room and the street, between private and public spaces, which civil society must admit if its citizens are to enjoy their right to a private life, but because the windows open onto the street it is a private life that is not freed from public responsibility. In looking through the windows Barrett Browning proclaims herself as, like her son, a 'Florentine'. The windows do not work to reveal that she is peripheral to the events that she sees, but rather to establish her as the poem's type of the true citizen, at once separate from the state and joined to it. The windows, as Helen Groth has recently suggested, establish the 'spatial division' between 'an abstract public self' and the self understood as a centre of 'inchoate private desires' on which Barrett Browning's liberalism is founded.[87] It is the civic ideal that many Victorian poems moved towards in their attempt to evade either of the uncomfortably intransigent ideals that their Romantic predecessors had left to them: either the uncompromising assertion of irreducible individuality that Byron celebrates in poems such as *Manfred*, or the contrasting ideal that informs the fourth act of *Prometheus Unbound*: 'Man, oh, not men, a chain of linked thought' (394). But it is a civic ideal that is, I think, first adequately expressed in *Casa Guidi Windows*.

# 6
# Realizing Romanticism

In his splendid study, *The Return of the Visible in British Romanticism*, William Galperin takes issue with the assumption that Romanticism may be definitively characterized by its rebellion against 'the tyranny of the eye'.[1] Romantic poets like Shelley may insist that their concern is with 'invisible nature', and 'perception', in poems such as 'Tintern Abbey', may give way to 'conception' as the 'eye', so keenly active in the poem's first paragraph, is supplanted by the 'I', and yet, Galperin argues, the repressed term always threatens to return. Objects resist their transmutation into symbols, or, in the terms Galperin borrows from Norman Bryson, the artist's attempt to subject all he sees to his commanding gaze is always likely to be frustrated by the intrusion of an insubordinate glance, which restores to the natural world its haphazard, uncontrollable contingency. Readers of Romantic poetry by women have pointed out that this willingness to subordinate facts to meanings is in any case a characteristic only of male artists. Stuart Curran, for example, celebrates the manner in which Charlotte Smith, in a poem such as *Beachy Head*, refuses to allow the details of the landscape to be absorbed within her theme. When her glance falls on 'the wood sorrel with its light thin leaves, / Heart-shaped and triply folded, and its root / Creeping like beaded coral' (361–3), what her eye sees is enough for her.[2] But Charlotte Smith, like the women poets who were her contemporaries, was largely forgotten by her Victorian successors, and though, in the work of the male poets who were remembered, the visible world is repressed only to make its sly returns, Galperin would accept, for his argument depends on it, the fact of the repression. In his reading of Constable's 'Haywain' (1820–1), for example, the spectator of the painting is disembodied, and allowed to survey the scene from an impossible vantage point, some fifty feet above the richly dappled surface of the Stour. The painter, just as readily as the poet Keats, seems able to employ 'the viewless wings of poesy' to lift him above the solid earth 'where men sit', and from that elevated vantage the crowded details of the canvas can resolve themselves into a deep and restful calm. Constable invites us to 'gaze' at the scene, and, if he alludes to the other mode of seeing, the glance, it is only by finding a place in the bottom left hand of the canvas for a spaniel, momentarily paused, as it goes along the bank about its doggy business, by the sight or the splash of the horse and cart. We may be invited to imagine the chaotic, material physicality of the world as it is perceived by that dog, but we are not given it to contemplate.

Galperin finds the richest presentations of a world that resists the unifying power of the imagination in the seventh book of *The Prelude*, 'Residence in London', but he does not try to disguise that, for Wordsworth, the assault on his ears of the 'Babel din' (1805, 157) of the city that resisted, except for brief moments, his power to reduce it to harmony is presented as a bewildering experience of imaginative impotence. It is a distressing, even if salutary, awakening, an extended version of the moment when the hero of Shelley's *Alastor* (1816) awakens from the dream in which he has melted into the 'dissolving arms' of the 'veiled maid':

> Roused by the shock he started from his trance –
> The cold white light of morning, the blue moon
> Low in the west, the clear and garish hills,
> The distinct valley, and the vacant woods,
> Spread round him where he stood.
>
> (192–6)

He opens his eyes on a world that painfully impresses him by its harsh clarity, and its indifferent externality. Similar moments are recorded in several poems by Tennyson, but, even in the earliest of them in which Tennyson is most evidently working within the tradition of his Romantic predecessors, the effect is slightly but distinctly different. In *Timbuctoo* (1829), for example, the city of the imagination, through which a river winds 'imaging / The soft inversion of her tremulous Domes' (227–8), wilts beneath the harsh gaze of 'keen *Discovery*', like Lamia transfixed by Apollonius's withering stare, until all its 'brilliant towers'

> Darken and shrink and shiver into huts,
> Black specks amid a waste of dreary sand.
> Low-built, mud-walled, Barbarian settlements.
>
> (242–4)

Even here the description of the city, not as dreamed but as seen by the first European eyes to have looked on it, has an imaginative vitality that at least modulates the regret expressed in the poem's elegiac conclusion: 'How changed from this fair City!' (245).

This is to say only what has been very generally recognized, most eloquently, perhaps, by Carol Christ, that the Victorian poets were much less willing than the Romantics to disregard, or to demean the evidence of their eyes.[3] Put another way, they were much less willing to co-opt the natural world as a screen onto which the self might expansively project itself. Hence, Tennyson's crusty reaction to Ruskin's description of Maud walking in the meadows as a fine example of the pathetic fallacy: 'For her feet have touched the meadows / And left the daisies rosy' (*Maud* (1855), 1, 434–5). His lines, he insisted, described the pink underside of the daisy's petals, turned by the tread of a foot or a long skirt that brushes the grass: 'Why, the very day I wrote it, I saw the daisies rosy in Maiden's Croft, and thought of enclosing one to Ruskin labelled "A pathetic fallacy" '.[4] Victorian poets may repeat the familiar Romantic complaint of the loss in adulthood of the sense of undifferentiated union with the natural world that marks childhood experience, but they do so less plangently, with a tougher sense that the child's vision of things is childish as well as childlike. So, Aurora Leigh no longer feels as a woman that grasshoppers are her playmates:

> now the creatures all seemed farther off,
> No longer mine, nor like me, only *there*,
> A gulph between us.
> 
> (7, 1098–1100)

That 'gulph' is, of course, the condition of realism, the aesthetic and ethical ideal of which Ruskin is the chief Victorian theorist. Byron, in a passing Wordsworthian mood, might write, 'to me / High mountains are a feeling', but for Ruskin the feeling that mountains inspired was not an invitation to merge his being with theirs but to study their geological formation. Browning is as suspicious as Ruskin of the notion that the multitudinous world should be put to the service of the poet's vision rather than vice versa. His 'garden fancy', 'Sibrandus Schafnaburgensis' (1842), for example, can be understood as a satire on the Romantic nature poem. Bored with a musty volume that he has been reading in the garden, Browning tosses it into the 'crevice' of a plum tree, where he knows that 'rain-droppings stagnate', and forgetfully leaves it there for a month. When he retrieves the volume, and lays it to dry in the sun, he gleefully notes how the life of the tree has invaded its pages. There is a toadstool 'stuck in his chapter six':

> How did he like it when the live creatures
> Tickled and toused and browsed him all over,
> And worm, slug, eft, with serious features,
> Came in, each one, for his right of trover?
> When the water-beetle with great blind deaf face
> Made of eggs the stately deposit,
> And the newt borrowed just so much of the preface
> As tiled in the top of his black wife's closet?
>
> (49–56)

The bugs and beasties that colonize the book are nature's revenge on the overweening claim of the Romantic poet that nature might be accommodated in a book, all its pullulating life absorbed into the words of a poem. But it is in a later poem, *Fra Lippo Lippi* (1855) that he most fully articulates his position.

The poem is so well known that commentary is scarcely necessary. To the prior's demand that he paint souls rather than bodies, Lippo retorts that the soul is not best honoured by ignoring or falsifying the body. It is an argument that Shelley would have thoroughly approved. The significant difference is that in Browning's poem the precept is so robustly acted out not just within the poem but by the poem. Shelley is as persuaded as Browning that artists are the product of their historical circumstances, and yet, even as he expresses the thought, he dematerializes it, until each word of a poem becomes 'a burning atom of inextinguishable thought'. One effect of throwing Sibrandus Schafnaburgensis' book into the pear tree was to expose it in all its material being 'With all the binding all of a blister, / And great blue spots where the ink has run' (42–3), in a lively satire on the notion that any text can approach the immaterial condition of thought. In *Fra Lippo Lippi*, the poem works most busily not to explicate but to act out the painter's aesthetic principles. His encounter with the watch is thickly realized, not just in the pressure of the grip on Lippo's throat, but in the rich possibilities of social relationship that Lippo explores as he wheedles, flatters, threatens, offers a lordly sixpence, and appeals to a code of masculine solidarity that requires its adherents to look with protective forbearance on fleshly frailties.[5] His personal history too is recounted through vivid, physical details, his Aunt Lapaccia and her 'stinger' of a hand (89), the 'half-stripped grape bunch' he eyes hungrily (115), and the feel of his monk's habit, its 'warm serge and the rope that goes all round' (100). So is his passionate devotion to his art: the sight of a characterful face makes his fingers itch for 'a bit of chalk / A wood-coal or the like' (37–8). And so is his historical situation, at the moment when patronage of the arts was passing from the Church to the merchant princes, the traders and bankers that ruled Italy's city states. Lippo lives his life passing between his convent, and 'the house that caps the corner' (18), the palace of Cosimo de Medici. That rich rendering of the material conditions that govern the artist's life and his work marks a decisive break with the Romantic focus on

> those passages of life in which
> We have had deepest feeling that the mind
> Is lord and master, and that outward sense
> Is but the obedient servant of her will.
> (*The Prelude* (1805), XI, 270–3)

But it is easier to explore the moment of that transition by inviting the return of a poet repressed into a footnote in Galperin's book, John Clare.

Galperin explains in that note that Clare is excluded from his study because of the 'lack of agency' in his work:

> For although Clare is certainly unique amongst his romantic contemporaries in his almost exclusive preoccupation with visible particularity, the fact that this particularity is, as John Barrell has shown, firmly rooted in a 'sense of place' puts substantial limits on its contestational function.[6]

It is precisely the 'contestational function' of Clare's poetry, and particularly the poems that he wrote in the years between 1825 and 1835, on which I wish to insist. But, as Galperin indicates, any such argument requires Clare to be recognized as quite other than the kind of poet he is most often represented as being. There are, and have been for some years, two tendencies evident in the critics of John Clare. One group, led by John Barrell, celebrates Clare as a local poet. For them, Clare's poems are uniquely valuable because through their diction and their syntax they express a mode of perception that would otherwise remain unarticulated. In reading these poems, the argument runs, we are allowed to see the world as it appeared to a particular social group, the agricultural labourers, at a particularly interesting time, the period during which the agricultural industry underwent the process of capitalization, and from a particular place, the village of Helpston in Northamptonshire.[7] Associated with this group are all those critics, some of them, like Seamus Heaney and Tom Paulin, poets themselves, who value above all Clare's use of the language that Helpston gave him, all those words sticky as frog-spawn – 'soodling', 'sloomy', 'gulsh'd', 'crizzling', 'crumping' – that lend the objects in Clare's poems a palpability in comparison with which the natural world as represented by other poets can seem bleached, faded into an idea.[8] A second group of critics, as yet a smaller one,[9] seems anxious that Clare should not be presented by modern critics in a way that so unnervingly recalls the stratagem of his first publisher, John Taylor, who marketed Clare's first volume of poems as the work of a peasant poet. For them, the crucial task is to establish John Clare's right to the place that he repeatedly claimed for himself, within the major tradition of English poetry, in 'the eternity of song' ('To a Poet').

Clare was, of course, a 'self-taught poet', but there is a sense, after all, in which all English poets of the modern period have been self-taught, there being no system of apprenticeship in literature of the kind that obtains in the fine arts. If we accept Keats's point, itself perhaps a response to those like Lockhart who accused him of lacking the education proper to a poet, that 'every man whose soul is not a clod' might claim to be a poet 'if he had loved, / And been well nurtured in his mother tongue' (*The Fall of Hyperion*, 13–15), then Clare, like Keats, might claim to be rather well-educated, well nurtured as he was not only in his mother tongue but in its poetry. Byron and Shelley had access to classical literature and to the literature of a number of modern European languages, but I do not think that either had the wide and deep familiarity with English poetry from the sixteenth century to his own time that Clare could claim. When, in 1831, Taylor sent him Southey's selections of the British poets 'from Chaucer to Jonson', Clare was pleased to find Surrey, the two Fletchers and Wither represented, and especially pleased by Browne's *Britannia's Pastorals*, but he was disappointed by the volumes: 'where is Suckling & where is Herrick & twenty more that ought to have been there'.[10] It is the response of an unusually well-read man.

Clare read for pleasure, but he read, too, because he had since his early youth bound himself apprentice in the craft of poetry. It was at precisely the time of this letter, 1831, that Clare was compiling the manuscript that, though it remained unpublished until 1978, constitutes his most substantial single volume, *The Midsummer Cushion*, and the poems collected there are those of a man who has mastered his craft.[11] Let me give three, brief examples, chosen almost at random. In the sonnet, 'Field

Thoughts', Clare praises, as he often does, wild flowers, which move him because their beauty is not produced by a gardener's care, and because they are tended by nothing

> But dews and sunshine and impartial rain...

It is a quiet line raised into monumental finality by its single epithet, a technique that in English poetry is much more commonly associated with poets steeped in the classics than with poets in the self-taught tradition. Or take a couplet from 'Pleasures of Spring':

> How beautiful the wind awakes and flings
> Disordered graces o'er the face of things

As John Barrell, among others, notes, Clare was fond of invoking an aesthetics of disorder, but in this couplet what strikes is how gracefully the enjambment disorders the pentameter lines. Or take the final line of 'St Martin's Eve', a rural idyll in the tradition of poems such as Burns's 'The Cotter's Saturday Night', but written in Spenserian stanzas. The poem closes as the revellers walk home:

> While every lanthorn flings long gleams along the snow

Clare hugely admired *The Eve of St Agnes*[12] and his line reveals how closely he has attended to Keats's handling of the final alexandrine of the Spenserian stanza. In the line 'And the long carpets rose along the gusty floor' (360), Keats cunningly acknowledges the extension of the line not just by the reference to the 'long' carpets, but by quietly repeating the idea of length in the word 'along'. Clare, as good poets, Eliot tells us, do, steals the effect, but puts it to use in a line of his own that is not at all imitative, a line, in fact, that most readers would find less studied than Keats's. I make these remarks only to challenge the notion that Clare lacked the 'agency' that critics assume in the work of his contemporaries, though it is odd that the point still needs making of a poet who, as early as 1822, could seriously consider 'imitating the styles of all the living poets as I got hold of them to read them...Southey and Crabb I fancy I can do to a tittle'.[13]

The confident expertise so repeatedly evident in *The Midsummer Cushion* is on the face of it an uncomplicated good. The presiding pathos underlying Gray's *Elegy* is that Gray, the super-educated don, fastidiously literate in several languages, must himself step forward to tell the 'artless tale' of the rural poor, because the poor cannot

adequately, in the 'uncouth rhymes' on the churchyard stones, memorialize their own lives. In the rural villages there are only those who
might have been poets, Miltons who, for lack of education, must
remain 'mute' and 'inglorious'. Clare, it might be said, by the mid-
1820s had broken down the barrier that Gray mourns between the
experience of the rural poor and the eloquence necessary to articulate
it.[14] But Clare repeatedly indicates that, however heartening such a
view might be, it is difficult to sustain, for it may be that the experience
of Gray's villagers is not simply hidden by their inability to articulate it,
waiting to be revealed by someone like John Clare who had miraculously learned to master the arts of eloquence, but rather that theirs is
an experience that is constituted by their inarticulacy, by their mute-
ness, and therefore an experience that is falsified precisely by virtue of
its being spoken.

The crucial matter for Clare is literacy. 'Both my parents was illiterate
to the last degree', he writes, and goes on to catalogue his father's reading
with unusual precision; the Bible, penny broadsheets, *Nixon's Prophecy*,
*Mother Bunch's Fairy Tales*, and *Mother Shipton's Legacy*.[15] It is an atten-
tiveness that is reproduced in the poems, as when 'The Village Doc-
tress' pores over 'Culpeppers Herbal' and 'Westleys Physic', and on
Sundays reads 'Bunyan's Pilgrim' or

> seeks her ancient prayerbook wrapt with care
> In cotton covers lest her hands should soil
> The gilded back full loath is she to spoil
> A book of which her parents took such heed
> *(Poems of the Middle Period, 3; 341)*

'The Cottager' has his prayer-book and Bunyan, too, and also Tusser's
*Husbandry* and *The Death of Abel*.[16] 'The Shepherd', when he sits by his
fire after work, sometimes 'takes up a book full of stories and songs', and
in the sonnet 'A Awthorn Nook' the nook is occupied by a shepherd
who 'on his elbow lolls to read / His slip of ballads bought at neighbouring fair'.[17] When Clare records a house like 'The Shepherd's Lodge' that
is entirely without books, he pauses to ponder the fact. Its tenant is

> To books unknown he never knows
> What they to thinking minds supply
> & yet his simple knowledge shows
> Much wiser men might profit bye
> *(Poems of the Middle Period, 3; 541)*

Clare notes, then, the reading habits of his neighbours, but he also notes his own, not just in his autobiographical writings, as in the twice-narrated story of how his reading of Thomson's *Seasons* made him a poet,[18] or in his journal, in which he planned to set down his 'opinion' of the books that he read, but in the poems themselves. In fact, Clare, more frequently than any of his contemporaries, more frequently even than Keats, presents himself in his poems as a reader, as a man who, when he returns home from a walk, is apt to 'reach down a poet [he] love[s] from the shelves', a copy of Thomson or Cowper ('The Holiday Walk'), who spends his evenings 'bending oer [his] knees', reading by the light of the fire, and, when he worked in the fields would often wish for rain so that he might get back to his books ('Labours Leisure').[19] Clare is happy to confess, as Wordsworth would never have done, to feeling the excitements of bookishness, 'cutting open with heart beating speed' the leaves of a 'brother poet's long-sought volume' ('The Pleasures of Spring'). When he takes his walks, he takes a book with him, and if the scenery is 'delicious' enough to persuade him to 'shut and put the volume bye', it is a fact worth noting ('On Visiting a Favourite Place').[20] Readerly habits are dear to him, especially the habit of marking a passage by turning down the corner of a page. When he reads out of doors some 'pocket poet' a plucked primrose serves 'Instead of doubling down to mark the place' ('The Pleasures of Spring'), and the same habit gives Clare a metaphor to define his own poetic purpose:

> How many pages of sweet natures book
> Hath poesy doubled down as favoured things ('Nature')[21]

My first point is the obvious one: that Clare himself in his poems repeatedly acknowledges that, if he is an expert reader of the book of nature, then he owes that expertise in some part to his habitual reading in other books, and especially the books of his brother poets. My second point is that Clare's reading complicates his relationship both with the natural world that he describes and with the community with which he shared it; both with his landscape and with his neighbours. I will begin with the neighbours.

Clare's lifelong love of Helpston did not prevent him either from feeling or on occasion from forcefully expressing his contempt for his fellow-villagers. He wrote to Taylor in 1822:

> I live here among the ignorant like a lost man in fact like one whom the rest seems careless of having anything to do with – they hardly dare talk in my company for fear I shoud mention them in my

writings & I find more pleasure in wandering the fields than in musing among my silent neighbours who are insensible to every thing but toiling & talking of it & that to no purpose[22]

Once again, this is a disposition that informs the poems. In 'Pleasures of Spring' there is an entirely characteristic distinction between the 'man of taste', an accomplished naturalist who takes with him on his springtime walks a 'pocket poet of some favoured muse', and the 'Hind' who scans his Bible 'wrapt in baize to keep the covers clean' for texts appropriate to the season, and the poem is characteristic too in that Clare's evident identification of himself with the man of taste underwrites his – in this case fond – detachment from the 'Hind'. Even John Barrell notes this tendency, but he tends to discount it. For him, Clare's introduction into his poems of figures such as 'Hodge', 'the swain', and 'the hind' is evidence only of a lingering contamination by the conventions of eighteenth-century landscape poetry, and he chooses to stress instead all those other characteristics of Clare's poetry that identify him with rather than detach him from his community; the use of dialect words, of a grammar of speech rather than of writing, the refusal to place the objects in his poems within any framing hierarchy.[23] But it seems fairer to accept that Clare's poems are not characterized by one or other of these habits, but by both, and to accept, too, that they are contradictory.

Clare will sometimes claim that poetry has an existence independent of language, so that the title of poet might justly be claimed by the illiterate, and even by the inarticulate:

> True poesy is not in words
> But images that thoughts express
> ('Pastoral Poesy', *Poems of the*
> *Middle Period*, 3; 581)

The image, unlike the word, is common to all, available even to the 'simplest'. In the same poem Clare suggests that poetry 'sings & whistles' before ever it 'talks aloud'. He is haunted here by a dream that Keats and Shelley also entertained, that a poem might be as natural, as untaught and unpremeditated, as birdsong, but for Clare the thought has an urgency not evident in his contemporaries. It prompts him in 'The Progress of Rhyme' to write poetry not about, but out of the nightingale's song:

> 'Wew-wew wew-wew chur-chur chur-chur'
> 'Woo-it woo-it' – could this be her

> 'Tee-rew tee-rew tee-rew tee-rew'
> 'Chew-rit chew-rit' – & ever new
> 'Will-will will-will grig-grig grig-grig'
>                 (*Poems of the Middle Period*, 3; 500)

This looks like a proto-modernist experiment, but it expresses a deep nostalgia for a lost time when the language of poetry was uncontaminated by the social and educational distinctions from which our ordinary language cannot be disentangled. And yet even in these lines Clare cannot fully assimilate language to birdsong, and in other moods he is willing to entertain the notion that for a poet to aspire to a language that evaporates, leaving no barrier between the reader and the natural world that it represents, is to pursue an impossible dream. It may be, Clare sometimes recognizes, that language, and in particular writing, cannot simply record the natural world, for to know a language, and to be able to read and write, is to have acquired a knowledge that informs each and every act of perception by which the natural world is known. Clare twice describes youngsters watching skeins of wild geese. In 'Schoolboys in Winter', the boys are 'Watching the letters that their journeys make'. The thought is expanded in 'March' in *The Shepherd's Calendar*, when the shepherd boy:

> marks the figurd forms in which they flye
> And pausing follows wi a wandering eye
> Likening their curious march in curves or rows
> To every letter which his memory knows

The flight of geese becomes a test case for Clare, marking his sense of how literacy cannot simply allow one to record pre-existing perceptions, because a knowledge of reading and writing informs the perception itself.[24] Yellowhammers' eggs prompt the same thought. In the sonnet sequence, 'A Walk', a cowboy triumphantly carries off a nest, excited by the mysteriously potent writing on the eggs, and in 'The Yellowhammers Nest' the 'pen-scribbled' eggs prompt a more literate observer to think of the 'scrawls' as 'natures poesy & pastoral spells'. The conclusion is clear; that when the hind and the man of taste look into a yellowhammer's nest they do not see the same eggs, and not even the cowboy sees the eggs as a member of a pre-literate culture would do. And a further conclusion follows. Clare was not only socially isolated in his village by his fame as a poet. His ability to articulate his world of itself rendered the world in which he lived crucially different from the world that his neighbours inhabited, and the more Clare developed his craft the more different the two worlds became.

Clare found, as had Robert Bloomfield, the poet with whom he most closely identified,[25] that the role of the peasant poet was a lonely one, a role that in itself served to isolate the poet from the communal village life that he celebrated. Like Bloomfield, Clare found himself occupying a position neither within the world of the village, nor within the literary world that both men associated with London, but somewhere between the two, at a remove equally from literary society and the community of the village. Clare was a greater poet than Bloomfield because he did not simply suffer this predicament, rather he allowed it to inform a substantial group of poems, which, for that reason, represent Clare's greatest achievement.

Clare, as Tom Paulin remarks, is 'both the poet of place and displacement',[26] and he is at his best when he is both at once. This is most obviously the case in the most widely discussed group of poems that Clare wrote, the poems named by Johanne Clare the 'enclosure elegies'.[27] Inevitably, and properly, the bulk of commentary on these poems has been historical and political in its bent, but it is worth remarking that contemplating the enclosed landscape of Helpston brought together for Clare with peculiar intensity the two contradictory emotions the coincidence of which seems to be the condition of his finest poetry. First, there is the object intimately known and deeply loved, and then there is that same object withdrawn from him, become blankly unfamiliar. Clare is, of course, pre-eminently the poet of familiar things, but he is also a poet who counts among the most potent items in his vocabulary the word, strange. It is the object at once familiar and strange that most excites him, and the enclosed landscape of Helpston is for him the most extreme example of such an object. This will seem a chilling remark to those like E.P. Thompson, who prize Clare because he 'conveys with extraordinary sensitivity the ways in which the psychic landscape of the village was savagely transformed by the enclosure of commons and open fields',[28] but it seems worthwhile to incur the risk of that response, and even to increase it. After all, Clare's best critics have themselves been apt to treat his hostility to enclosure as a metaphor – John Lucas, for example:

The hundred years between 1750 and 1850 is the century of dictionaries, of grammatical rules, and of the standardizing of pronunciation. As I have elsewhere remarked this is, in short, the period when language is being enclosed.[29]

For Lucas, Clare's hostility to orthographic and grammatical conventions, and to 'that awkward squad of pointings called commas colons semicolons'[30] is of a piece with his hostility to the enclosure of the open fields of Helpston, and in both cases it is a hostility that marks Clare's solidarity with the ordinary villagers, unlanded and uneducated. But the metaphor opens more complex possibilities. The century that Lucas refers to is, after all, also the century in which the laws of copyright were gradually formulated, in which published writings were, to extend the metaphor, enclosed. Clare's father who 'could sing or recite above a hundred' ballads[31] lived in an unenclosed literary landscape, but Clare, as his troubled relations with Edward Drury, Taylor, and Hessey indicate,[32] tried staunchly, if with little success, to establish his own title to his poems. For Clare's father, ballads and songs were the property not of an individual but of the community. His skill as a ballad-singer earned him social prestige, not an income. But, for his son, literature, like the enclosed landscape of Helpston, had undergone the process of capitalization. Edward Drury put the matter bluntly:

> My view of these poems is to consider them as wares that I have bought which will find a market in the great city. I want a broker or a partner to whom I can consign or share the articles I receive from the manufacturer ...[33]

Clare often expressed his contempt for the notion that the value of poetry might be determined by market forces,[34] but he could not afford to ignore in practice the new status of poetry as a market commodity.

Clare, then, was at once an agricultural labourer and a manufacturer of wares that found their market in 'the great city', and those two, scarcely consistent roles produced the complex position out of which Clare's poems are written. In the great poem that records his removal from Helpston to Northborough, 'The Flitting', he writes:

> I sit me in my corner chair
> That seems to feel itself from home

The chair is an old possession, its contours and Clare's frame comfortably adapted one to the other by the habit of long years, but it becomes for Clare a poetically charged object at the moment when a disconcerting strangeness is superimposed on its familiarity, when it feels itself 'from home', 'at loss', 'ill at ease'.[35] It is at this moment that it becomes the appropriate chair on which to imagine Clare sitting as he writes his strongest poems.

As almost all his readers have noticed, Clare never writes better than when he writes about birds, and in particular about birds' nests. Clare claims:

> I found the poems in the fields
> And only wrote them down
> (*The Shepherd's Calendar*)

He found the poems, then, as he took his daily walks, in precisely the same way that he found the birds' nests, the discovery of which these poems record, and the poems, Clare must want us to notice, are like the nests, woven together from humble natural materials, and like the eggs that the nests contain they own a fresh perfection of form that delights us when we come across them. These are, then, amongst Clare's most natural poems, but they are also amongst his most literary, for it is in writing these poems that Clare most fully articulates his sense of his own distinctive place amongst his fellow poets. He begins his sonnet, 'The Wren', by addressing them:

> Why is the cuckoos melody preferred
> & nightingales rich song so fondly praised
> In poets ryhmes Is there no other bird...

He makes the same point in one of his bird lists, when he describes the 'Sky Lark' as 'a bird that is as much of use in poetry as the Nightingale'.[36] He protests against the thinness of the selection of birds that do service in the poems of his contemporaries – Wordsworth's cuckoo, the skylark that Wordsworth shares with Shelley, and the nightingales of Coleridge and Keats – and responds with a flock of poems that mocks in the very variety of birds celebrated the meagreness of the symbolic imagination.[37]

The selection of British birds that the Romantic poets make is thin, but it is not arbitrary. They choose birds that can be heard without being seen: the cuckoo hidden in the leaves, the nightingale lost in the gathering gloom, and the skylark that sings from a height at which, as Shelley puts it, one 'feels' rather than 'sees' its presence. Wordsworth offers an explanation when he discusses his own poem to the cuckoo, in which he asks of the bird, 'Shall I call thee bird / Or but a wandering Voice?': 'This concise interrogation characterizes the seeming ubiquity of the voice of the Cuckoo, and dispossesses the creature almost of a corporeal existence; the imagination being tempted to this exertion of her power by a consciousness in the memory that the Cuckoo is almost perpetually heard throughout the season of Spring, but seldom becomes an object of sight' (Preface to *Poems* of 1815). These poems celebrate the possibility that poetry might free itself from the merely temporal circumstances, the 'weariness, the fever, and the fret', out of which it was produced. Just as the cuckoo's invisibility renders it for Wordsworth not a bird but simply a 'wandering voice', so poetry is offered as a 'mystery' through which the constraints of earthly life may be transcended, in which it is possible to leave behind all the limiting material weight of ordinary existence in order to experience what Shelley calls 'unbodied joy'. Even mortality itself may, in this view of things, be transcended by the song of the bird or the art of the poet: 'Thou wast not born for death, Immortal Bird!'. It is true that this group of poems characteristically ironizes the drive towards transcendence. The poets acknowledge that they cannot become the birds whose songs they celebrate, that they remain planted on the ground, stuck within their bodies.[38] Nevertheless, their poems locate the lyric impulse in the ambition to escape a merely 'corporeal existence', and may even suggest that such an attempt might be 'half' successful:

> Teach me half the gladness
> That thy brain must know,
> Such harmonious madness
> From my lips would flow,
> The world should listen then – as I am listening now.
> ('To a Skylark', 101–15)

Clare is characteristically hostile to such claims. For him, the action of even the simplest of flowers, the daisy, has more power to withstand time than the poet ('The Eternity of Nature'). But it is in his poems on birds and birds' nests that Clare most fully adumbrates his own dissenting position. His first and crucial tactic is his refusal to listen contentedly to the song of an unseen bird. The music of the nightingale prompts Clare to go 'Creeping on hands and knees through matted thorns' until he finds a spot from which he can watch the nightingale as it sings, and 'marvel that so famed a bird / Should have no better dress than russet brown' ('The Nightingale's Nest'). Clare is willing to agree with his contemporaries that birds may be 'poet-like' ('The Yellowhammer's Nest'), but poets, in Clare's view of things, are not released from their bodies by their music any more than the nightingale is freed from its russet brown feathers. Whatever Keats might have thought, the nightingale is not 'viewless': it is just that he did not know where to look for it, or did not look hard enough. Clare's insistence on finding and describing the birds' nests works still more strongly to ground song in the material facts of life; the need for food and shelter, and the overriding obligation to feed and to protect one's offspring. When Clare inspects a nest with that delighted exactitude of his, noting how the pettichap builds its nest from 'small bits of hay / Pluckt from the old propt-haystacks pleachy brow' and 'withered leaves' that 'from the snub-oak dotterel yearly falls / & in the old hedge-bottom rot away', fashioning the materials into a shape like an 'oven', lining it with 'feathers warm as silken stole', and contriving a 'snug entrance', 'Scarcely admitting e'en two fingers in', he is doing more than paying the natural world the tribute of his rapt attention. In such passages he is making his own eloquent plea against an aesthetics of transcendence. He works out in these poems a view of his own craft in terms of which the more exalted claims of his contemporaries appear childish, like the boys who think that if they could fly so high as a skylark they would build their dwellings 'on nothing but a passing cloud', and live there:

> As free from danger as the heavens are free
> From pain & toil – there would they build & be
> & sail about the world to scenes unheard
> Of & unseen
>
> ('The Sky Lark')

But the lark itself rests content with its 'low nest', built amongst 'the russet clods' and hidden in the corn.

Clare is always alert to, and suspicious of, the ease with which natural objects are diminished when a symbolic status is bestowed on them by poets. In Shelley's 'To a Skylark', for example, the skylark which sings its song as it mounts ever higher into the sky underwrites the drive towards transcendence that impels so much of Shelley's verse. Clare retorts in his journal, 'It is often reported that the Sky lark never sings but on the Wing this report is worth little truth like a many others I saw one this morning sing on the ground'.[39] In Keats's 'Ode to a Nightingale' the nightingale sings at night to secure its invisibility, and to underwrite the poet's separation from the workaday daytime world, but, Clare reminds us, 'the Nightingale sung as common by day as night & as often tho it's a fact that is not generaly known'. He makes the observation at the beginning of a passage that gleefully satirizes the process by which types of beauty so easily become independent of the objects that gave rise to the ideal:

> Londoners are very fond of talking about this bird & I believe fancy every bird they hear after sunset a Nightingale I remember when I was there last while walking with a friend in the fields of Shacklewell we saw a gentleman & lady listning very attentive by the side of a shrubbery & when we came up we heard them lavishing praise on the beautiful song of the nightingale which happened to be a thrush but it did for them.[40]

Song, as Clare well knew, offers no magical escape from a world of 'pain and toil', and in his poems about birds and their nests he quietly rebukes any such claim. But the poems do more. By repeatedly tracing the song-bird to its nest, Clare articulates his recognition of the intimate connection between his poetry and his village, between his song and the material conditions of his life. Hence, in this group of poems, Clare might be thought to reconcile the apparent contradictions that I began by addressing. He appears in them as a poet aware of, and responsive to, the work of his peers, and yet a poet fully conscious of his own distinctive place amongst them, and thus more than able to sustain the modest claim that he makes in 'The Progress of Rhyme': 'My harp though simple was my own'. And he also appears in these poems as a countryman, and as a writer whose authority is grounded in his intimate familiarity with a locality; with its language and with its landscape. To refuse either of these aspects of Clare's poetry is, it might be thought, to make the mistake that Clare seems to imply was too often made by his fellow-poets: it is to suppose that the bird might be separated from its nest. Clare was both a poet and a man of Helpston, and in him these two identities were inseparable.

This is a heartening view, but for all that it remains unconvincing. Its defectiveness is best indicated by pointing to another characteristic of this group of poems. Clare repeatedly represents the boys of Helpston, himself among them in his remembered boyhood, as pathologically addicted to bird-nesting. The cowboy singing in triumph as he carries off in his hat his obscene trophy, the 'stubbly nest' of a yellowhammer ('A Walk'), is not monstrous, but at worst a case of arrested development. Schoolboys, Clare tells us in the sonnet 'Sedge Birds Nest', are 'In robbing birds & cunning deeply skilled'. All summer long they patrol the fields 'In their birdnesting rounds' ('The Landrail'), and a nest, once seen, is safe from them only if their approach to it is barred by an enraged bull ('The Wild Bull'), or if the climb to the nest is so difficult that 'down they sluther' before they have reached it ('The Raven's Nest'). But it is ground-nesting birds who most move Clare; birds such as the lark, the fern owl, the peewit or the pettichap:

> Its nest close by the rut gulled waggon road
> & on the almost bare foot-trodden ground
> ('The Pettichaps Nest')

He is affected by the apparent vulnerability of these nests, that somehow survive though 'horses trample past them twenty times a day', and that remain even though built on open ground so hard to see that

> you and I
> Had surely passed it on our walk today
> Had chance not led us to it

In the sonnet, 'The Meadow Hay', Clare represents himself as just such a bird, stretched in 'the new mown swath' only 'a minute from the path', and humming a song which prompts a passer-by to pause wonderingly as he passes, and then move on:

> Unthinking that an idle rhymester lies
> Buried in the sweet grass
> (*Poems of the Middle Period*, 4; 253)

It is a pleasantly relaxed sonnet, lacking the tense alertness that characterizes Clare's nesting birds and his own best poems, and it is the tension that offers the strongest indication that he and the birds share the same landscape, a landscape intimately known, and a landscape to which they are supremely adjusted, and yet nevertheless a landscape in which both Clare and the birds remain vulnerable, and under threat.

My point in the end is a simple and a sad one. It is not possible to understand Clare as an English poet amongst other English poets, distinguished from them only by a knowledge of the English countryside that they could not match, and neither is it possible to understand him as a villager amongst his fellow villagers, remarkable amongst his neighbours only in that he, unlike them, was able to articulate their common experience. Clare on occasion strikes each of these attitudes. He may sometimes claim a place in the literary community, as when he begins a sonnet to an admired fellow writer, 'Friend Lamb', and, rather more often, he may claim a place in the village community, as one of the 'merry folks' 'circling round the fire' ('St Martins Eve'). But his true place, and the place from which he writes his most compelling poems, is neither of these, but an uncomfortable position in which familiarity and estrangement coincide, a place in which, as Clare puts it in 'I am',

> Even the dearest that I love the best
> Are strange – nay rather stranger than the rest.

*The Midsummer Cushion* was not published until 1978. In 1835 a selection of the poems, a rather weak selection, had been collected in *The Rural Muse*, the last of the four volumes of Clare's poems to appear in his lifetime. From 1837 until his death in 1864, with one brief respite, Clare was an inmate of insane asylums, first at High Beech in Epping Forest, where he was under the care of Dr Matthew Allen (a close acquaintance of Tennyson who visited High Beech while Clare was there, though there is no evidence that the two poets met), and later at the Northampton asylum. In these long years he was all but forgotten. His seems a sad but entirely special story, too individual to be of interest to the literary historian. But I doubt that this was the case. First, Clare's failure, even after the success of his first two volumes, to earn a living as a poet was a consequence of the disastrous collapse of the market for volumes of poetry that affected almost all his younger contemporaries. Tennyson was not able to support himself by his literary earnings until he was in his early forties, and Browning not until he was in his fifties. The difference is that they, unlike Clare, were able to support themselves in their chosen profession from other sources. Other poets, such as Keats's friend, John Hamilton Reynolds, and Beddoes, took up alternative professions, the law or medicine. Such people either continued to write poetry in their free time, or not. Others still, such as Darley, became journalists. Clare's lack of education meant that no such possibilities were available to him. The realism of Clare's natural description is, in one sense, equally distinctive, grounded in his intimate possession of a single landscape, the landscape in and around the Northamptonshire village of Helpston, in which he lived for the first forty years of his life. And yet he describes a landscape that is at once familiar and estranged, a landscape through which the poet moves both as proprietor and trespasser, and hence a landscape that he recognizes and that yet fills him with astonishment, and this is the landscape that pervades the poetry of the Victorians.

He did not, of course, share their education, but another difference seems equally important. He did not share their piety. Clare was for a time attracted by a non-conformist preacher, but was content most often to describe himself as a 'Church and King' man. His poems are sprinkled with tributes to God both as his creator and the creator of the natural world, but these seem, if not perfunctory, then either vaguely reverential or loosely pantheistic. He studies natural objects such as ferns or birds' nests with a scholarly exactness that Ruskin, had he known of it, would surely have admired, but, whereas Ruskin always insists that his realism is grounded on his faith, and that he studies geology, for example, because to learn the principles of rock formation is to gain an insight into the mind of God, Clare's fascination with the pettichap's nest seems sufficient to itself. The distinctive piety of the early Victorian poets provides the subject of the next chapter.

# 7
# Christening Romanticism

Elizabeth Barrett's *Poems* of 1844 ends with a long, lyric celebration of the death of the pagan Gods, 'The Dead Pan'. Explicitly, her rebuke is aimed at Schiller:

> Let no Schiller from the portals
> Of that Hades call you back,
> Or instruct us to weep all
> At your antique funeral.
> > Pan, Pan is dead.
> > (220–4)

But the reprimand spreads outwards to include Keats, whose hymn to Pan (*Endymion*, 1, 232–306) was gruffly acknowledged by Wordsworth as 'a pretty piece of paganism', Shelley whose 'Song of Pan' was published by Mary in 1824, and the whole of that attempt by the second generation Romantics to locate in Greek mythology a life-affirming alternative to Christian spirituality that Marilyn Butler has called 'the cult of the south'. Barrett fondles the pagan gods, with their resonant epithets and appurtenances, but only as a way of bidding them farewell. They are 'grey old gods', and poets 'grow colder if they name you' (153), because Aphrodite and Cybele and Pan himself can have in the mid-nineteenth century only an artificial, fictional life:

> Earth outgrows the mythic fancies
> Sung beside her in her youth,
> And those debonair romances
> Sound but dull beside the truth.
> > (232–5)

Hare and Connop Thirlwall, the translators of Niebuhr, inspired the Trinity men they tutored with an enthusiasm for all things German. Julius Hare, in particular, was a notorious advocate for the merits of *Wilhelm Meister*.[2] The interest of the Apostles would have been quickened when the brothers Charles and Arthur Buller joined their group, for they had been tutored by Carlyle during the period when he was at work on his translation.[3] Of still more weight was the fact that by 1829 both of the men regarded by the Apostles as the spiritual fathers of their society were at work on novels directly influenced by *Wilhelm Meister*. John Sterling did not publish *Arthur Coningsby* until 1833, and F.D. Maurice published *Eustace Conway* a year later, but both novels had existed in draft form for some years previously.[4] Sterling and Maurice found in *Wilhelm Meister* a new kind of novel, a novel that was, as all its readers noted, in large part autobiographical, but a novel the protagonist of which could be robustly but not unfairly described by Carlyle as 'a milksop, whom, with all his gifts, it takes an effort to avoid despising'. It is the distinctive blend of autobiographical intimacy and blank narrative indifference, 'wrinkled' from time to time, in Carlyle's memorable phrase, 'by a slight sardonic grin', that was seized on by Sterling and Maurice as the germ that made their own novels possible.[5] They recognized the possibility of a novel that might function as a distanced, sardonic autobiography, and yet represent the experience of the central character as representative rather than merely personal. When he sent a copy of his novel to Richard Chenevix Trench, Maurice explained it as an expression of his desire 'to have more deep and affectionate sympathy with every state of feeling through which I or any dear friends have passed'.[6] In the novel itself the depth of the sympathy is more apparent than its affectionateness, but the nature of Maurice's project is clear: his plan was to write a novel that embodied as completely as possible not just his own experience, but the experience of his group. *Wilhelm Meister* offered him, as no other novel available to him could, a formal model for such an enterprise. But it was a model that neither Maurice nor Sterling was prepared to endorse without qualification.

Maurice's and Sterling's novels decisively part company with their model in two ways. First, the greater part of his 'apprenticeship' is spent by Wilhelm in exorcizing his infatuation with the stage. Wilhelm spends his time in the company of travelling players, staying with them in second-rate inns, and experiencing the complex pleasures available in the chaotically disordered bedrooms of the company's actresses. Maurice and Sterling seem to have had no more of Goethe's hearty relish for such things than Carlyle, in whom the spectacle of 'players and libidinous actresses and their sorry pasteboard apparatus for beautifying and enlivening the "moral world"' provoked 'a feeling mild and charitable as that of a starved hyena'.[7] The apprenticeships of Conway and Coningsby are a good deal more earnest and a good deal more dignified. Secondly, *Arthur Coningsby* and *Eustace Conway*, unlike *Wilhelm Meister*, end unhappily. Neither Coningsby nor Conway succeeds in developing a fully rounded character, nor in finding his proper place in the social world: both remain to the end out of unity with themselves.

Arthur Coningsby's task is to outgrow his youthful infatuation with the French Revolution. Residence in Paris and exposure to the reality of French revolutionary politics effectively accomplish this, but at the end of the novel Coningsby is left desolate, contemplating a solitary life in the wildernesses of America. His history is offered as a warning of the danger that attends 'the pursuit of rational ideals of good government', 'the danger of following any rule but that which is written in the heart' (1, 245). As a young radical he is determined to bring about 'a future unconnected with the past' (1, 127), and, in consequence, he finds that his political pursuits have broken 'the continuity of his mind' (1, 84). By the end of the novel he is forced to recognize that the breach is irreparable. He is separated from his country, where he is wanted for treason, from his young cousin, Isobel, who had once loved him but who judges his conduct unforgivable, and he is separated too from his Christian faith. He sets out for America with no greater hope than that of finding a space where he can live out his days in the exercise of an astringent self-contempt.

*Eustace Conway* seems a more optimistic tale. Like Coningsby, the young Conway believes that the crucial question confronting him is, 'How a nation is to be governed in order that it may be happy' (1, 76). But he is a post-revolutionary, convinced from the first that systems of government are to be changed non-violently, by persuasion. In his radical period he commits no misdemeanour more serious than boring his family by his endless prate of 'the greatest happiness of the greatest numbers'. His radicalism is nine-tenths affectation, and his political theories do not survive his brother's ridicule. He gives up politics and goes in for debauchery, 'galvanised by a Byronic battery' (1, 235). This is the nadir of Conway's career. He is brought to despair, and contemplates suicide. His regeneration begins when he is committed to prison to await trial, falsely accused of a crime in fact committed by the leader of the Benthamite reformers. In prison he meets a man called Kreuzner, who extricates him from atheism by converting him to 'German spiritualism', a

belief in the omnipotence of the individual will. At the last, he returns
to orthodox Christianity, won over by the wise counsels of the Reverend Wilmot, and this final conversion seems to promise a happy
ending. But Conway, reviewing his career, notes that at every stage of
his progress, from Benthamite radicalism, to German metaphysics, and
back to the religion of his childhood, he seems only to have gained
'more arrogance'. He remains to the last a victim of what Maurice considered the cardinal sin, a 'foul devotion to self' (3, 272).

Neither novel resolves the problems of its central character. They
cannot do so because of the kind of novels they are. They are bildungsromane, and for Maurice and Sterling the bildungsroman cannot
properly admit of a solution because it is itself a symptom of the disease. They chose to write this kind of novel because it permitted them
to explore a diseased self-consciousness, but the only successful resolu-
tion that such a novel permits is the hero's arrival at a state of harmonious self-cultivation, and the notion that self-cultivation might be the
end of life was an outrage to Maurice's and Sterling's Christian piety. In
1850, Maurice greeted the publication of the *Prelude* in a manner oddly
muted for so ardent a Wordsworthian. He described the poem as 'the
dying utterance of the half century we have passed through',

> the expression – the English expression at least – of all that self-
> building process in which according to their different schemes and
> principles, Byron, Goethe, Wordsworth, the Evangelicals (protestant
> and Romanist), were all engaged, which their novels, poems, experi-
> ences, prayers, were setting forth, in which God, under whatever
> name, or in whatever aspect He presented Himself to them, was still
> the agent only in fitting them to be world-wise, men of genius,
> artists, saints.[8]

Two things here are worth noting. First, the qualification, 'the English
expression at least', which suggests that Maurice still thinks of *Wilhelm
Meister* as the other chief expression of this tendency, and second,
Maurice's scarcely concealed distaste for any 'self-building process',
which, because it is conceived as an end in itself, reduces the status of
God to that of an agent helping the individual along his path towards
personal self-fulfilment, or, as Maurice crushingly terms it, the state of
being 'world-wise'. It is unsurprising that Maurice continues, 'For us
there must be something else intended'.

Like *Wilhelm Meister*, *Arthur Coningsby* and *Eustace Conway* are cen-
trally concerned with the attempt to find some relation between the

individual's inward sense of himself and the individual in his social role. While Coningsby is a radical revolutionary he believes that the individual is wholly defined by his social relations. When he goes to France, he finds there a people who have 'no existence at all except with relation to others' (2, 101), and is forced to concede the shallowness and the moral instability of such a position. He recovers a sense of the lonely 'I', a self that cannot be taken up in any political or social relationship, but he can do nothing with it, and is reduced ultimately to an equal and indiscriminate contempt for 'the world without and the world within' (3, 371). In his utilitarian period, Conway 'proclaimed social arrangements all important' (1, 142). When he falls under the spell of Kreuzner, the German metaphysician, he recovers his sense of himself, but finds that the world has become a vacuum inhabited only by his own omnipotent and isolated will. The solution to his problem is offered to him in the novel's final volume by the wise old cleric, the Reverend Wilmot. All his early life Wilmot had been haunted by the question, 'What am I?' It is a question that can only be answered by recognizing ourselves as at once separate from our social relationships and involved in them, and this will remain an impossible paradox to anyone not able to grasp that the individual finds his relationship with other individuals through his relationship with God. Conway comes to understand this, but he cannot feel it, because he has severed the relationship between himself and his Maker. The bildungsroman is the kind of novel that explores the fate of such people, people who have lost their sense of a personal relationship with God, and so have fallen victim to what Sterling calls a 'diseased and sleepless self-consciousness'. Goethe may believe that a human being might be self-fulfilled, but Maurice and Sterling would rather accept the conclusion of Coningsby's French mistress: 'we seek in vain to construct for ourselves a binding and supporting law out of our own tastes, impulses, notions while we turn from that which exists without us, based eternally on the Being of God, and reflected in every human heart' (3, 353). Self-development for Goethe is the road to happiness, for Maurice and Sterling it is a fatal detour. Their bildungsromane can only end unhappily, for unhappiness is the inevitable end of a life devoted to bildung.

Wilhelm Meister recognizes in Hamlet his ideal self: Hamlet is the only role that he can act with complete success. In Goethe's novel, *Hamlet* becomes an ur-bildungsroman. It is, Wilhelm tells us, more like a novel than a play: its hero is endowed with 'sentiments' rather than 'character', its action is propelled by 'events' rather than 'deeds', and it has 'in some measure the expansion of a novel'.[9] Sterling follows Goethe in introducing a discussion of Hamlet into his novel. Coningsby and Madame de Valence agree in describing Hamlet as 'the Prometheus of the modern world', 'the magnified representation of the thoughts, passions, misgivings and moral instincts of the universal soul. All around him exist but in relation to him, and vary in importance according to the flux and reflux of his mind' (3, 138). Both Goethe and Sterling acknowledge *Hamlet* as the prototype of the kind of novel they are writing, but whereas Wilhelm expresses for Hamlet an unbounded enthusiasm, Coningsby and Madame de Valence seem to regard it with a horrified fascination.

Maurice and Sterling were both clear under what 'name' or 'aspect' God presented himself to Goethe. He seemed to them an exponent of the religion of art, substituting, in such episodes as the funeral of Mignon, rituals for sacraments, subordinating the good to the beautiful, and practising, in consequence, a cool indifference to whatever means his characters might employ so that they arrive at the one goal of human life, the creation of themselves as finished works of art. In *Arthur Coningsby* there is a series of scenes in which paintings or sculptures are juxtaposed with living men and women. The effect is to expose the danger that a contemplation of the finished, reposeful creations of art will obscure one's perception of the restless, unfinished condition of living people, or, alternatively, that, if the incongruity is noted, the temptation to turn away from the real world to seek solace in the contemplation of inert statues will prove too strong. Art is the religion that has sustained Madame de Valence, Coningsby's mistress, first by occluding her perception of the real nature of the revolutionary leaders, and afterwards by offering her a refuge from her duty to confront the political realities of the Revolution. Maurice seems not to have shared Sterling's interest in the fine arts, but still Wilmot takes pains to disabuse Conway of the notion that 'poetry is religion' (3, 39).

Goethe presented himself to these men both as a model and a threat, as an inescapable model and as a threat the more dangerous because they found it so seductive. They did not know the *Prelude*. For them, *Wilhelm Meister* was the most complete embodiment of a literary project that they recognized as the principal legacy to them of their Romantic predecessors. But it was a project that they were already suspicious of. It was surely a symptom of this complex response rather than simple modesty that made Maurice 'almost ashamed' to send his novel to Trench. Later, in November 1838, Trench wrote to Maurice confessing his own troubled response to Goethe:

> the power his works, and still more his life has to persuade one that there is another wisdom besides the wisdom of Christ, another object of life besides conformity to Him, I sometimes find almost overpowering, and the temptation terrible, so that one hardly recovers for many days, and after many struggles and prayers, a right and healthy tone of spirit.[10]

Ian H.C. Kennedy was the first to point out that the original title of Tennyson's *Supposed Confessions of a Second-rate Sensitive Mind*, which added the information that the mind was 'not in union with itself', echoed Carlyle's translation of the first volume of *Wilhelm Meister*, the *Wanderjahre*. Kennedy went on to trace a network of correspondences between Goethe's novel and the poems of Tennyson's Cambridge period.[11] Tennyson's *Supposed Confessions* shares with the novels by Maurice and Sterling a detachment from the experience that it records at times rueful, at times acerbic. His perspective is aggressively announced in the poem's title, in its ascription of the confession to 'a second-rate sensitive mind'. Despite his admiration of the poem, Arthur Hallam disliked this title for its 'quaintness', and insisted that it was, in any case, 'incorrect'. He saw no need to placate the hostile reader by presenting a confessional lyric as though it were a dramatic soliloquy, for he was confident that the mood displayed in the poem was 'the clouded season of a strong mind' rather than 'the habitual condition of one feeble and "second-rate"'.[12] But Hallam may not have been quite disinterested in his criticism, for the poem describes a spiritual crisis, and the spiritual crisis of 1829 that can be documented was undergone not by Tennyson but by Hallam himself. Hence, one guesses, Hallam's nervous insistence that the mood of the poem is that of a 'strong' rather than a 'second-rate mind', and that it offers a record of 'those particular trials that are sure to beset men who think and feel for themselves at this epoch of social development'.

But it is not just self-defensive in Hallam to describe the experiences that Tennyson's poem expresses as representative rather than merely personal. The novels by Maurice and Sterling record similar spiritual crises, and such experiences were not confined to fiction. They seem to have been endemic amongst Tennyson's Cambridge contemporaries, particularly amongst those who became Apostles. There is evidence in letters and poems that in the years from 1829 to 1831 a religious crisis of some kind was experienced not just by Arthur Hallam but by John Kemble, Richard Chenevix Trench, Richard Monckton Milnes, and Henry Alford.[13] The experiences that these men describe are so similar that it is easy to list their common characteristics.

First comes the awakening of the Apostle to a sense of his own sinfulness. This agonized moment of self-recognition is not prompted by any particular sin, but is simply a product of a new sense of himself as fallen. Almost always this discovery is presented with an odd ambivalence, as if it were at once a confession of unusual depravity and a back-handed boast.[14] The reason is not hard to find. What prompts the condition is a new understanding that his culture is at odds with his religion, that his intellectual sophistication has isolated him from the possibility of a simple, unthinking faith. Hence, the confession of religious despair becomes a boast of intellectual achievement.

Secondly, the recognition of his own sinfulness provokes in the Apostle a nostalgia for some earlier time of happy innocence when faith seemed instinctive. The troubled soul sees around him others who seem never to have lost this happy state. Hallam recognizes such a figure in his old schoolfriend, Gaskell, who is preserved, it seems, from Hallam's torments by his unintellectual cast of mind. More commonly, the Apostle contrasts his own state with the happy innocence enjoyed by children, or by women. Hallam praises women, such as his fiancée Emily Tennyson, who are saved by their lack of education from any dangerous encroachment of the serpentine understanding into the domain where the intuitive reason ought properly to rule supreme.[15] Most often the representative of the state of innocence is a child, and the recognition of his own depravity fosters in the Apostle a yearning to regress to the condition of infancy. A poem by Milnes ends with an especially flagrant expression of this fantasy. He imagines Heaven as populated exclusively by the kind of putti who cluster on the ceilings of Italian churches, 'cherub forms in infant guise'. The reward of the blessed will be to escape in the afterlife the burden of their adult bodies, and to reassume the idyllic chubbiness of infancy. Again, this impulse is ambivalent, because a regression to infancy, although it promises escape from the painful awareness of his own sinfulness from which the Apostle suffers, also threatens the intellectual sophistication on which these young men rather evidently pride themselves, which is why the envy that Hallam expresses for the spiritual state of Gaskell, or of Emily Tennyson, or of a Highland child, is the kind of envy that is entirely compatible with a sense of his own superiority. Hallam's 'I saw a child upon a Highland moor' is distinctive not at all in its envy for the state of childhood, but because the poem registers Hallam's acute recognition that the envy is factitious. The dream that he might become a child again rests on the assumption that, as a child, he might somehow retain an adult sense of the value of childhood.[16]

We are offered accounts of a spiritual malaise that does not seem susceptible to any effective cure. Most often, what is imagined is a reunion with the commonalty of unthinking, orthodox believers, and an end to the painfully intense self-consciousness from which the Apostle suffers. But it is precisely their self-consciousness that defines them, so that the wish to be like other people is counteracted by an unwillingness to lapse into anonymity. In most confessional literature the spiritual experience that these young men record, the sudden recognition of oneself as utterly sinful and cut off from God, is the prelude to an experience of conversion. This group of writings is distinctive in its failure to record the second experience.[17] The explanation is once again to be found in the odd ambivalence with which they record their despairs. If the recognition of one's own sinfulness is at once a confession of depravity and a proof of finer spiritual sensitivities than the common folk are gifted with, then the experience of feeling cut off from God becomes in itself a paradoxical mark of election. These young men seem to have practised a curious kind of evangelicalism in reverse: they formed themselves into an exclusive group of believers united somewhat complacently by their common experience of religious despair.

Tennyson's *Supposed Confessions* is written out of this common experience. Like Maurice's *Eustace Conway* it is an expression of a desire to sympathize with 'every state of feeling through which I or any dear friends have passed', and like the novels by Maurice and Sterling it is marked by a sardonic detachment from those states of feeling, a detachment that Tennyson had learned, as the original title of his poem gives the clue, from his reading of *Wilhelm Meister*. In Tennyson, as in Maurice and Sterling, the detachment is made possible by a clear understanding that the intense self-consciousness that propels these confessional documents, much as it may result in self-abasement, is in itself the expression of spiritual pride.[18] Maurice notes wonderingly at the end of his novel that Eustace Conway's painful and undignified progress from utilitarianism to orthodox Christianity has not served at all to moderate his self-regard, that at each stage in his career he seemed only 'to have gained more arrogance'. Tennyson's poem, even more clearly than Maurice's novel, reveals the impulse to self-abasement evident in all these documents as the reflex of spiritual pride. 'Is not my human pride brought low?', the young man asks. But he knows all the same that if his dead mother could speak, she would tell him:

> That pride, the sin of devils, stood
> Betwixt me and the light of God!
>                         (109–10)

He claims that such a charge is no longer applicable:

> I think that pride hath now no place
> Nor sojourn in me. I am void,
> Dark, formless, utterly destroyed.
>                         (120–22)

Even here one may feel that a recalcitrant satisfaction in the sublime obscurity of his inner desolation stands in the way of true penitence. When he goes on to explain why he is unable to find consolation in common orthodoxy, his grandiloquence strikingly reveals how his pride, far from having been eradicated, has found much to feed on in his despair:

> Why not believe then? Why not yet
> Anchor thy frailty there, where man
> Hath moored and rested? Ask the sea
> At midnight, when the crisp slope waves
> After a tempest, rib and fret
> The broad-imbased beach, why he
> Slumbers not like a mountain tarn?
> Wherefore his ridges are not curls
> And ripples of an inland mere?
> Wherefore he moaneth thus, nor can
> Draw down into his vexed pools
> All that blue heaven which hues and paves
> The other?
>                         (123–35)

Hallam may have read this with some disquiet, for Tennyson seems to have borrowed the mountain tarn from one of Hallam's poems, the sixth of his 'Meditative Fragments', written probably in the autumn of 1829. Hallam's poem was provoked by his irritation that Robert Robertson's sister, Anne, did not share his enthusiasm for Wordsworth. He reconciles himself to her indifference by reflecting that she has never known the spiritual agonies necessary for a just appreciation of the poet, and he ends his poem hoping that she never will, that she will keep through life the 'innocent joy' that is so perfectly reflected in her 'face, like an unruffled mountain tarn'.[19] Anne Robertson must have been quite as good-natured as Hallam thought her if she accepted this as a compliment. In borrowing the simile, all that is left for Tennyson to do is to make explicit the contrast between small, sheltered lakes and the ridges of the mighty sea. In case anyone should miss the sleight of hand by which the speaker converts self-denigration into a species of vainglory, Tennyson allows to play behind the passage Byron's proud sense of himself as oceanic in comparison with Wordsworth, Coleridge and Southey: 'I wish they would exchange their lakes for ocean'. *Supposed Confessions* ends with the speaker still roundly accusing himself:

> O weary life! O weary death!
> O spirit and heart made desolate!
> O damned vacillating state!

Even without so very apostrophic a style most readers would be alert to the element of self-fondling in these lines. The speaker is presenting himself as Hamlet-like, and Hamlet is, after all, a hero, indeed as Goethe and Sterling insist, the peculiarly modern hero, 'the modern Prometheus'.

Tennyson had learned from *Wilhelm Meister* how to construct a representative protagonist, and Goethe would have shown him, too, how the sympathy with which he viewed such a protagonist might remain wholly unsentimental, even astringent. But, for Tennyson just as much as for Maurice and Sterling, Goethe was not simply a model to be imitated, he was also exemplary of one particular 'state of feeling' that it was necessary to supersede. Goethe's conflation of religion and art – his calm assumption that both are human creations, and that it is with religion as it is with art: that variety is best which best serves human purposes – was a state of feeling that required not only to be sympathized with, but to be exposed. The proud scepticism that distinguishes Tennyson's speaker in his youth is scepticism of a characteristically Goethean kind. He held then that:

> It is man's privilege to doubt
> If so be that from doubt at length,
> Truth may stand forth unmoved of change,
> An image with profulgent brows,

> And perfect limbs, as from the storm
> Of running fires and fluid range
> Of lawless airs, at last stood out
> This excellence and solid form
> Of common beauty.
>
> (142–50)

He imagined that truth might solidify, like the world out of chaos, or as, say, Cellini's Perseus achieved its perfect form, out of the 'running fires' of molten bronze. His project is like God's or like the artist's, like both indiscriminately because in his youth he failed, like Goethe, to distinguish between the two. But the lines are informed by a later awareness that the Goethean project is blasphemous. The truth he had hoped to find is figured by a statue with 'profulgent brows' and 'perfect limbs', the kind of Greek or Renaissance statue that Goethe revered, and its triumphal beauty is strikingly at odds with the Christian embodiment of truth, a figure dimly discerned in the poem's opening lines, 'Patient of ill and death and scorn', his brow girt round with thorns.

Tennyson's speaker grounds his acceptance of the need for religious belief on 'Our double nature', on the fact of human self-consciousness. Human beings, like all other animals, are mortal, but unlike other animals they know that this is the case, so that life would seem pointless to us were it not given meaning by religion. But this is still to view religion as a kind of art, and to reduce the seeker after God to a kind of connoisseur, whose business it is to compare:

> All creeds till we have found the one,
> If one there be? Ay me! I fear
> All may not doubt, but everywhere
> Some must clasp Idols. Yet, my God,
> Whom call I Idol?
>
> (176–80)

Paul Turner suggests that Tennyson uses the word idol here in its Baconian sense to refer to false mental images,[20] but that seems not quite right. All creeds, the speaker implies, are aesthetic objects, statues, that become idols for anyone too weak-minded to retain a sense that they are only works of art. The idolater confuses the sign with what it signifies, the creed with the human mystery that the creed attempts to make sense of. But this Goethean view of things comes up short against the recognition that there is a religion quite unlike art, because it is true, and can therefore command a belief that does not have its origin in a confusion of categories: 'Yet, my God, / Whom call I Idol?'

Like Hallam, Tennyson presents his religious crisis through Coleridge. Sinfulness is the issue rather than particular sins, and sinfulness, as Coleridge had taught him, is a disposition of the will. In *Aids to Reflection* (1825), Coleridge argues that the will is properly described as supernatural in that it is itself the origin of its own state, and hence distinct from all natural things which are subject to the law of cause and effect. But in the fall of man, an event that is repeated in the life of each and every one of us, the will loses, or more precisely is perceived as having lost, its supernatural quality, and becomes a part of nature, its state determined by the laws of cause and effect. Tennyson's speaker may imagine that some 'Devil' has brushed the dew of innocence from him, but he quickly realizes that the only supernatural agency at work was his own supernatural will: 'Myself? Is it thus? Myself?'. He accuses God of failing to heed his mother's prayers on his behalf: 'Why pray / To one who heeds not, who can save / But will not?' It is a question that cannot be answered: it must remain, as Coleridge insists, a mystery. The question ought to be addressed elsewhere, for then the speaker would realize that it is his own heedlessness, not God's, that ought to concern him. His own will ought to have responded to his mother's prayer, but his own will seems dead in him:

> The joy I had in my freewill
> All cold, and dead, and corpse-like grown...
>
> (16–17)

This is exactly phrased. His freewill, being itself supernatural, cannot die, only his 'joy' in it, his sense of it, seems dead. But it feels the same: it feels as if his will has been bleakly naturalized, like a living body become a thing, a corpse. So, he is left to wish despairingly that 'grace' would drop from God's 'O'erbrimming love / as manna on [his] wilderness', knowing that if only he could shed 'tears of penitence' he would experience grace, knowing that all he has to do to become penitent is to pray, but unable to find in himself the will to pray, because the will feels dead inside him.

It is not so for everyone, and it was not always so. The general Apostolic sense of being removed from the community of the faithful is realized in Tennyson's poem more poignantly than in similar poems by

Hallam and Trench, and so too is the wish to become once more a child. What is more, by making the representative of the faithful the speaker's mother, Tennyson is able to fuse the two emotions:

> Thrice happy state again to be
> The trustful infant on the knee!
> Who lets his rosy fingers play
> About his mother's neck, and knows
> Nothing beyond his mother's eyes.
> They comfort him by night and day;
> They light his little life alway;
> He hath no thought of coming woes;
> He hath no care of life or death;
> Scarce outward signs of joy arise,
> Because the Spirit of happiness
> And perfect rest so inward is;
> And loveth so his innocent heart,
> Her temple and her place of birth,
> Where she would ever wish to dwell,
> Life of the fountain there, beneath
> Its salient springs, and far apart,
> Hating to wander out on earth,
> Or breathe into the hollow air,
> Whose chillness would make visible
> Her subtil, warm, and golden breath,
> Which mixing with the infant's blood,
> Fulfils him with beatitude.
> Oh! sure it is a special care
> Of God, to fortify from doubt,
> To arm in proof, and guard about
> With triple-mailed trust, and clear
> Delight, the infant's dawning year.
>
> (40–67)

The thought is entirely typical of a group of Apostolic poems, though Tennyson may have in mind a particular passage from *Aids to Reflection*.[21] What distinguishes this from similar sentiments expressed by, say, Milnes is the control that Tennyson exerts over what may seem a weakly regressive emotion. It is not so much a matter of the packaging – opening a passage with a 'thrice happy state' that closes with a 'triple-mailed trust' – as of the syntactic confidence that can quietly hold a single sentence through 22 octosyllabic lines. The trinity that begins and ends the passage is made up of the mother, the child, and the spirit of happiness that exists between them and within them both. It exists unknown, in the warm interchange of their breath. True happiness, the lines tell us, can only be unknown: to see our breath, for it to condense into mist, is a sign that the spirit of happiness is no longer in its element, that the air around it is chilly. The union of mother, child and happiness figures – perhaps it embodies – the most mysterious of Christian dogmas, the trinity, the God who is three in one, a truth that the mind of the adult can scarcely grasp, but a truth that the child, or so Tennyson would have it, can absorb quite unconsciously.

It is Tennyson's control of his materials that everywhere distinguishes his poem from other Apostolic poems of spiritual crisis. The crucial decision was to write the poem as a dramatic monologue, encouraging the reader to inspect rather than simply to witness the confession, and, just as important, the monologue form gave Tennyson a licence to leave the speaker's crisis unresolved. But almost as critical is the choice of verse form. The poem is written in regular tetrameters, but the rhyme scheme is fractured. It begins as if it were going to be a poem in couplets, but the third line ends in 'me' and does not find its rhyme until the 'misery' of line 8. Occasionally, the poem slips into another form. Lines 19–26 are written in interlocking quatrains. Throughout, the promise of a regular rhyme scheme is held out only long enough for the reader to register frustration when it is withdrawn. The effect is exacerbated by Tennyson's admission into the poem of half-rhymes harsher than he elsewhere allows himself – in lines 161–2, to give just one example, 'whence' is offered as a rhyme for 'pains' – and the rhymes are sometimes so far separated that only the alertest ear could catch them. Often the two devices are combined. A scarcely audible half-rhyme links 'were' of line 68 with 'prayer' of line 72, and then there is a long lapse before the pattern is completed in 'dare' of line 78. A sequence even more demanding on the ear links 'man' in line 124 with 'tarn' of line 129 and 'can' in line 132. Tennyson seems to allude to his own rhyme scheme in lines that describe the dead mother's anxiety as she watches from Heaven her son's stormy progress through life:

> Thou … seest me drive
> Through utter dark a full-sailed skiff
> Unpiloted i'the echoing dance
> Of reboant whirlwinds.
>
> (94–7)

It may have been to call attention to these lines that Tennyson, a poet sparing in neologism, allowed himself the coinage 'reboant', that is, 're-bellowing', echoing but echoing harshly, like his own rhyme scheme. Such formal artfulness works to separate Tennyson from his speaker. It co-operates with the poem's title to establish *Supposed Confessions* as a dra-matic poem, or, as Isobel Armstrong terms it, an example of the Victorian double poem. Armstrong first puts this notion into practice in a brilliant reading of Browning's *Pauline*, a reading that establishes *Pauline* as a close counterpart to *Supposed Confessions*. Both are religious poems that fail to become conversion poems because the speaker can find no escape from a self that is 'progressively fictionalised and experienced as alone and pri-vate'.[22] The task that remained, the task that serves better than any to define Victorian religious poetry, was to discover a mode of religious experience that joins one to society rather than separates one from it.

## III

This is the task that Tennyson addresses quite directly in *The Two Voices*. The most striking difference from *Supposed Confessions* is technical. The spasmodic, broken form of the earlier poem is replaced by regular tetrameter triplets, a tricky verse form, sustained by Tennyson with unfaltering smoothness through a poem that was eventually to consist of more than 460 lines. This is not just a demonstration of technical vir-tuosity, it produces the poem's most interesting effect. For its first 400 lines the poem records a dialogue within the soul in which the speaker attempts to stand firm against the seductive power of a voice that tries to persuade him that, in a world without meaning, suicide is the only rea-sonable course of action. But the verse is too smooth to distinguish the tempting voice from the voice that seeks to resist it. The two voices merge insidiously into a single voice that makes of every triplet a couplet followed by a long, dying fall, a couplet always followed by a dead echo of itself. There is no effective counter to this voice until the introduction of a 'little whisper silver-clear' in line 428. The little whisper handles triplets quite differently, completing in the third line a rising movement that the couplet cannot contain, so that each stanza overflows into hap-piness. The one voice replaces the other when the speaker opens the shutters, and sees – it is Sunday morning – a family walking to church:

> One walked between his wife and child,
> With measured footfall firm and mild,
> And now and then he gravely smiled.

The prudent partner of his blood
Leaned on him, faithful, gentle, good,
Wearing the rose of womanhood.

And in their double love secure,
The little maiden walked demure,
Pacing with downward eyelids pure.

(412–20)

Almost all modern readers find this vision of the bourgeois family transformed into the Holy Family banal, and it is hard not to sympathize with their response. But as he watched them, the speaker of the poem tells us, 'I blessed them', and at once he hears the whispering voice of prayer. The allusion to *The Ancient Mariner* fixes Tennyson's claim that his is, like Coleridge's, a conversion poem. But Tennyson is intent on re-writing the conversion poem for a new generation in which conversion will signify not simply a re-discovery of faith, but a reunion with the faithful.[23] If Tennyson's poem fails to satisfy, it is because his representation of the faithful remains weakly emblematic. Browning addresses the same theme more energetically in a poem that was not published until 1850, and has found even less favour with modern readers than *The Two Voices*, *Christmas-Eve*.

Like *The Two Voices*, *Christmas-Eve* recalls *The Ancient Mariner*. The speaker witnesses a lunar rainbow from which Christ materializes (the rainbow is a common emblem of Christ, its refraction of white light into colour figuring the incarnation). Holding the hem of Christ's robe he is transported first to Rome and then to Germany:

As a path were hollowed
And a man went weltering through the ocean,
Sucked along in the flying wake
Of the luminous water-snake.

(501–4 and 777–80)[24]

It is a poem about the choice of faith but that decision is interpreted as a choice between congregations: it is a question of which 'company', 'goodly' or otherwise, one should go with to church.

The speaker shelters from a squall of rain in the porch of a Congregational chapel. He chooses to attend the service that is about to begin only because he is put out by the way that the lower-class worshippers glare as they push past him. Sanctimoniousness is irritating, especially in one's social inferiors:

> I very soon had had enough of it,
> The hot smell and the human noises,
> And my neighbour's coat, the greasy cuff of it...
>
> (139–41)

Worst of all is 'the preaching man's immense stupidity'. He flings out of the stuffy chapel into the cool night air. The rain has stopped and above him the night sky is a turmoil of clouds and moonlight. He feels that he has entered 'God's church door', not the 'lath-and-plaster' porch of the chapel with its absurd superscription, 'Mount Zion', but the temple of nature:

> Oh, let men keep their ways
> Of seeking thee in a narrow shrine –
> Be this my way!
>
> (372–4)

The mimicry of the Romantic rejection of the shabby conventionalism of established religion in favour of a solitary communion with natural 'immensities' is obvious enough. But visionary isolation is no longer the badge of the prophet, it is the mark of the snob. When Christ appears to him, it seems at first a mark of special distinction, confirmation that he has a dispensation to worship God in his own way. It is only later that he understands it as a sign that he is a lost sheep. Christ first takes him to Rome, where he witnesses a religion reduced to its forms, and then to Germany, to a small town very like Göttingen, where he hears a professor very like David Friedrich Strauss lecture. The exposure to German Higher Criticism warns him of the opposite danger, religion reduced to a rationalist morality. His first thought is that Christ is teaching him a lesson in tolerance. He must learn to recognize beneath all the flummery of the Mass as it is celebrated at St Peter's a love for the Saviour in which he can unite with the Catholic worshippers, and to detect even in the professor's lecture a vestige of true religious faith: 'If love's dead there, it has left a ghost' (1071). But, 'While I watched my foolish Heart expand / In the lazy glow of benevolence' (1166–7), the hem of Christ's robe slips from his grasp, and he finds himself back in the Chapel, where, he assumes, he had fallen asleep during the sermon. His task, he realizes, is to choose his Church: not to imagine the kind of Church that might perfectly suit him, but to choose the best of what is available. And he chooses the Congregational chapel, its stupid preacher, and his ramshackle flock. The poem ends when he lays down his pencil, and joins in the singing of the last hymn:

> I put up pencil and join chorus
> To Hepzibah tune, without further apology,
> The last five verses of the third section
> Of the seventeenth Hymn of Whitfield's Collection,
> To conclude with the doxology.

He chooses Whit(e)field's hymn book, I suspect, because its title, *Hymns for Social Worship*, underlines the transition from solitary authorship to communal singing that concludes the poem.

The widespread dissatisfaction with *Christmas-Eve* has focused on the poem's form. The *Athenaeum* (April 6, 1850) warned early that the 'form of doggrel – carried to excess by strange and offensive oddities of versification – is not that in which the mysteries of faith, doubt, and eternity can be consistently treated'. Recent critics have agreed. Ian Jack holds that 'the free metrical form which Browning has chosen is completely unsuited to his subject-matter', and Lee Erickson finds it appropriate to the 'Hudibrastic satire' of the poem's grotesque rendering of the chapel congregation, but at odds with its conclusion.[25] Most of the poem is written either in couplets or quatrains, though with many irregularities, but it is the metre and the rhyming that shock; 'enough of it' rhyming with 'cuff of it' (139, 141), 'Testament' forcing a daring archaism in 'vestiment' (120–1), and 'Manchester' chiming with 'haunches stir' (231, 234). Most of the lines are either octo- or decasyllabic, and either three-beat or four-beat, but when Christ appears the line shrinks to three syllables, 'He was there' (431), and many expand to twelve or thirteen syllables. In comparison, *Hudibras* is regular.

Browning described *Christmas-Eve* as 'a Christmas story *in verse*' (March 11, 1850), which in itself suggests, as Jack and Erickson point out, that he thought of it as similar to Dickens's Christmas stories, and especially the most famous of them, *A Christmas Carol*, written for the Christmas of 1843.[26] Christ takes the poem's speaker on a journey very like the journeys on which the Spirits of Christmas take Scrooge. But it is the difference that strikes. Dickens is fully at one with his material, whereas the 'doggrel' of *Christmas-Eve* seems designed to dramatize Browning's discomfort with his. In 1850 the porch of the chapel had been absurdly narrow, 'Four feet long by two feet wide' (17), which, Jack suggests, persuaded Browning in later editions slightly to increase its dimensions to 'Six feet long by three feet wide'. But the alteration was surely intended to mute the echo of the most ridiculed couplet in Wordsworth, the couplet from *The Thorn*, in which the precise dimensions of the pond are given: 'I've measured it from side to side: / 'Tis three feet long, and two feet wide', lines that had been selected by Coleridge as in themselves refuting the theory according to which they were written, the notion that poems should be written in the language actually used by those in 'low and rustic' life.[27] The echo serves to dispel any thought that Browning has chosen his verse form in the naïve belief that it is somehow appropriate to the ragged congregation of the little Chapel that, at the end of the poem, he chooses to join. Rather, it expresses the discomfort of any attempt to 'join chorus', to fit one's thoughts and feelings to a particular tune. Metre, Wordsworth's Preface tells us, is 'regular and uniform', and, unlike diction, which is 'arbitrary and subject to infinite caprices', is obedient to 'certain laws'. He and Coleridge found metre best authenticated in natural regularities, the pulse or the rhythm of breathing. But Browning chooses metres at once capricious and mechanical:

> A tune was born in my head last week,
> Out of the thump-thump and shriek-shriek
> Of the train, as I came by it, up from Manchester...
>
> (249–51)

And this, or something like it, is the tune of his poem. It is a metre that most readily voices his contempt for his fellow-Christians, who live in the 'squalid knot of alleys'(32) behind the chapel, the 'shoemaker's lad, discreetly choking,' anxious not to disturb the preacher by his coughing, the 'old fat woman', who twirls her thumbs faster and faster, keeping time with the sermon, and the man who unties the handkerchief knotted under his chin to expose 'a horrible wen inside it' (173–82). It can never modulate into anything softer than a rough, half-comic affection. But it is this that gives the poem its own kind of awkward honesty.

It was the first substantial poem that Browning wrote after his marriage, and after the death of his mother in March, 1849. The poem is a public reaffirmation of the faith in which his mother had raised him, for it was the influence of his Scottish Presbyterian mother that prompted his father to leave the Church of England for the York Street Congregational Church in Walworth that Browning attended in his youth. When his son was to be baptised in 1849 in Florence he took some care to search out a service as like as possible to those that George Clayton had conducted at Walworth. The Walworth Chapel was not at all like 'Mount Zion' in *Christmas-Eve*, but an establishment genteel enough for Browning's sister to walk to services accompanied by a servant whose duty it was to carry her prayer book. But Browning could be as impatient with the sermons. He is remembered biting the rail of his pew in an agony of boredom and frustration. By the time he was fifteen he had discovered Shelley and atheism, and had even managed to disturb the faith of a much older friend, Sarah Flowers (who nevertheless recovered well enough to write the hymn, 'Nearer, My God, to Thee'), but the atheism was short-lived. *Pauline* of 1833 is marked throughout by fashionably intense and vague expressions of religious guilt.[28] *Christmas-Eve* is quite different, because it is not a poem about faith so much as a poem about communion. It focuses less on the speaker's relationship with God than his relationship with his fellow-Christians, and in particular on the need not just to affirm one's own belief, but to do so as a member of a particular congregation. The position that the poem takes seems to be at least as much his wife's as his own. Indeed, it is glossed most easily not by his letters but by Elizabeth's, as when she wrote to Robert in 1846. I quote at length, because the poem is almost a versification of the letter.

Dearest, when I told you yesterday, after speaking of the many-coloured theologies of the house, that it was hard to answer for what *I* was ... I meant that I felt unwilling, for my own part, to put on any of the liveries of the sects. The truth, as God sees it, must be something so different from these opinions about truth – these systems which fit different classes of men like their coats, & wear brown at the elbows always! – I believe in what is divine & floats at highest, in all these different theologies – & because the really Divine draws together souls, & tends so to a unity, I could pray anywhere & with all sorts of worshippers, from the Sistine chapel to Mr. Fox's, those kneeling & those standing. Wherever you go, in all religious societies, there is a little to revolt, & a good deal to bear with – but it is not otherwise in the world without, – &, *within*, you are especially reminded that God has to be more patient than yourself after all. Still you go quickest there, where your sympathies are least ruffled and disturbed – & I like, beyond comparison best, the simplicity of the dissenters ... the unwritten prayer ... the sacraments administered quietly & without charlatanism! & the principle of a church, as they hold it, *I* hold it too, quite apart from state-necessities ... pure from the Law. Well – there is enough to dissent from among the dissenters – the Formula is rampant among them as among others – you hear things like the buzzing of flies in proof of a corruption – & see every now & then something divine set up like a post for men of irritable minds & passions to rub themselves against, calling it a holy deed – you feel moreover bigotry & innocence pressing on you on all sides, till you gasp for breath like one strangled –. But better this, even, than what is elsewhere – *this* being elsewhere too in different degrees, besides the evil of the place. Public & social prayer is right & desirable – & I would prefer, as a matter of custom, to pray in one of those chapels, where the minister is simple-minded & not controversial – certainly wd prefer it.[29]

But Browning finds a metre, rhymes and a form that admit the need that worship should be 'public and social' while fully expressing what it feels like to be pressed on all sides by those with whom one has no fellow-feeling except for the deep obligation that they must be recognized as one's fellow Christians. So, he writes a dream vision, a favourite form of his favourite Shelley, the form of *Queen Mab*, *The Revolt of Islam*, and *The Triumph of Life*, a form that in Shelley establishes the poet's prophetic isolation from his fellows, but re-works the genre so that the dreamer, when he awakes, does not find himself bleakly exposed to a world that refuses to echo back to him his imaginings. Rather, he awakens to a moment of comic, social embarrassment. He finds that he has fallen asleep during the sermon.

*Christmas-Eve* is a robust, idiosyncratic, awkward poem. It could only be by Browning. But the decision with which it ends, the resolve to go together to the kirk with a goodly company, or a company, if not goodly, then at any rate good enough, has a representative value. It acts out with an almost clumsy honesty a need widely felt amongst Browning's contemporaries to find a religious faith that does not separate them from but joins them with their fellow human beings, which is why Victorian architecture is so strongly marked, unlike the Georgian architecture that preceded it, by its church buildings. But Browning, as he sits so awkwardly in his pew, has for me a still wider representative value. He assumes in the religious sphere a very similar posture to that assumed by his wife, as she surveys Italian politics from her Florentine window, neither quite separate from the citizenry that parade along the streets beneath her, nor yet quite subsumed within them. And it is a posture that has something in common with Clare's when he surveys a landscape that is at once familiar and strange, at once his own and utterly alien from him. In all three modes one detects a reaction against the extremes of Romantic individualism, but in none does this betoken a retreat into social cosiness, but something at once less comfortable and more intelligent than that.

# 8
# Domesticating Romanticism

The Victorian poets were distrustful of the contempt for established religion that is strident in Shelley, pervasive in Byron and Keats, and detectable in muted form even in Wordsworth and Coleridge. They were still more nervous of another characteristic common to the second generation of Romantic poets: their espousal of a sexual freedom that seemed to verge on licentiousness. How is one to imagine poets so devoted to the ideal of marriage as Tennyson and the Brownings responding to, for example, Shelley's *Epipsychidion*?

> I never was attached to that great sect,
> Whose doctrine is that each one should select
> Out of the crowd a mistress or a friend,
> And all the rest, though fair and wise, commend
> To cold oblivion, though it is in the code
> Of modern morals, and the beaten road
> Which those poor slaves with weary footsteps tread,
> Who travel to their home among the dead
> By the broad highway of the world, and so
> With one chained friend, perhaps a jealous foe,
> The dreariest and the longest journey go.
>
> (149–59)

In this final chapter I will address this, the most dangerous of Romantic legacies, and in its most dangerous form. By 1830 many of the first readers of Thomas Moore's life of Byron were aware, if only by rumour, of Byron's relationship with his half-sister Augusta, and similar relationships figure prominently in poems by Byron and by Shelley. The sexual licence that the younger Romantics claimed extended, so it seemed, even to incest.

I begin with a particular legacy, with the copy of *The Revolt of Islam* owned by Arthur Hallam and bequeathed, after his early death, to his friend and fellow Apostle, Henry Alford. Like Hallam, Alford was a minor poet, but he lived to earn a more substantial reputation as Dean of Canterbury Cathedral and as the English editor of the Greek Testament. The book was doubly precious to Alford who revered both Hallam and Shelley, and when he married on March 10, 1835, he chose it as his wedding gift to his wife, first inscribing on the flyleaf some blank verse lines that explained its special value to him.[1] What was he thinking of, this pious, conventional young clergyman, giving into the hands of his bride a copy of *The Revolt of Islam*, a fiercely anti-clerical poem dedicated to the ideals of the French Revolution? It is true that the poem that he wrote on the fly leaf ends with a warning. Fanny is advised:

> to shun
> Only the error's of the poet's creed,
> Yielding free duty to his code of love.

But these errors, as Alford must have seen them, occupy a very large part of Shelley's poem. If they are shunned, Shelley's visionary epic becomes a love poem, and it is as a love poem that Alford offers it to his bride.

It must have seemed peculiarly appropriate to his own circumstances, for his bride, Frances Alford, was also his first cousin. Alford's mother had not long survived his birth, and for much of his childhood Alford lived in his uncle's house, learning to think of his cousins as his brothers and sisters. Almost Alford's first memory was of being introduced, as a boy of three, to his new-born cousin, Fanny. In his best known poem *The School of the Heart*, Alford celebrates an intimacy with his wife that had its origins in their shared infancy, a time when they lived 'Like two babes passing hand in hand along / A sunny bank of flowers'.[2] He surely chose his wedding present because he recognized the love of Laon and Cythna as prefiguring his own love for his cousin and his bride. It would be more comfortable, though not quite safe, to accept Alford's ignorance of the fact that in the first version of Shelley's poem Laon and Cythna had been brother and sister, and their relationship frankly incestuous, but in any case the revised version only lightly disguises the bond of kinship between them.[3] Alford's decision to give to his wife on their wedding day a copy of Shelley's poem urging her to read it, 'every page with inly fervent heart', stands as a striking enough illustration of the problem of transmission that I want to explore.

Incest was a fashionable theme when Shelley began work on *Laon and Cythna*,[4] but we may suspect that its importance for him was prompted by something more than a taste for the modish. The love of a brother for a sister aptly figures the argument that Shelley pursues in his 'Essay on Love',[5] where he insists that love is an emotion that has its origin in narcissism. Love is the instinct within us that, 'from the instant that we live, more and more thirsts after its own likeness'. There is within each of us 'a soul within our soul', a mirror reflecting back to us our own identity, 'not only the portrait of our external being but an assemblage of the minutest particles of which our nature is composed'. We are driven to love by our need that this internal image should be embodied in some outward form, that the mirror within should be supplemented by a mirror without, and we might find in the coincidence of inward and outward reflections a delightful repose. 'This is the invisible and unattainable point to which love tends,' writes Shelley: unattainable in life, perhaps, but in art, in the consummation of Laon's love for his sister, Cythna, Shelley can represent the perfect blending of 'two restless frames in one reposing soul' (*The Revolt of Islam*, 2658).[6] The kinship of the two lovers works simply to enforce their 'likeness' one to another, for that likeness is the condition of the consummation that Shelley describes, an ecstatic moment in which recognition of the self becomes indistinguishable from recognition of the other, a moment of plenitude in which we lose all sense of the presence within us of 'the chasm of an insufficient void', our consciousness of which defines on all other occasions our common humanity.

It is characteristic of Shelley's poems that their motive power is love. The poems drive towards 'the invisible and unattainable point to which love tends', for that point outside which 'there is no rest nor respite to the heart over which [love] rules' is the only point at which the poem can close. Love is a quest, and the poem can end only when the quest is completed, or abandoned. An elegiac poem such as *Alastor* takes the second route. It ends when 'the passionate tumult of a clinging hope' is exchanged for 'pale despair and cold tranquility' (717–18). But *Prometheus Unbound* ends triumphantly with the reunion of Prometheus and Asia who prepare to retreat to their cave where they will gaze into each other's eyes and read the 'hidden thoughts' that are at once and indistinguishably the thoughts of the self and of the other, and *Epipsychidion* ends in a breathless proleptic rush in which Shelley conjures up just such a consummation of his own love for Emily. At such moments the poems come to rest, Laon and Cythna blending themselves into 'one reposing soul', and the hero of *Alastor* achieving a condition in which 'no mortal pain or fear/Marred his repose' (640–1). When Prometheus and Asia retire to their cave 'time and change' will still operate, but only as a topic of conversation: the lovers will remain themselves 'unchanged', and mutability will have dissolved into a murmur, its only function to soothe their rest (III, iii, 10–63). Such repose is offered by the poems as a version of immortality, but it is an 'immortality' that, as the final lines of *Epipsychidion* make explicit, is synonymous with 'annihilation'. The 'insufficient void' is filled, and without it nothing 'urges forth the powers of man to arrest the faintest shadow of that without the possession of which there is no rest nor respite to the heart'. The presence of that void within us makes it impossible to rest content, but, as the 'Essay on Love' insists, to rest content is to succumb to a living death, to become the 'sepulchre' of oneself.

Love, Shelley would have us believe, can re-constitute the world, but only, it would seem, for so long as it remains unfulfilled, for so long as the point to which it tends remains unattainable. Cythna leads her successful revolution before she is reunited with her brother. Asia is impelled not just by her love of Prometheus but by her separation from him to visit Demogorgon's cave and so unleash the power that will overthrow Jupiter. Laon and Cythna at last consummate their love in compensation for the failure of their revolutionary project; Prometheus and Asia, more happily, are reunited once their project has triumphed, but in both cases love can be fulfilled only when the lovers have escaped from history, for history is a process of change, and those who participate in it do so because they are urged forth by their consciousness of a void within them that demands to be filled. If it seems otherwise in *Epipsychidion*, that is because this poem admits a willingness never entertained by the younger, less disillusioned Shelley to retreat from the world to an island, and to exchange the ambition to reform the world for a dream of private joy. When the soul is reunited with its 'heart's sister' (*Epipsychidion*, 415), it knows at last 'respite and repose'. It finds joy but at the cost of undoing what Timothy Clark has called 'Shelley's politics of want'.[7] The soul is at last freed from stress, but at the cost of obliterating the one impulse that has the power to mould the world to a new likeness, the stress of unsatisfied desire.

Lévi-Strauss follows Freud in identifying the prohibition of incest as the act which initiates human society. The incest taboo is the point of transition between nature and culture, between the static sovereignty of nature and the dynamic process of civilization. The prohibition of incest is crucial because it enforces exogamy, marriage outside the tribe, and hence it institutes the process of exchange on which human society is founded. 'The exchange of brides,' as Lévi-Strauss puts it, 'is merely the conclusion to an uninterrupted process of reciprocal gifts, which effects the transition from hostility to alliance, from anxiety to confidence, and from fear to friendship'.[8] To prohibit incest is to abandon a static ideal of self-subsistence for an ideal of reciprocity. It follows that to dream of marrying one's sister is to dream of a return to a state of nature, a happy state where there is no giving in marriage. The builder of the tower where Shelley dreams of taking up residence with his Emilia lived in just such a world:

> for delight,
> Some wise and tender Ocean-King, ere crime
> Had been invented, in the world's young prime,
> Reared it, a wonder of that simple time,
> An envy of the isle, a pleasure-house,
> Made sacred to his sister and his spouse.
> (*Epipsychidion*, 487–92)

To live in such a place is to know delight, but 'the calm delight of flowers and living leaves … And semi-vital worms' (*Prometheus Unbound*, II, iv, 36–8). It is to resign one's place within a world that permits change, that other world that Shelley repeatedly summons into being all through his career, a world that is the arena for a dynamic interplay of opposing forces, the world so thrillingly invoked in 'Ode to the West Wind'. And it is as well to remember that in that poem the creative tempest of the autumn wind is powered by the wind's separation from his 'azure sister of the spring'.

For Lévi-Strauss the prohibition of incest is crucial because it institutes a system of exchange, but for a poet, despite John Taylor Coleridge's suspicions about the Shelleyan ménage on Lake Geneva,[9] the primary objects of exchange are not women but words. In a striking passage at the very end of *The Elementary Structure of Kinship Relations* Lévi-Strauss connects the two. Rules against incest are, he argues, a branch of the rules of grammar: 'women themselves are treated as signs, which are *misused* when not put to the use reserved to signs, which is to be communicated'. He goes on boldly to suggest that women are the primary signs, and hence that the prohibition of incest is the necessary precondition of the institution of language: 'the emergence of symbolic thought must have required that women, like words, should be things that were exchanged'. If women are no longer quite like words, this is not because of a change in women but a change in language. Under the impact of scientific civilization the 'signifying function' of words has become 'common property', and one unfortunate consequence has been to 'impoverish perception'.[10]

Lévi-Strauss rehearses here a thought to be found in Shelley's *A Defence of Poetry*, where Shelley describes the process by which words 'become, through time, signs for portions or classes of thoughts instead of pictures of integral thoughts', a process that ends only when language has become 'dead to all the nobler purposes of human intercourse'. For Shelley, it is the peculiar business of the poet to resist this process, and the poet resists most forcefully by making new metaphors (278). The coincidence of thought here between Lévi-Strauss and Shelley is unsurprising. In both it derives from a keen sense of the connection between eroticism and writing, between love and language. That recognition may even be shadowed in the passage I have just quoted, in the use of the phrase 'human intercourse', but elsewhere it is far more explicit. The poet's peculiar function for Shelley is to re-discover the eroticism of language: poetry 'strips the veil of familiarity from the world and lays bare the naked and sleeping beauty, which is the spirit of its forms' (295). The thought is common enough, its insistently erotic expression is peculiarly Shelleyan,[11] and one of its effects is to alert us to the full sense of the word 'familiarity'. The poet removes the veil of familiarity from the world, and, as he does so, the world is recognized not as a sister but as a bride. The poet achieves this by constructing a language 'vitally metaphorical, that is, it marks the before unapprehended relations of things' (278). The poet brings into kinship through metaphor words hitherto unrelated. The poet's language is defined by such passages as the practice of a kind of verbal exogamy, it effects marriages outside the tribe, 'it marries', for example, 'exultation and horror, grief and pleasure, eternity and change' (295).

We might say, then, that Shelley, like Lévi-Strauss, was interested in incest as the condition of exogamy. Incest, the calm joy of the Ocean-king as he wandered the Aegean isle with his sister and his spouse, remains for Shelley both an origin and a goal. But as an origin it is irrecoverable, and as a goal it is unattainable, and in that resides its value. It creates within us the void without which there would be no motive force to urge us forth 'to arrest the faintest shadow of that without the possession of which there is no rest nor respite to the heart'; it supplies the want without which 'man becomes the living sepulchre of himself'. The prohibition of incest becomes, on this account, a benign defence against closure, a safeguard of that condition of unceasing becoming that is Shelley's version of Godwinian perfectibility and that is celebrated by him in poem after poem. It sanctions his determination to go on until he has been stopped by providing him with the necessary assurance that he never can be stopped.[12]

This is an attractive account of Shelley's activity, especially for modern readers, and it is in important ways a true one, but it fails in the end to persuade. For there is in Shelley's work, surely, a desire for closure quite as strong as a resistance to it, a desire that the spring heralded by the West wind of autumn be eternal at least as powerful as any recognition that it, too, is just a passing season. Nor are these two impulses in Shelley antithetical, but rather alternative reflexes of a single condition.

Shelley's verse is distinctive in its use of two kinds of figurative language. In one, Shelley supplies a series of signs, each of which seeks union with the object he addresses, and each fails, fades into darkness, and its place is supplied by its successor. The poem becomes a shower of fading sparks, propelled forward by its own insufficiency.[13] The other kind is finely described by Empson as 'that "self-inwoven" simile employed by Shelley, when not being able to think of a comparison fast enough he compares the thing to a vaguer or more abstract notion of itself, or points out that it is its own nature, or that it sustains itself by supporting itself'.[14] In *Prometheus Unbound*, Shelley describes how:

> Like to a child o'erwearied with sweet toil
> ...
> The spirit of the earth is laid asleep...
>
> (IV, 263–5)

The spirit is a sleeping child, and it is like one. The two parts of the simile perfectly mirror one another in a celebration of the spirit's perfect autonomy. But it is the desire for just such a state, in which the self recognizes its ideal mirror image and self and image can merge in 'one immortality / And one annihilation', that generates the rapid, breathless slippage between signs that characterizes Shelley's alternative mode. The two figurative modes are united in that both express Shelley's rejection of an alternative metaphorical ideal, in which the two terms of the metaphor are bound together both by likeness and difference, the ideal described by Coleridge as 'the harmonious reconciliation of opposite or discordant qualities'. If, as Shelley repeatedly invites us to do, we accept that language and love are intimately connected, and that something more than a loose analogy connects linguistic and erotic practices, then we might say that Shelley's two figurative modes are united in their opposition to the possibility of a stable union founded at once on likeness and difference, by their opposition, that is, to the Christian ideal of marriage. Which brings me back to the oddity that Henry Alford should have chosen to present to his bride on their wedding day a copy of Shelley's *Revolt of Islam*.

The fullest exploration of Shelleyan eroticism by a successor is not to be found in Alford's poetical works, but in a poem written by Tennyson, probably in 1829. *A Lover's Tale* was to have been the last and the longest poem in Tennyson's volume, *Poems*, 1832. In the event, and despite the protests of his friends, he decided to withdraw it at the last moment, when the volume was already in proof, and did not finally publish it until 40 years later. In 1832 the poem was a fragment in three parts. The first describes a walk taken by the poem's speaker, himself a poet, with the cousin whom he loves. In 1832 the speaker is unnamed, but when the poem was at last published he is identified as Julian. Julian walks with his cousin, Cadrilla, through a gorgeous landscape, intent on finding the perfect occasion to declare his passion, but all day long he defers the moment, until the two sit down together on the shore of a small lake. Happy and inattentive, Julian listens to the sound of his cousin's voice. Only gradually does the import of what she is saying force itself upon him. Cadrilla has received a proposal of marriage from Lionel, a friend of both cousins, and she has accepted. His dreams shattered, Julian faints, and knows nothing until he awakes to find Lionel tenderly ministering to him. He stutters out his congratulations and hurries away, retreating into the nightmare world described in the poem's second and third parts, a world in which reality and hallucination merge, as do marriage and funeral, two rituals which become, in Julian's unhinged perception giddily confused.[15]

Julian and Cadrilla are Shelleyan lovers, each the mirror image of the other. Tennyson follows Shelley in locating the origin of Julian's love in narcissism, but he confesses it more flagrantly than even Shelley dared. Julian looks into Cadrilla's eyes in order 'To worship mine own image, laved in light, / The centre of the splendours'. He may add that this idol of himself is 'all unworthy / Of such a shrine' (1, 63–7, 1832), but the gallantry serves only to underline the egoism. He dreams, in a passage even more awash with Shelleyan echoes than the rest of the poem, of a consummation of his love, but the consummation he imagines is a penetration of the self by the self, the consummation enjoyed by 'the rose', when,

> drunk with its own wine, and overfull
> Of sweetness, and in smelling of itself,
> It falls on its own thorns.
>
> (1, 265–7)

Unlike Laon and Cythna, Julian and Cadrilla are only cousins; their consanguinity remains within respectable bounds. But this serves in

Tennyson's poem only to make possible a specularity more perfect than even Shelley conceived. The two were born 'on the same morning, almost the same hour' (1, 192), the children of two sisters. Cadrilla's mother dies in childbirth. Immediately afterwards, Julian's father dies, so that now the two babies can share a single mother and a single father, and may be laid together in a single cradle, less cousins than a miracle of nature, identical twins of opposite sex.

Julian loves Cadrilla as his mirror image, but to see oneself reflected in a mirror, to recognize oneself, is inevitably to recognize the otherness of that self, and Julian is by no means willing to admit the otherness of Cadrilla. That unnerving moment when the infant for the first time sees itself in a mirror and responds to its reflection 'in a flutter of jubilant activity', can occur as early as the age of six months,[16] and so it is fitting that Julian's nostalgia should focus most fondly on the time before his memory begins, on the time that he can know only from the reports of others, who can describe to him how:

> we slept
> In the same cradle always, face to face,
> Folding each other, breathing on each other,
> Hearts beating time to heart, lip pressing lip,
> Dreaming together (dreaming of each other
> They should have added), till the morning light
> Sloped through the pines, upon the dewy pane
> Falling, unsealed our eyelids, and we woke
> To gaze upon each other.
>
> (1, 252–60)

He is nostalgic for the time before he can remember, because that is the time when he could not know his separateness from Cadrilla, the time before he had learned to distinguish himself from his reflection. He looks back to his infancy, which is, as Tennyson famously knew, the time before language – in *In Memoriam* he defines the infant etymologically as one who 'has no language but a cry'.

*The Lover's Tale* is a wordy poem – even in its unfinished state it extends over more than a thousand lines – but its wordiness is produced by Tennyson's employment of two tactics, both of them derived from Shelley. First, as in *Epipsychion*, a recognition of the inadequacy of language generates a spate of words. Julian denies that his love can be 'cabined up in words and syllables', and his recognition of the futility of language itself produces a massively sustained burst of eloquence. He is driven to eloquence in his anxiety to celebrate speechlessness, for the love to which he aspires is perfectly available only to the speechless infant. It is because his love cannot be spoken, that Julian can only defer the moment when he will declare himself to Cadrilla, and it is that deferral that produces the poem's second tactic, for it generates the landscapes that occupy so much of the poem. As he walks along, every object that he sees becomes a fetish, a substitute for the passion that he cannot speak. The landscape is charged with his own erotic yearnings. Because it is denied any other expression, his love overflows, flooding the world, transforming each and every object in it into the sign of an unspoken thought, into the kind of sign of which poems are made. Like *Alastor* or *Epipsychidion*, the first part of Tennyson's poem can be understood as a sequence of metaphors organized by the fact that the breathless array of vehicles with which we are presented have each a single tenor, Cadrilla, Emilia, the heart's sister, and propelled forward by the inadequacy of any possible vehicle to adumbrate a truth which is defined by its being ineffable. In the second and third parts of the poem, Tennyson, still following Shelley, explores the nightmare that is as intimately connected to the dream as the shadow to the object that casts it. His model now is the madman's speech in *Julian and Maddalo*. Julian is deprived of his love object, deprived of the one referent that made sense of all his words, and in consequence his language runs mad: the literal and the figurative, reality and dream, merge, blur and intermingle. It is a poetic language lapsed into chaos, but chaos of a peculiar kind, of a kind, as Shelley puts it in *Julian and Maddalo*, 'such as in measure is called poetry'.

*The Lover's Tale* is an encyclopaedic set of variations on Shelleyan themes, but there is something odd about it. Julian's plight is presented sympathetically, and yet throughout the poem verges on parody. The poem is a prime example of what John Bayley has described as the 'implicit humour' of Tennyson's poetry, a humour that derives from a covert sense that the poems are 'sending up their own subject matter'.[17] There is a brutal comedy in Tennyson's poem that lurks, as it were, beneath its surface. Julian is driven mad by the discovery that the woman of his dreams had dreams of her own, and that his own love, quite perfect because unspoken, has been found wanting in comparison with that of a lover willing to express his love in the public and no doubt conventionally approximate language that, on such occasions, is the only alternative to silence. Julian remains a Shelleyan poet, but his rhapsodies are consistently undercut by Tennyson's awareness that, precisely because of the unspeakable intensity of his emotions, Julian is not at all cut out to make Cadrilla an ideal husband, and that on the whole she will be a good deal better off with Lionel. In *A Lover's Tale* Tennyson rehearses the defining features of Shelley's erotic poetry flamboyantly, enthusiastically, but not quite seriously.

*A Lover's Tale*, it might be thought, exemplifies the peculiar difficulty that confronted the Victorian poets in their dealings with their Romantic inheritance, and also their preferred solution. It was not a legacy that they felt free to disclaim, for – and in this they were unlike their Romantic precursors – they were grateful children, and they honoured their poetic parents. But their legacy included frankly subversive material, of which Shelleyan incest is as good an example as any, that challenged them to find some means of accommodating it within their own, more cautious, less impetuous negotiations with the received ideas of the reading public. Tennyson, as it were, frees himself from the legacy of Shelleyan eroticism by acting it out. It is the same tactic that I have identified on several occasions in this book, most obviously perhaps in the Spanish episode in which the Cambridge Apostles seemed, as if by an unspoken corporate decision, to have agreed to free themselves from Romantic revolutionary politics by enacting them. But it seems entirely unlikely that Henry Alford had anything similar in mind when he presented his wife with his copy of *The Revolt of Islam*. It is a gift that is explicable only if we accept that Alford did not, at least consciously, entertain the notion that it might be construed as an invitation to his wife, Fanny, to act out in the marriage bed the ecstatic, incestuous consummation enjoyed by Shelley's Laon and Cythna. The poem that Alford wrote on the fly leaf of the book begins:

> Beloved, to whose wedded hand I trust
> This treasure of sweet song...

He entrusts the book to her, but he trusts too, in the other sense, trusts that somehow, as she reads, his wife will transform Shelley's subversive visionary epic into a paean to quiet, domestic joy. He seems to ground this unlikely confidence on the fact that, before it belonged to him, the book had belonged to Arthur Hallam: 'Blessed eyes / Have looked upon its pages'. Alford trusts that the gaze of his dead friend will have disinfected the book of its 'errors', and re-consecrated it to the service of religious and moral values of which Shelley would surely have been surprised to find himself a proponent.

Shelley could not have foreseen the manner in which Tennyson or Alford was to read his poems, but he foresaw at least that it would be unforeseeable, that, after 'one age' has taken from a poem all that 'their peculiar relations enable them to share', another age succeeds, 'and new relations are ever developed, the source of an unforeseen and an unconceived delight' (291). This book has tried to trace some of these relations. *A Lover's Tale*, for example, is an imitative poem. The imitation is affectionate, and yet there is a constant pressure diverting the poem from copy towards parody. It demonstrates a paradoxical method of winning free from a predecessor, not by avoiding his poetic habits, but by flamboyantly displaying how completely they can be assumed. It is an instance of just one of the many forms that poetic influence can take. Alford's present to his wife suggests a quite different manner of accommodating the work of a predecessor.

It seems true and significant that the Romantic interest in the love between siblings was transformed into an interest in love between first cousins. First cousins, after all, as Jane Austen shows in one of the earliest treatments of the theme, *Mansfield Park* (1814), may marry. When lovers become cousins rather than siblings their love may be accommodated by the social and legal mechanisms that oblige private emotion to conform to public rules. It is a transformation that marks one strong characteristic of the early Victorian re-writing of Romanticism. Victorian writers are far less ready than poets such as Byron and Shelley to assert their individuality by demonstrating the inability of any social forms to contain it. I have described similar kinds of transformation repeatedly, in, for example, my discussion of the transformation of revolutionary poetry into a poetry of citizenship.

But even here differences are as apparent as similarities. *A Lover's Tale*, for example, concerns two cousins who do not respond to their cousinship in the same way. For Julian, Cadrilla is the mirror image of himself, and hence his one true love. For Cadrilla, the same fact has produced in her sisterly feelings that have prevented her from ever imagining Julian as her wedded partner. It is Julian's point of view that Tennyson chooses to articulate, but other writers choose Cadrilla's. In Disraeli's *Henrietta Temple*, Ferdinand Armine runs into debt, and repairs his fortunes by proposing to a charming young cousin who is also happily an heiress. But his love for his cousin, Katherine, cannot survive his meeting once again with Henrietta Temple, whom he had fallen in love with at first sight. It was a love, they both at last agree, too much like that of brother for sister. 'Your mother is my mother', Katherine explains, and in accepting Armine's offer she had 'looked upon [their] union only as a seal of that domestic feeling'. She is content to end their engagement and resume their relationship as 'kinsfolk' (Book 4, ch. 14). Lorenzo in L.E.L.'s *The Improvisatrice* is betrothed, like Victor Frankenstein, to a young orphan who has been brought up since infancy in his father's house. He 'loved her as a brother loves / His favourite sister', but finds that love to be a pale thing in comparison with the passion that the improvisatrice inspires in him:

> I thought of her not with that deep,
> Intensest memory love will keep
> More tenderly than life. To me
> She was but as a dream of home, –
> One of those calm and pleasant thoughts
> That o'er the soldier's spirit come;
> Remembering him, when battle lowrs,
> Of twilight walks and fireside hours.
>
> (1399–406)

For Cadrilla, for Ferdinand Armine and Katherine, and for Lorenzo, to love someone as a brother or a sister is incompatible with married love. They substitute for the Shelleyan notion of passion produced by the perception that the object of one's love is identical with oneself, the more sociable notion that love requires difference, and that it might be inhibited in those too closely bound by ties of kinship.

And yet this, too, is not a settled pattern. When Aurora Leigh at last confesses her love to her cousin Romney, their embrace signals a union scarcely less intense than the unions of Shelley's lovers with the sisters of their soul.

> There were words
> That broke in utterance ... melted, in the fire;
> Embrace, that was convulsion ... then a kiss ...
> As long and silent as the ecstatic night, –
> And deep, deep, shuddering breaths, which meant beyond
> Whatever could be told by word and kiss.
>
> (9, 719–24)

It is an intensity that seems produced rather than obstructed by the fact that they are cousins, brought up together as brother and sister in the house of Romney's mother.

There is yet another possibility, articulated by Henry Alford both in his poem *The School of the Heart*, and in his life. Trollope explains it. 'Cousins are almost the same as brothers,' writes Trollope in *The Vicar of Bullhampton* (1869–70), 'and yet they may be lovers'. He adds that the 'idea of cousinly intimacy to girls is undoubtedly very pleasant, and the better and the purer is the girl, the sweeter and pleasanter is the idea'. By presenting her with his copy of *The Revolt of Islam*, Alford chose to remind his wife that she was also his cousin, and he surely did so not at all because he expected consanguinity to lend an added erotic intensity to their relationship, but because he recognized the erotic instinct as the most powerful and hence most dangerous of human emotions, and believed that in a marriage that grew out of a strong familial attachment there was every chance that the erotic instinct would be properly chastened and subdued. He looked forward to sharing with his wife, 'a lasting quiet joy,' and added, 'for nothing can be lasting that is not quiet'.[18]

Romantic siblings become Victorian cousins. It seems a simple enough change, but it masks diversity, and it is this diversity that I have tried all through this book to explore. In my conclusion I will change tack, and ask what, if anything, the writings of the period have in common.

# Conclusion

At last I turn, somewhat reluctantly, to the task that the wise and generous reader of my first manuscript noticed that I had shirked. I had set out no 'period-defining theory': all I had done was to write a series of essays on some of the writing produced between 1824 and 1840 that most interested me. I had not even attempted as much as Virgil Nemoianu in 1984, who, although he accepts that the label he attaches to the writing of these years, the 'Age of Biedermeier', does not name a literary movement, still claims for it a loose coherence, a 'Grundgefühl'.[1] I decided to place my last chapter, 'Domesticating Romanticism', at the very end of my book in part as an acknowledgement of Nemoianu, for what can be a clearer instance of the 'taming of romanticism' than the replacement of an erotic love between brother and sister, an incestuous love that can never be socially accommodated, by a love between first cousins that, as Henry Alford found, can enjoy the blessing of the church, the approval of his family, and be happily acknowledged by all his parishioners.

And yet I cannot quite bring myself wholeheartedly to agree with Nemoianu's characterization of the period, in part because his account of the Romanticism that was tamed seems wholly implausible. Nemoianu claims the authority of Abrams, Bloom, and Hartman, but his Romanticism is a good deal more colourful than theirs. At its core is a drive towards a 'paradisial recovery of unity', and, like a very different kind of core, it proves 'unstable and explosive', which 'explains why early death becomes almost a norm': 'Core romanticism results in suicide, misadventure, disease, drugs, madness, and the guillotine'.[2] But Keats, it seems proper to note, was not snuffed out by Romanticism any more than by an article: he died, like many before him and many afterwards, of tuberculosis. Kleist may have killed himself, but so too did Beddoes, and so, almost certainly, did Letitia Landon, and it was

Clare, not Wordsworth, who was, for more than twenty years, confined in an asylum for the insane.

That final chapter was also intended as an acknowledgement of Harold Bloom. This has been a book, in part, about influence. Bloom's theory of influence, the strongest such theory that has yet been produced, was derived from a study of the poetry of these very years, and, for Bloom, as he puts it somewhat gnomically, 'poetry is the enchantment of incest, disciplined by resistance to that enchantment'.[3] Bloom worked out his theory in a series of books that appeared in the 1970s: *The Ringers in the Tower: Studies in Romantic Tradition* in 1971; *The Anxiety of Influence* in 1973; *A Map of Misreading* in 1975; and *Poetry and Repression: Revisionism from Blake to Stevens* in 1976. They are not, I suspect, books that are these days much read, and that is surely because two kinds of literary critic have found them antipathetic. Historicist critics have found little to interest them in a theory that insists so strenuously on the autonomy of the aesthetic sphere, and feminist critics have been equally unattracted by so very Kiplingesque a theory, a theory that represents literary history as a series of encounters in which two strong men are brought face to face, a 'battle between strong equals, father and son as mighty opposites, Laius and Oedipus at the crossroads'.[4] In the work of critics such as Angela Leighton, Marlon Ross, and Anne Mellor, mothering replaces fathering as the influential verb, and the transactions between women poets and their precursors are presented as tender, expressions of gratitude rather than challenges to mortal combat.

I have no wish to fight with Nemoianu or with Bloom, but, as Bloom would anticipate, I would like to swerve away from them. I had a third reason for closing my book with a chapter that centred on a discussion of *A Lover's Tale*. It is a poem in which Tennyson's lover is more interested in the origin of his love than in its outcome. His dream is that he and Cadrilla might somehow recover their shared infancy, and return to the time when they slept

> In the same cradle always, face to face,
> Folding each other, breathing on each other,
> Hearts beating time to heart, lip pressing lip,
> Dreaming together (dreaming of each other
> They should have added), till the morning light
> Sloped through the pines, upon the dewy pane
> Falling, unsealed our eyelids, and we woke
> To gaze upon each other.
>
> (1, 252–60)

In this, it seems to me a poem entirely characteristic of its period. The writing of the years from 1824–40 shares a preoccupation with origins.

Bloom insists, and he is quite right to insist, that poems originate from other poems; that the writing we write now is produced by the writing that has already been written. All through this book I have been concerned with the relations between writers and their precursors, but quite deliberately in a piecemeal fashion. In the first chapter, through a discussion of biographical and frankly fictional accounts of the Romantic poets, I laid out my premise; that the Romantic poets were at once remembered and forgotten, honoured and satirized, by their successors. In the following chapters the writers of the period are shown assuming the full range of these postures, from Barrett Browning's tart rejection in 'The Dead Pan' of an aesthetic that preferred pagan fictions to Christian truths (Chapter 7) to her future husband's embarrassing apostrophe to Shelley in *Pauline*, 'Yet, sun-treader, all hail! From my heart's heart / I bid thee hail!' (Chapter 5). But it is the mixed response that I have pointed to as most characteristic. Even in *Pauline*, after all, Browning bids 'adieu' to his Shelleyan youth with a regret strongly qualified by the triumphant chuckle with which he claims his freedom from his hero. More usually, in Browning, the rejection of the heroic predecessor is accompanied by feelings of guilt. Hence the theme of apostasy, endemic in Browning's early work, that I encounter in Chapter 5 in my discussion of *Strafford*. In the novels by Bulwer and Disraeli that I discussed in Chapter 4, heartfelt admiration of Byron coincides with satirical caricatures of the Byronic poet and the Byronic hero in the persons of Lord Alhambra and Sir Reginald Glanville.

The couplet from Lord Alhambra's poem that Grey admires is clearly a parody of poems like *The Corsair*, and parody is a common device. Parodists, of course, are almost always anxious to claim that parody is the sincerest form of flattery, but they protest too much. If parody is a compliment, it is at least a double-edged one. *A Lover's Tale* (Chapter 8) is not so much an imitation as a parody of the Shelleyan erotic poem, and in this is it typical of Tennyson's early verse so much of which verges on parody. Even Keats, a much more powerful influence on Tennyson than Shelley, is imitated with an exuberance that verges on the comic, so that Tennyson's Mariana occupies a position oddly in between a figure like Keats's Madeline, enclosed in her bedchamber and absorbed in erotic anticipation, and a comic grotesque such as Dickens's Miss Havisham. But the most spectacular achievement of Tennyson and his friends was to extend their practice of parody from poetry to life, as in their ill-fated Spanish adventure (see Chapter 5).

It was in that chapter, too, that I found, in *Casa Guidi Windows*, the most comprehensive exploration of the range of possibilities open to a poet in her dealings with her predecessors. For Barrett Browning the poets of the past are at once an inspiring example, and a provocation: 'I kiss their footsteps, yet their words gainsay'. The freedom that she claims for the modern poet is paradoxical. The modern poet recognizes herself as belated. Barrett Browning writes her poem almost half a century after Byron had roused Italy to reassert its nationhood, and she writes from the city in which Dante had written more than five hundred years before. Poets, she accepts, are produced by history, and yet she insists on her freedom and finds it in the power to re-write the literary history by which she is bound.

And yet, for all Bloom's claims, literary history cannot fully be extricated from other kinds of history. It cannot even quite be separated from political history. As I point out in Chapter 3, Macaulay proclaimed the end of history a hundred and fifty years before Fukuyama. For him, English history ended in 1832, with the passing of the Great Reform Bill, 'the Revolution which brought the Parliament' at last and finally 'into harmony with the nation'. But history then, as now, tends not to stop when it is told to, and in *Felix Holt* and *Middlemarch* George Eliot finds in the same event not an end but a beginning. In Chapter 5, I identify that Act, and a series of legislative measures that preceded it, as the origin of the political ideal that was to remain paramount for more than a century, the ideal that I term the idea of citizenship. But it is an idea that, Barrett Browning robustly insists, had its true origin not in Westminster but in France. For her, as for Carlyle, Whig history, in its insularity, represents in itself an act of forgetting. It was a common enough response. In Chapter 1, I located it even where it might have been least expected, in novels in which Caroline Lamb, Mary Shelley, and Disraeli contrived to recall Byron and Shelley without ever indicating that both had agreed in identifying the French Revolution as, in Shelley's words, 'the master plot of the epoch in which we live'.[5] But it was Carlyle rather than Barrett Browning who most belligerently challenged the collective amnesia, and Chapter 2 centres on the book in which he did so most forcibly, his history of the Revolution.

Writing has its origin in earlier writing, in literary history, and also in history of other kinds, but it also has more prosaic origins; in printing presses, and in the offices of the publishers who decide whether the manuscript submitted to them should be set in type, bound, and sold. The period that I have studied coincides with the time during which publishing became fully industrialized. The Romantic poets had been belated participants in what was still for them in important ways a manuscript culture. Two of Coleridge's most important poems, 'Kubla Khan' and 'Christabel', made their mark on the poems of Coleridge's contemporaries long before 1817 when they were finally published, because they circulated in manuscript. Blake came to be recognized as a poet when an important manuscript came into the possession of the Rossetti family. Wordsworth's poems often circulated for many years in manuscript form before they were printed, the greatest of them all, the *Prelude*, not appearing in print until after his death. Many of the best-known poems of Keats and Shelley were also first printed posthumously, in 1848, when Monckton Milnes published his *Life, Letters and Literary Remains of John Keats*, and in 1839, when Mary Shelley brought out her *Poetical Works of Percy Bysshe Shelley*. That so many of these poems existed, during their writers' lives, only as manuscripts, is an indication, of course, of the commercial failure of their printed publications. But many of their successors were scarcely more successful. Browning and Tennyson were able to see their early volumes in print only because they were prepared to subsidize their publication. They could afford to do this, but it is also true that they felt that they had to. By 1830 the claim to be a poet was authenticated not by writing poems, but by printing them.

So it is that a writer in these years, meditating on the origin of his craft, is as likely to find it in Old Monmouth Street as in an impulse from a vernal wood. Dickens, in the character of Boz, haunts the old clothes shops for which the street was famous, because it is there, he tells us, that he finds the raw material of his stories, and what gives point to the thought is that it is at once a fanciful suggestion and a literal truth: once the clothes have become too ragged to be sold as garments they are bought by the paper manufacturers. The Romantic poets were apt, like Coleridge at the end of 'Frost at Midnight', to locate in the natural cycle of the seasons a type of the order that their poems seek to emulate:

> Therefore all seasons shall be sweet to thee,
> Whether the summer clothe the general earth
> With greenness, or the redbreast sit and sing
> Betwixt the tufts of snow on the bare branch
> Of mossy apple tree.

But his successor, Carlyle, was as likely to meditate on the industrial cycle of paper manufacture: 'is it not beautiful to see five million quintals of Rags picked annually from the Laystall; and annually, after being macerated, hot-pressed, printed on, and sold, – returned thither; filling so many hungry mouths by the way?'.

The first effect of the industrialization of publishing was massively to increase the power of the publisher. When Edward Moxon refused the manuscript of *Paracelsus* – even Tennyson, despite his popularity at Cambridge, had proved a poor investment: 'of 800 copies that were printed of his last [*Poems*, 1833], some 300 only have gone off' – it was a black day for Browning, because by 1835 Moxon was almost the last serious publisher in London prepared to publish volumes by young poets. Poets, it seemed, like handloom weavers before them, were to become victims of industrialization. Seen in this light, the feminizing of poetry that I explore in Chapter 3 is susceptible of a more cynical explanation. The feminine voice came to dominate poetry at precisely the period in which it became scarcely possible for poets to earn a living from the practice of their profession, and their earnings could scarcely amount to more than what Catherine Gore calls, in the title of one of her novels, *Pin Money*.

Novelists survived the crisis better, but their situation, too, changed. The fashionable novels that I discuss in Chapter 4 are such characteristic products of the age in part because the novelists who wrote them are so conscious of their new status as manufacturers of consumer products. They are characteristic, too, because the fashionable novel is better understood as a literary kind that was invented and developed not by a writer but by a publisher, Henry Colburn, who, as it were, merely sub-contracted the task of supplying the words for the novels to his authors. I suspect that an awareness of the newly subordinate position of the writer seeps into their fictions. Disraeli's and Bulwer's heroes masquerade as Byronic dandies, as did Disraeli and Bulwer themselves, but, as Andrew Elfenbein has pointed out, the masks that they assume are in one aspect rather unByronic.[6] They are extravagantly and self-consciously effeminate. It is hard to think of Byron ever claiming, as Disraeli did, never to have thrown a ball in his life, or a Byronic hero, like Bulwer's Pelham, boasting that, when he stepped into a Parisian gutter, he had no recourse except to scream until someone helped him out. Bulwer and Disraeli between them have some claim to have invented camp, and both no doubt found complex gratifications in this kind of self-display, but on one level it seems best understood as a means by which they accommodated themselves to the changed status of the writer in the fashionable world that they both aspired to enter. They could no longer dream of prowling, like Byron, the drawing rooms of London as a literary lion: the most they could hope for was that they might be adopted as a pet.

Books, as the writers of this period were forced to recognize, have their origin in the economics of publishing, or, as Vivian Grey puts it, 'Consols at 100 were the origin of all book societies'. But writers were interested, too, in tracing the origin of their writing in a much more homely way. As I point out in Chapter 4, the prophecy with which Barrett Browning ends *Casa Guidi Windows* is not spoken from an abstract, elevated site of prophetic inspiration but from the drawing room of her own house, where she stands, looking out of the window with her infant child. Such moments are wholly typical. Browning despairs of ever finding a way to complete *Sordello* satisfactorily as he squats 'on a ruined palace-step / At Venice', and notes how the metre of *Christmas-Eve* was modelled on the 'thump-thump and shriek-shriek / Of the train, as I came by it, up from Manchester' (Chapter Seven), and Tennyson records how he shaped his version of the Godiva legend as 'he waited for the train at Coventry'.

It is a trait evident enough in the most characteristic periodicals of these years, *Blackwood's*, *Fraser's* and *John Bull*. In the reviews that dominated the previous age, the *Edinburgh* and the *Quarterly*, comment was massively impersonal, its only origin the abstract space of right reason. But in the new magazines the editorial viewpoint is not divinely ubiquitous and invisible: it may even be given a name as in *Fraser's* Oliver Yorke or *Blackwood's* Christopher North. The new magazines claim an origin in the habits of conviviality that have brought together the contributors, and in which the readers are invited to share. *Fraser's Magazine* is presented as an all but accidental product of Fraser's dinners, and *Blackwood's* of the lavish hospitality to be found at Ambrose's Tavern in Edinburgh during the long nights of conversation that John Wilson records in his *Noctes Ambrosianae*. Both magazines celebrate an intellectual culture that they are happy to trace to its origins in the humble, material pleasures of the table and the glass. But except, briefly, in Chapter 4, where I consider Carlyle's dealings with *Fraser's*, there has been little consideration of periodicals in this book – it is its single biggest omission.

Whatever he may have suggested in his letters, in *Sartor Resartus* itself Carlyle seems content enough that his first major philosophical work should appear serialized in a lively but unpretentious magazine. Had he decided otherwise he would have been untrue to his hero Teufelsdröckh, who is happy to muse on his philosophy of clothes while scanning the newspapers, and glugging beer in a humdrum Weissnichtwo coffeehouse. Teusfelsdröckh is proud of his own humble origins, and Carlyle too, it may be, was pleased enough that his first major philosophical work should originate in the pages of *Fraser's*. He was, after all, soon to note with evident delight that the French Revolution itself might be explained as an effect of the 'gospel according to Jean-Jacques', but might just as easily be accounted for as an inevitable consequence of constipation: 'scanty, ill-baked loaves, more like baked Bath bricks, – which produce an effect on the intestines!'.

It is a period in which writers are pleased to locate the origin of even the greatest events in the humble, material circumstances of life, and to point out that their own writings have origins very similar. This was my preoccupation in my sixth chapter. It is a theme that for me is most movingly treated in the poems of John Clare, and in particular in his poems about birds' nests. John Clare, crawling through tangled undergrowth, disregarding the thorns that scratch and impede him, intent only on finding the bird whose song he is listening to, and happier still if he happens to find its nest, is an exemplary figure. It does not disappoint him that the nightingale should have no better dress than 'russet brown'. Rather, the nightingale's drab feathers are a salutary and pleasing confirmation that even the most beautiful music might have humble origins, and that it is the writer's task not to disguise those origins but to search them out.

One important characteristic of the writing of these years is, then, its concern to name its origins, whether the origin is located in the writings of the past, in the publishing industry of the present, or in the domestic life of the writers. But writers, like the rest of us, name their beginnings only as a way of electing their ends. The Romantics were apt to mystify the question of where their poems originated from. As Shelley puts it in 'A Defence of Poetry':

> A man cannot say, 'I will compose poetry'. The greatest poet even cannot say it: for the mind in creation is as a fading coal which some invisible influence, like an inconstant wind, awakens to transitory brightness: this power arises from within, like the colour of a flower which fades and changes as it is developed, and the conscious portions of our nature are unprophetic either of its approach or its departure.

Here, the origin of poetry is at once unknowable and wholly internalized. It is an event quite inexplicable and an event that occurs only within the mind of the poet. It is because of such notions that the Romantics were able to take seriously what Shelley calls 'that bold and true word of Tasso: Non merita nome di creatore, se non Iddio ed il

Poeta' [No-one deserves to be called a creator except God and the Poet]. Only poetic creation resembles divine creation, presumably, because in both cases creation is ex nihilo. And just as poems are without origins, so they are without ends. A poet, as Shelley has it, sings like a nightingale for its own delight, and the pleasure that it gives to others is always in some sense accidental, however happy the accident may be. Their successors supplied their writings with origins because they were unwilling that writing should have no end, and the origins they chose reveal the ends that they most wished for.

Writing for them does not have a secret, inexplicable origin enclosed in the mind of the poet, rather it originates from the world that we all share; a world of books and of book publishers, and a world in which writers, like the rest of us, need to eat and sleep, look after their children, and earn the money to do these things, and, when it is published, the writing is returned to the world from which it came. Writing has its origin in a shared world, and achieves its proper end only when it is recovered by that world. This was the notion underlying my fifth chapter, in which I discussed poets for whom the duty to practise their vocation was inseparable from their duty to act as responsible citizens, and it was also central to my final two chapters. In Chapter 7 I focused on religious emotion, the soul's lonely grapplings with God, but the exemplary poem here was *Christmas-Eve*, in which the prelude to the divine vision is Browning's revulsion at the 'greasy cuff' of his neighbour, and its proper end his repentant decision to join his voice with that neighbour's in the singing of a psalm. In the final chapter I turned from religious to erotic emotions, emotions that in Shelley, and even at times in Coleridge and Keats, are experienced most intensely in sleep, when the mind is self-enclosed, and freed from the painful realization that the world cannot offer any object adequate to the intensity of the poet's desire. But for their successors it is not enough that love be felt, nor even that it be returned. Love is completed only when it restores the lover to the social world from which it had abstracted him. It is completed, that is, only when it ends in marriage.

This is all that I feel able to do by way of offering a 'period-defining theory', and it is, even by my own estimation, not much. Does it amount to a theory at all? Not really, at most to what Nemoianu calls a 'Grundgefühlung', a vague sense that the books I have discussed have various things in common combined with a troubled awareness that these common characteristics can be identified only at the cost of radical over-simplification. It is, of course, its failure to achieve a single distinctive character, and its resistance to having one thrust upon it, that has left the literary period from 1824 to 1840 so vulnerable to the great imperial powers that adjoin it. Its territory has been partitioned, and its writers reduced to conscripts forced to serve in opposing armies. They are read either as late Romantics or early Victorians. And yet I would not wish, even if I could, to preserve the period by claiming for it a distinctive and dominating presence of its own. To me the looseness of the only kind of coherence that can be claimed for it is in itself an attraction.

Perhaps, I ought to end with a confession. It would please me rather than otherwise if the modest little period that I have studied, 'a quiet buffer', as Herbert Tucker puts it, 'between more turbulent Romantic and Victorian zones',[7] were suddenly to become militant, take on the big powers on its borders and impose on them its own vagueness. The pleasure that I found in my work for this book came from glimpsing as I read quite unexpected patterns, some of which I have traced in its successive chapters. It is a pleasure that comes from the freedom to bring together very different texts, and it may be a condition of that freedom that the period with which I was concerned has not been granted a strong theoretical constitution.

# Notes

## Introduction

1. For a history of the fluctuations in Hemans's reputation, and the recent revival of interest, see *Felicia Hemans: Selected Poems, Letters, Reception Materials*, ed. Susan J. Wolfson (Princeton and Oxford: Princeton University Press, 2000), pp. xiii–xxi.
2. See *http://www.rc.umd.edu/reference/anthologies/hemans.htm* for the discussion thread.
3. Herbert F. Tucker, 'House Arrest: The Domestication of English Poetry in the 1820s', *New Literary History*, 25 (1995), 521–48, pp. 521–2.
4. Virgil Nemoianu, *The Taming of Romanticism: European Literature and the Age of Biedermeier* (Cambridge, Mass.: Harvard University Press, 1984), p. 18.
5. Hallam Tennyson, *Tennyson: A Memoir* (London: Macmillan, 1897), 1, p. 4.
6. Harold Bloom, *The Western Canon: The Books and School of the Ages* (London: Macmillan, 1994), p. 250.
7. Andrew Bennett, *Romantic Poets and the Culture of Posterity* (Cambridge: Cambridge University Press, 1999).
8. Michael O'Neill, ' "A Storm of Ghosts": Beddoes, Shelley, Death and Reputation', *Cambridge Quarterly*, 28 (1999), 102–15.
9. See the article on Colburn in the *Dictionary of National Biography*.

## 1  Memorializing Romanticism

1. Walter Jackson Bate, *John Keats* (London: Oxford University Press, 1963), p. 694. For a recent discussion of the manner in which *Adonais* functioned to control Keats's posthumous reputation, see Kim Wheatley, *Shelley and His Readers: Beyond Paranoid Politics* (Columbia and London: University of Missouri Press, 1999), pp. 151–95.
2. *Remarks on the Exclusion of Lord Byron's Monument from Westminster Abbey*, 1844. For a detailed history of the affair, see Doris Langley Moore, *The Late Lord Byron: Posthumous Dramas* (London: John Murray, 1961), pp. 207–13, 502–3, 506–7.
3. The best account of the matter is given by Sylva Norman, *The Flight of the Skylark: The Development of Shelley's Reputation* (Norman, Oklahoma: University of Oklahoma Press, 1954).
4. Echoes of the phrase are identified in Steven E. Jones's hypertext edition of *The Last Man*, to be found at http://www.rc.umd.edu/editions/mws/lastman/ed
5. Thomas Medwin, *The Shelley Papers: Memoir of Percy Bysshe Shelley, and original poems and papers by Percy Bysshe Shelley* (London: Whitaker, Treacher and Co, 1833), pp. 78–9.
6. William Clyde De Vane, *A Browning Handbook* (London: John Murray, 1935), p. 244.

7.  *The Letters of Percy Bysshe Shelley*, ed. Frederick L. Jones (Oxford: Clarendon Press, 1994), I, p. 220.

8.  Thomas Jefferson Hogg, *The Life of Percy Bysshe Shelley* (London: Edward Moxon, 1858), 1, p. 22. All subsequent references are to this edition. Thomas Medwin, *Memoir of Shelley*, p. 3. *The Works of Thomas Love Peacock* (London Constable, 1934), 8, pp. 47–8. All subsequent references are to this edition. Peacock's *Memoirs of Percy Bysshe Shelley* first appeared in *Fraser's Magazine* in June 1858, January 1860, and March 1862.

9.  Edward John Trelawny, *Records of Shelley, Byron, and the Author,* ed. David Wright (Harmondsworth: Penguin, 1973, first published 1878), p. 319. Wright is quoting here from the earlier *Recollections of the Last Days of Shelley and Byron* of 1858. Twenty years later, Trelawny's memory was very different. Byron suffered from 'Tendon Achilles', a condition that made it impossible for him to walk on his heels: 'except this defect, his feet were perfect', p. 246.

10. The probabilities are canvassed by Wright in his introduction, pp. 32–3. Doris Langley Moore persuasively insists that his claim to have inspected the corpse is a lie. See *The Late Lord Byron*, pp. 92–3.

11. *Conversations of Lord Byron with the Countess of Blessington* (London: Colburn, 1834), p. 6. All subsequent references are to this edition.

12. Thomas Moore, *The Letters and Journals of Lord Byron with Notices of his Life* (London: John Murray, 1873), pp. 651–2 (note). All subsequent references are to this, the one volume edition.

13. Doris Langley Moore offers a full bibliography of these works, *The Late Lord Byron*, pp. 525–33. For accounts of, and selections from them, see *Lives of the Great Romantics by their Contemporaries*, volume 2, *Byron*, ed. Chris Hart (London: William Pickering, 1998), *His Very Life and Voice*, ed. Ernest Lovell (London: Macmillan, 1954), and Norman Page, *Byron: Interviews and Recollections* (London: Macmillan, 1985).

14. *The Halliford Edition of the Works of Thomas Love Peacock*, ed. H.F.R. Brett-Smith and C.E. Jones (London: Constable, 1924–34), 9, pp. 82–3.

15. Leigh Hunt, *Lord Byron and Some of His Contemporaries* (London: Henry Colburn, 1828), p. 184. All subsequent quotations are from the edition.

16. *Life, Letters and Literary Remains of John Keats*, ed. Richard Monckton Milnes (London: Edward Moxon, 1848), p. xix. All subsequent references are to this edition.

17. *The Halliford Edition of the Works of Thomas Love Peacock*, ed. H.F.R. Brett-Smith and C.E. Jones (London: Constable, 1924–34), 9, p. 73.

18. *The Letters of Percy Bysshe Shelley*, 1, 178–81. It is very likely that, prior to this outburst of indignation, Hogg had been encouraged in his attempts by Shelley himself. Shelley certainly tried to persuade Mary Shelley, his second wife, to establish a sexual relationship with Hogg. If so, the duplicity of Hogg's treatment of the incident is at least understandable.

19. Lord David Cecil, *The Young Melbourne: and the Story of his Marriage with Caroline Lamb* (London: Constable, 1954), p. 158.

20. Lady Caroline Lamb, *Glenarvon (1816)*, introduced by James L. Ruff (Delmar: Scholar's Facsimiles and Reprints, 1972), 3, p. 53. All references are to this edition which is a facsimile of the first edition of 1816. There is now a modern edition of the novel, edited by Frances Wilson (London: J.M. Dent, 1995).

21. *The Journals of Mary Shelley*, ed. Paula R. Feldman and Diana Scott-Kilvert (Oxford: Clarendon Press, 1987), pp. 476–7.

22. *The Novels and Selected Works of Mary Shelley* (London: William Pickering, 1996), 4, *The Last Man*, ed. Jane Blumberg with Nora Crook, p. 7. All subsequent references are to this edition.

23. There has been a widespread effort to minimize the autobiographical significance of *The Last Man* made by critics understandably suspicious of the manner in which writing by women is so often represented simply as a reflection of their personal lives, but the case for an autobiographical reading, made most persuasively by Mary Poovey, seems to me completely convincing. See Mary Poovey, *The Proper Lady and the Woman Writer: Ideology As Style in the Works of Mary Wollstonecraft, Mary Shelley, and Jane Austen* (Chicago: University of Chicago Press, 1984).

24. *Glenarvon*, 3, pp. 82–3. This is the only extant version of the letter, but Leslie A. Marchand accepts that it is by Byron and includes it in his edition of *Byron's Letters and Journals*, 2, (London: John Murray, 1973), p. 242. For Marchand's reasoning, see his note.

25. Benjamin Disraeli, *Venetia* (London: Longman, Green and Co, 1881), p. 429. All subsequent references are to this edition.

26. *The Works of Lord Macaulay*, ed. Lady Trevelyan (London: Longman, Green and Co, 1875), 5, p. 391.

27. A point made by Malcolm Kelsall, 'The Byronic Hero and the Revolution in Ireland: The Politics of *Glenarvon*', *The Byron Journal*, 9 (1981), pp. 4–19. Kelsall's article is the first to offer a serious account of the novel, and it remains, for me, the most perceptive. Frances Wilson offers a comprehensive survey of accounts of the novel in her edition, pp. 375–96.

28. Thomas Pakenham, *The Years of Liberty: The Story of the Great Irish Rebellion of 1798* (London: Hodder and Stoughton, 1969), pp. 170–83.

29. *Byron's Letters and Journals*, ed. Leslie A. Marchand, 3 (London: John Murray, 1974), pp. 248–9. For additional evidence of Byron's admiration for Lord Edward Fitzgerald, see his sonnet to George IV, 'To be the father of the fatherless'.

30. On Lord Edward Fitzgerald, see Stella Tillyard, *The Citizen Lord: Edward Fitzgerald, 1763–1798* (London: Chatto and Windus, 1997).

31. It is possible to suggest a quite different time scheme for the novel if the historical references are ignored, and one focuses instead on Venetia as a representation of Byron's daughter, Ada. In that case the novel begins in the spring of 1824, when she was ten years old, and, significantly, the spring of Byron's death. This may be a rash assumption, but it is less so than it seems. Disraeli's Lady Annabel who has studiously raised her daughter in total ignorance of her father rather clearly recalls her namesake, Byron's wife. Both Annabels are at once paragons of British womanhood and women who demand as the price of their approval a surrender to their own narrow and self-righteous notion of what is acceptable in behaviour and opinion. In the novel Venetia first gazes on her father when she finds a portrait of him in a room that her mother keeps locked. Her historical counterpart was enlightened more dramatically when, on her twentieth birthday, her mother sent her the portrait of Byron in Albanian dress having hitherto kept her in complete ignorance of her father. This was in 1835, and it is

hard not to think that Disraeli knew of the event, and alluded to it in the novel that he published two years later.

32. See Morton D. Paley, 'Mary Shelley's *The Last Man*: Apocalypse without Millennium' in *The Other Mary Shelley*, ed. Audrey A. Fisch, Anne K. Mellor and Esther H. Schor (New York: Oxford University Press, 1993), pp. 107–23.

33. Compare, for example, P.B. Shelley's note to *Queen Mab*, VI, 45–6: 'It is exceedingly probable, from many considerations, that this obliquity will gradually diminish, until the equator coincides with the ecliptic: the nights and days will then become equal on the earth throughout the year, and probably the seasons also. There is no great extravagance in presuming that the progress of the perpendicularity of the poles may be as rapid as the progress of intellect; or that there should be a perfect identity between the moral and physical improvement of the human species'.

34. Critics have disagreed as to whether *The Last Man* should be understood as a conservative satire on the radicalism of Godwin and Percy Shelley. The conservative case is most persuasively put by Lee Sterrenburg, 'The Last Man: Anatomy of a Failed Revolution', *Nineteenth Century Fiction*, 33 (1978), pp. 324–47, and by Pamela Clemit, *The Godwinian Novel: The Rational Fictions of Godwin, Brockden Brown, and Mary Shelley* (Oxford: Clarendon Press, 1993), pp. 183–210. Clemit seems right to argue that Shelley's fable satirizes radicalism and conservatism both. It is a satire not on a particular political position, but on the human disposition to attach so much importance to their political differences.

35. Virgil Nemoianu, *The Taming of Romanticism: European Literature and the Age of Biedermeier* (Cambridge, Mass.: Harvard University Press, 1984), p. 28.

# 2  Historicizing Romanticism

1. The anachronism is less startling than it seems. Macaulay's is the most finished expression of a version of English history, commonly described as Whig history, which was already quite fully developed by his predecessors, in particular by Henry Hallam in *The Constitutional History of England from the Ascension of Henry VII to the Death of George II* (1827), and Sir James Mackintosh in *The History of the Revolution in England in 1688, Comprising a View of the Reign of James II* (1834). On this tradition, see J.W. Burrow, 'A Heritage and its History', in his *A Liberal Descent: Victorian Historians and the English Past* (Cambridge: Cambridge University Press, 1981), pp. 11–35. In my account of Macaulay's history, I am indebted to Burrow. On Macaulay's indebtedness to Mackintosh's and Fox's earlier histories, see Hugh Trevor Roper's introduction to his abridged edition of Macaulay's *History* (Harmondsworth: Penguin, 1974).

2. Sir George Otto Trevelyan, *The Life and Letters of Lord Macaulay* (London: Longman, Green and Co, 1889), p. 347.

3. Introduction to Trevor Roper's edition, p. 8.

4. A phrase from Macaulay's essay, 'Sir James Mackintosh' used by William Madden to define the chief quality of Macaulay's prose. See 'Macaulay's Style' in *The Art of Victorian Prose*, ed. George Levine and William Madden (New York: Oxford University Press, 1968), pp. 127–53.

5. J.W. Burrow, *A Liberal Descent*, p. 80. Compare Jane Milgate, *Macaulay* (London and Boston: Routledge and Kegan Paul, 1973):

> Throughout the *History* we are aware of a movement towards an established goal, a bringing of the story forward to a point where historian and reader are one in their shared knowledge of nineteenth-century men and events. This point of unity is both narrative and narrative means, since it controls the perspective from which events are recounted: author and reader both look at the past from the vantage point of the nineteenth century and use it as their standard for comparison, explanation, and evaluation. (p. 128)

6. It is a point that becomes explicit on the several occasions when Macaulay alludes directly to the French Revolution in order to establish it as a happily foreign phenomenon. For example, in a review of Henry Neele's *The Romance of History: England* (1828), Macaulay laments the historical tradition that he derives from Plutarch that holds up Greece, especially Sparta, and Rome as ideal exemplars of republican virtues. He adds that the 'transactions of the French Revolution, in some measure, took their character from these works', without which the 'government of a great and polished nation would not have rendered itself ridiculous by attempting to revive the usages of a world which had long passed away, or rather of a world which had never existed except in the descriptions of a fantastic school of writers'. The English are immune from this disease: 'We have classical associations and great names of our own which we can confidently oppose to the most splendid of ancient times'. *The Works of Lord Macaulay*, ed. Lady Trevelyan (London: Longman, Green and Co, 1875), 5, pp. 138–9.

7. Mill, *London and Westminster Review*, 27 (July 1837), pp. 17–53; Morgan, *Athenaeum*, 20 May 1837, pp. 353–5; *Christian Examiner*, 23 (January 1838), pp. 386–7; Christopher North/John Wilson, *Blackwood's*, 42 (November 1837), pp. 592–3; Thackeray, *The Times*, 3 August, 1837, p. 6; Merivale, *Edinburgh Review*, 71 (July 1840), pp. 411–45; *Monthly Repository*, ns 11 (September 1837), pp. 219–20; *Literary Gazette, and Journal of the Belles Lettres*, no. 1062 (27 May 1837), pp. 330–2. All the reviews are unsigned. Mill, Morgan, Thackeray, and Merivale are quoted from *Thomas Carlyle: The Critical Heritage*, ed. Jules Paul Seigel (London: Routledge and Kegan Paul, 1971), pp. 52, 47, 48, 74, 48–9, 81. *The Christian Examiner*, *Blackwood's*, *Monthly Repository*, and *Literary Gazette* are quoted from *The Critical Response to Thomas Carlyle's Major Works*, ed. D.J. Trela and Rodger L. Tarr (Westport, Ct and London: Greenwood Press, 1997), pp. 57, 55, 56, 53, 49.

8. *The Critical Response to Thomas Carlyle's Major Works*, p. 55.

9. *The French Revolution* in the Ashburton edition of *Thomas Carlyle's Works* (London: Chapman and Hall, 1885–88), 3, p. 203. All subsequent references are to this edition.

10. John Sterling, *Arthur Coningsby: A Novel* (London: Effingham Wilson, 1833).

11. *Thomas Carlyle: The Critical Heritage*, pp. 78–9.

12. *Monthly Review*, ns 2 (August 1837), pp. 543–8, *The Critical Response to Thomas Carlyle's Major Works*, p. 52; *Thomas Carlyle: The Critical Heritage*, p. 60.

13. *The Collected Letters of Thomas and Jane Welsh Carlyle*, ed. C.R. Sanders and K.J. Fielding, 9 (Durham, North Carolina: Duke University Press, 1981), p. 116. Hereafter, *Letters*.

14. *Thomas Carlyle: The Critical Heritage*, p. 61.

15. Mark Cumming in his *A Disimprisoned Epic: Form and Vision in Carlyle's French Revolution'* (Philadelphia: University of Pennsylvania Press, 1988), the best existing account of the work, offers an alternative account of the same characteristic when he describes the *History* as torn between the 'Ptolemaic' pull of traditional generic categories and a 'Copernican' recognition that all genres must be redefined in order to accommodate the new facts of the modern world. See 'The Critic as Copernicus', pp. 15–30.

16. In a perceptive comparison between Carlyle and Macaulay as historians Robin Gilmour stresses the difference between Macaulay's past tense and the present tense in which Carlyle very often writes. See Robin Gilmour, *The Victorian Period: The Intellectual and Cultural Context of English Literature, 1830–1890* (London and New York, Longman, 1993), pp. 31–40.

17. The opening sentence of Dickens's novel of the French Revolution, *A Tale of Two Cities*.

18. On this, see Carol Collins's unpublished University of Glasgow doctoral thesis,'Duality in the Writing of Thomas Carlyle and Charles Kingsley'.

19. John Holloway, *The Victorian Sage: Studies in Argument* (London: Macmillan, 1953), pp. 41–9.

20. Introduction to *The History of England*, p. 26.

21. *The Critical Response to Thomas Carlyle's Major Works*, pp. 51 and 53; *Thomas Carlyle: The Critical Heritage*, p. 59 (note).

22. John Sterling, *London and Westminster Review*, 33 (October 1839), pp. 1–68; *Thomas Carlyle: The Critical Heritage*, p. 111.

23. *The Examiner*, 17 September and 1 October, 1837, pp. 596–8 and 629–30; *The Critical Response to Thomas Carlyle's Major Works*, p. 54.

24. Quoted in J.A. Froude, *Thomas Carlyle: A History of His Life in London* (London: Longman's, Green and Co, 1902), I, p. 43.

25. *The Critical Response to Thomas Carlyle's Major Works*, p. 49.

26. *The Critical Response to Thomas Carlyle's Major Works*, pp. 50 and 52.

27. *Thomas Carlyle: The Critical Heritage*, p. 48; *The Critical Response to Thomas Carlyle's Major Works*, p. 52.

28. *The Works of Lord Macaulay*, 5, p. 138.

29. *Thomas Carlyle: The Critical Heritage*, p. 52; *American Biblical Repository*, ns 7 (1842), pp. 233–4, and *Boston Quarterly Review*, 1 October 1838, pp. 407–17, quoted from *The Critical Response to Thomas Carlyle's Major Works*, pp. 58 and 63.

30. Albert J. LaValley, *Carlyle and the Idea of the Modern: Studies in Carlyle's Prophetic Literature and its Relation to Blake, Nietzsche, Marx, and Others* (New Haven: Yale University Press, 1968), pp. 139–64.

31. Mark Cumming, *A Disimprisoned Epic*, p. 51.

32. A suggestion made by John D. Rosenberg, *Carlyle and the Burden of History*, p. 7. In his survey of the various nominations to the role of hero Cumming notes that J.A. Heraud proposes Napoleon and John Clubbe Goethe, before offering his own suggestion that Carlyle's hero is 'the human being as symbolmaker', *A Disimprisoned Epic*, pp. 68–9.

33. Benjamin Disraeli, *The Revolutionary Epick and Other Poems*, ed. W. Davenport Adams (London: Hurst and Blackett, 1904). All references are to this edition.
34. *The Critical Response to Thomas Carlyle's Major Works*, p. 49, and *Thomas Carlyle: The Critical Heritage*, pp. 66–7.
35. For a full account of Dickens's borrowings, see Michael Goldberg, *Carlyle and Dickens* (Athens, Georgia: University of Georgia Press, 1972), pp. 100–24.
36. The script of the play is unpublished, but Collins re-wrote it as a novella, and published it with an introduction in which he describes the play in performance and notes the differences between it and the narrative version. See Wilkie Collins, *The Frozen Deep, and Other Tales* (London: Chatto and Windus 1875).
37. *Byron's Letters and Journals*, ed. Leslie A. Marchand, 8 (London: John Murray, 1978), p. 78.
38. James Anthony Froude, *Thomas Carlyle: A History of his Life in London 1834–1881*, 2 vols (London: Longman Green and Co, 1902) 1, pp. 32–3 and 48.
39. *The Collected Letters of Thomas and Jane Welsh Carlyle*, 2, p. 437. I borrow Carlyle's description of the feeling that often overtook him as he proceeded with his translation of *Wilhelm Meister*.

# 3 Feminizing Romanticism

1. *Edinburgh Review*, 50 (1829–30), pp. 32–47.
2. Marlon B. Ross, *The Contours of Masculine Desire: Romanticism and the Rise of Women's Poetry* (New York and Oxford, Oxford University Press, 1989), pp. 267–309.
3. Isobel Armstrong, *Victorian Poetry: Poetry, Poetics and Politics* (London: Routledge, 1993), pp. 318–32; Stuart Curran, 'Women readers, women writers', in *Cambridge Companion to British Romanticism*, ed. Stuart Curran (Cambridge: Cambridge University Press, 1993) pp. 177–95; Angela Leighton, *Victorian Women Poets: Writing Against the Heart* (London and New York, Harvester Wheatsheaf, 1992); Anne K. Mellor, *Romanticism and Gender* (London and New York, Routledge, 1993); Susan J. Wolfson, '"Domestic Affections" and "the Spear of Minerva": Felicia Hemans and the Dilemma of Gender' in *Re-Visioning Romanticism: British Women Writers, 1776–1837*, ed. Carol Shiner Wilson and Joel Haefner (Philadelphia: University of Philadelphia Press, 1994), pp. 128–66; and *Felicia Hemans: Selected Poems, Letters, Reception Material*, ed. Susan J. Wolfson (Princeton and Oxford: Princeton University Press, 2000).
4. Anne K. Mellor, *Romanticism and Gender*, p. 123 and 145; Susan Wolfson, '"Domestic Affections" and "the Spear of Minerva": Felicia Hemans and the Dilemma of Gender', p. 145; Angela Leighton, *Writing Against the Heart*, pp. 25–6.
5. Mellor confronts the problem directly, and boldly insists that 'Hemans' popularity rested on a broader social recognition of the general truth of her vision', her demonstration, that is, of the destructive nullity of the domestic ideal, but, for all its boldness this is unpersuasive.
6. Harriet Owen, *Memoir of the Life and Writings of Mrs Hemans* (Edinburgh: Blackwood, 1844), p. 56.

7. *The Poetical Works of Mrs. Hemans* (London: Frederick Warne, 1873), p. 398. All references are to this edition in which the lines are not numbered. Line numbers are supplied for ease of reference from the Chadwyck-Healy English Poetry Database.

8. Isobel Armstrong, *Victorian Poetry: Poetry, Poetics and Politics*, p. 331; Anne K. Mellor, *Romanticism and Gender*, p. 142.

9. Jerome J. McGann, *The Poetics of Sensibility: A Revolution in Literary Style* (Oxford and New York: Clarendon Press, 1996), pp. 218–19. McGann misquotes Jeffrey's 'serenity of expression' as 'severity of expression', a less accurate and hence less interesting description.

10. Felicia Hemans, *Records of Woman: With Other Poems*, ed. Paula R. Feldman (Lexington: University of Kentucky Press, 1999), p. xx.

11. Marlon B. Ross, *The Contours of Masculine Desire*, p. 279; Anne K. Mellor, *Romanticism and Gender*, pp. 137, 141.

12. The oddest example of this habit of accommodating irreconcilable points of view is the inclusion of a third citizen, who had, one would have suspected, strayed into Hemans's play from Shelley's *Charles I*, had not *The Siege of Valencia* been published a year earlier. He takes a grim satisfaction in a siege that has reduced his city to famine: 'These are the days when pomp is made to feel/Its human mould!' (p. 102).

13. Angela Leighton, *Writing Against the Heart*, p. 17.

14. *Edinburgh Magazine*, 3 (1819), p. 443.

15. *Edinburgh Magazine*, 3 (1819), p. 576. Byron thought Hemans's poetry manly enough to prompt feeble plays on her name; 'Mrs Hewoman', 'your feminine He-Man', *Letters and Journals of Lord Byron* (London: John Murray, 1977), 7, pp. 158, 183.

16. For a condensed statement of Southey's imperialist aspirations see 'The Vision', the second part of *The Poet's Pilgrimage to Waterloo*. On Hemans and imperialism, see Tricia Lootens, 'Hemans and Home: Victorianism, Feminine "Internal Enemies", and the Domestication of National Identity' in *Victorian Women Poets: A Critical Reader*, ed. Angela Leighton (Blackwell, Oxford, 1996), pp. 3–23.

17. *The Poetical Works of Mrs. Hemans*, ed. W.M. Rossetti (London and New York: Ward, Lock and Co, 1873), Introduction, p. xxvii.

18. Marlon B. Ross, *The Contours of Masculine Desire*, p. 267. Hemans's essay appeared in *The New Monthly Magazine and Literary Journal*, ns 3 (1834), pp. 1–5.

19. Angela Leighton, *Writing Against the Heart*, pp. 24–5.

20. L.E.L., *The Improvisatrice and Other Poems* (Third Edition, London: Hurst Robinson and Co, 1825), pp. 29–30. All references are to this edition in which the lines are not numbered. For ease of reference, line numbers have been supplied from the Chadwyck-Healy English Poetry Database.

21. Marlon B. Ross, *The Contours of Masculine Desire*, p. 292.

22. *The Poetical Works of William Wordsworth*, 4, ed. E. de Selicourt and Helen Darbishire (Oxford: Clarendon Press, 1947), p. 461.

23. The best introduction to Landon and her work is by Glennis Stephenson, *Letitia Landon: The Woman Behind L.E.L.* (Manchester: Manchester University Press, 1995).

24. *New Monthly Magazine*, 32 (1831), p. 546. From Bulwer's review of Landon's *Romance and Reality*.

25. The importance of *Corinne*, like many other things, was first pointed out by Ellen Moers. See *Literary Women* (New York: Doubleday, 1976), pp. 173–210. On Madame de Stael's reclamation of the figure of Sappho, see Margaret Reynolds, ' "I lived for art, I lived for love": The Woman Poet Sings Sappho's Last Song', in *Victorian Women Poets: A Critical Reader*, pp. 277–306.
26. L.E.L., *The Golden Violet, with its Tales of Romance and Chivalry, and Other Poems* (London: Hurst, Robinson and Co, 1827), p. 238. Lines in this edition are not numbered. For ease of reference line numbers have been supplied from the Chadwyck-Healy English Poetry Database.
27. *The Troubadour, Catalogue of Pictures and Historical Sketches* (Third Edition, London: Hurst Robinson and Co, 1825), p. 244. All subsequent references are to this edition. This volume has been omitted from the Chadwyck-Healy database so line numbers are not given.
28. McGann and Riess offer a witily perceptive description of the style; 'It is cold and sentimental at the same time, flat and intense, like the photographs of Cindy Sherman'. *Letitia Elizabeth Landon: Selected Writings*, ed. Jerome McGann and Daniel Riess (Peterborough, Ontario: Broadview, 1997), Introduction, p. 29.
29. Very occasionally Landon constructs a quite different landscape, in 'Gladesmuir', for example:

> Where the forest ends,
> Stretches a wide brown heath, till the blue sky
> Becomes its boundary; there the only growth
> Are straggling thickets of the white-flowered thorn
> And yellow furze: beyond are the grass-fields,
> And of yet fresher verdure the young wheat; –
> These border round the village.

But in order to write like this Landon has to use a quite different diction and a quite different rhythm.
30. *The Venetian Bracelet* (London: Hurst, Robinson and Co, 1829). This volume is quoted here and subsequently from the Chadwyck–Healy Poetry Database.
31. L.E.L., *The Fate of Adelaide, a Swiss Romantic Tale, and Other Poems* (London: Hurst Robinson and Co, 1827). All subsequent references are to this edition in which the lines are not numbered. For ease of reference line numbers are taken from the Chadwyck-Healy Poetry Database.
32. Angela Leighton discusses Elizabeth Barrett's stiff retort to Landon in her *Elizabeth Barrett Browning* (Brighton: Harvester, 1986) pp. 23–4.
33. One recalls the monster's address to the body of the dead Frankenstein, in which the word has a similar ambiguity, 'generous and self-devoted being'.
34. Marlon B. Ross, *The Contours of Masculine Desire*, p. 274.
35. *Letters and Journals of Lord Byron*, ed. Leslie A. Marchand, 6 (London: John Murray, 1976), p. 106.
36. *Letters and Journals of Lord Byron*, 6, p. 234.
37. *Letters and Journals of Lord Byron*, 9 (1979), p. 125.
38. *Letters and Journals of Lord Byron*, 7 (1977), p. 182.
39. *Letters and Journals of Lord Byron*, 6, p. 237.
40. *Letters and Journals of Lord Byron*, 7, p. 183.

41. *Letters and Journals of Lord Byron*, 7, p. 202, and 8 (1978), p. 148.
42. *The Keats Circle: Letters and Papers 1816–1878*, ed. Hyder Edward Rollins (Cambridge, Mass.: Harvard University Press, 1948), 1, p. 92.
43. *The Keats Circle: Letters and Papers 1816–1878*, 1, p. 97.
44. *The Letters of John Keats*, ed. Hyder Edward Rollins (Cambridge: Cambridge University Press, 1958), 2, p. 327.
45. For an incisive description of the collapse of the poetry market, and a less persuasive explanation of it, see Lee Erickson, *The Economy of Literary Form: English Literature and the Industrialization of Publishing, 1800–1850* (Baltimore and London: Johns Hopkins University Press, 1996), pp. 19–48.
46. Michael O'Neill, '"A Storm of Ghosts": Beddoes, Shelley, Death and Reputation', *Cambridge Quarterly*, 28 (1999), 102–15, p. 109. Compare Donald J. Lange, 'Darley: Some Re-Appraisals', *Durham University Journal*, 72 (1974), 61–70, in which he points to Darley's 'personal and existential isolation … in a mass-industrial, urban society dominated by a cerebral and overly technological culture'.
47. *The Complete Poetical Works of George Darley*, ed. Ramsay Colles (London: Routledge, 1908), Introduction, p. xi. All subsequent references are to this edition. Line numbers have been supplied from the Chadwyck-Healy English Poetry Database.
48. On the reawakening of interest in pastoral drama in the period, see Jeffrey N. Cox, *Poetry and Politics in the Cockney School* (Cambridge, Cambridge University Press, 1998), pp. 123–45.
49. Claude Colleer Abbott, *The Life and Letters of George Darley, Poet and Critic* (London: Oxford University Press, 1928), p. 224.
50. A good general account of Darley's poetry is given by Mark Storey, 'George Darley: The Burial of the Self', *Keats–Shelley Memorial Bulletin*, 31 (1980), 22–38. By far the most perceptive account of his poetry is by Leslie Brisman, 'George Darley: Buoyant as Young Time' in *Romantic Origins* (Ithaca and London: Cornell University Press, 1978), pp. 183–223.
51. Brisman brilliantly locates in Darley's recognition of his own poetic smallness the metaphor that presides over all his work. See *Romantic Origins*, pp. 183–223.
52. Brisman offers an extended analysis of this passage, identifying it as a central confession of the belated, miniature status that, for Brisman, becomes the unlikely foundation of Darley's odd achievement. See *Romantic Origins*, pp. 189–96.
53. All references are to Thomas Lovell Beddoes, *The Works*, ed. H.W. Donner (London: Routledge and Kegan Paul, 1935).
54. In fact, Beddoes's first volume of poems, *The Improvisatore*, was published in 1821, pre-dating by three years Landon's *The Improvisatrice*, but there seems to be no influence. Beddoes's poem is simply a succession of verse romances in three 'fyttes' loosely connected by virtue of being sung by the same minstrel.
55. Northrop Frye points out that in Beddoes's work the most penetrating 'intuitions' are usually articulated by the heroine. See *A Study of English Romanticism* (New York: Random House, 1968), p. 57.
56. Hallam Tennyson: *Tennyson: A Memoir* (London: Macmillan, 1897), 1, p. 4.
57. Published after 1832 in a revised form under the title 'The Day-Dream'.

58. Lionel Stevenson, 'The "High-Born Maiden" Symbol in Tennyson', in *Critical Essays on the Poetry of Tennyson*, ed. John Kilham, pp. 113–25.

59. Carl Plasa, '"Cracked from side to side": Sexual Politics in "The Lady Of Shalott"', *Victorian Poetry*, 30 (1992), 247–63.

60. Herbert F. Tucker, 'House Arrest: The Domestication of English Poetry in the 1820s', *New Literary History*, 25 (1995), 521–48, in which Tucker describes Tennyson as 'this studious son of Hemans', p. 542. He argues that in 'Mariana' Tennyson subverts Hemans's domestic ideal by realizing the domestic architecture and appurtenances of the grange in a manner inconsistent with Hemans's 'homes', which must be abstractly and vaguely rendered in order to constitute a set of values rather than a building. It is a suggestive argument, but L.E.L.'s descriptions of domestic interiors and gardens are characteristically more detailed than Hemans's.

61. Isobel Armstrong, *Victorian Poetry: Poetry, Poetics and Politics*, p. 327.

62. A phrase that, as Christopher Ricks notes, was borrowed by Eliot for 'Whispers of Immortality'. 'Thomas Lovell Beddoes: "A Dying Start"', *The Force of Poetry* (Oxford: Clarendon Press, 1984), 133–62, p. 141. Ricks wonderfully amplifies Frye's sense of Beddoes's isolation, the sense that his characters, and his poems, speak into a 'void'. The word 'alone', he suggests, is amongst the most powerful items in his vocabulary, pp. 157–62. I would add only that it is an isolation as much culturally as psychologically produced.

63. *New Monthly Magazine*, 40 (1834), p. 1.

64. *Edinburgh Review*, 99 (Oct., 1829), p. 32.

# 4 Fashioning Romanticism

1. On the difficulties that arose from the coincidence of a definition of literature as writing produced disinterestedly and a new acceptance that the writers were professional and had a right to be expect reward for their labours, see Paul Keen, *The Crisis of Literature in the 1790s: Print Culture and the Public Sphere* (Cambridge: Cambridge University Press, 1999), pp. 76–134.

2. *Isabella*, 137 and 125–6; *A Defence of Poetry, Shelley's Poetry and Prose*, ed. Donald H. Reiman and Sharon B. Powers (New York and London: Norton, 1977), p. 503.

3. On Colburn and his marketing techniques, see M.W. Rosa, *The Silver Fork Novel: Novels of Fashion preceding* Vanity Fair (New York: Columbia University Press, 1936), pp. 178–206.

4. *Byron's Letters and Journals*, ed. Leslie A. Marchand (London: John Murray), 9 (1979), p. 198.

5. *Byron's Letters and Journals*, 10 (1980), p. 12.

6. *Byron's Letters and Journals*, 8 (1978), p. 187.

7. All references are to *Don Juan*, ed. T.G. Steffan, R. Steffan and W.W. Pratt (Harmondsworth: Penguin, 1973).

8. Andrew Bennett, *Romantic Poets and the Culture of Posterity* (Cambridge: Cambridge University Press, 1999).

9. It had been a favourite joke of Byron's at least since *Beppo* (1818), where he refers to the 'twenty-score / Of well-bred persons, called *"the World"'* (470–1).

10. *Vivian Grey* (London: Henry Colburn, 1826), 2, p. 166. This is the second edition of the novel, which was published anonymously, and re-prints the first. All references are to this edition.

11. *Pelham, or The Adventures of a Gentleman* (London: Henry Colburn, 1835), revised edition with a new introduction and notes.

12. *Pelham; or The Adventures of a Gentleman* (London: Henry Colburn, 1828), 1, p. 109. All references are to this, the first edition.

13. *Women as They Are; or, The Manners of the Day* (London: Henry Colburn and Richard Bentley, 1830), 1, p. 136. All references are to this, the second edition of the novel, which re-prints the first.

14. Michael Sadleir, *Bulwer: A Panorama: Edward and Rosina, 1803–1836* (London: Little, Brown and Co, 1931), p. 125. Sadleir offers a helpful introduction to the fashionable novel. For more comprehensive treatments see M.W. Rosa, *The Silver Fork School: Novels of Fashion preceding* Vanity Fair, and Alison Adburgham, *Silver Fork Society: Fashionable Life and Literature, 1814–1840* (London: Constable, 1983). I am indebted to both.

15. Quoted by Robert Blake, *Disraeli* (London: Methuen, 1969, first published 1966), p. 57.

16. Catherine Gore, *Cecil: or The Adventures of a Coxcomb* (London: Richard Bentley, 1845), p. 102. This is the one-volume edition. The novel was first published in 1840.

17. Edward Bulwer, *England and the English* (Paris: Baudry's European Library, 1834), p. 253.

18. R.H. Horne, *A New Spirit of the Age* (London: Smith, Elder and Co, 1844), 1, p. 235.

19. Edward Bulwer, *England and the English* (Paris: Baudry's European Library, 1834), p. 253.

20. Lord Normanby, *Yes and No: A Tale of the Day* (London: Henry Colburn, 1828), I, pp. 135–6. The adverbial suffix in 'gentlemanly' is italicized presumably to mark the word as itself a vulgarism, a low form of 'gentleman-like'.

21. In fact, *Journal of the Heart* is a miscellany rather than a novel, a sort of scrapbook for a fashionable novel, and retains a certain interest on that account.

22. Lady Charlotte Bury, *Journal of the Heart* (London: Colburn and Bentley, 1830), 2, p. 93.

23. *Benjamin Disraeli Letters 1815–1834*, ed. J.A.W. Gunn, John Matthews, Donald M. Schurman, M.G. Wiede (Toronto, Buffalo, London: University of Toronto Press, 1982), p. 155.

24. Robert Blake, *Disraeli*, pp. 37–40.

25. *Blackwood's Edinburgh Magazine*, July, 1826. Horne took a more jovial view of Colburn's marketing stratagems. He notes, for example, that Catherine Gore's novels 'are as sure to come out with the earliest spring and winter advertisements, as the scribe of the mysterious "Evening Paper" is sure, by some inexplicable means, to anticipate the merits of every one of Mr. Colburn's new publications', *A New Spirit of the Age* (London: Smith, Elder and Co, 1844), 1, pp. 232–3.

26. Robert Blake persuasively suggests that Disraeli refers to the reception of *Vivian Grey* in *Contarini Fleming*: 'With what horror, with what blank despair, with what supreme appalling astonishment did I find myself for the first time in my life the subject of the most reckless, the most malignant, and the most adroit ridicule', *Disraeli*, p. 42.

27. Andew Elfenbein, *Byron and the Victorians*, pp. 221–9. Elfenbein also makes a brief comparison between *Sartor Resartus* and the fashionable novel, p. 103.

28. Mr. Edward Lytton Bulwer's Novels; and Remarks on Novel Writing, *Fraser's Magazine* 1 (1830), 509–32. Maginn sent Carlyle this and several other issues of *Fraser's* in 1830, just as he was beginning the first draft of *Sartor Resartus*.

29. It is a fascination that the young Dickens shared. Boz has 'a particular attachment towards Monmouth Street', because the old clothes he sees displayed in the shop windows incite him to imagine the lives of their first owners. One window shows 'a few suits of clothes' which must, he deduces' have once belonged to the same owner: 'There was the man's whole life written as legibly on these clothes, as if we had his autobiography engrossed on parchment before us'. The clothes provide the material from which the parchment is made, and they also dictate the novel to be written on it. 'Meditations in Monmouth Street' in *Sketches by Boz* (1833–6).

30. Not a perception original to Byron and Bulwer, of course. Both were widely read in eighteenth-century literature, and would have been familiar with *The Beggar's Opera* and *Jonathan Wild*.

31. Catherine Gore, *Pin Money* (London: Colburn and Bentley, 1831), Preface. *The Westminster Review* challenged her right to the comparison (Oct. 1831) disturbed perhaps by her at times more dashingly Byronic wit– she describes 'good plain English principles', for example, as 'a sort of verbal lullaby by which [the British public] delights to hum its senses asleep' (*Women As They Are*, 1, 278–9). The spelling 'Austin' seems almost as common as 'Austen' in the period.

32. From the notice of the novel in the *Courier*, n°. 13635 (16 April 1835).

33. *The Letters of Mary Wollstonecraft Shelley*, ed. Betty T. Bennett (Baltimore: Johns Hopkins University Press, 1980–88), 3 vols, 2, p. 80, and p. 151.

34. *The Journals of Mary Shelley, 1814–1844*, ed. Paula Feldman and Diana Scott-Kilvert (Oxford: Oxford University Press, 1987), p. 557.

35. It is not simply a one-way influence. Bulwer was one of the last in that long procession of young men who over the years came to sit at the knee of Mary Shelley's father to receive the benefit of his advice. He was drawn to her father, it seems, not so much by his philosophy, for Bulwer was at this time a convinced Benthamite, but by his novels, and most of all by *Caleb Williams*, which is the most important single model for most of Bulwer's early fiction, as it was, of course, for Shelley's. Bulwer's first novel pays transparent homage to *Caleb Williams* in the very name of the character who gives the novel its name, *Falkland*, and, like Godwin's Falkland, Bulwer's is an honourable man who is guilty of an action for which he can make no reparation. He persuades a married woman to elope with him, and, when her husband discovers the affair, she suffers a haemorrhage and dies. The plot of *Pelham* hinges on the murder of a brutish squire, and the suspicion that falls on Pelham's admired friend, Glanville. In another act of

homage the squire is named Tyrrell. In *Paul Clifford* the attack on a judicial system that punishes youthful misdemeanours by sending the culprit 'to a place where, let him be ever so innocent at present, he was certain to come out as much inclined to be guilty as his friends could desire', and of which 'the especial beauty' is its aptness 'to make no fine-drawn and nonsensical shades of difference between vice and misfortune' (Chapter 7), develops one of the major themes of *Caleb Williams*, and Clifford himself, a man of energy and talent who finds that the only profession available to him in which he can express these virtues is that of the highwayman, is a character who owes much to Godwin's Captain Raymond. To use Pamela Clemit's term, both Shelley and Bulwer were exponents of 'the Godwinian novel'. See Pamela Clemit, *The Godwinian Novel: The Rational Fictions of Godwin, Brockden Brown, Mary Shelley* (Oxford: Clarendon Press, 1993).

36. 'Elizabeth Brownrigge: a Tale', *Fraser's Magazine*, 6, 21 (August 1832) 67–88. My quotations are drawn from the dedication 'To the Author of "Eugene Aram"'.
37. 'Mr. Bulwer's Novels – Eugene Aram', *Edinburgh Review*, 55, 109 (April 1832) 208–19.
38. Letter of 15 March, 1836, *The Clairmont Correspondence*, ed. Marion Kingston Stocking, 2 vols (Baltimore: Johns Hopkins University Press, 1995), vol. II, p. 341.
39. See Jane Dunn, *Moon in Eclipse: A Life of Mary Shelley* (London: Weidenfeld and Nicolson, 1978) pp. 306–7.
40. P. B. Shelley's preface to *The Cenci*.
41. George Eliot, 'The Morality of *Wilhelm Meister*', *Leader* (21 July 1855) 703, reprinted in George Eliot, *Selected Essays, Poems and Other Writings*, ed. A.S. Byatt and N. Warren (London: Penguin, 1990) pp. 307–10.

# 5   Civilizing Romanticism

1. Students entering Oxford had to subscribe to the thirty-nine articles. At Cambridge, students had to swear to be *bona fide* members of the Church of England before they could take their degree. Attendance at chapel was compulsory in both institutions.
2. Hallam Tennyson, *Tennyson: A Memoir* (London: Macmillan, 1897), 1, p. 209.
3. All quotations from Tennyson's poems are taken from *The Poems of Tennyson*, ed. Christopher Ricks (London: Longmans, 1969).
4. *Critical Review*, 26 (August, 1799), p. 475.
5. These matters are discussed at length in my *The Politics of Romantic Poetry: In Search of the Pure Commonwealth* (Basingstoke: Macmillan, 2000 – now Palgrave).
6. Tennyson's memory of a comment by Hallam, quoted in *Tennyson: A Memoir*, 1, pp. 92–3. Hallam Tennyson reports that his 'father did not view the political situation as gloomily as did Arthur Hallam', and tells an anecdote in which Tennyson and his brothers are rebuked by the new Somersby vicar for celebrating the passing of the Bill by ringing the church bells in the middle of the night. Hallam may be right, but it may equally well be

that Tennyson had become embarrassed by his youthful opposition to a very moderate measure of Parliamentary reform. The ringing of church bells at night might as easily signal alarm as celebration.

7. *The Letters of Arthur Henry Hallam*, ed. Jack Kolb (Columbus, Ohio: Ohio State University Press, 1981), p. 372.

8. *Athenaeum* (1828), p. 33. Subsequent page references are included in the text.

9. T. Wemyss Reid, *The Life, Letters and Friendships of Richard Monckton Milnes, First Lord Houghton* (London, 1896), 1, p. 50.

10. *Thomas Carlyle's Works*, 4, *The Life of John Sterling* (London, 1885), p. 52.

11. *Life, Letters and Friendships*, 1, p. 77.

12. *The Letters of Arthur Henry Hallam*, p. 301. The edition of *Adonais* is described by Ruth S. Graniss, *A Descriptive Catalogue of the First Editions in Book Form of the Writings of Percy Bysshe Shelley* (New York, 1923), pp. 72–3. Monckton Milnes records that the poem was printed from a copy brought back by Hallam from Pisa (*Life Letters and Friendships*, 2, 433). In a letter to Trench Donne describes the publication as a corporate Apostolic venture: 'Tennant *cum sex aliis* reprinted *Adonais* in five hundred copies, and the impression was very successful' (Mary Chenevix Trench, *Richard Chenevix Trench: Letters and Memorials* (London, 1888), 1, p. 42). R.J. Tennant became an Apostle on 29 November 1828.

13. Hallam's poems are quoted from *The Writings of Arthur Hallam*, ed. T.H. Vail Motter (London: Oxford University Press, 1943).

14. Shelleyan echoes in 'The Poet' are pointed out by Paul Turner, *Tennyson* (London, 1976), and by M.A. Lourie, 'Below the Thunders of the Deep: Tennyson as Romantic Revisionist', *Studies in Romanticism*, 18 (1970), 7–9.

15. The allusion, as Ricks points out, is to *Revelation*, xix, 12–16, in which the name written on the thigh is 'King of Kings', *The Poems of Tennyson*, p. 223, note.

16. *Athenaeum* (1829), 207. I quote this text which differs in minor particulars from the poem as it appears in Trench's *The Story of Justin Martyr and Other Poems* (London, 1835) and his *Poems* (London, 1865).

17. Hallam wrote to Charles: 'Your philosophical indifference respecting the affairs in which I have been engaged seems to me to be so exalted, that probably anything I could tell you on that subject would hardly modify your yawning'. *The Letters of Arthur Henry Hallam*, pp. 376, 379, 380, 382.

18. In Trench's *Poems* (1865) this poem is dated 1829, before Trench's embarkation for Gibraltar, but by 1865 Trench may not have wished to recall his active participation in the venture.

19. Thomas Carlyle, *Life of John Sterling*, p. 74.

20. For various accounts of the Spanish adventure, see *Richard Chenevix Trench; Letters and Memorials*, 1, 65–109; Carlyle's *Life of John Sterling*, pp. 53–74; Hallam Tennyson, *Alfred Lord Tennyson: A Memoir* (Cambridge, 1897), 1, pp. 51–5; Benjamin DeMott, 'The General, the Poet, and the Inquisition', *Kenyon Review*, 24 (1962), 442–56; A.J. Sambrook, 'Cambridge Apostles at a Spanish Tragedy', *English Miscellany*, 16 (1965), 115–23; Robert Bernard Martin, *Tennyson: The Unquiet Heart* (Oxford, 1980), pp. 115–23.

21. Thomas Carlyle, *Life of John Sterling*, p. 53.

22. Trench rejoiced when Kemble at last renounced Bentham, and added, 'He is the only one who upheld for a long space of time the most degrading system

of philosophy that ever was framed, without having his heart or mind impoverished or coarsened by it' (*Richard Chenevix Trench: Letters and Memorials*, 1, 37).

23. *Letters of Arthur Henry Hallam*, pp. 387–8.

24. In a letter dated June 16, 1831, four months after his return from Gibraltar, Trench confessed to Kemble, 'I hate the Orangemen, who are sanguinary and violent, and yet I see in them the last hope of Ireland' (*Richard Chenevix Trench: Letters and Memorials*, 1, 97). In late 1832 Trench left Ireland after his father's steward had been murdered by republicans and he had awoken one morning to find 'a couple of graves dug in our lawn, with a coffin traced in the sod between them, being a sort of very lively *memento mori* to my father and self' (*Richard Chenevix Trench: Letters and Memorials*, 1, 113).

25. *Letters and Memorials*, 1, p. 80 and pp. 91–2.

26. *Letters of Arthur Henry Hallam*, p. 532.

27. *Letters and Memorials*, 1, p. 103.

28. *The Writings of Arthur Hallam*, pp. 104–5.

29. Tennyson wrote two sonnets in support of the Poles, 'Blow ye the trumpet, gather from afar', and 'How long, O God, shall men be ridden down'. He ends 'Hail Briton!' execrating the Czar and bemoaning the fate of 'the Polish virgin'. Trench, too, has a sonnet, 'Poland, 1831', beginning 'The nations may not be trod out' (*Poems* [1865], p. 85), but he recognized and insisted on the difference between the Polish and Spanish revolutions. The Spanish have no conception 'of a *nation*, as anything different from a horde of human beings aggregated together for mutual interest' whereas the Poles have the advantage of 'a nationality strongly and distinctly expressed' (*Letters and Memorials*, 1, p. 99).

30. *Letters and Memorials*, 1, p. 102.

31. *Letters and Memorials*, 1, p. 96.

32. *Letters of Arthur Henry Hallam*, p. 522 and p. 513.

33. *The Letters of Alfred Lord Tennyson*, 1, p. 69. There are useful summaries of Saint-Simonian ideas in Hill Shine, *Carlyle and the Saint-Simonians* (Baltimore: Johns Hopkins Press, 1941), and in John Kilham, *Tennyson and the Princess: Reflections of an Age* (London, 1958), though Kilham understands Tennyson's remarks rather oddly as 'meaning no more than that Saint-Simonism is both a product of the social evils abounding at the time and an attempt to solve them' (p. 25).

34. *Letters of Arthur Henry Hallam*, p. 683.

35. Quoted by Peter Allen, *The Cambridge Apostles: The Early Years*, p. 90.

36. *Letters and Memorials*, 1, p. 73.

37. *Tennyson: A Memoir*, 1, p. 54.

38. See 'In The Valley of Cauteretz', the poem that Tennyson wrote when he re-visited the valley in 1861.

39. *Tennyson: A Memoir*, 1, p. 55.

40. Herbert F. Tucker, *Tennyson and the Doom of Romanticism* (Cambridge, Massachussetts, 1988), p. 154.

41. The process of revision is well discussed by Paul F. Baum, *Tennyson Sixty Years After* (Chapel Hill, University of North Carolina Press, 1948), pp. 75–82, and by Philip Gaskell, *From Writer to Reader* (Oxford, Oxford University Press, 1978), pp. 118–41.

42. Benjamin DeMott is the one critic who has suggested that the episode had a formative impact on Tennyson's literary career, but he traces its significance for Tennyson in a reading of another poem that Tennyson may have begun to write in the Pyrenees, 'The Lotos-Eaters'. See 'The General, the Poet, and the Inquisition', pp. 450–1.

43. For example, Paul Turner in his 'Some Ancient Light on Tennyon's "Oenone"', remarks on the 'general incongruity of tone between the Judgement passage and the rest of the poem', and adds: 'From the pastoral we are suddenly transported not merely into the epic, but into the philosophical dialogue', *JEGP*, 61 (1962), 57–72, pp. 71–2.

44. *Letters and Memorials*, 1, p. 73.

45. *Athenaeum*, 1828, p. 194.

46. *Letters and Memorials*, 1, p. 30.

47. Compare DeMott's summary of the lesson that the young Cambridge men learned from their Spanish escapade: 'they had discovered nothing except the complication of political affairs, the familiar truth that the act of distinguishing good from evil, right action from wrong action, is a thoroughly arduous labour for the brain'. But it was at least a lively demonstration that 'the right does not exist in a Platonic world where everyone knows and worships the good', 'The General, the Poet, and the Inquisition', pp. 456, 450.

48. Tennyson, *The Critical Heritage*, ed. J.R. Jump (London, 1967), p. 75.

49. *Letters and Memorials*, 1, p. 81. Donne himself had married his cousin shortly after leaving Cambridge at the age of twenty-one, and had already begun to cultivate a life devoted to scholarly domesticity. He became the role model for his fellow-Apostles. Sterling could not go to Spain himself, because he had just become engaged. Hallam shortly after the Pyrenean adventure proposed to Tennyson's sister, Emily, and was accepted. Trench was already betrothed to his cousin, Frances, although he was unable to make his engagement public until 1832.

50. *Letters and Memorials*, 1, p. 86.

51. *Letters of Arthur Henry Hallam*, p. 411.

52. The fullest account of the episode is given in a letter by Merivale printed in *The Letters of Arthur Henry Hallam*, pp. 338–9.

53. The poem is quoted by Peter Allen, *The Cambridge Apostles: The Early Years*, pp. 121–2.

54. Isobel Armstrong, *Victorian Poetry: Poetry, Poetics and Politics* (London and New York: Routledge, 1993), pp. 25–161. Armstrong's innovatory insistence on placing Victorian poems and poetics within the politicized culture of Victorian England, whatever my local disagreements with her, informs this whole chapter, as it does so much recent criticism of Victorian poetry.

55. *The Brownings' Correspondence*, ed. Philip Kelley and Ronald Hudson (Winfield: Wedgestone Press), 3 (1985), pp. 134–5. Fox had shown Browning the appalled but fascinated comments made by Mill on the copy of *Pauline* that Fox had sent Mill for review.

56. Lee Erickson has deftly shown how the blank verse is adapted to Macready's idiosyncratic delivery, which cut against the metre, very widely varied the emphasis, and further broke up the metrical line by frequently introducing what came to be known as 'the Macready pause'. In all this, as Erickson

indicates, the verse of *Strafford* prepared the way for the verse of the later monologues. See Lee Erickson, *Robert Browning: His Poetry and his Audiences* (Ithaca and London: Cornell University Press, 1984), pp. 41–4.

57. Furnivall reports, on Browning's own authority, that he wrote 'almost all' the life printed under Forster's name, and in 1892 re-printed it for the Browning Society, with an introduction by C.H. Firth as *Robert Browning's Prose Life of Strafford* (London: Kegan Paul, Trench and Trubner, 1892). Quotations are from this edition. For discussions of the extent of Browning's assistance see William De Vane, *A Browning Handbook*, pp. 62–3; William S. Peterson, 'A Re-examination of Robert Browning's Prose Life of Strafford', *Browning Newsletter*, 3 (1969), 12–22; Michael Hancher, 'Notes on the Prose Life of Strafford', *Browning Newsletter* 4 (1970), pp. 42–5; Bruce S. Busby, 'A Note to the Editor of *Thomas Wentworth, Earl of Strafford*', *Studies in Browning and His Circle*, 5 (1977), 65–70.

58. The refraction of light into colour is widely recognized as providing a metaphor central to Browning's poetics. See W.O. Raymond, '"The Jewelled Bow": A Study in Browning's Imagery of Humanism', *PMLA*, 70 (1955), pp. 115–30; Park Honan, *Browning's Characters: A Study in Poetic Technique* (New Haven: Harvard University Press, 1960), pp. 189–98; Richard Cronin, *Colour and Experience in Nineteenth-Century English Poetry* (London: Macmillan, 1988), pp. 84–95.

59. 'The Lost Leader', probably written in 1843, the year in which Browning suggested to Horne that he choose as the epigraph to his chapter on Wordsworth in *The New Spirit of the Age* one of Milton's descriptions of the 'arch apostate', Satan. See John Woolford and Daniel Karlin, *Robert Browning* (London and New York: Longman, 1996), pp. 7–8. As Woolford points out, 'In his early work, Browning's presentation of radical thought is complicated by a near-obsession with apostates from its principles', *Browning the Revisionary* (Basingstoke: Macmillan, 1988 – now Palgrave), p. 19.

60. Browning would have known the fragment from its inclusion in the *Miscellaneous Poems* by Percy Bysshe Shelley, which were produced in a pirated publication by William Benbow in 1826, Browning's copy of which survives in the Taylor Collection.

61. On this, see Lee Erickson, *Robert Browning: His Poetry and His Audiences*, and John Woolford, *Browning the Revisionary*, pp. 28–56.

62. *The Brownings' Correspondence*, 3, p. 134.

63. On Browning's 'set', see John Maynard, *Browning's Youth* (Cambridge, Mass., and London: Harvard University Press, 1977), pp. 96–112. It contained at least one other member of unusual talent, Alfred Domett, who was to become Prime Minister of New Zealand, and was, as the annotations he made on his copy of *Sordello* reveal, a reader of formidable intelligence. The annotations are recorded by Ian Jack in his edition of the poem.

64. The meeting with Aprile is more heavily revised for the edition of 1888 than any other section of the poem, and the revisions accentuate the process by which the differences between the two men are blurred, but the effect is already apparent in 1835.

65. John Woolford argues persuasively that the rival impulses should be located not just in Browning's characters but in the poet himself. See 'The Problem of Power', *Browning the Revisionary*, pp. 1–27.

66. The best treatment of the political import of *Sordello* is in John Lucas's, 'Politics and the Poet's Role', *Literature and Politics in the Nineteenth Century*, ed. John Lucas (London: Methuen, 1975), pp. 7–44.

67. Daniel Stempel suggests that Browning has specifically in mind the diorama, a popular contemporary entertainment. See '*Sordello*: The Art of the Makers-see', *PMLA*, 80 (1965), 554–61.

68. Herbert Tucker in perhaps the best discussion of the poem properly insists that 'the way to meaning in *Sordello* is through its style, not around or above or in spite of it', and he points out how one of the characteristics of that style is to call attention to itself, in lines such as these:

> Nor slight too much my rhymes– that spring, dispread
> Dispart, disperse, lingering over head
> Like an escape of angels! (III, 593–5)

*Browning's Beginnings: The Art of Disclosure* (Minneapolis: University of Minnesota Press, 1980), 86–7. It may be, however, that Tucker is too ready to suppose that if a poem avoids closure it has achieved its only proper end.

69. From the article on *Sordello*, consulted by Browning, in the *Biographie Universelle*, quoted by Jack, 2, 166.

70. Lee Erickson, *The Economy of Literary Form*, pp. 42–7.

71. Compare the 'forgotten vest' that falls from a ship, and, as it soaks in the water, slowly loses its colour: 'how the tint loosening escapes / Cloud after cloud!' (3, 17–18).

72. In poems such as 'An Italian in England', 'An Englishman in Italy', 'The Lost Leader', the 'Parleying' with 'Bubb Doddington', *Prince Hohenstiel Schwangau*, and even possibly *The Ring and the Book*. On these last two poems, see Flavia Alaya, 'The Ring, the Rescue, and the Risorgimento: Reunifying the Brownings', *Browning Institute Studies*, 6 (1978), 1–41.

73. *The Letters of Elizabeth Barrett Browning*, ed. Frederic G. Kenyon (London: Smith, Elder and Co, 1897), 2, p. 358. She explains in another letter how it came about that *Poems Before Congress* was written solely by her:

Robert and I began to write on the Italian question together, and our plan was (Robert's own suggestion!) to publish jointly. When I showed him my ode on Napoleon he observed that I was gentler to England in comparison to what he had been, but after Villafranca (the Palmerston Ministry having come in) he destroyed his poem and left me alone, and I determined to stand alone. What Robert had written no longer suited the moment, but the poetical devil in me burnt on for an utterance.

(*The Letters of Elizabeth Barrett Browning*, 2, pp. 368–9).

74. The complicating factor was that her father's wealth came from his ownership of large West Indian slave plantations. When the slaves were emancipated in 1833, her father was forced to give up his Hertfordshire country house, and the family moved to rented accommodation, first in Sidmouth, and then in London in Wimpole Street. It is worth noting, as one of the few actions that speak to his credit, that her father supported the emancipation despite the financial consequences to himself.

75. See Elizabeth Barrett Browning's letters to John Kenyon, February 8, 1845, to Mary Russell Mitford of the same day, to Miss Stansfield, the representative

of the Leeds Anti-Corn Law committee of women who had first extended the invitation, of February 10, and to Mary Russell Mitford the following day. It is in this last letter that she most fully reveals her shame and humiliation; 'What was the folly called my "poetical reputation," in comparison to the duty to which I was invited?'. *The Browning's Correspondence*, 10 (1992), pp. 60–8.

76. She was also exercised by slavery in the Unites States, an evil to which her own family history no doubt made her especially sensitive, in poems such as 'The Runaway Slave at Pilgrim's Point' (1848), and 'A Curse for a Nation' (1860). It is perhaps the first of these and 'The Cry of the Children' that she has in mind, when she allows Romney Leigh to mock both the social utility and the authenticity of such verse:

> You gather up
> A few such cases, and, when strong, sometimes
> Will write of factories and of slaves, as if
> Your father were a negro, and your son
> A spinner in the mills.
>
> (*Aurora Leigh*, 2,192–6)

77. *The Brownings' Correspondence*, ed. Philip Kelly and Ronald Hudson, 3, p. 25.
78. *Corinne, or Italy*, translated by Sylvia Raphael (London: Oxford University Press, 1998), pp. 38, 103, 97.
79. *Valperga: or, The Life and Adventures of Castruccio, Prince of Lucca*, ed. Nora Crook, *The Novels and Selected Works of Mary Shelley* (London: William Pickering, 1996), 3, p. 221.
80. *Casa Guidi Windows* has been well edited by Julia Markus (New York: The Browning Institute, 1977). Her introduction and notes provide the best account of the poem's political background. All quotations are taken from this edition. In a brilliant reading of Barrett Browning's Italian poems, Sandra Gilbert argues that she found in the Risorgimento an allegory both of her own personal life and of her literary endeavour. For Gilbert, Barrett Browning tells through Italian politics the story of her own risorgimento both as a woman and a poet. This account of the poems seems to me convincing, but not in itself adequate, because it does not register strongly enough the demand that Barrett Browning consistently made of herself, and that Romney Leigh recognized had been fulfilled in Aurora's new poem in which she 'showed [him] something separate from [herself]' (8, 606). See 'From Patria to Matria: Elizabeth Barrett Browning's Risorgimento', *PMLA*, 99 (1984), pp. 194–211. Esther Schor's article, 'The Poetics of Politics: Barrett Browning's *Casa Guidi Windows*', *Tulsa Studies in Women's Literature*, 17 (1998), 305–24, is valuable not least in its brave reinstatement of *Casa Guidi Windows* as a political poem.
81. Isobel Armstrong, *Victorian Poetry: Poetry, Poetics and Politics*. For Armstrong's definition of the double poem, see pp. 11–21.

82.     Oh, God! that thou wert in thy nakedness
        Less lovely, or more powerful, and couldst claim
        Thy right, and awe the robbers back, who press
        To shed thy blood, and drink the tears of thy distress. (IV, xlii)

83. Mazzini's motto, as Barrett Browning records in 1, 499.
84. Dorothy Mermin, *Elizabeth Barrett Browning: The Origins of a New Poetry* (Chicago and London: University of Chicago Press, 1989), p. 163.
85. The first part of the poem was written in 1847 and offered immediately to *Blackwood's*, but was rejected. It cannot be demonstrated that, before she published the two parts of the poem in 1851, she revised the first, but I think it likely that she did, not at all as a means of denying the 'discrepancy' between the two parts of the poem, but in order to establish that discrepancy as the poem's point.
86. As Steve Dillon and Katharine Frank point out, *Casa Guidi Windows* is Barrett Browning's most emphatically Carlylean poem, especially in its desire that a leader appear, whether he be 'last peasant or first Pope' (1, 835) who will in his own person embody Italian unity. See 'Defenestrations of the Eye: Flow, Fire, and Sacrifice in *Casa Guidi Windows*', *Victorian Poetry*, 35 (1997), 471–92.
87. Helen Groth, 'A Different Look– Visual Technologies and the Making of History in Elizabeth Barrett Browning's *Casa Guidi Windows*', *Textual Practices*, 14, 1 (2000), 31–52, p. 36.

# 6 Realizing Romanticism

1. William H. Galperin, *The Return of the Visible in British Romanticism* (Baltimore and London: Johns Hopkins University Press, 1993).
2. See Stuart Curran, 'The I Altered' in *Romanticism and Feminism*, ed. Anne K. Mellor (Bloomington, Indiana: Indiana University Press, 1988), pp. 185–207.
3. See Carol T. Christ: *The Finer Optic: The Aesthetic of Particularity in Victorian Poetry* (New Haven and London: Yale University Press, 1975), and, edited with John Jordan, *Victorian Literature and the Victorian Visual Imagination* (Berkeley and London: University of California Press, 1995).
4. Hallam Tennyson, *Tennyson: A Memoir* (London: Macmillan, 1897 – now Palgrave), I, p. 511. The snatch of conversation is recalled here by Thomas Wilson.
5. See the discussion of the poem in Herbert Sussman, *Victorian Masculinities: Manhood and Masculine Poetics in Early Victorian Literature and Art* (Cambridge and New York: Cambridge University Press, 1995), pp. 82–97.
6. *The Return of the Visible in British Romanticism*, p. 287, note 12.
7. John Barrell, *The Idea of Landscape and the Sense of Place, 1730–1840: An Approach to the Poetry of John Clare* (Cambridge: Cambridge University Press, 1972). Amongst those in broad agreement with Barrell is John Lucas in his *John Clare, Writers and Their Work* (Plymouth: Northcote House, 1994), though Lucas may be more properly placed in between the two groups of critics that I distinguish.
8. Seamus Heaney, [Bicentenary Thoughts], *John Clare Society Journal*, 12 (1993); Tom Paulin, 'John Clare in Babylon' in Paulin's *Minotaur: Poetry and the Nation State* (London: Faber, 1992).
9. See in particular Kelsey Thornton, 'The Complexity of John Clare' in *John Clare: A Bicentenary Celebration*, ed. Richard Foulkes (Nothampton: University

of Leicester Press, 1994), pp. 41–56, Paul Chirico, 'Writing Misreadings: Clare and the Real World' in *The Independent Spirit: John Clare and the Self-Taught Tradition*, ed. John Goodridge (Newcastle: The John Clare Society and The Margaret Grainger Memorial Trust, 1994), pp. 125–38, and Eric Robinson, 'John Clare's Learning;, *John Clare Society Journal*, 7 ( July, 1988), 10–25.

10. *The Letters of John Clare*, ed. Mark Storey (Oxford: Clarendon Press, 1985), p. 185. For Clare's own collection of books, see David Powell's *Catalogue of the John Clare Collection in the Northampton Public Library* (Northampton, 1964).

11. All quotations from this volume are taken from John Clare, *Poems of the Middle Period, 1822–37*, ed. Eric Robinson, David Powell, and Paul Dawson (Oxford: Clarendon Press, 1996), two volumes, forming volumes 3 and 4 of the Clarendon edition of Clare's poetry.

12. See *The Letters of John Clare* ed. Mark Storey, p. 189.

13. *The Letters of John Clare*, p. 231.

14. On the relation between Clare's poems and Gray's 'Elegy', see R.J. Ellis, 'Plodding Plowmen: Issues of Labour and Literacy in Gray's "Elegy"' in *The Independent Spirit: John Clare and the Self-Taught Tradition*, pp. 27–43, and John Goodridge, ' "Three cheers for mute ingloriousness!": Gray's *Elegy* in the Poetry of John Clare', *Critical Survey*, forthcoming.

15. *John Clare By Himself*, ed. Eric Robinson and David Powell (Manchester: Carcanet, 1996), p. 2.

16. *Poems of the Middle Period*, 3, pp. 414–18.

17. *Poems of the Middle Period*, 4, pp. 138–9, 309.

18. *John Clare By Himself*, pp. 9–10, and Mark Storey, 'Edward Drury's "Memoir" of John Clare', *John Clare Society Journal*, 9 (1992), p. 15.

19. *Poems of the Middle Period*, 3, p. 397; 4, p. 331.

20. *Poems of the Middle Period*, 3, pp. 561–5 (563).

21. *Poems of the Middle Period*, 3, pp. 48–68; 4, p. 163.

22. *The Letters of John Clare*, p. 230.

23. John Barrell argues powerfully that Clare's growing maturity as a poet is evidenced by his becoming 'more able to emancipate himself from the influence of Goldsmith, and to discover a language of his own' in *The Idea of Landscape and the Sense of Place, 1730–1840: An Approach to the Poetry of John Clare*, p. 120. Similarly, for John Lucas, such expressions are merely 'linguistic traps', *John Clare*, p. 46.

24. I am indebted to Paul Chirico's discussion of this passage in his 'Writing Misreadings: Clare and the Real World'. Clare may well be recalling the story of Palamedes, who is reputed to have invented the alphabet when watching the flight of a flock of cranes, which suggested to him the possibility of letters.

25. On the relationship between the two poets, see John Lucas, 'Bloomfield and Clare' in *The Independent Spirit: John Clare and the Self-taught Tradition*, pp. 55–68.

26. Tom Paulin, 'John Clare: A Bicentennial Celebration', in *John Clare: A Bicentenary Celebration*, pp. 69–78.

27. Johanne Clare, *John Clare and the Bounds of Circumstance* (Kingston and Montreal: McGill-Queen's University Press, 1987).

28. E.P. Thompson, [Bicentennial Thoughts], *John Clare Society Journal* 12 (1993), p. 31.

29. John Lucas, 'Clare's Politics' in Hugh Haughton, Adam Phillips, and Geoffrey Summerfield (eds), *John Clare in Context*, p. 211.
30. *The Letters of John Clare*, p. 421.
31. *John Clare By Himself*, p. 2.
32. Drury's relationship with Clare is described by Edward Storey, *A Right to Song: The Life of John Clare* (London: Methuen, 1982) especially pp. 121–31. Clare's publishers, Taylor and Hessey, particularly Taylor who edited Clare's first three volumes, have been much maligned by Clare's admirers for their treatment of him. They are ably and in many ways persuasively defended by Zachary Leader in his *Revision and Romantic Authorship* (Oxford: Clarendon Press, 1996), pp. 206–61.
33. Quoted in Edward Storey, *A Right to Song: The Life of John Clare*, p. 128.
34. Most movingly perhaps in the triple sonnet, 'To the Memory of Bloomfield', *Poems of The Middle Period*, 4, pp. 181–4.
35. The first two phrases are from 'The Flitting', the third from 'The Mores'.
36. *The Natural History Prose Writings of John Clare*, ed. Margaret Grainger (Oxford: Clarendon Press, 1983), p. 139.
37. Amongst the birds celebrated by Clare are the blackcap, the bumbarrel, the chiff-chaff, the crow, the fern-owl, the firetail, the hedge-sparrow, the heron, the kingfisher, the landrail, the lark, the missel thrush, the moorhen, the nightingale, the nuthatch, the peewit, the pettichap, the quail, the raven, the redcap, the reed-bird, the robin, the sand-martin, the snipe, the swallow, the wagtail, the woodpecker, the wryneck, the yellowhammer. Many of the bird poems are collected in John Clare, *Bird Poems* (London: The Folio Society, 1980). Wordsworth is more various than the other poets in his bird observations, and he, like Clare, on occasion finds their nests. See, for example, his 'A Wren's Nest'.
38. A point well made by William A. Ulmer, 'Some Hidden Want: Aspiration in "To a Skylark"', *Studies in Romanticism*, 23 (1984), 245–58.
39. *The Natural History Prose Writings of John Clare*, p. 239.
40. *The Natural History Prose Writings of John Clare*, pp. 36–7.

# 7 Christening Romanticism

1. See Stephen Prickett, *Romanticism and Religion: The Tradition of Coleridge and Wordsworth in the Victorian Church* (Cambridge: Cambridge University Press, 1976), pp. 91–119.
2. Richard Chenevix Trench records his relief that Julius Hare, when he left Trinity to become vicar of Hurstmonceux, did not 'preach from "Wilhelm Meister"', but delivered 'excellent, plain, and practical sermons'. See *Richard Chenevix Trench: Letters and Memorials*, ed. Mary Chenevix Trench (London: Kegan Paul, Trench and Co, 1888), 1, p. 161.
3. Charles Buller became an Apostle on December 2, 1826, and Arthur Buller on February 16, 1828.
4. In February, 1830, Trench wrote to William Bodham Donne: 'You have read probably all, or part of, Sterling's novel, and perhaps Maurice's'. Donne replied in April that he had never met Maurice, but that Sterling had been 'so kind as to show me a portion of [his novel] in the summer that I thought

admirable'. See *Richard Chenevix Trench: Letters and Memorials*, 1, pp. 52 and 61–62. Donne must mean the summer of 1829. Both novels were published in three volumes; *Arthur Coningsby* (London: Effingham Wilson, 1833), and *Eustace Conway* (London: Richard Bentley, 1834). References to the novels are to these, which remain the only editions. Parallels between 'Supposed Confessions' and *Eustace Conway* are indicated by Kenneth McKay, *Many Glancing Colours: An Essay in Reading Tennyson* (Toronto, Buffalo, and London: University of Toronto Press, 1988), pp. 45–47. McKay also has useful remarks on the Apostolic response to Goethe. So far as I know, the first English novel directly to borrow the form of *Wilhelm Meister* is the second part of Disraeli's *Vivian Grey* (1827), and Disraeli returns to the Goethean bildungsroman in *Contarini Fleming* (1831). Scott had already borrowed Goethe's character Mignon for his *Peveril of the Peak* (1821), but Scott seems uninfluenced by the form of Goethe's novel.

5. From Carlyle's preface to the first edition of *Wilhelm Meister's Apprenticeship*, *The Works of Thomas Carlyle* (London: Chapman and Hall, 1907), 22, p. 6.

6. *Richard Chenevix Trench: Letters and Memorials*, 1, p. 158.

7. *The Collected Letters of Thomas and Jane Welsh Carlyle*, 2 (Durham, North Carolina: Duke University Press, 1970), p. 437.

8. *The Life of Frederick Denison Maurice*, ed. Frederick Maurice (London: Macmillan, 1881), 2, p. 59.

9. See *Wilhelm Meister's Apprenticeship*, Book V, Chapter 7.

10. *Richard Chenevix Trench: Letters and Memorials*, 1, pp. 158 and 270.

11. Ian H.C. Kennedy, 'Alfred Tennyson's Bildungsgang: Notes on his Early Reading', *Philological Quarterly*, 57 (1978): 82–105. In Chapter 8 of the *Wanderjahre*, Wilhelm encloses, in a letter to Natalia, papers that are described in Carlyle's translation as 'the confessions of some mind not yet in unity with itself'. Kennedy's suggestion that this confession is similar to that offered in Tennyson's poem is less persuasive.

12. From Hallam's review of Tennyson's *Poems*, 1830, *The Writings of Arthur Hallam*, ed. T.H. Vail Motter (London: Oxford University Press, 1943), p. 196.

13. Hallam gives the most direct account of his crisis in a letter to Gladstone written on March 18, 1829, *The Letters of Arthur Henry Hallam* (Ohio State University Press: Columbus, Ohio, 1981), pp. 282–3. He gives a verse account of the experience in a series of poems published by his father under the title 'Meditative Fragments'. See especially Fragments I and III, *The Writings of Arthur Hallam*, pp. 33–4 and 36–7. Hallam's religious despair was accompanied by a fear, reported to his friends, that he was going mad, and by temptations towards suicide. In August, 1829, he visited a lunatic asylum, hoping apparently that the experience would have a prophylactic effect, *The Letters of Arthur Henry Hallam*, pp. 304, 323, and 312. The visit is also recorded in a poem entitled, significantly, 'Lines Addressed to Alfred Tennyson'. Tennyson suffered from a fear that the insanity of his father might be a heritable condition, and it may be that this shared anxiety sealed the friendship between Hallam and Tennyson: they became intimate at precisely this time. In the spring of 1830, John Kemble wrote to Trench complaining of a 'thick roof between [him] and God'. Curiously, his letter seems to have crossed with a letter from Trench in which Trench made, more obscurely, the same confession.

Trench gave a fuller account of his feelings in a letter to William Bodham Donne. See *Richard Chenevix Trench: Letters and Memorials*, 1: pp. 53, 56, and 59–60. But Trench offered his fullest account retrospectively, in two poems included in his *The Story of Justin Martyr and Other Poems* (London: Edward Moxon, 1835), the title poem, and a poem entitled 'Addressed on leaving Rome to a Friend residing in that City', *The Story of Justin Martyr and Other Poems*, pp. 9–26, and 98–104. Monckton Milnes seems not to have been much given to religious gloom, arriving early at that elegant religious creed he was in the habit of describing as 'Puginian scepticism', so that when in an untitled poem beginning 'Six years, six cycles of dead hours', he lays claim to an experience of religious agony, his testimony is revealing. See *Poems of Many Years* (London: Edward Moxon, 1844, after the volume had been printed for private circulation in 1838), pp. 12–16. Milnes may not have been particularly religious, but he was intensely clubbable, and such a poem indicates that in the club to which he was proudest to belong, to which his book was dedicated, the Apostles, experience of religious agony was a prized attribute. Henry Alford, a younger Apostle, elected in 1830, seems to have been blessed from very early in life with a deep and untroubled religious faith, and yet in the first book or 'lesson' of his *The School of the Heart*, a poem first published in 1835, he lays claim to a rather similar religious crisis, *The Poetical Works of Henry Alford* (London: Edward Strahan, 1868), pp. 1–84.

14. In Trench's 'Justin Martyr', the notion that the young man's misery is a consequence of him setting himself 'a loftier aim / Than the blind lives of men may claim / For the most part' is registered quietly enough. But elsewhere, as in Hallam's letter to Gladstone and Kemble's to Trench, it can result in an uncomfortable blend of explicit self-abasement and covert self-congratulation.

15. All these men were great admirers of Coleridge, and tended to understand their despair as a consequence of the understanding having usurped the function properly performed by the reason. In his letter to Trench, Kemble confesses that his faith remains a matter of the 'understanding'. Hallam invokes the same distinction in the third of his meditative fragments, addressed to his schoolfriend, Gaskell, when he claims that in him the diabolical understanding fascinates with its 'serpentine, thought-withering gaze' 'the sovran rational eye'.

16. See Monckton Milnes, *Poems of Many Years*, p. 16. In Trench's 'Justin Martyr', Trench records a death wish that is described wholly in terms of a regression to infancy:

> And death grew beautiful to me,
> Until it seemed a mother mild,
> And I like some too happy child –
> A happy child, that, tired with play,
> Through a long summer holiday,
> Runs to his mother's arms to weep
> His little weariness asleep.

See also *The Writings of Arthur Hallam*, pp. 55–7.

17. Trench's 'Justin Martyr' is an exception to this rule, but the conversion it describes seems oddly perfunctory.
18. The same recognition underlies *St Simeon Stylites*, but in the later poem it is expressed satirically.
19. 'Meditative Fragments', VI, 140–1, *The Writings of Arthur Hallam*, p. 74.
20. Paul Turner, *Tennyson* (London: Routledge and Kegan Paul, 1976), p. 53.
21. A passage from the 'sequelae' to the ninth of the 'Aphorisms on Spiritual Religion':

> the great fundamental truths and doctrines of religion, the existence and attributes of God and the life after death, are in Christian countries taught so early, under such circumstances, and in such close and vital association with whatever makes or marks reality for our infant minds, that the words ever after represent sensations, feelings, vital assurances, sense of reality – rather than thoughts, or any distinct conception. Associated, I has almost said identified, with the parental voice, look, touch, with the living warmth and pressure of the mother, on whose lap the child is first made to kneel, within whose palms its little hands are folded, and the motion of whose eyes its eyes follow and imitate – (yea, what the blue sky is to the mother, the mother's upraised eyes and brow are to the child, the type and symbol of an invisible heaven!) – from within and without these great first truths, these good and gracious tidings, these holy and humanizing spells, in the preconformity to which our very humanity may be said to consist, are so infused that it were but a tame and inadequate expression to say, we all take them for granted.

S.T. Coleridge, *Aids to Reflection*, ed. H.N. Coleridge (London; William Pickering, 1848), 186–7.
22. Isobel Armstrong: *Victorian Poetry: Poetry, Poetics and Politics* (London and New York: Routledge, 1993, pp. 113–26, p. 125.
23. Ricks notes the allusion to Coleridge, and points out, too, that in an earlier version that was completed by 1833 the poem ended after some 300 lines with the speaker's doubts unresolved. The conclusion, in which faith is re-discovered, was added at some point before the first publication of the poem in 1842. *The Poems of Tennyson*, pp. 522 and 540 (note).
24. It is not simply the reference to the water-snake noted by Jack that recalls Coleridge, but the means of propulsion. Browning's speaker is 'sucked along', and so is the mariner's boat: 'The air is cut away before, / And closes from behind' (424–5).
25. Ian Jack, *Browning's Major Poetry* (Oxford: Clarendon Press, 1973), p. 127; Lee Erickson, *Robert Browning: His Poetry and His Audiences* (Ithaca and London: Cornell University Press, 1984), p. 120.
26. *The Poetical Works of Robert Browning*, IV, ed. Ian Jack, Rowena Fowler and Margaret Smith (Oxford, Clarendon Press, 1991), p. 325; Lee Erickson, *Robert Browning: His Poetry and his Audiences*, p. 120.
27. See Chapter XVII of *Biographia Literaria*.
28. On Browning's religious upbringing, see John Maynard, *Browning's Youth*, pp. 51–62.

29. *The Brownings' Correspondence*, ed. Philip Kelly and Scott Lewis, 13 (Winfield: Wedgestone Press, 1995), pp. 253–4.

# 8  Domesticating Romanticism

1. Alford's poem is printed in *The Poetical Works of Henry Alford* (London: Strahan, 1868), pp. 131–2, under the title 'Written in a Copy of "The Revolt of Islam"'. Frances Alford remembers the book as given to her not on her wedding day, but on her first wedding anniversary, in her *Life of Henry Alford* (London, Oxford and Cambridge: Rivingtons, 1874), p. 105.
2. *The Poetical Works of Henry Alford*, p. 3.
3. The poem was first published under the title, *Laon and Cythna*, but was withdrawn by its publisher, Ollier, who feared prosecution, and re-issued under the title *The Revolt of Islam* with references to Cythna as Laon's sister removed together with some of Shelley's more extravagant blasphemies.
4. On this, see John Donovan, 'Incest in *Laon and Cythna*: Nature, Culture and Desire', Keats–Shelley Review, 2 (1987), 49–90.
5. *Shelley's Prose or The Trumpet of a Prophecy*, ed. David Lee Clark (Albuquerque: University of New Mexico Press), pp. 169–71. All references to Shelley's prose are to this edition.
6. All quotations from Shelley's poetry are taken from *The Poetical Works of Percy Bysshe Shelley*, ed. Thomas Hutchinson, revised by G.M. Matthews (London: Oxford UP, 1970).
7. Timothy Clark, *Embodying Revolution: The Figure of the Poet in Shelley* (Oxford: Clarendon Press, 1989). Crucial to Clark's argument throughout his book is his persuasive presentation of Shelley's insistence that human beings are characterized by their capacity for unlimited desire as the notion through which Shelley is able to unify the erotic and the political energies of his verse.
8. Claude Lévi-Strauss, *The Elementary Structure of Kinship Relations*, translated by Bell, von Sturmer, and Needham, revised edition (London: Beacon Press, 1969), p. 68.
9. See John Taylor Coleridge's unsigned review of *The Revolt of Islam* in the *Quarterly*, *Shelley: The Critical Heritage*, ed. James E. Barcus (London and Boston: Routledge and Kegan Paul, 1975), pp. 124–35.
10. Claude Lévi-Strauss, *The Elementary Structure of Kinship Relations*, pp. 492–7.
11. Shelley may have in mind Coleridge's description, in Chapter XIV of *Biographia Literaria*, of Wordsworth's ambition in his contributions to *Lyrical Ballads*, 'to awaken the mind's attention from the lethargy of custom' by 'directing it to the loveliness and the wonders of the world before us; an inexhaustible treasure, but for which, in consequence of the film of familiarity and selfish solicitude, we have eyes yet see not, ears that hear not, and hearts that neither feel nor understand'. The significant difference from Shelley is that Coleridge chooses, in place of an erotic language, a language that invests the thought with religious resonance by its echo of the psalmist. The connection made by Shelley between love and language has been often remarked, for example by Roland A. Durkheim, who argues that for Shelley the 'creative, imaginatively identifying use of language … is the

quintessential act of love' in his *Shelley's Poetry of Involvement* (Urbana, Chicago and London, University of Illinois Press, 1980), p. 33. The relationship has been most fully explored by William A. Ulmer in his *Shelleyan Eros: The Rhetoric of Romantic Love* (Princeton: Princeton University Press, 1990).

12. 'I always go on until I am stopped, and I never am stopped,' Shelley told Edward Trelawny in his *Recollections of the Last Days of Shelley and Byron*, ed. Edward Dowden (London: Henry Froude, 1906), p. 45.

13. For an extended exhibition of this technique see *Epipsychidion*, 1–123, but such passages are only extreme manifestations of Shelley's liking for metaphors that admit their own deliquescence, the kind of metaphor explored by William Keach in his chapter, 'Evanescence: Melting, Dissolving, Erasing', *Shelley's Style* (New York and London: Methuen, 1984), pp. 118–53.

14. William Empson, *Seven Types of Ambiguity* (Harmondsworth: Penguin, 1961), p. 160. The 'self-inwoven simile' is again only the most extreme manifestation of that quirk of Shelleyan style ably explored by William Keach in his chapter 'Reflexive Imagery', *Shelley's Style*, pp. 79–117.

15. For the tangled publication history of *A Lover's Tale*, see *The Poems of Tennyson*, ed. Christopher Ricks (London: Longman, 1969), p. 299. Quotations are taken from Ricks's edition. Cadrilla, when the poem was at last published, was re-christened Camilla. Julian and Lionel are distinctively Shelleyan names, as in *Julian and Maddalo*, *Rosalind and Helen*, and *The Boat on the Serchio*. In later life Tennyson claimed to have written his poem before ever he had read Shelley, but commentators on *A Lover's Tale* concur in dismissing this as a lapse of memory.

16. See Jacques Lacan, *Ecrits: A Selection*, translated by Alan Sheridan (London: Tavistock, 1977), pp. 1–2.

17. John Bayley, 'Tennyson and the Idea of Decadence' in *Studies in Tennyson*, ed. Hallam Tennyson (London: Macmillan, 1981 – now Palgrave), pp. 186–205.

18. *The Life of Henry Alford*, p. 84.

# Conclusion

1. Virgil Nemoianu, *The Taming of Romanticism: European Literature and the Age of Biedermeier* (Cambridge, Mass., and London: Harvard University Press, 1984), p. 14.

2. *The Taming of Romanticism*, p. 27.

3. *The Anxiety of Influence: A Theory of Poetry*, second edition (New York and Oxford: Oxford University Press, 1993, first published 1973), p. 95.

4. Harold Bloom, *The Anxiety of Influence*, p. 11.

5. *The Letters of Percy Bysshe Shelley*, ed. F.L. Jones (Oxford: Clarendon Press, 1964), 1, p. 504. The letter was addressed to Byron.

6. Andrew Elfenbein, 'Silver-Fork Byron and the Image of Regency Culture' in *Byromania: Portraits of the Artist in Nineteenth- and Twenieth-Century Culture*, ed. Francis Wilson (Basingstoke: Macmillan, 1999 – now Palgrave), pp. 77–92.

7. Herbert F. Tucker, 'House Arrest: The Domestication of English Poetry in the 1820s', *New Literary History*, 25 (1995), 521–48.

# Index